THE TEACHERS' HANDBOOK FOR ENVIRONMENTAL STUDIES

THE TEACHERS' HANDBOOK FOR ENVIRONMENTAL STUDIES

G. A. PERRY former Head of Rural Studies Department, Berkshire College of Education

E. JONES Head of Science Department, Summerfield College of Education

A. HAMMERSLEY Head of Geography Department, St. Katharine's College of Education, Liverpool

BLANDFORD PRESS · LONDON

First published in 1968
Revised edition 1971
3rd edition (revised) 1974

167, High Holborn, London WC1V 6PH

ISBN 0 7137 3499 X

Printed in Great Britain by Fletcher & Son Ltd, Norwich
and bound by Richard Clay (The Chaucer Press) Ltd, Bungay, Suffolk

CONTENTS

ACKNOWLEDGMENTS

The publishers wish to thank the following for the pictures they kindly supplied:

Aerofilms Ltd., Figs. 3:10, 3:11, 3:12, 3:13

D. A. Avon, Fig. 7:53

Forestry Commission, Figs. 3:5, 3:6, 3:7, 3:8

Charles Frank Ltd., Fig. 4:36

T. Gerrard & Co. Ltd., Fig. 4:59

Longworth Scientific Instrument Co. Ltd., Fig. 4:63

Countryside Commission, Crown Copyright, Fig. 3:18

Fig. 3.9 compiled from information supplied by Holiday Fellowship, Methodist Youth Camps, Youth Hostels Association

Figs. 4:24a, b, c, 4:25a, b, c, 4:26 reproduced by courtesy of Kodak Limited from the booklet *Developing Printing Enlarging*

Fig. 4:34 reproduced from the Ordnance Survey Map with the sanction of the Controller of H.M. Stationery Office, Crown Copyright reserved

Preface

This handbook is intended as a guide for the teacher in his approach to environmental studies with children in the 9–13 age group. The emphasis is on the practical discovery of information within the local environment, the meaningful handling of ideas and information, followed by the ever-broadening concepts of these against a national and world background. The book draws attention in an essentially practical way to the investigational possibilities of the 'total' environment. The Teachers' Guides offer suggestions for the teacher in dealing with the series of class books. These books suggest ways in which children may discover information, contain further necessary information for the widening of their studies, and are presented in an attractive format, with lavish use of colour. Another function for these children's books is to provide the background information for the programmed texts written by Colin Kefford in the course of work sponsored by the Nuffield Foundation 'Resources for Learning' Project. He has contributed a section in Chapter 2 of this book on 'A Programmed Approach to Environmental Studies'.

Colour slides in folio form (Slidefolios) and film loops are a part of the overall additional teaching aids published by The Slide Centre in association with this scheme. A more detailed description of available aids is given on p. 274 of this book.

Teachers who wish to treat some particular aspect of environmental studies in much greater detail will find extensive lists of film strips, slides, films, film loops, wall charts and books for reference in the associated Teachers' Guides. From these lists appropriate selections can be made.

The authors wish to thank Charles Rickitt of The Slide Centre Ltd., for his assistance with illustrations, Mr. P. D. Bivand, Head of the Design Workshop at Summerfield College of Education, for the information and diagrams relating to the making of apparatus and Mr. T. K. Bailey, Senior Lecturer in Biology at Summerfield College, who kindly read the proofs.

Finally, it should be pointed out that although lists of material available and addresses are believed to be correct at the time of going to press, changes in this information are likely to occur.

G.A.P.
E.J.
A.H.

PREFACE TO SECOND EDITION

The preparation of this Handbook for its second edition has provided an opportunity for various additions, deletions and amendments to be made to the text and illustrations. An additional chapter, dealing with methods of study of the environment in the past, has been contributed by Lawrence Taylor and Don Steel, Senior Lecturers in the History Department of the Berkshire College of Education, while the section on programmed learning has been revised by Colin Kefford, now Headmaster of the Augustus Smith Middle School, Berkhamsted, Hertfordshire. The lengthy lists of vehicle registration numbers, index marks and international registration letters have been removed, since these are readily available in the *A.A. Members' Handbook*. Additions and corrections have been made to the lists of useful addresses provided in various sections of the book. It is hoped that these changes will add to the value of this Handbook in providing suggestions and details of resources concerning Environmental Studies for teachers and students.

The General Editor wishes to thank (*a*) various correspondents who have suggested additions to the lists of addresses (*b*) the authors who have revised their sections of the book and (*c*) Miss Vera Frampton and Mr. John Goulding of Blandford Press who have given invaluable help in the production of this second edition.

July, 1970 Gordon A. Perry

PREFACE TO THIRD EDITION

The ever-increasing interest of educationalists and others in the environment has ensured the continuing popularity of this Handbook. In preparation for its third edition a major revision has been made of the lists of resources and useful addresses. In addition all measurements are now shown in metricated form. Every effort has been made to ensure accuracy at the time of going to press, but readers are invited to inform the editor of any amendments that could be incorporated in the next edition.

The General Editor is grateful for information which has been sent in by correspondents, firms, societies and associations, and wishes to thank Miss Vera Frampton and Miss Daphne Phillips of Blandford Press for their tireless efforts in the revision of this Handbook.

September, 1973 Gordon A. Perry

1 The Importance of Environmental Studies

THE GULF BETWEEN EDUCATION AND LIFE

The idea that in learning with understanding, one should move from the familiar to the less familiar, is a generally accepted one, and today most teachers make earnest efforts to link education with life. In the early days of compulsory education however, government grants for the schools were dependent on standards reached in prescribed grant-earning subjects. The requirements were so narrow that they influenced adversely not only the curriculum but the methods used. The committal to memory of great numbers of unrelated facts, bearing little or no relevance to the life and experience of the children concerned, led inevitably to the separation of the subjects of the curriculum and barred the way to correlation.

Many writers have drawn attention to these serious defects in the teaching methods of the past. In his book *Education* (Pelican Books) W. O. Lester Smith points out that 'the grammar schools still, as Charles Lamb described those of his day, revolved "in a perpetual cycle of declensions, conjugation, syntaxes and prosodies, while the elementary schools drilled their children in the three Rs with rod and regimentation".' Sir Oliver Lodge has described in an article (*Strand Magazine*, February 1925) how after a dame-school education which consisted of mechanical tasks such as writing out lists of the kings of England with their dates and memorising passages from a geography book, he went on to a grammar school where he worked at practically nothing else but Latin and Greek until he left school at the age of fourteen. H. M. Burton in *The Education of the Countryman* (Kegan Paul) describes how country children 'were drilled like their brothers and sisters in the towns, in classes of forty to seventy, until they could work sums in complicated multiplication, of long division, of money. ... The height of their ambition in history and geography was to be able to reel off stupendous lists of dates or of capes and bays. To this not very liberal curriculum might be added, for the fortunate, singing, mensuration, "object lessons", drawing and (for the girls) plain needlework.' As recently as 1927 Aldous Huxley's *Proper Studies* (Chatto and Windus) deplored the existence in many schools of the wide gap between education and life. In such schools, Huxley avers: 'Passively, with his forty or fifty dissimilar and unique companions, he (the child) sits at his desk while the teacher pumps and mechanically repumps information into his mental receptacle.'

OFFICIAL ENCOURAGEMENT FOR ENVIRONMENTAL STUDIES

Although until comparatively recently little had been done in many schools in using the environment for teaching purposes, yet official reports and documents have been encouraging this approach for many years. In 1918 a Committee appointed by the Prime Minister reported that the best preparation for the study of science at secondary school was a course of nature study, as practical in character as possible and aiming to arouse an interest in natural phenomena and developing the powers of observation. In *Rural Education*, published by the Board of Education in 1926, praise is given to geography teaching which includes special studies of natural features, crops, resources and occupations of the school district. The author points out that children's interest is thereby aroused and the knowledge gained allows useful comparisons to be made with data for other districts and countries.

A year later, the Board published the *Handbook of Suggestions for Teachers* (H.M.S.O.), which advocated that every child should know of the history of his own village, town or county, and that visits should be made if possible, to the scene of historic events and to historic remains to help to create atmosphere and to make history live. It was claimed that much of the outdoor work done in arithmetic could help with geography teaching, including the interpretation by the children of Ordnance Survey maps.

The *Report on the Primary School* (Hadow Report) (H.M.S.O. 1931) recommended visits to places of interest in the neighbourhood to give realism to the children's lessons in history, geography and nature study.

Education and the Countryside (H.M.S.O. 1934) pinpoints two main reasons why the environment should have a profound influence on the content of education in rural areas. First, children are always interested in the processes going on around them, and these processes are fundamental to civilisation. Secondly, the wise educational use of the environment can provide a wider intellectual horizon which can be the basis of interest and enjoyment for the individual throughout his life.

In 1937 the Board of Education produced a new edition of *Handbook of Suggestions for Teachers* (H.M.S.O.), which advocated the full use of the historical, geographical and scientific possibilities of the school's neighbourhood. Not only should visits be paid to near-by centres of interest, but in addition teachers should make constant reference to the environment to illustrate their teaching.

The pamphlet *Schools and the Countryside* (H.M.S.O. 1958) urged schools to make full use of the educational opportunities of the environment, whether the schools were rural or urban in character.

In the following year, *Primary Education* (H.M.S.O.) insisted that children in their environment should be encouraged to search, to observe, to study closely and to talk about their experiences. Attention is particularly directed to the use of the environment in the teaching of history, mathematics, geography and natural history.

There are many references to environmental studies in *Children and their Primary Schools: Plowden Report* 1967 (H.M.S.O.). It is pointed out that the curiosity of children about their environment often leads on to studies in depth. The Report recognises a twofold change in primary education – first, the increasing variety of subject-matter, and secondly, a new approach to learning. The physical environment of a school, and of the children who attend it, contains a vast complex of objects and phenomena. Whether we are thinking in terms of the natural world of living forms or of the realm of man-made objects, the Report is adamant that the approach must be through 'learning by discovery'.

THE ATTITUDE OF SOME FAMOUS EDUCATIONALISTS

The works of several well-known educational philosophers and writers contain references to the importance of the effect of environment on a child's development.

Pestalozzi maintained that when the teacher had grasped the starting-point he could, given a certain amount of basic knowledge, easily educate himself by observation and self-guided practice. This would enable him to guide his pupils to learning by similar methods.

Froebel recognised two facets of a pupil's activity. In one, the child's environment supplies material for his mind to work on, and in the second, his reactions to this material have an effect of modification, to a greater or lesser extent. Understanding of the nature and purpose of anything is dependent on the appreciation of its relationship with other things, and Froebel insists that a child must 'study things in their natural connexion'.

Montessori emphasises the importance of children's activity in the learning process. All too often children are forced to sit in a classroom in a state of passivity and any activity on their part may be regarded as play rather than work. This philosophy lends support to the activity of discovery. Such activity is implicit in the environmental studies approach to integrated learning.

Piaget points out that anyone who wishes to learn efficiently must organise his material, and must adapt himself to the things and information around him. The learner is altered to some degree in this process. There must be continuous interaction between the learner and his environment, and as the child is involved in new experiences so his mind is affected to some degree and his picture of the world is gradually built up.

Piaget, together with educational researchers such as Isaacs, Baldwin, Luria and Bruner, assures us that most primary school children need the experience of concrete situations if learning is to be efficient.

THE VALUE OF ENVIRONMENTAL STUDIES

As teachers have developed the use of the environment in their teaching, many names have been suggested and used for this type of approach. Some of these titles achieved popularity for a time and then faded somewhat from the educational scene, while some are currently in use and may be with us in the future. Among these titles are: Local Studies; Social Studies; Rural Studies; Environmental Science and Environmental Studies. The term used for this approach is comparatively unimportant, provided that we mean the use of the environment in providing integrated and meaningful studies.

In Colleges of Education the term 'Environmental Studies' is increasingly used to describe courses which are provided for the majority of students to show how the demarcation barriers of various subjects may be overcome. It is encouraging to see less insistence on courses in 'curriculum subjects' and a move towards an integrated approach to learning for those who will soon be planning courses for classes of their own.

The content of our schools' curricula developed largely from the few traditional subjects which were regarded as essential for a child. To these, as the years passed, were added extra subjects until timetables became overloaded. At certain fixed intervals during the school day there was a change from one subject to another, often with no sign of relevance, and this pattern was followed day after day and year after year.

Experiences and problems in life never appear neatly labelled as 'mathematical', 'geographical' or 'scientific'. Yet this is the way in which we have tended to educate. The artificiality of subject teaching can be largely overcome in the primary school by the integrated approach of environmental studies. For example, it is impossible to understand fully the town in which one lives without an appreciation of such aspects as the history of its settlement and its buildings, the geography of its site, the occupations of its people, its cultural provision and so on.

In the series of Teachers' Guides, some suggestions are offered for the integration of 'subjects' in various aspects of environmental studies.

'THE NUFFIELD APPROACH'

With the help of grants from the Nuffield Foundation, investigations have been made into possible changes in the teaching of science, and suggestions have been incorporated in series of teachers' and children's books. The emphasis is placed on observation and study of and experimentation with materials and organisms of the child's environment. Measurement and recording of data, and the interpretation of simple statistics are encouraged.

A further project, sponsored by the Nuffield Foundation, is concerned with 'Resources for Learning'. Colin W. Kefford has worked on a programmed approach to Environmental Studies, which was investigated as one of the developments by the Project. This approach is outlined in chapter 2 and is treated more fully in *A Programmed Approach to Environmental Studies: Guide to Programmes* by Colin Kefford, published by Blandford Press.

2 The Learning Partnership

In the teaching of traditional subjects by traditional methods, the teacher's task is straightforward and simple. The class is a single unit over which the teacher has control and command. The timetable dictates the amount of time which the teacher shall spend on one particular subject; at the end of this period of time there is often an abrupt change to another subject, whose content appears to have little relevance to that of the preceding lesson. The amount of information to be absorbed is decided by the teacher and the children's retention of this will be great or small according to their interest and ability.

THE ROLE OF THE TEACHER IN ENVIRONMENTAL STUDIES

The environmental studies approach places greater demands on the teacher. Activity no longer involves a single unit working *en masse*, but rather a number of groups or a greater number of individuals working on different aspects of a theme. Under such a system the teacher is rarely the dominant figure, but has complicated functions, some of which we can examine briefly now.

1 To arouse the children's interest in their environment and to raise challenging problems in connection with it

One might imagine that all children brought up in the country have great understanding and knowledge of country things and that, similarly, children in an urban environment are naturally interested in their surroundings. A few questions put to groups of children soon reveal that this is not so. If, however, teachers are prepared and able to interpret the pattern of natural and man-made things of any environment, then the children will respond with enthusiasm. The problems or topics for investigation may arise from newspaper articles brought to school, from visits to the school by various people (nurse, dustman, road safety officer, overseas visitors, etc.), or maybe from the teacher's prearranged plan for a study of the neighbourhood. A limited problem such as 'Why do farmers in this area grow so many market garden crops?' or 'Why is our town such an important shopping centre?' may be attempted. The limits of the problem will extend rapidly as work proceeds.

2 To discuss the approach to problems or topics

As soon as a problem or topic has been decided upon, then the teacher must join in discussion with the class to decide the method of tackling the work. With children who are unused to this approach, the teacher may have to contribute a good deal, and should therefore have some suggestions in reserve. It is wise to summarise on the blackboard any decisions made so that all the class is aware of what is intended.

3 To organise the working groups

Here the teacher's knowledge and understanding of the abilities and the attitude to work of the children will be of great help in forming the working groups. According to the amount of work involved in the subdivisions of the topic, so the numbers in each group will vary. In some cases, individual work may be the answer. Where a group contains three or more children it may be wise to see that a responsible child acts as leader. The teacher will ensure, too, that the groups encompass children of mixed ability. Work cards are often a useful means of guiding the children along the main lines of enquiry.

4 To arrange visits or expeditions

Visits involving work away from the classroom and the school are an essential part of environmental studies. The teacher must therefore be prepared to decide how many visits are necessary, the venues, the length of time to be spent there and whether the whole class or merely groups shall be involved. The question of transport may arise, and the permission of the Head will naturally be sought. Under certain conditions it may be possible for groups of children to make short local visits unaccompanied by the teacher, but obviously the possibilities of accidents must be borne in mind if such visits take the children beyond the school boundaries. Suggestions concerning the planning of longer visits are given in another chapter of this book. Expeditions are of little value unless adequate preparation has been made and children have a clear idea of the observations to be made and work to be done.

5 To provide reference material for the children's use

To give depth to the work a comprehensive supply of books, maps, charts, pamphlets, specimens, models, encyclopaedias, etc., appropriate to the studies must be available in the classroom. The teacher should make every effort to obtain the material in good time. It may be necessary to approach the county library, various associations and commercial firms, the local museum, the county archivist and other possible sources. If children are encouraged to write to firms for pamphlets or brochures, then the teacher should see that only one letter, clearly expressed and legibly written, arrives at each firm concerned. Where help is needed from experts, then the teacher must ensure that the question is a limited one that can be answered briefly, that a stamped addressed envelope is enclosed and that a letter of thanks is sent afterwards. Suggested sources of reference material will be listed under particular sections in the series of Teachers' Guides.

6 To provide materials needed for practical work

During their work the groups of children will be recording in various ways. They may be engaged on descriptive writing, the construction of graphs, sketching, painting, model-making, photography in black and white or colour, or recording on tape. The teacher should try to plan for the materials needed to be available at the time when required in the classroom or while at work in the environment. The methods of making group and class records will be considered in another chapter of this book.

7 To arrange for visiting speakers

Depending on the aspect of environmental studies involved in the work, it is often possible to enlist the help of visiting speakers. They might include, possibly, a farmer, a policeman, a doctor, a councillor, a youth leader, an industrialist, a shopkeeper, a local government official, a miner or quarry worker, a water board official, a fireman, a park-keeper, a transport driver and others. When contacting a potential visitor, the teacher should make clear what work is being done by the class and what is expected of the speaker. The children should be encouraged to ask as many questions as possible. It is worth noting that various animal welfare associations are prepared to send speakers to schools, free of charge, on request.

Possible sources for speakers

(*a*) Apply to the Town Clerk, the Clerk of the Rural District Council or to the Clerk of the County Council, as appropriate, requesting speakers on aspects of local government.

(*b*) Apply to the Head Postmaster if a postman is required.

(*c*) Apply to the Chief of the Fire Brigade for the visit of a fireman.

(*d*) Apply to the Chief Constable for the visit of a policeman or the road safety officer.

(*e*) Apply to the Local Chamber of Commerce for a speaker on industry.

(*f*) Apply to the Head of Department of a local University or College of Technology or College of Education for possible help.

(*g*) For a suitable farmer apply to the appropriate National Farmers' Union Regional Information Officer:

Chief Regional Information Officer: E. E. Milner, Agriculture House, Knightsbridge, London, SW1X 7NJ Tel.: 01–235 5077

Northern

Cumbria, Lancashire, North Riding and Durham, Northumberland, Yorkshire (East Riding), Yorkshire (North Riding No. 2), Yorkshire (West Riding).

P. Williams, Agriculture House, Salters Lane South, Haughton-le-Skerne, Darlington, Co. Durham, DL1 2AA. Tel.: Darlington (0325) 65132

Midland

Cheshire, Derbyshire, Herefordshire, Leicestershire, Northamptonshire, Nottinghamshire, Oxfordshire, Shropshire, Staffordshire, Warwickshire, Worcestershire.
R. A. Wright, 43, Upper Tything, Worcester. Tel.: Worcester (0905) 24324

East Midland

Bedfordshire and Huntingdonshire, Buckinghamshire, Cambridgeshire, Essex, Hertfordshire, Lincs, (Holland), Huntingdonshire (Ramsey), Isle of Ely, Lincolnshire, Norfolk, Peterborough and District, Rutland and Stamford, Suffolk.
J. W. Rodgers, 22, St. Faith's Lane, Norwich, NOR 09P. Tel.: Norwich (0603) 25430.

South-West

Cornwall, Devon, Dorset, Gloucestershire, Somerset, Wiltshire.
R. Maslen, London Buildings, Market Place, Chippenham, Wiltshire. Tel.: Chippenham (0249) 4034

South-East

Berkshire, Central Southern, Hampshire, Isle of Wight, Kent, Sussex (East)
G. N. Jobling, Avebury Chambers, 6A, St. Peter Street, Winchester, Hampshire. Tel.: Winchester (0962) 66992.

Wales and Monmouth

Anglesey, Brecon and Radnor, Caernarvonshire, Cardiganshire, Carmarthenshire, Denbighshire, Flintshire, Glamorgan, Merioneth, Monmouthshire, Montgomery, Oswestry, Pembrokeshire.
D. G. Lloyd, M.B.E., Agriculture House, 19, Severn Street, Welshpool, Montgomeryshire. Tel.: Welshpool 2001. Home: Gobowen (069182) 315.

Scotland. Request name and address of N.F.U. Area Secretary from National Farmers' Union of Scotland, 17, Grosvenor Crescent, Edinburgh, 12.

(*h*) Cadbury Bros. Ltd., Schools Department, Bournville, Birmingham, 30.

(*i*) International Wool Secretariat, 6, Carlton Gardens, London, W.1.

(*j*) R.S.P.C.A., 105, Jermyn Street, London, S.W.1.

(*k*) Universities Federation for Animal Welfare, 230, High Street, Potters Bar, Herts.

(*l*) Speakers may be available from the British Red Cross and also St. John Ambulance Brigade. Enquiries should be made at the County or City headquarters: the addresses will be found in the local telephone directory.

(*m*) Local branch of the Historical Association. Apply for information to the headquarters' address, 59A, Kennington Park Road, London, S.E.11 or ask for local secretary's address at your library.

(n) Local history society, local branches of Geographical and Geologists Associations: addresses available from your library.

8 To discuss and guide the progress of each group

The more experienced teacher may find that he has to guide, say, up to a dozen different studies all equally important. This needs a great deal of patience, and the ability to switch quickly from one aspect to another. At times, the interest of a group may be flagging, or another group may need further ideas to develop their plans. Questions may arise, and if the teacher cannot suggest reliable sources for the answers, he may have to seek these from his own reference books or from an appropriate reference library. As the children work towards the completion of the topic in hand, the teacher must constantly evaluate progress, for without this action environmental studies methods could well produce superficial results, comparing unfavourably, perhaps, with traditional methods of subject teaching. The newly qualified teacher and the student are advised to work with the children in larger and therefore fewer groups.

9 To initiate and develop discussion and debate

During work of this kind, the teacher should also encourage the whole class, on occasions, to discuss the development of the topic in hand. Opportunities may arise, too, for a planned debate on questions arising from the study. The subjects might involve such ideas as the advantages of village life, traffic problems in towns, the destruction of wild life and so on. The main speakers should be chosen with care, but as many as possible of the class should be encouraged to take part.

10 To persuade each group of children to explain their work to the rest of the class

It is important to maintain the unity of the work, and to help in this, a spokesman from each group should be chosen to report on progress to the rest of the class. If the study is not a lengthy one, then this passing on of information can be left until the end of the work.

11 To provide facilities for displays or exhibitions of the work carried out

The culmination of a period of environmental study should be a display or exhibition of the work achieved. At first, the children will need help from the teacher in selection and lay-out of work, but usually the groups will enjoy displaying their work for the benefit of their classmates, of other classes in the school and perhaps for parents to see. It is helpful if some extra flat-top tables, peg-board and pin-board sheets, supplies of backing paper, drawing pins, etc., can be provided so that the children are able to make a worth-while display.

12 To draw together the various aspects of the work and to summarise the results

This is very important, for it is easy for groups to work in isolation, and to fail to see what has really been achieved by the efforts of the class. In experimental work, too, it is possible for children to carry out instructions and reach a result which has little relevance for them.

13 To link the work with the wider world

Critics of environmental work point out that it can be extremely narrow and parochial in its outlook. The teacher's task is to link the work undertaken, the information gained and the ideas formulated, with the wider world. Farming at home leads on to farming in the rest of the world; studies of citizenship proceed to a study of world affairs; village life in Britain can be compared with the rural scene overseas and so on. As the speed of communication increases, the world becomes 'smaller and smaller'; as teachers we must see that the world, in its physical, biological, sociological and political aspects, becomes more and more familiar to those we teach.

THE ROLE OF THE CHILD IN ENVIRONMENTAL STUDIES

Many of the points which would normally be discussed under this heading have been touched on when considering the role of the teacher. The functions of the children in the class can be summarised as follows:

1 To suggest approaches to the topic

Give credit to children who put forward useful ideas. These can be built up as a blackboard list.

2 To work as part of a small group

Here the child must be prepared either to act as a leader and apportion work or to accept instructions and carry them out to the best of his ability. The idea of working constructively as part of a small team rather than as an individual in direct competition with about forty others appeals to many children and is a valuable beginning to the concept of 'team-work'.

3 To learn to handle reference material

One of the aims of education should be to help us to find information when we require it. Children should be helped to understand the indexing system of books, the best reference book to use for particular types of information, the use of encyclopaedias, the symbols of maps and so on.

4 To experiment, investigate and discover for himself

The challenge of this type of work is the personal quest for information. Where experimental work is possible in the classroom or out-of-doors, this should be undertaken. Much information can be discovered in the environment by observation and by enquiry. If the problem presented to the child is an interesting one, then he will make a real effort to solve it.

5 To see the relevance of his own work to that of the rest of the group and of the class

The planning of the work and the summing up are of great importance if the child is to understand the value of what he is asked to do.

LEARNING TOGETHER

Oral activity on the part of the teacher and receptive passivity on the part of the child are recognised as a poor educational method. In work such as we have been considering, there should be 'give and take' at all stages. Question and answer, discussion between individuals and the teacher, or discussion in large or small groups, lecturettes by the children and class debates are all vital parts of 'learning together'.

For the teacher embarking on this method of teaching, there may be the worry that he has not attained the necessary breadth of knowledge. He has left the safety of the prepared lesson where selected information is passed to the children. Now he must be prepared to deal with situations outside his previous experience and to attempt to answer questions of various degrees of difficulty on a variety of subjects. The cause for worry over this disappears rapidly if the teacher is prepared to learn with the children as the work proceeds. Many teachers who have used these methods admit freely that their own education has been greatly improved by discovering with the children.

TEAM-TEACHING

The idea that a school should consist of a series of box-like rooms, similar in size, in each of which a class of approximately forty children is faced by the same teacher for a year, has been losing ground during recent years. We are moving in thought and design towards an 'open plan' system where larger rooms may be used as such or may be divided by plastic folding doors into smaller units in which a variety of activities can take place. Linked with this development is the system of team-teaching, where groups of staff members join together to plan and carry out environmental study work, making the most of the particular interests and abilities of each member of the team. For some periods, parallel classes may be grouped as one so that basic instruction can be given. Thereafter, the large unit may divide into smaller groups, class divisions being forgotten and the work of a certain number of these groups will be guided by the various members of the teaching team. Thus we may have some groups working on local history aspects and directed by a teacher whose interest this is. In a similar way teachers interested, say, in art and craft, in geography, in science can take part in these studies.

It is obvious that such work will be planned well in advance by the teaching team, so that the maximum value may be obtained. Areas will be allocated for practical work such as painting, sketching and modelling, while space must be found for an information room which will have books, pamphlets, charts, maps, specimens, film strips, slides, etc., available for reference and use. Such teaching of course, can function more efficiently in a purpose-built school, but by adaptation and improvisation many schools are making successful, if limited, progress on team-teaching with the integration of subjects.

A PROGRAMMED APPROACH TO ENVIRONMENTAL STUDIES

This section has been contributed by Colin W. Kefford, Headmaster of the Augustus Smith School, Berkhamsted, and formerly Senior Lecturer in Education at Coventry College of Education.

Introduction

To many teachers the title of this section may seem to embody a contradiction in terms. They will argue that the nature of programmed learning is such as to constrain and restrict the enquiry and the discovery through experience which is the essence of environmental studies. They will point an accusing finger at the many dull, repetitive, conditioning 'programs' which have come to this country from across the Atlantic and while they may concede that, where the aim is simply the acquisition of a skill or the rote learning of established facts, programmed learning can play an effective role, they will stoutly reject any suggestion that its techniques could be employed to further creative thinking or to encourage a positive attitude towards scientific enquiry.

It is not difficult to appreciate the reasons why such opinions have gained wide support since, during its emergent years, programmed learning surrounded itself with an aura of mistrust and suspicion; mistrust because many teachers believed that programmed learning meant a return to formal instruction; suspicion because they feared that automatons labelled 'teaching machines' might threaten their status in the classroom. Despite this initial resistance, programmed learning is now beginning to establish itself, not as a rival to the teacher but as a teaching method which, if exploited positively, could bring immense benefit to the teaching profession and to successive generations of children and students.

Defining programmed learning

Probably the most important single factor which has contributed to the increasing acceptance of programmed learning in this country is the way in which its definition has evolved and broadened. In the early days programmed learning referred to a method of conditioned study which employed a programme, structured in a precisely defined manner, validated to a point at which it achieved a predetermined success level and presented according to a prescribed and detailed formula. Today programmed learning may be defined as a technique for structuring learning situations whereby any materials which are used are subject to revision and improvement in the light of empirical testing.

This broad definition means that programmes can be of many different kinds, ranging from the classical Skinnerian linear type programme with its restrictive mode of presentation, its highly structured frames and its 'shaped' responses, to the film or film-strip which has been edited and revised in the light of audience reaction. It means that the teacher in the classroom who has been careful to analyse and adapt his teaching methods on the evidence of the degree of learning achieved by his pupils has always been applying one of the basic principles of programmed learning, viz. validation.

This is not to suggest that programmed learning has nothing new to offer. In the first place no teacher has sufficient time at his disposal to construct and validate even some of his material to a point at which successful learning can be virtually guaranteed. It therefore follows that much of the teaching in this country could be improved in terms of effective learning potential. Secondly, a large proportion of our teaching force is relatively young and inexperienced. This is particularly true at the primary school stage.

The young teacher straight from college is faced with the responsibility of providing for the basic needs of perhaps forty children over a wide range of subjects. It is unrealistic to suppose or expect that he can cope adequately without help, yet all too often that help is not forthcoming and he is forced into a situation in which he abandons the principles of good teaching in favour of the security which exercises from a textbook may offer. This is not to suggest that there should be an attempt to standardise the curriculum and our methods of teaching for that would be a negation of the principle of individuality which is basic to our educational system. What is implied is the need to make available for all teachers the best resources for learning which can be devised. One of those resources is programmed learning.

'Teaching machines'

A second factor which has contributed to the increasing acceptance of programmed learning has been the growing realisation that programmed learning and 'teaching machines' are not synonymous. In the past, schools have often rejected the concept of programmed learning simply because they believed that it entailed the use of expensive machinery. Machine manufacturers gave credence to the belief by stressing the motivational value of a mechanical aid and by implying the need for cheat-proof devices. Subsequent research has given us a more balanced viewpoint and has thereby demolished many of the more extravagant claims made by those with vested interests in specific types of machinery. It must be stressed that the most important factor demanding consideration by any teacher contemplating the use of programmed materials is not what kind of machine should be employed but rather what kinds of programmes are available to suit the specific needs of his pupils.

The use of programmes for environmental studies

Despite what has been written so far, there will be many teachers who feel that there is a dichotomy existing between the concept of programming, with its apparent emphasis upon the efficient learning of information, and the objective implied in the study of an environment which is the engendering of a positive attitude towards learning and scientific enquiry through experience.

Let us examine a realistic and fairly typical situation. A young teacher in charge of a class of forty 9- and 10-year-old children in an unstreamed suburban primary school decides to undertake a study of the immediate area around the school as a 'centre of interest'. He is convinced of the value of 'discovery' methods and believes that the children should be given the opportunity to pursue their own particular interests. He begins his planning by undertaking his own survey of the area, thereby assessing the likely lines along which such a project may develop. At once he is struck by the magnitude of the situation and realises that he cannot cater for all the possible lines of enquiry and interest which may emerge. Nevertheless, there appear to be some topics which are likely to be more fruitful than others and he attempts to plan for developments in the children's thinking along these broad lines. His advance planning may include the provision of reference materials, facilities for experimentation, opportunities for expeditions and enlisting the help of experts. His approach is thoughtful, competent, realistic and enthusiastic.

After a preliminary discussion the first expedition is undertaken by the entire class. The children are told that, in the course of their walk, they are to find for themselves as many items of interest as possible. Their route lies along the High Street, past the church, under the railway bridge by the station, to the outskirts of the town where the road leading to the river is flanked by a new housing development on one side and by a farm on the other. The walk is undertaken in a spirit of high adventure and many exciting discoveries are made about places and things which have hitherto escaped the children's notice.

Back at the school it is quickly apparent to the young teacher that the walk has achieved its motivating objective but it is also clear to him that his advance planning has not been sufficiently thorough or extensive. While the interests of some groups are adequately catered for by the arrangements which he has made, other children have genuine lines of enquiry for which he has not provided. Faced with this situation it is not uncommon for the teacher to suggest that the children should pursue their enquiries in the library where he hopes that they may find some of the answers. Weeks later, on Open Evening, the parents are duly impressed by the colourful display of work relating to 'Our Neighbourhood' but to the discerning observer too many of the topic booklets appear to contain no more than a host of traced drawings and some long passages of adult prose, all too obviously culled from an encyclopaedia in the library.

This pattern of events has been repeated many times in schools up and down the country and no teacher who has had such an experience can feel complacent about the outcome. Yet basically the fault is not his. His partial failure, in effect, reflects the failure of a system which has not taken sufficient account of the needs of teachers and has not provided them with adequate resources.

Let us look again at the teacher with his class of forty youngsters who have just returned from their initial expedition. This time the teacher has at his disposal a comprehensive series of programmed materials which deal with many specific aspects of an environmental study and which are backed by a small library of reference works which provide an extension and enrichment of the subjects covered by the programmes. The programmes themselves have been written in such a way that they guide and stimulate the pupil to learn while at the same time providing some basic information necessary to the pupil's understanding of the topic. Given these kinds of resources the teacher is in a position to provide every child in the class, either as an individual or as a member of a small group, with follow-up material which is relevant to his interests. He will know that the content has been carefully analysed and will lead the child forward in a meaningful manner by providing further opportunities for discovering and experiment arising out of open-ended questioning and suggestions.

The programmes

The concept of producing programmes of this kind has called for a new approach in the field of publishing since a number of factors have emerged which must make the traditional textbook obsolescent. Among these factors may be numbered the following:

1. There must be the facility for a pupil to make frequent responses, whether by writing an answer, by looking at a slide, by listening to a tape or by carrying out an experiment.

2. The programme must be sufficiently flexible to enable the class teacher who has a knowledge of local conditions to adapt and amend the material to suit those circumstances.

3. The format of the programmes must be standardised to the extent that, where amendments seem desirable to the teacher, he can incorporate his own work at appropriate points in the programme through the use of standard duplicated materials, and can also remove any of the printed sections which appear inappropriate to his pupil's needs.

4. The mode of presentation must be basically simple in order to eliminate for the pupil, as far as possible, the hazard of operational or handling difficulties.

5. Provision must be made for the pupil to retain some record of the work which he has done in connection with a programme, without making the programme itself expendable.

6. Provision must be made to enable the teacher to keep a record of each child's progress and evidence of his achievement level.

7. Supplementary and enrichment materials in the form of slides, tapes, film-loops and other equipment must be made available in conjunction with the publication of the programmes.

To meet these requirements the programmed materials are produced as follows:

(*a*) The programmes are printed on standard size paper with holes punched so that they can be accommodated in a normal loose-leaf ring book. This ensures that pages can be added or extracted according to the needs of the pupils.

(*b*) In programmed sequences the answer side of any page can be masked by the simple expedient of a strip of cardboard.

(*c*) Two inexpensive and expendable Work Booklets accompany each programme pack. Facilities which these provide include:

(1) *A Time Sheet* on which the pupil can record the time spent on work related to the programme.

(2) *Assessment Section* answer spaces. Analysis of these answers enables

the teacher to draw a comparison between pre- and post-programmes performance.

(3) *A Visit Study Sheet.* This sheet is designed to promote careful observation by the child in the course of an initial visit.

(4) *A Summary Section.* The centre four pages of each Work Booklet contain a summary of the main contents of the programme and are retained by the pupil for his subsequent use.

(5) *Response Spaces.* These provide appropriate spaces where the pupil can record his responses to the programme.

(6) *Review Sheet Answer Spaces.* The Review Sheets, completed at intervals throughout the programme, provide the means by which the teacher can assess the progress of each pupil.

(*d*) A set of Teacher's Notes accompanies each programme pack and includes the following features:

(1) A statement indicating the age range and ability level for which the programme is designed.

(2) A statement specifying the objectives of the programme.

(3) A detailed list of all equipment necessary for the effective completion of the programme.

(4) A statement concerning the validation statistics.

(5) An outline of a possible procedure to be adopted in the classroom when using the programme.

(6) Information relating to supplementary and enrichment materials.

(7) Answers and Marking Keys in respect of the Assessment Section and the Review Sheets.

(*e*) Supplementary materials in the form of Slidefolios and Film Loops are produced in association with the publication of the programmes and are available from The Slide Centre Ltd., Portman House, 17, Brodrick Road, London, S.W.17.

Validation

Prior to publication all the programmes were submitted to a careful process of validation and details relating to that procedure are made available in the Teacher's Notes.

Part of that validation was done in a Nuffield Foundation-sponsored 'Resources for Learning' experiment at Binley Junior School, Coventry, over a period of one year. At the school unstreamed classes of 9 to 11-year-old children made a study of the school's environment with the help of programmed materials. In addition, other schools throughout the country assisted in the validation of individual programmes and on the basis of an analysis of the children's reactions and progress, coupled with teachers' comments and criticisms, the material in the programmes has been revised and edited. This has enabled a clear statement to be made about the effectiveness of the materials in their final published form.

Moreover, it is hoped that teachers who use the published programmes will submit them to a further process of validation by analysing the results achieved by their own pupils and by subsequently amending the materials to suit their individual requirements. Only in this way will the maximum potential of the programmes be realised.

Programme format

On p. 28 can be seen an example of a page from one of the programmes. It is reproduced at this point in order to give an indication of the kind of format which will be used in many of the programmes and to enable comment to be made about the mode of responses.

It will be seen that there is a vertical line dividing the page into two parts. The information and problems appear on the left-hand side of the page while the answers appear to the right of the vertical line. It will be found that the provision of a simple mask effectively covers the answer side of the page but allows the child to reveal successive single answers as he works down the page. Each unit of information and questioning is called a 'frame' and it will be seen that the page consists of two frames – nos. 142 and 143.

The frames reveal just two of the several techniques which may be employed to elicit responses. In frame 142 the programmer is seeking to reinforce an item of information which has been introduced in the preceding frames. This is done by requiring the pupil to complete a sentence by responding with a key word. In frame 143, however, the approach is quite different. In this case the programmer is testing the pupil's ability to apply what has been learnt in this section by posing a practical and relevant problem. Other techniques employed in the programmes include the use of open-ended questioning, reference back to the teacher for discussion, the performance of a task, the collection and analysis of information and the construction of equipment. Indeed, at frequent points throughout the programmes, the programmer deliberately requires that the pupil shall get up from the desk at which he has been sitting and pursue his enquiries beyond the narrow confines of the classroom. In this way the concept of fieldwork becomes a practical reality.

The adaptation of programmes to meet local circumstances

Page 28 also serves as an example of a point in a programme at which a

(142) It is best not to take a traffic census by yourself at a .... because the traffic is travelling in so many directions.	roundabout

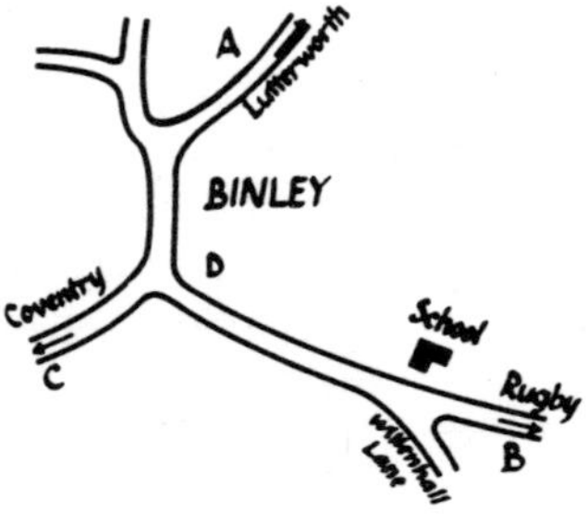

(143) Say which of the four points – *A, B, C* or *D* – you would go to in order to take a traffic census to provide the following information:	
1. All traffic travelling through Binley to Coventry.	1. *C*
2. Traffic travelling to Lutterworth.	2. *A*
3. Traffic travelling from Coventry to Rugby and Willenhall Lane.	3. *D*
4. Traffic from Rugby to Binley.	4. *B*

(*From a programme entitled 'Traffic'*)

teacher might wish to adapt the material to suit local circumstances. Frame 143 shows a sketch-map which relates to the Binley area of Coventry since that is the area in which the Nuffield experiment relating to the use of programmed materials is taking place. For the children at that school the sketch-map is relevant and meaningful. It will be apparent that children in other parts of the country will also be able to answer that frame if they have successfully learnt the material contained in that section of the programme but clearly it would be desirable, for example, that children in a school in central Watford should have a sketch-map relating to central Watford. This is a case where the class teacher can adapt the content of the programme by extracting this particular page and by replacing it with a duplicated sheet showing a sketch-map of the area around his own school.

Scope of the programmes

The ultimate range of programmes will be determined in the light of the needs of teachers and pupils alike but the following 10 titles have already been published:

1. Traffic
2. The Highway Code for Pedestrians
3. Farmers and their Animals
4. Farmers and the Crops they Grow
5. The Growth of Railways
6. Railways Today
7. Weather Recording
8. Houses and their History
9. Building a House
10. The Growth of Roads

The role of the teacher

One question which inevitably arises in any situation where the use of programmed materials is contemplated concerns the role of the teacher. It has already been stressed that the concept involved in the provision of programmed materials stems from the need to equip the teacher and his pupils with more and better resources for learning. The concept does not imply a weakening of the relationship between teacher and pupil by excluding the teacher from the learning process and replacing him with a programmed text. Nor does it imply, as the Plowden Report would seem to suggest, that programmed learning can do only the routine tasks. But the Report does rightly stress that what is important is that teachers should have greater opportunities 'to exercise their influence more constructively'.

> The motive for learning may arise from the children, or may be stimulated by discussion between teacher and children. The teacher can help children to become aware of problems, and to recognize the need for specific knowledge. At that point a programme might provide knowledge, techniques and practice in them. . . .
>
> *Children and Their Primary Schools*, para. 729
> *Plowden Report published by H.M.S.O.*

In the production of the programmes in this 'Environmental Studies' series the view is taken that the programmes themselves should play a positive part in forging the link between pupil and teacher. For this reason the programmes frequently refer the pupil to the teacher with such phrases as 'Go and discuss this answer with your teacher' or 'Show this to your teacher and ask his advice.' In this way the child will become increasingly aware of the teacher's role as a guide and friend who can be consulted as the occasion demands. Nevertheless, the programmed materials remain under the ultimate control of the teacher since he is the person who decides at what point any individual or group of pupils should undertake a particular programme.

It is anticipated that teachers will quickly come to appreciate the advantages to be gained from a situation in which pupils can work at a level appropriate to their ability, at a pace which is not predetermined by the 'average' of the class, and in the pursuit of learning, the motive for which is intrinsic.

3 Outdoor Work: the Environments Available

ARRANGING VISITS IN LOCAL AND MORE DISTANT AREAS

The whole essence of an environmental study is that initially the pupils should visit and study the local area and extend from this to more distant parts of the world. In rural areas this field study of the locality is comparatively easy; but in urban districts there is a need for careful supervision because of the traffic hazards. The children should be warmly and comfortably dressed and for any excursion into the country, other than a very short one, hiking clothing – an anorak, strong boots with good woollen stockings, sweater, a hat and gloves – is desirable. Wellingtons and capes are not recommended. They are uncomfortable when used for long periods and are cold. A haversack or rucksack for carrying equipment and specimens is another essential. Throughout such an excursion the Country Code should be observed.

'The Country Code'

Guard against all risk of fire.
Keep dogs under proper control.
Avoid damaging fences, hedges and walls
Safeguard water supplies.
Go carefully on country roads.
Fasten all gates.
Keep to the paths across farm land.
Leave no litter.
Protect wild life, wild plants and trees.
Respect the life of the countryside.

The booklet is obtainable from Her Majesty's Stationery Office.

The children need careful briefing before these excursions. It is very useful to give them a duplicated list of things to be found out, problems to answer, drawings to make, locations and habitats to find, and the route to be followed.

These local visits can be to any place of interest. Below is a list of some of these localities.

pond	pit heaps	near-by mansion
lake	road	local industry
river	road verge	street
stream	lane	neighbourhood
canal	park	town centre
water tank	gardens	market

playground	playing fields	fire station
waste ground	farm	post office
rubbish tips	church	railway station

Apart from visits to the local environment, half-day and full-day trips add to the possibilities of a discovery topic. The visit should be planned with the children in mind. Younger children (under 10) find a journey of normal school hours sufficient, but for older children longer journeys can be undertaken. For a long journey, train travel is more convenient than bus travel, for there is plenty of space for writing and exercise and toilet facilities are on the spot. Special party fares are available on the train and it is generally possible to get open-plan carriages which make supervision easier. Containers and water, to which fruit squash can be added, are supplied free.

Many teachers prefer to use coaches as costs are generally lower, but the itinerary needs to be carefully thought out to include all the necessary stops.

The idea for the visit may arise from discussion with the parents. First the Local Education Authority should be asked for written permission through the School Governors. Then the parents should be notified of the idea of the outing and written permission obtained for each child to join the party. The route should be worked out and time allowed for refreshment and toilet necessities. Many excursions suffer from having a too crowded itinerary. The object of the expedition should be clear and the children's attention should be directed to the important features perhaps by a questionnaire.

In a museum visit the children should be directed to the significant items (see section on museums p. 41). School uniform is good dress for many of these occasions as it makes 'head counting' easy. Adequate supervision is essential and many schools arrange for dining-room helpers or nursery helpers or even parents to come along so that the staffing rota is no more than fifteen children to one adult.

Insurance is very necessary. Most Local Authorities insure their teachers against third-party risk when organising school journey parties. Some also insure against loss of baggage or money, accidents or illness and cancellation of tours; but it is necessary to check exactly how much insurance has been taken out so that any gaps can be filled by a private insurance. The travel agent can usually recommend a reliable insurance company.

Below is a list indicating the kinds of places that may be visited.

1. LONDON

London is a natural place for such a visit. Some suggested venues are:

(a) The usual sights and a trip along the river. Much useful information and maps can be obtained from: The Corporation of London, Information Centre, 5 St. Paul's Churchyard, London, E.C.4; London Transport, Public Relations Division, 55 Broadway, London, S.W.1.

(b) The Markets. Information can be obtained from Covent Garden Market, London, W.C.2., Billingsgate Market, London, E.C.3, Smithfield Market, London, E.C.1.

(c) The Roman Wall can be seen at the following points: the General Post Office, King Edward Street; Roman Wall House, Crutched Friars; the St. John Cass College, Cooper's Row; the Crescent, Trinity Place and the Wardrobe Tower, Tower of London. Portions of the wall as rebuilt in medieval times are to be found at All Hallows Churchyard, London Wall; in the churchyards of St. Alphage and of St. Giles', Cripplegate; Warwick Square, and Amen Court.

(d) Ships

(i) *The Cutty Sark*, Greenwich Pier, S.E.10.
The last and most famous of the old Clippers with a small museum of her contemporaries and a fine collection of figureheads. Mondays to Saturdays, 11–6; Sundays, Good Friday and Boxing Day, 2.30–6. Closed Christmas Eve. Special rates for parties. Unaccompanied children not admitted.

(ii) H.M.S. *Discovery*, Victoria Embankment, W.C.2.
Scott's first ship and a museum of his Antarctic voyages. Daily 1–4.30. Organised parties with a guide.

(iii) National Maritime Museum, Romney Road, Greenwich, London, S.E.10.
This has a good collection of ship models, figureheads, seascapes and portraits, navigational instruments and charts. Mondays to Saturdays 10–6. Sundays 2.30–6.0.

(e) Houses of famous men

(i) Carlyle's House, 24, Cheyne Row, Chelsea, S.W.3.
Thomas Carlyle lived here for nearly 50 years. His clothes in his wardrobe and, on the top floor, his double-walled refuge from the noises of town. Wednesdays to Saturdays 10–1 and 2–6; Sundays 2–6 or dusk, if earlier. Closed Boxing Day and Christmas Day.

(ii) Dickens' House, 48, Doughty Street, W.C.1.
Dickens' home from 1837 to 1839. A Dickens library, mss., letters, his furniture and reproduction of Dingley Dell Kitchen. Mondays to Saturdays only 10–5. Closed Bank Holidays and Easter weekend.

(iii) Flamstead House, Greenwich Park, S.E.10.
The old Royal Observatory built by Wren in 1676 for the Rev. John Flamstead, the first Astronomer Royal. The Octagon Room is as it was in his day. The Greenwich Meridian runs across the courtyard. Here is the National Maritime Museum's collection of historic telescopes and astronomical instruments. Mondays to Saturdays 10–6; Sundays 2.30–6. In winter the house closes at 5.30. Closed Christmas Eve.

(iv) Hogarth's House, Hogarth Lane, Chiswick, London, W.4.
This was the painter's country house for 15 years. Drawings, engravings and some relics. Mondays to Saturdays 11–6. Sundays 2–6 (Oct.–April, close at 4).

(v) Dr. Johnson's House, 17, Gough Square, London, E.C.4.
This is a Queen Anne house in which Johnson compiled his dictionary. Closed Bank Holidays and Sundays.

(vi) Keats' House, Keats Grove, Hampstead, London, N.W.3.
Two years of Keats' creative life were spent here. Mondays to Saturdays. 10–6. Closed Boxing Day.

(vii) Wellington Museum, Apsley House, Hyde Park Corner, W.1.
Personal relics of the Duke in his own splendid house. The pictures include three

superb works by Velasquez. Mondays to Saturdays 10–6; Sundays 2.30–6. Organised school parties free.

(viii) Wesley's Chapel and House, City Road, E.C.1.
John Wesley died here in 1791. Mondays to Saturdays 10–1 and 2–4. Chapel daily 8–dusk.

(f) The Tower of London

Tower of London Armouries, Tower of London, E.C.3.
Arms and armour from the Middle Ages onwards. Mondays to Saturdays, November–February 9.30–4. Mondays to Saturdays, March–October 9.30–5 (Sundays 2–5).

(g) Museums

(i) British Museum and Print Room, Great Russell Street, W.C.1.
The Rosetta Stone, the Portland Vase, Magna Charta, the Elgin Marbles, Nelson's Log-Book, Scott's Diary, Engravings of the masters. Mondays to Saturdays 10–5; Sundays 2.30–6.

(ii) The Commonwealth Institute, Kensington High Street, London, W.8.
Provides a series of display galleries and lessons on the galleries, which are booked in advance. Cinema shows are also given. Applications for these services should be made to the Education Officer.

(iii) Geffrye Museum, Kingsland Road, Shoreditch, E.2.
An instructive museum of furniture and furnishings arranged in chronological order as specimen rooms from 1600 onwards. Tuesdays to Saturdays 10–5; Sundays 2–5.

(iv) Geological Museum, Exhibition Road, South Kensington, S.W.7.
Primarily a museum for the student of geology and mineralogy, but of great general interest. Mondays to Saturdays 10–6; Sundays 2.30–6. Lectures can be arranged. on application to the Museum Lecturer.

(v) Horniman Museum, London Road, Forest Hill, S.E.23.
An ethnographical museum. Man: his arts, crafts and religions. Zoology. Aquaria. Many musical instruments from all parts of the world. Free lectures and concerts in winter. Tuesdays to Saturdays 10.30–6; Sundays 2–6. Open Good Fridays.

(vi) Imperial War Museum, Lambeth Road, S.E.1.
A visual record of the Empire and Commonwealth in two world wars. Its art collection includes most of the modern masters. Photographs, library, models, actual weapons and relics. Mondays to Saturdays 10–6; Sundays 2–6.

(vii) Museum of London Transport, Syon Park, Middlesex.

(viii) National Army Museum, Royal Hospital Road, Chelsea, London, SW3 4HT.

(ix) Natural History Museum, Cromwell Road, London, S.W.7.
Lessons are given by qualified teachers on any subject covered by the museum. In order to arrange lessons for under-13s teachers should apply to the Teacher in Charge, Children's Centre, British Museum (Natural History), Cromwell Road London, S.W.7.

(x) Rotunda Museum, Woolwich Common, S.E.18.
Guns, early rockets, muskets, rifles and arms of all kinds and periods. Armour and ship models. Mondays to Saturdays 10–12.45 and 2–5; Sundays 2–5. (October to March until 4.) Unaccompanied children under 14 not admitted.

(xi) Royal Air Force Museum, Hendon Aerodrome, N.W.9

(xii) Science Museum, Exhibition Road, South Kensington, S.W.7.
The application of science to industry and to everyday life. 'Puffing Billy', the 'Rocket', replicas and working models. Mondays to Saturdays 10–6; Sundays 2.30–6.

(xiii) Victoria and Albert Museum, Cromwell Road, South Kensington, S.W.7.
Fine and applied arts of all periods; Raphael cartoons, a fine collection of

paintings and drawings by Constable. English miniatures and water-colours. An excellent print room. Mondays to Saturdays 10–6; Sundays 2.30—6.

(h) London Airport

Information can be obtained from London Airport, Hounslow, Middlesex.

For adults there is the *London Appreciation Society*, 8, Scardale Villas, Kensington, London, W.8, which organises visits on Saturday afternoons to places of historic and modern interest in and around London.

2 THE SEA-SHORE

This makes an excellent place for an educational visit. All aspects of the study can be covered – historical and geographical, aesthetic and scientific. Collections of shells, pebbles, seaweed and sea animals can be made. The form of the coast is another interesting study with cliff forms, shape, undercutting, caves and the shape of the beach. Pebbles can be identified and random samples taken of the numbers of the different types of stones. A profile can be measured down the beach (see Chapter 4). Animal life, seaweeds and the nature of the beach materials can be plotted alongside the profile (Fig. 3:1). If the school is near the seaside these profiles can be

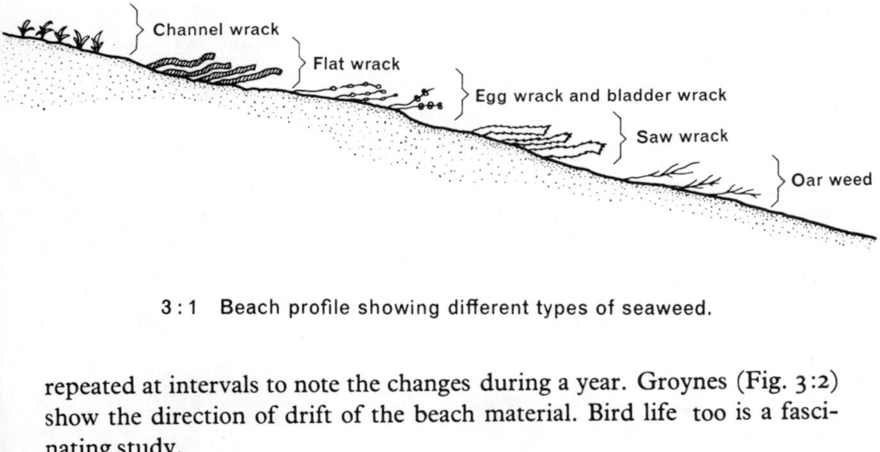

3:1 Beach profile showing different types of seaweed.

repeated at intervals to note the changes during a year. Groynes (Fig. 3:2) show the direction of drift of the beach material. Bird life too is a fascinating study.

The seaside town is a study in itself. Where is the nucleus of the town? What kinds of house-types are present? How many different types of shops are present? Where are they? What is the history of the town? How many industries are there? Why is there a tourist industry here? Where do the visitors come from? What evidence is there of the importance of the industry? What is the shape of the promenade? How many hotels and cafés are there? Was there a fishing industry? Is fishing still carried on? How many buses and trains run to the town? How often do they run?

3:2 A groyne. The beach material is piled up against one side of the groyne.

3 A RIVER VALLEY

A coach trip could be made from the source to the mouth of the river. This trip may have to be split into two or more parts. Studies would be made where the river was accessible. The water, animal life, nature of the bottom, could be sampled, measurements made of the rate of flow, depth and width of the river, and the land use in the valley could be mapped. Observations could be made of the relationship of the geology and land use, settlement sites, and the position of the road and railway.

4 FARM VISITS

Contacts can sometimes be made through the National Farmers' Union, County Headquarters. The addresses are in the telephone directory. These visits are of great importance for children living in large towns. More details of this can be found in Teachers' Guide 1.

3:3 House types. The older ones are grouped together along the main road.

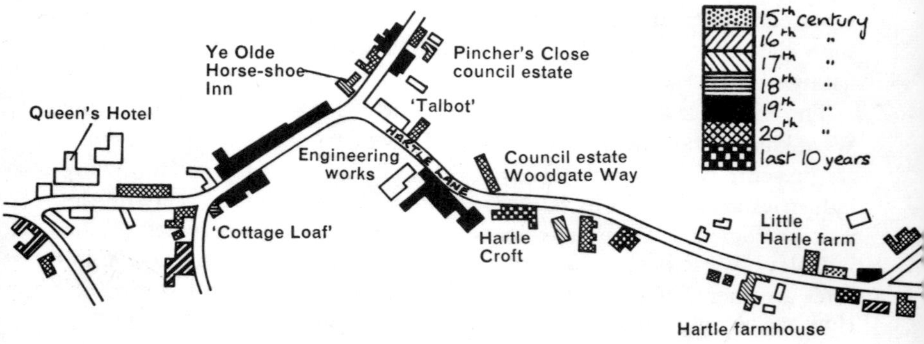

5 ZOO VISITS

Zoo visits can be wonder-provoking for younger children or places of real investigation for older pupils. The following list indicates some of the main points of interest in the Zoos.

The Young Zoologists Club, London Zoo, Regent's Park, London, N.W.1, has some 4000 members throughout the country aged between 9 and 18. It provides tours and lectures in the school holidays, a magazine and six tickets annually for London Zoo and Whipsnade. There is a reduced subscription for groups. Some other zoos may offer similar facilities; where these exist details may be obtained from the zoos concerned.

Bedfordshire

Whipsnade Park Zoo, nr. *Dunstable.* The Zoological Society of London's country zoo, specializing in herd animals. This was the first drive-in zoo in Britain.

Berkshire

Windsor Safari Park, St. Leonards, *Windsor.* It was opened in 1969 by Billy Smart's New World Circus Ltd. The dolphins are worth visiting.

Buckinghamshire

Flamingo Gardens and Zoological Park, Weston Underwood, *Olney*. This is an important bird collection specialising in water fowl and cranes, and a collection of hoofed animals, including European bison and members of the Camel family.

Cheshire

The North of England Zoological Society, *Chester.* It is noted for its Pachyderm House, its Tropical House and its plants. There is a water-bus service which carries visitors around the zoo.

Devonshire

(i) *Exmouth.* Exmouth Zoo, Sea Front, Exmouth. Begun as a branch of Paignton Zoo, it was bought in 1962 by Kenneth Smith, who has collected animals with Gerald Durrell.

(ii) *Paignton.* Paignton Zoological and Botanical Gardens, Paignton. The zoo, owned by an educational trust, also incorporates a fine botanical collection. Residential courses are run for VIth form students in Biology, day courses for secondary school pupils, and lecture demonstrations are also held.

(iii) *Torquay.* Aqualand (Aquana Research Ltd.), Beacon Quay, Torquay. There is a good collection of local marine fish.

Dorset

(i) *Abbotsbury* Swannery, Abbotsbury.

Essex

(i) *Colchester.* Colchester Zoo, Stanway Hall, Colchester. A good general collection, specializing in the big cats. It also has a small museum.

(ii) *Widdington.* Mole Hall Wildlife Park, Widdington, nr. Newport. A small mixed collection of animals. Note especially the waterfowl and fine groups of flamingoes and woolly monkeys.

Gloucestershire

(i) *Bourton-on-the-Water.* The Birdland Zoo Gardens, Bourton-on-the-Water. A superb bird collection in the middle of this beautiful village. Noted for its Tropical House, free-flying macaws and penguin tank where penguins can be seen swimming under water.

(ii) *Slimbridge.* The Wildfowl Trust, Slimbridge. Peter Scott's famous collection of waterfowl, the largest of its kind in the world. Observation towers and hides give unique opportunities of watching the birds, including large migrant populations of geese.

Hampshire

Marwell Zoological Park, Fisher's Pond, Colden Common, Nr. *Winchester.* A major new collection of hoofed animals, including many rarities. This is a drive-round park like Whipsnade, not 'drive-through', like safari parks. The collection also has Siberian tigers and other cat species, and some Australian and South American animals.

Lancashire

(i) *Blackpool* Tower Co., Ltd., Empress Buildings, Blackpool. There is an excellent aquarium with many of the local Fylde coast fish. Also see the indoor zoo on the top floor of the Tower. This has recently been modernised and is well worth a visit.

(ii) *Blackpool* Municipal Zoological Gardens. Like Marwell, this was another major zoo opened in 1972. It is by far the largest Municipal Zoo in the country, and Phase 1 is now completed, covering 12 hectares. It is a general collection of elephants, giraffes, lions, tigers, etc. and a large beautifully landscaped tropical bird house.

(iii) *Manchester.* Belle Vue (Manchester) Ltd., Zoological Gardens, Belle Vue, Manchester, 12. The services of an Educational Officer are available and full details are obtainable on request.

(iv) *Morecambe.* Marineland, Morecambe. Aquarium, reptiles, young chimpanzees in summer, sea lions and dolphins.

(v) Winged World, New Heysham Head Entertainment Centre, *Heysham.* One of the best collections of soft-billed birds in Europe. Some of the birds are confined by light only, while visitors remain in comparative darkness.

(vi) *Bolton Aquarium*, Museum and Art Centre, Civic Centre, *Bolton.*

Leicestershire

Twycross. Zoo Park (Twycross Ltd.), Norton-Juxta-Twycross, nr. Atherstone, Warwickshire. Conducted educational tours can be booked. The instruction of mentally retarded and spastic children is a speciality of the zoo. The zoo specializes in South American primates and the anthropoid apes.

Lincolnshire

Cleethorpes. Cleethorpes Marineland and Zoo Ltd., Humberston, Grimsby. School parties are welcomed and conducted parties can be arranged at no extra charge.

(ii) *Skegness.* Skegness Natureland, North Parade, The Promenade, Skegness. An interesting collection of marine mammals kept in sea water. There is also an excellent small aquarium and a Tropical House. The owner is George Cansdale, the well-known broadcaster and lecturer.

London

(i) The Zoological Society of London, *Regent's Park*, London, N.W.1. This is the major zoo of Britain. For school parties applications should be made to the Education Officer at Regent's Park.

(ii) *Battersea.* Children's Zoo.

(iii) *Crystal Palace.* Children's Zoo.

Norfolk

Great Witchingham. The Norfolk Wildlife Park, Great Witchingham. It specialises in the exhibition of British and European fauna. This is also the home of the Pheasant Trust, a major collection of exotic pheasants.

Northants

Peakirk. The Waterfowl Gardens, Peakirk, nr. Peterborough. This is the Wildfowl Trust's other collection of waterfowl, used mainly as a breeding nursery.

Oxfordshire

Burford. The Cotswold Wild Life Park. Opened in 1970; the setting is excellent and the collection of birds in particular has great potential. Now has white rhinos and zebras and a reptile house.

Somerset

(i) *Bristol.* Clifton and West of England Zoological Society, Zoological Gardens, Bristol. Special bookings can be made for parties. This is one of the major zoos in Britain, set in beautiful gardens. Note especially the white tigers, okapis and rhinoceroses, all of which breed regularly.

(ii) *Rode.* The Tropical Bird Gardens, Rode, nr. Bath. A fine bird collection, noted for its breeding successes in the parrot family.

Surrey

(i) *Chessington.* Chessington Zoo Ltd., Chessington. A major collection with many new exhibits, including an interesting British wild life section.

(ii) *Farnham.* Birdworld, Holt Pound, Farnham. A new and interesting small bird garden with a good collection of perching birds.

Sussex

(i) *Brighton.* Brighton Aquarium, Marine Parade, Brighton. A 1000-seat dolphinarium was added in 1969.

(ii) *Halland.* The Bentley Wildfowl Collection, Halland, Lewes. This is a very interesting waterfowl collection in a natural setting.

(iii) Drusilla's Animal Collection, Berwick, *Alfriston.* This is a well-run Children's Zoo which has modernised and improved the cage exhibits and added a good penguin pool, water fowl ponds and large guinea pig exhibit.

Wiltshire

Longleat. The Lions of Longleat, Warminster. Starting with groups of lions in this famous park, the collection now includes groups of giraffe, zebra and baboons; also hippos, sea lions and a chimpanzee island in the lake.

Warwickshire

Birmingham. Birmingham Zoo, Cannonhill Park, Pershore Road, Birmingham 29. This is a small offshoot of Dudley Zoo, a mixed collection which includes gibbons, cats, camels and kangaroos. A model zoo, beautifully kept.

Worcestershire

Dudley. The Dudley Zoological Society Ltd., Dudley Zoo, Dudley. In addition to the zoo there is also an aquarium and a children's zoo. There are facilities for conducted parties and feature films about the zoo are shown throughout the country. Those interested should contact the General Manager.

Yorkshire

(i) Flamingo Park Zoo, *Kirby Misperton,* Nr. Malton. A feature of the zoo is the Model Farm which shows a collection of cattle, sheep, pigs and poultry of the lesser-known and the well-known breeds.

(ii) Harewood Bird Garden, Harewood House, *Leeds.* This is a beautifully designed collection of aviaries and paddock enclosures in the grounds of Harewood House, which is itself open to the public; a large penguin pool with underwater viewing and a very attractive little tropical house. The Garden has a well-organised lecture service for schools and teaching facilities on the spot.

Ireland

(i) *Dublin.* The Royal Zoological Society of Ireland, Phoenix Park, Dublin. An excellent general collection in a beautiful setting, including a 3 hectare lake. There is a well-stocked Children's Corner, with a special staff to answer questions.

(ii) *Belfast.* Bellevue Zoological Gardens, Belfast. Britain's oldest and largest municipal zoo.

Channel Islands

Jersey. The Jersey Wildlife Preservation Trust, *Les Augres Manor*, Jersey. This zoo specialises in the preservation of rare species of animals which might otherwise become extinct. The zoo was started by Gerald Durrell, the well-known animal collector and author.

Scotland

(i) *Edinburgh.* The Royal Zoological Society of Scotland, Zoological Park, Murrayfield, Edinburgh 12. Talks can be arranged for parties. Special features are the largest collection of penguins in Britain, the Carnegie Aquarium and the Children's Farm. The zoo also has an unusually comprehensive labelling system.

(ii) *Glasgow.* The Zoological Society of Glasgow and West of Scotland, Calderpark, Uddington, Glasgow. A fairly small mixed collection in an attractive setting, with tropical, reptile and nocturnal houses.

(iii) *Aberdeen.* The North of Scotland Zoological Society Ltd., Hazlehead Park, Aberdeen. Guided tours are given on request. The Zoo's educational function is an important part of its activities. Still a small collection, now being modernized and improved.

(iv) *Dundee.* Camperdown Children's Zoo, Camperdown Park, Dundee. Started by the Corporation as an educational facility. Lectures are given at the zoo's field study centre with walks along a nature trail.

(v) Highland Wild Life Park, Kincraig, Kingussie, Inverness-shire. This is the third high-quality collection opened in 1972 14 km. south of Aviemore in beautiful Scottish moorland scenery. The aim is to show indigenous Scottish animals, including those found there since the last Ice Age which have since disappeared, such as wolves, bears and reindeer. You first drive through an 80-hectare enclosure mainly populated by red deer and wild horses, after which you see other exhibits on foot. Very well run and well worth a visit.

Wales

Colwyn Bay. The Welsh Mountain Zoo and Botanic Gardens, Flagstaff Gardens, Colwyn Bay. Guided tours are given by arrangement. This is a good and still growing general collection, with reptile, parrot and tropical houses, and an excellent natural history museum.

6 VISITS TO PORTS

Visits can be arranged to most ports which are controlled by the British Transport Docks Board. Applications should be made to the Port Director or Docks Manager at the addresses below:

HULL DOCKS
Docks Manager, P.O. Box No. 1, Kingston House Tower, Bond Street, Hull, HU1 3ER. (Tel. 0482 27171)

GOOLE DOCKS
Docks Manager, Dock Office, Goole, Yorks., DN14 5BB. (Tel. 0405 2691)

GRIMSBY DOCKS, IMMINGHAM DOCKS
Docks Manager, Grimsby, Lincs. (Tel. 0472 59181)

KING'S LYNN DOCKS
Docks Manager, Dock Office, King's Lynn, Norfolk, PE30 2EU. (Tel. 0553 2636)

LOWESTOFT HARBOUR
Docks Manager, Custom House, Lowestoft, Suffolk. (Tel. 0502 2286/7)

SOUTHAMPTON DOCKS
Port Director, Dock House, Canute Rozd, Southampton, SO9 1PZ. (Tel. 0703 23844)

PLYMOUTH (MILLBAY) DOCKS
Docks Manager, Dock Office, Millbay Docks, Plymouth, Devon, PL1 3EF. (Tel. 0752 62191)

SOUTH WALES PORTS
(Newport, Cardiff, Barry, Port Talbot, Swansea)
Port Director, South Wales Ports, Pierhead Building, Bute Docks, Cardiff, Glam., CF1 5TH. (Tel. 0222 42544)

GARSTON DOCKS
Docks Manager, Docks Office, Garston, Liverpool, L19 2JW. (Tel. 051–427 5971)

FLEETWOOD DOCKS
Docks Manager, Dock Office, Fleetwood, Lancs., FY7 6PP. (Tel. 039–17 2323)

BARROW DOCKS, SILLOTH DOCKS
Docks Manager, Dock Office, Ramsden Dock Road, Barrow-in-Furness, Lancs., LA14 2TW. (Tel. 0229 12911)

AYR HARBOUR, TROON HARBOUR
Docks Manager and Harbour Master, Dock Office, Ayr, Ayrshire. (Tel. 0292 67261)

Full information about the British Transport Docks is obtainable from British Transport Docks Board, Melbury House, Melbury Terrace, London, NW1 6JY.

Avonmouth Visits to Avonmouth last approximately two hours and children under the age of 14 are not allowed.

Information is obtainable from The Port of Bristol Authority, St. Andrew's Road, Avonmouth, Bristol, BS11 9DQ.

Liverpool Mersey Docks Harbour Board, Dock Office, Liverpool, 3.

Manchester A visit to Manchester Docks lasts two hours and departure times are 10.00 a.m. and 2.00 p.m. Tours run from February to November each year. A party must not consist of more than 50 pupils. The starting-point for all tours is at the South 6 Dock gate in Trafford Road, Salford, 5, where parties will be met by a guide. Enquiries should be addressed to the Public Relations Officer, Manchester, Ship Canal Co., Ship Canal House, King Street, Manchester, M2 4WX.

Full-length tours can be arranged by the Co-operative Travel Service, New Century House, Manchester M60 4ES, to whom applications for fuller information should be made.

Belfast Guided tours for school parties are provided at Belfast. For full information write to The Executive Officer, Belfast Harbour Commissioners, Corporation Quay, Belfast.

Glasgow At Glasgow parties must not exceed 40 in number and, if aged under 16, must remain in their coach. For details of school visits write to Clyde Port Authority, Marketing Department, 16 Robertson Street, Glasgow, G2 8DS.

Southampton Sightseeing tours of shipping in Southampton Docks are organised from the Royal Pier by Star Boats, 1 Cranbury Buildings, Cranbury Place, Southampton and Favourite Boat Cruises, Royal Pier, Southampton.

7 MUSEUM VISITS

Museums provide excellent information on local history, general knowledge, geography and science. There is a series of specialised museums to which a useful visit could be made. These are listed in the *National Benzole Book on Museums* edited by Sir Hugh Casson. The main ones are noted below.

Brixham Museum, Devon, tells of the history of fishing, shipping and of Brixham itself.

The Shuttleworth collection of old war planes is situated at the Old Warden Aerodrome, nr. Biggleswade, Bedfordshire.

Museum of English Rural Life, Whiteknights Park, Reading, Berks.

The Tramway Museum, Cliff Quarry, Crich, Derbyshire.

National Motor Museum, Beaulieu and Maritime Museum, Buckler's Hard, Hants.

The Cromwell Museum, Market Square, Huntingdon.

The Waterways Museum, Stoke Bruerne, Towcester, Northants.

Ironbridge Gorge Museum, Church Hill, Ironbridge, Shropshire.

Great Western Railway Museum, Farringdon Road, Swindon, Wilts.

The York Museums (Railway and Castle).

The Welsh Folk Museum, St. Fagans, Cardiff.

The Highland Folk Museum, Kingussie, Inverness-shire.

Haslemere Educational Museum, Haslemere, Surrey.

North of England Open Air Museum, Beamish, Co. Durham.

Avoncroft Museum of Buildings, Bromsgrove, Worcs.

Weald and Downland Open Air Museum, Singleton, Sussex.

Abbots Hall Museum of Rural Life of East Anglia, Stowmarket, Suffolk.

Museum and visitor centre, Morwellham Quay, nr. Tavistock, Devon.

Roman Palace Museum, Fishbourne, Sussex.

A list of the other museums can be found in:

Museums & Galleries in Great Britain and Northern Ireland (Index Publishers Ltd.).

Directory of Museums and Art Galleries in the British Isles (Museums Association), 1948

Guide to London Museums and Galleries (H.M.S.O.).
Museums Calendar (Museums Association).
Individual City Guides to Museums are also available.

In recent years museums have given a great variety of services to schools which include loans, particularly useful for historical topics, lectures, questionnaire tours, lessons, film shows and fieldwork. Their post cards and guides are useful teaching material. A list of the museums providing these services is given below. Further details are available from the Hon. Sec., Group for Educational Services in Museums, City Museum, Bristol, BS8 1RL.

ENGLAND (except London)

AYLESBURY
County Museum, Church Street, Aylesbury, Bucks.

BATH
The American Museum, Claverton Manor, Bath, BA2 7BD, Somerset.

BIRMINGHAM
City Museum and Art Gallery, Congreve St., Birmingham, B3 3DH.

BRADFORD
City Art Gallery and Museum, Cartwright Memorial Hall, Bradford, BD9 4NS, Yorks.

BRIGHTON
Schools Loan Service, Northgate House, Church Street, Brighton, BN1 1UE.

BRISTOL
City Museum, Queen's Road, Bristol, BS8 1RL.

CAMBRIDGE
County Museum Service, 9 Castle Street, Cambridge.

CHELTENHAM
Cheltenham Art Gallery and Museum, Clarence Street, Cheltenham, Glos.

COLCHESTER
Colchester and Essex Museum, The Castle, Colchester, CO1 1TJ, Essex.

DERBY
Derbyshire Museum Service, Park Grange, Duffield Road, Derby, DE3 1AB.
Museum and Art Gallery, Strand, Derby.

DEVON
Devonshire County Council Natural History Museum, Babbacombe Road, Torquay.

DURHAM
Bowes Museum, Barnard Castle, Co. Durham.

EAST SUSSEX
Schools Museum Service, Westfield House, Baron's Down, Brighton Road, Lewes, Sussex.

HASLEMERE
Educational Museum, Haslemere, Surrey

IPSWICH
Ipswich Museum, High Street, Ipswich, Suffolk.

KINGSTON UPON HULL
Hull Museums, 23–24 High Street, Hull.

LEEDS
Schools Museum Service, Municipal Buildings, Leeds, LS1 1AA.

LEICESTER
Schools Service, Belgrave House, Church Road, Belgrave, Leicester.

LETCHWORTH
Museum and Art Gallery, Broadway, Letchworth, Herts.

LIVERPOOL
City of Liverpool Museum, William Brown Street, Liverpool, L3 8EN.

LUTON
Museum and Art Gallery, Wardown Park, Luton.

MANCHESTER
Art Gallery Centre, The Athenaeum, 81 Princess Street, Manchester, M1 4HR.
Manchester Museum, The University, Oxford Road, Manchester, M13 9PL.
Manchester Museum of Science and Technology, 97 Grosvenor Street, Manchester, M1 7HF.

NEWPORT, Mon.
Schools Museum Service, Museum and Art Gallery, John Frost Square, Newport, Monmouthshire, NPT 1PA.

NORWICH
The Castle Museum, Norwich, NOR 65B.

NOTTINGHAM
Natural History Museum, Wollaton Hall, Nottingham, NG8 2AE.
Nottinghamshire County Educational Museum Service, Gedling House, Gedling, Notts., NG4 4AD.

OXFORD
City-County Museum Service, Fletcher's House, Woodstock, Oxon., OX7 1SN.

PLYMOUTH
City Museum and Art Gallery, Tavistock Road, Plymouth, Devon, PL4 8AJ.

PORTSMOUTH
Portsmouth City Museums, Alexandra Road, Portsmouth, Hampshire.

READING
Museum and Art Gallery, School Service Section, Yeomanry House, Castle Hill, Reading, Berks., RG1 7TA.

ROTHERHAM
Schools Officer, Education Offices, Wellgate, Rotherham, Yorkshire.

ST. ALBANS
Verulamium Museum, St. Albans, Herts.

SHEFFIELD
City Art Galleries, Weetwood, Eccleshall Road South, Sheffield, S11 9PL.
City Museum, Weston Park, Sheffield, Yorks., S10 2TP.

TAUNTON
Educational Museum and Art Service, Weir Lodge, Staplegrove Road, Taunton, Somerset.

TEESSIDE
Dorman Museum, Teesside.

WAKEFIELD
West Riding School Museum Service, 71c Northgate, Wakefield, Yorkshire.

WARWICK
County Museum, Market Place, Warwick.

WORCESTERSHIRE
Hartlebury Castle, Kidderminster, Worcs.

SCOTLAND

EDINBURGH
Schools Museum Service, Royal Scottish Museum, Chambers Street, Edinburgh, EH1 1JF.

GLASGOW
Museum and Art Gallery, Kelvingrove, Glasgow, C3.

PAISLEY
Museum and Art Galleries, High Street, Paisley.

WALES

National Museum of Wales, Cathays Park, Cardiff, CF1 3NP.

LONDON (see also section on 'London', p. 32)

Bethnal Green Museum, Cambridge Heath Road, London, E.2.
British Museum, London, WC1B 3DG.
British Museum (Natural History), Cromwell Road, London, SW7 5BD.
Commonwealth Institute, Kensington High Street, London, W8 6NQ.
Geffrye Museum, Kingsland Road, London, E2 8EA.
Geological Museum, Exhibition Road, London, S.W.7.
Horniman Museum, Forest Hill, London, SE23 3PQ.
Imperial War Museum, Lambeth Road, London, SE1 6HZ.
London Museum, Kensington Palace, The Broad Walk, Kensington Gardens, London, W8 4PX.
National Gallery, Trafalgar Square, London, W.C.2.
National Portrait Gallery, St. Martin's Place, London, WC2H OHE.
National Maritime Museum, Greenwich, London, SE10 9NF.
National Army Museum, Royal Hospital Road, London, S.W.3.
Passmore Edwards Museum, Romford Road, Stratford, London, E15 4LZ.
Science Museum, South Kensington, London, SW7 2DD.
Tate Gallery, Millbank, London, S.W.1.
Victoria and Albert Museum, Cromwell Road, South Kensington, London, SW7 2RL.
(Details of the services available will be supplied on writing to the Museum Education Officer.)

An example of the services provided is that of the Bristol Schools Museum Service. The Service is provided free of charge to schools and colleges in Bristol and to the borderline areas in N. Somerset and S. Gloucestershire. There is a children's room fitted with visual aid equipment, laboratory benches with sinks, water, gas and electricity. At the beginning of each term a circular letter is sent to all junior and secondary schools in the area and to infant and special schools on request. This circular gives details of the various services for the term.

SERVICES OFFERED BY THE BRISTOL SCHOOLS MUSEUM SERVICE

The lesson service

(*a*) Lessons listed in the termly circular are given by the organisers in the museum. A range of topics in biology, history, archaeology, geology and geography is offered each term and schools make their requests for them.

(*b*) The class with its own teacher comes to the Schools' Room and after an introduction to the subject by the organiser, lasting perhaps half an hour or so, individual work begins. The children are taken in small groups (usually 6–10) to the museum galleries to see and discuss relevant displays and for the remainder of the time, work on specimens in the Children's Room. Work-sheets when provided are prepared with the age and ability of the children, who are coming for the lesson, in mind. The teacher participates in these activities.

(*c*) Morning sessions begin at 10 a.m. and afternoon sessions at 2 p.m. A visit normally lasts 1½–2 hours. All necessary equipment is provided.

(*d*) Schools using the lesson service:

(i) Primary schools generally have little difficulty in arranging for a morning or an afternoon session at the museum.

(ii) Secondary schools can and do make similar arrangements but times of the visits are often arranged to fit in with their timetable.

The loan service

(*a*) *Contents*

The material included in the School Loan Collection is especially prepared for the use of the teacher in the classroom. It includes museum specimens, models, photographs and slides, and composite display cases. Wherever possible material for handling is presented. The subjects covered are again biology, history, archaeology, geology and geography. Art teachers frequently borrow some of the items. The cases are designed by the appropriate organiser and constructed in the museum workshops, by the Department's own conservation assistant.

(*b*) Applications to borrow and confirmations of booking are made on specially printed cards.

(*c*) *Administration of the Loan Service*

Items are circulated weekly in term-time. The Museum has the permanent use of a delivery van from the Corporation Transport Department. For convenience Bristol is divided into five delivery areas, red, white, blue, green and yellow – and delivery cards are correspondingly coloured.

Saturday clubs are run (*a*) for Juniors (aged 4–10) and (*b*) for Seniors (aged 10–13). They meet each Saturday in term-time in the Schools' Room from 10–11.30 a.m. There is no charge for membership and all the materials used (pencils, notebooks, etc.) are provided. Membership is limited to 50 club members. Handling specimens are available and in addition to the gallery displays, films or slides may be shown. Books borrowed from the Bristol School Library Service may be used. Usually, one half-day excursion connected with the work is arranged each month (e.g. to Aust Cliff to collect fossils, to local woods for toadstools, to the zoo, etc.). After the age of 12, really keen members join the Junior Section of the British Naturalists' Society (age limits 12–21) with which the Museum is closely associated.

Special lectures are arranged for school children, and they are given in the Museum Lecture Theatre (seating 400) by visiting speakers. The four lectures for older primary children take place in school time in the Autumn term. The lecture for secondary school children is given in the Spring term.

Competitions are arranged by the Organisers with the help of the Schools Museum Service Advisory Committee. Details of the competitions are given in the leaflets distributed to schools, the local press, etc. Entries are judged by a sub-committee of the Advisory Committee and prizes are awarded in various age and subject groups.

Students. Student-teachers from Bristol University and Colleges of Education in Bristol and Bath visit the Museum with their tutors for lecture-demonstrations about the Schools Museum Service and the principles involved in planning museum lessons and in preparing loan material. A number of them borrow loan material during their periods of teaching practice.

Courses for teachers. It has been felt for some time that the number of children reached by the teaching service was very small in proportion to the total school population of the City, and so the department has begun a series of teacher training courses, in conjunction with the University of Bristol Institute of Education. So far successful courses have been run in Geology, Natural History and History. In each case the use of the Museum has been emphasised.

The City Museum also co-operates in holiday play schemes, using the museum's collections as a basis for many types of creative work.

QUESTIONNAIRES FOR CHILDREN'S USE

An example page from a Questionnaire provided by Verulamium Museum, St. Albans, Herts.

BUILDING MATERIALS AND CONSTRUCTION

1. What materials were used in mosaics?
2. How many kinds of tiles were used in Roman buildings?
3. What kind of glass was used for windows?
4. What were water-pipes made of?
5. What kind of wood was used in Roman timber houses?
6. What is the name of the material plastered on walls?
7. What colour was Roman mortar?
8. Why were flints and mortar used for buildings at Verulamium?

WEAPONS AND TOOLS

1. Draw a weapon used by a Roman soldier
2. Make a list of tools which are like those workmen used today
3. Draw a bow brooch. Why was the bow steeply curved?

NOTE: *Museum questionnaires are basically intended to help schools in follow-up work.*

8 VISITS TO LOCAL INDUSTRIES

These visits can be of great value and are arranged through local contacts. The Personnel Officer usually deals with these enquiries. The industry can be investigated from the historical and scientific point of view as well as from the geographical one.

These questions may be asked:

Why is the industry established here? Where do the raw materials come from and in what quantities? What is produced? How is the product made?

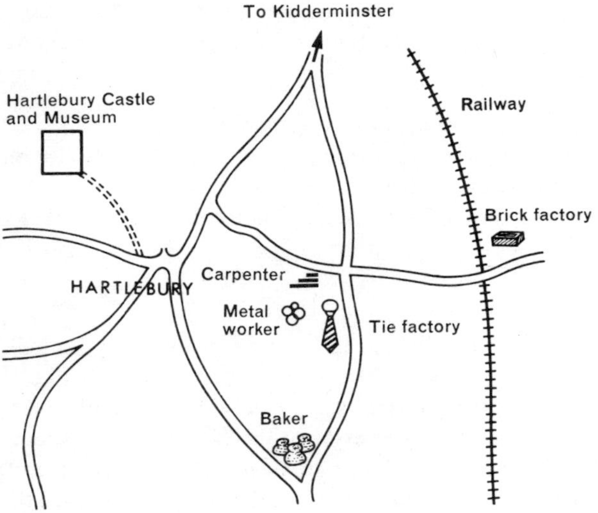

3 : 4 The location of the industries in Hartlebury village, Worcestershire.

How were these things formerly made? Where do the finished products go? How many people are employed in the factory? Do they live in the neighbourhood? Is the factory modern or old? How are the product's raw materials transported?

Fig. 3:4 shows how this information can be mapped.

9 NATURE RESERVES

Nature reserves in Britain are of three main kinds:

National Nature Reserves are statutorily established and managed by the Nature Conservancy Council.

Local Nature Reserves are also statutorily established, in this case by local authorities.

Other nature reserves are managed by voluntary conservation organisations, principally the Royal Society for the Protection of Birds (The Lodge, Sandy, Beds.) and the various County Naturalists' and Conservation Trusts for which the Society for the Promotion of Nature Reserves (The Manor House, Alford, Lincs.) acts as a co-ordinating centre.

Nature reserves are by no means always the best place for field-work and many alternative areas may be available. Some local education authorities have acquired sites specifically for field teaching and many others have agreements with owners on the educational use of their land. These sites are far too numerous to list but information about them can usually be obtained from:

(*a*) your local planning authority;
(*b*) the adviser or other person in your l.e.a. with responsibility for environmental studies;
(*c*) the secretary of your Local County Naturalists' or Conservation Trust.

National Nature Reserves

One of the main functions of the Nature Conservancy Council is to establish, maintain and manage National Nature Reserves. The Council is a governmental body, financed by grant-in-aid from the Department of the Environment, and is the successor to the Nature Conservancy first set up by Royal Charter in 1949. There are nearly 140 National Nature Reserves, covering over a quarter of a million acres. These reserves are the nucleus of a series of sites of national importance for nature conservation, for study and research, or for both these purposes. Some are the best available examples of different types of countryside, others contain unusual communities of wild plants and animals, and yet others include impressive natural features such as rock exposures, gorges and landslips.

Visitors to the reserves are welcomed wherever and whenever their presence does not conflict with conservation or research or with the interests of owners or tenants; but obviously some wild plants and animals are highly sensitive to human disturbance and it is not always possible to allow unrestricted access. The selected list of National Nature Reserves below distinguishes those where public or other footpaths provide access or where there is open access. Some have special facilities of interest to teachers such as nature trails, leaflets and reserve centres. A permit is required to visit all other National Nature Reserves and for parts of many of the reserves listed below away from paths. Applications for permits should be made to the appropriate Regional Office. The day-to-day running of most reserves is in the hands of a warden, and teachers intending to take parties on nature trails, etc. should contact him (or the Regional Office) in advance of a visit. Reconnaissance visits by teachers are always encouraged.

The headquarters of the Nature Conservancy Council are at 19 Belgrave Square, London SW1X 8PY. A leaflet about the work of the Council, another on 'Visiting National Nature Reserves' and a reading list on nature conservation can be obtained on request from that address or from the Education Officer, Attingham Park, Shrewsbury, SY4 4TW.

NATIONAL NATURE RESERVES

Symbols
† Descriptive leaflet available
* Nature Trail
‡ Reserve centre or field museum

ENGLAND
East Anglia
Regional Office: 60 Bracondale, Norwich, NOR 58B.
Huntingdon and Peterborough
Castor Hanglands Woodland and grass heath.
† Permit required except for Ailsworth Heath.
Holme Fen Fen.
*‡ Permit required except for nature trail.
Lincs
Saltfleetby–Theddlethorpe Dunes Dunes.
† Unrestricted access, except during Ministry of Defence Operations.
Norfolk
Bure Marshes Marsh.
†* Permit required except for nature trail.
Holkham Coastal marshes and sand-dunes.
† Unrestricted access, except to farmland.
Scolt Head Island Shingle, dunes and saltmarsh.
†* Access to Ternery restricted during breeding season (May–July inc.).
Winterton Dunes Dunes. †
Suffolk
Cavenham Heath Heath.
Permit required to visit Ash Plantation and Tuddenham Heath.
Walberswick Heathland and marsh.
† Permit required away from Public Rights of Way.
Westleton Heath Heath
† Permit required away from picnic area and Public Rights of Way.
Midlands
Regional Office: Attingham Park, Shrewsbury, Shropshire, SY4 4TW.
Worcestershire
Wren's Nest Limestone geology.
Permit needed to carry out scientific work and collect specimens.
North
Regional Office: Merlewood Research Station, Grange-over-Sands, Lancs, LA11 6JU.
Lancs
Ainsdale Sand Dunes. Dunes
†*‡ Permit needed away from Public Rights of Way and concessionary paths.
Roudsea Wood Mixed wood.
† Permit required away from Public Rights of Way.
Northumberland
Lindisfarne Dunes, estuary sands and mudflats. †
Westmorland
Moor House Moorland.
†* Permit required away from Public Rights of Way.
Yorks
Upper Teesdale Moorland, arctic alpine flora, woodland.
†* Permit required away from Public Rights of Way.
South
Regional Office: Foxhold House, Thornford Road, Crookham Common, Newbury, Berkshire, RG 158EL

Hants
Old Winchester Hill Downland and woodland. †*‡
Oxfordshire
Aston Rowant Chalk grassland, woodland.
*‡ Permit needed away from paths.
Wilts
Pewsey Downs Chalk downland.
South-East
Regional Office: Zealds, Church Street, Wye, Ashford, Kent, TN25 5BW.
Herts
Tring Reservoirs Reservoirs, marsh.
†* Permit required away from paths.
Kent
Blean Woods Woodland.
Permit required away from paths.
Ham Street Woods Woodland.
Permit required away from paths.
High Halstow Coastal and woodland.
† Permit required away from paths.
Stodmarsh Marsh.
† Permit required away from paths.
Wye and Crundale Downs Chalk grassland.
†*‡ Permit required away from paths and open access area on Broad Downs.
Sussex
Kingley Vale Downland and yew wood.
†*‡ Permit required for Bow Hill.
Lullington Heath Heath.
† Permit required away from paths.
South-West
Regional Office: Roughmoor, Bishop's Hull, Taunton, Somerset, TA1 5AA.
Devon
Axmouth-Lyme Regis Under-Cliffs Down and cliff.
† Permit required away from paths.
Braunton Burrows Dunes.
†* Unrestricted access on foot.
Yarner Wood Oak wood.
*‡ Permit required other than for nature trails.
Dorset
Studland Heath Dunes, heath. †*‡
Somerset
Bridgwater Bay Saltmarsh, estuary.
† Permit required to visit Stert Island.
Ebbor Gorge. Limestone gorge, woodland.
†‡ Permit required away from marked paths.

WALES
North Wales
Regional Office: Penrhos Road, Bangor, Caernarvonshire, LL57 2LQ.
Anglesey
Newborough Warren–Ynys Llanddwyn Dunes.
†* Permit required away from Rights of Way.
Caernarvonshire
Cwm Idwal Arctic alpine flora, mountain, lake. *
Snowdon–Y Wyddfa Mountain and woodland. *

Merioneth
Cader Idris Arctic alpine flora, mountain.
Coed Ganllwyd Oak wood and gorge.
Coedydd Maentwrog Oak wood. *
Morfa Dyffryn Dunes.
Permit required away from Rights of Way.
South Wales
Regional Office: Plas Gogerddan, Aberystwyth, Cardiganshire, SY23 3EB.
Cardiganshire
Dyfi Estuary, dunes, bog. †*‡
Glamorgan
Gower Coast Sea cliffs. *
Oxwich Dunes and fen. †*‡
Pembrokeshire
Skomer Island Island, sea-bird colonies.
* Landing fee. Permit if other than nature trail.

SCOTLAND
All Regional Offices: 12 Hope Terrace, Edinburgh, EH9 2AS.
Aberdeenshire
Sands of Forvie Dunes.
† Permission required to visit reserve during nesting season and in late summer and autumn.
Angus
St Cyrus Dunes. *
Dumfries-shire
Caerlaverock Saltmarsh.
† Access to part of Reserve by permit only.
Inverness-shire
Cairngorms Pinewood and arctic alpine.
†*‡ Access restricted to parts of Reserve in late summer and autumn.
Craigellachie Birchwood and moor. *
Rhum Island.
†* Permission required to visit parts of Reserve away from Loch Scresort area.
Ross and Cromarty
Beinn Eighe Pinewood and arctic alpine. †*
Corrieshalloch Woodland gorge. †
Inverpolly Arctic alpine, woodland, lake.
†*‡ Permission required to visit Drumrunie in late summer and autumn.
Stirlingshire
Loch Lomond Lake and islands.
†* Permit required for parts of mainland.

A LIST OF BOTANICAL GARDENS

ENGLAND
Cambridgeshire *Cambridge*. The University Botanic Gardens, Cambridge. Guides can be provided at the cost of £1, from Mondays to Fridays after 5 p.m. and on Saturdays after 1 p.m.
Devon *Paignton*. Paignton Zoological and Botanical Gardens, Paignton, Devon. Well known as a zoo; gardens very interesting especially the Tropical House.
Chelsea, London *Chelsea Physic Gardens*, Swan Walk, Chelsea, London, S.W.3. It is not open to the general public, but can be open to school parties on application to the Trustees, London Parochial Charities, 3 Temple Gardens, Temple, London, E.C.4. There is an excellent herb garden.

Surrey *Kew*. The Royal Botanic Gardens, Kew, Surrey. School parties are admitted free. They are the finest botanical gardens in the world.
Wisley The Royal Horticultural Society Garden, Wisley, Ripley, Woking, Surrey. It is a garden and centre of research. School parties are admitted free.
Oxford University Botanic Garden, Oxford. There is an important arrangement of the plants in systematic order.
Warwickshire *Birmingham*. Birmingham Botanical Gardens, Westbourne Road, Edgbaston, Birmingham, 15. A good collection of alpines and rhododendrons.
Yorkshire *Harrogate* The Northern Horticultural Society's Gardens, Harlow Car, Harrogate, Yorkshire. Applications must be made to the Director.

IRELAND
Dublin. National Botanic Gardens, Glasnevin, Dublin, 9. Guided tours can be arranged for school parties.

SCOTLAND
Edinburgh. The Royal Botanic Garden, Edinburgh, 2. The gardens have been specially arranged for education of the general public.
Glasgow Botanic Gardens, Glasgow. There is a chronological arrangement of plants which is of great interest to school parties.
Ross-shire The National Trust for Scotland, Inverewe, Poolewe, Ross-shire. Information can be obtained from The Warden, Inverewe Stage House, Poolewe, Western Ross. (Tel. Poolewe 249.)

10 NATURE TRAILS

ENGLAND

BEDFORDSHIRE
1 MAULDEN WOOD, Ampthill Forest (147/073370). 13 km. S. of Bedford on A6. All year. 1½–3 km. No dogs. Management of mixed coniferous and broadleaved forest. Forest trail for schools. Guide from Head Forester, Wood End, West End, Haynes. (Tel.: Wilstead 285.)
2 SANDY. 09.00–17.00 hours. All year (not Sat. and Sun. in Oct.–Mar.). Sundays Apr.–Sept., members only. 1 or 2½ km. Oak and mixed woodland, heath, farmland. E. of Sandy on A603. Guide from Royal Society for Protection of Birds, The Lodge, Sandy, Beds. Car park.

BUCKINGHAMSHIRE
3 CHURCH WOOD, Hedgerley. All year. 1 to 2 km. Woodland developed naturally, warblers, woodland flora. Start in village of Hedgerley, follow lane opposite pond for ½ km. Key (deposit) from Mrs. Hatson, 2, Deans Cottages, Hedgerley. Guide from Royal Society for Protection of Birds, The Lodge, Sandy, Beds.
4 COOMBE HILL, Aston Clinton (SP 849066). All year. 1¼ km. Chalk grassland, with patches of clay. Beechwood. Spectacular views of Vale of Aylesbury. 5½ km. N.E. of Princes Risborough, 2½ km. W. of Wendover, S. of B4010. Guide from local booksellers or by post from the National Trust Area Office, Hughenden Manor, High Wycombe, Bucks.
5 EMBERTON PARK, Olney. All year. 1½ km. Waterwide habitat for wildfowl, other birds and flora. Starts 1 km. S. of Olney on A509 (SP 887507). Guide at trail or from Newport Pagnell Rural District Council, 7, Station Road, Newport Pagnell.
6 HALTON WOOD, Chiltern Forest (159/889091). All year. Management of mixed coniferous and hardwood forest. Whole area open for pedestrian use and a forest trail for schools. Car park. Guide from Chief Forester, Forest Lodge, Upper Icknield Way, Aston Clinton, Aylesbury.
7 BOARSTALL DECOY, Boarstall, nr. Aylesbury. 7th February–15th September. 1 km. Woodland walk in relic part of ancient Bernwood forest; wildfowl. Trail is set

in new Conservation Centre of the Wildfowlers Association of Great Britain and Ireland. Starts at Decoy Cottage at Centre, off Boarstall Road, $\frac{1}{3}$ km. from junction with B4011, 3 km. N. of Oakley Village (SP 623147). Guide at Decoy Cottage. Entrance charge.

8 WENDOVER FOREST (SP 889080). All year. $\frac{1}{2}$ hr.–1$\frac{1}{2}$ hrs. Scenic walks among broad leaves and conifers. Four trails, inc. school trail. Guide from Head Forester, Forest Lodge, Aston Clinton, Aylesbury. No dogs.

CAMBRIDGESHIRE

9 COE FEN, Cambridge. All year. 1$\frac{1}{4}$ km. Common grazing land for townspeople's use for several centuries. Riversides and meadows. Starts at car park near children's paddling pool on Coe Fen within City of Cambridge. Guide from Cambridgeshire and Isle of Ely Naturalists' Trust, 1, Brookside, Cambridge.

10 HAYLEY WOOD, Little Gransden (295536). All year. 1$\frac{1}{2}$ km. Pure oxlip wood and boulder clay, coppice management. Take B1046 to water tower 1$\frac{1}{2}$ km. W. Longstowe (295536). Down Hayley Lane to Cottage and level-crossing; wood beyond. Guide from Cambs. and Isle of Ely Naturalists' Trust, as above, between 09.30–16.30 hours.

11 NORWOOD ROAD RESERVE, March (417980). All year. 1 km. Nesting sites of resident and migrant birds in urban setting. Marshland scrubs. Starts behind March railway station. Guide from Cambs. and Isle of Ely Naturalists' Trust, as above.

12 PARADISE, Cambridge (446574). All year. 1 km. Wet meadow and marshland with belts of willow and alder scrub on W. bank of river Granta, close to Coe Fen (above). Starts from car park near children's paddling pool on Coe Fen within City of Cambridge. Guide from Cambs. and Isle of Ely Naturalists' Trust, as above.

13 ROSWELL PITS, Ely. All year. 1$\frac{1}{2}$ or 4 km. Very varied plant and animal life. Waterfowl. Closely connected with history of Ely. Starts near bottom end of hard road in Springhead Lane, Ely. Guide from Cambs. and Isle of Ely Naturalists' Trust, as above. Also on sale in Ely Cathedral.

14 WANDLEBURY. All year. 1$\frac{1}{2}$ or 2$\frac{1}{2}$ km. Chalk, grassland, beechwood, Iron Age fort, giant redwood. Starts 3 km. S. of Cambridge on Cambridge/Haverhill Road, A604. Guide at Wandlebury or from Cambridgeshire Trust as above.

15 WICKEN FEN. 5 km. W. of Soham, A1123 and A142. 300 hectares of wetland reserve. Plant, insect and bird life. Variety of habitats supporting birds characteristic of scrub, marshland, reedbeds, open water. Laboratory and lecture rooms, and observation tower (apply Resident Warden/Naturalist: Lt.-Col. C. E. Mitchell, Lode Lane, Wicken, Ely). (Tel.: Soham 274.)

CHESHIRE

16 CAPESTHORNE, Macclesfield. In the grounds of Capesthorne Hall, home of the Bromley Davenport family. Admission charge. Hall extra. Sun.–April to September inclusive and Bank Holidays. Weds. and Sats.–May to September inclusive. Descriptive leaflet from Hall Manager, Capesthorne Hall, Macclesfield, Cheshire SK11 9JY. (Tel.: Chelford 221.)

17 CHEADLE HULME, Cheadle. All year. 3$\frac{1}{2}$ km. Bridle-path through pastureland. Variety of tree species, plants and birds. Hedgerows and associated animal life. Starts at Farnham Close, Cheadle Hulme. Guide from Parks Superintendent, Cheadle and Gatley U.D.C., Parks Department, Bruntwood, Cheadle.

18 DELAMERE (SJ 549705). Forest trail starting from Forest Museum at Linmere Forest Office, 1 km. W. of Delamere Station, which lies on B5152 Frodsham–Tarporley road. An old Crown woodland holding magnificent Scots and Corsican pines, midway between Northwich and Chester. (Forestry Commission.)

19 ETHEROW COUNTRY PARK, Romiley, nr. Stockport. All year. 2 km. Valley containing reservoir. Very varied plant and animal life. Sailing and angling. Trail within the park starts at end of Montagu Street, Compstall, off B6104. Guide

from Clerk of Bredbury and Romiley U.D.C., George Lane, Bredbury, Stockport, SK6 1DL.

20 LYME PARK, Disley, nr. Stockport. All year. 2½ km. Moorland and parkland adjacent to ancestral hall. Plants, trees and birds. Herd of red deer. Commences near car park, numbered guide-posts. Guide from dispenser on trail or from Office, Lyme Hall, Lyme Park, Disley, Nr. Stockport.

21 NESTON ROCK CUTTING, Wirral Country Park, Mellock Lane, Neston, Wirral (297774). All year. 1¼ km. Deep rock cutting, plant life, insects, birds, geology. Guide from Head Ranger, Wirral Country Park, 4, Station Cottages, Thurstaston, Wirral.

22 TATTON PARK, Knutsford. All year. 2½ km. Mixed woodland, streams and meres. Bird life. Booklets at start. Parking fee. Details of opening hours of Park from County Hall, Chester or Manager, Tatton Park, Knutsford.

23 WOODBANK PARK, Stockport. All year. 1½ km. Parkland with river and mixed woodlands; plants, trees and birds. Commences outside Woodbank Hall, numbered guide-posts, car park off Park Lane. Guide from dispenser on trail or from Parks and Recreation Department, Woodbank Hall, Woodbank Park, Stockport, SK1 4JR.

24 THURSTASTON, Wirral Country Park, Wirral (SJ 239835). All year. 2½ km. Birds and estuarine flora and fauna. Mainly for schoolchildren, but being developed for adults. Junior Guide from Head Ranger, Wirral Country Park, as above.

CORNWALL

25 COOMBE VALLEY, nr. Bude (SS/210117). All year. 2½ km. Typical North-Cornish valley. Oak woodland, coniferous afforestation. Cornwall Naturalists' Trust Guide from local bookshops.

26 COTEHELE, W. Bank of Tamar. 13 km. S.W. of Tavistock, 22 km from Plymouth via Saltash Bridge. 2½ km. National Trust/Shell circular walk through woods surrounding a romantic 14th-century house on upper reaches of River Tamar. Woods and gardens are open. House open April–mid-October. Booklet available from National Trust shops and principal Shell garages in Devon and Cornwall.

27 LANHYDROCK. 4 km. S. of Bodmin. B3268, overlooking valley of River Fowey. 3 km. National Trust/Shell circular walk through park and woods surrounding Lanhydrock House which is also open April to mid-October. Refreshments. Booklet from National Trust shops and principal Shell garages in Devon and Cornwall.

28 TRELISSICK, 6½ km. S. of Truro on B3289. 4 km. National Trust/Shell circular walk (with optional shorter route) through park and woods beside River Fal. Trelissick Gardens also open March to October. Refreshments. Booklet from National Trust shops and principal Shell garages in Devon and Cornwall.

CUMBERLAND

29 FRIARS CRAG. Keswick-on-Derwentwater. All year. 2½ km. Mixed woodland. Lakeshore walk. Aquatic and woodland birdlife. Historical associations of Derwentwater and mining. Beautiful natural viewpoint. Memorial to Canon Rawnsley, co-founder of the National Trust. Car park. Illustrated guide from all National Trust and National Park Information Centres (2 in Keswick) or from the National Trust Area Office at Broadlands, Borrans Road, Ambleside, Westmorland.

30 JOHNNY WOOD, Borrowdale. All year. 4 km. Superb viewpoint 280 m., natural oak forest, regenerated woodland, open fell, rich bird and plant life. Walk begins and ends at car park in Seatoller on B5289 Keswick–Buttermere Road (245138). Regular bus service Seatoller–Keswick. Guide from all National Trust and National Park Information Centres, or from National Trust Area Office, as above.

31 LAUNCHY GHYLL FOREST TRAIL, Thirlmere. All year. 1 km. Forest management and wildlife. Starts Thirlmere West Road, Leaflet at trail. Organised by Manchester Corporation Waterworks, Manchester, M60 2JU.
32 MOOR HOUSE NATIONAL NATURE RESERVE. All year. Week-days only unless by appointment. 1 km. Pennine moorland – part of Moor House National Nature Reserve – used for experimental purpose (ecological research). Start at Moor House Field Station, Garrighill, Alston. Guide from Officer in Charge, or Warden. (Tel.: Alston 435.)
33 NETHER WASDALE, at foot of Wastwater, north shore, on 'C' road. Lake District Naturalists' Trust. All year. Two circular routes, 2½ km. each. Mixed woodland on lakeshore, rough fell, a small lake, pasture, bog and riverside. Leaflet from all National Trust and National Park Information Centres, or from National Trust Area Office, as above.
34 SWIRLS FOREST TRAIL, Thirlmere (316168). All year. 1¼ km. Woodland management and wildlife. Starts at A591. Leaflet at trail. Organised by Manchester Corporation Waterworks, as above.

DERBYSHIRE
35 LATHKILL DALE. All year. 8 km. Marsh plants, mixed wood, river, farmland. Take footpath from Lathkill Dale Hotel, Over Haddon. Guide from Peak National Park Office and Information Centres, as above.
36 PADLEY GORGE. All year. 10–11 km. Relict oak wood, bryophytes, invertebrates, moorland, stream. Starts on National Trust Longshaw Estate, Fox House, near A625/A6011 junction. Guide from Peak National Park Office and Information Centres, as above, or City Museum, Sheffield, 10.
37 TIDESWELL DALE NATIONAL PARK TRAIL. All year. 2½ km. (takes about ½ to ¾ hour). Situated between Tideswell and Millers Dale, just off B6049 road. Former quarry site. Geology, flora, fauna, local ecology as well as attempting to show problems of land use in a National Park. Guide from Peak National Park Office or Information Centres, as above.

DEVON
38 ARLINGTON COURT. 11 km. N.E. of Barnstaple. Open 1st April–14th October, daily between 11.00–18.00 hours, except Sats. 3 km. Parkland shrubs and trees, lake, Heronry and wildfowl. Start at the Court (611405) where booklets are available. Car park.
39 BELLEVER FOREST WALK, Postbridge (175/656773). All year. 1½–5 km. Managed conifer woodland in Dartmoor Forest; wildlife and archaeology. Guide at site or from Forestry Commission, Flowers Hill, Brislington, Bristol, 4. (Tel.: 78311.)
40 BERRY HEAD COUNTRY PARK, Brixham, Torbay. All year. Limestone, downland turf, blackthorn, scrub, sea cliff, birds and plants. Circular walk starts at Exposition Centre in car park. Leaflet available from Warden or from Resort Services Dept., Lymington Rd., Torquay.
41 BOLBERRY DOWN, between Salcombe Harbour – B3197 – and Hope, S. Devon. All year. 2½ km. National Trust/Shell coastal walk along cliffs near Salcombe, ending on beach at Soar Mill Cove. Booklet available from National Trust shops and principal Shell garages in Devon and Cornwall.
42 BRAUNTON BURROWS NATIONAL NATURE RESERVE. (S.W. Region, Nature Conservancy). All year. (*a*) The Flagpole Trail – sand-dunes. 2½ km. Starts from American Road car park at 163/463349. (*b*) The Lighthouse Trail – flora and sea-shore. 2½ km. Starts from S. end of American Road at 163/465325. Booklet covering both trails, from Warden, Pounds Mead, Hills View, Braunton. (Tel.: Braunton 812552.)
43 DUNSFORD WOOD. Devon Trust Nature Reserve. 11 km. W. of Exeter on Exeter–Moretonhampstead road. All year. 1½–4 km. Woodland and riverside

walk. Noted for wild daffodil display in spring months. Entrance at Steps Bridge Leaflets on site at week-ends during daffodil time or by post from Executive Secretary, D.T.N.C., 2, Pennsylvania Road, Exeter, EX4 6BQ.

44 EGGESFORD FOREST. All year. Three walks, 1½ km. each. Long established commercial woodlands on valley sites. Map ref. SS 693103 (two walks) and SS 673119. Guide at car park at start, or from Forestry Commission, District Office, Barnstaple.

45 HARTLAND FOREST, Hartland. All year. 2½ km. Moorland afforestation, marshy areas, open rides. Start SS 273201. Explanatory notices on walk. Car park at start.

46 HEDDON VALLEY. Devon Trust Nature Trail over National Trust land. All year. 1½–3 km. Woodland, water-meadows, open moorland, river and coastal walk. Adjoining Hunters Inn, Martinhoe, N. Devon. Booklets available from Hunters Inn or by post from Mr. H. Machin, The Gate House, Lee, Ilfracombe.

47 HEMBURY WOODS. 3 km. N. of Buckfastleigh, A38, 1½ km. S. of A384. 2½ km. National Trust/Shell circular walk through typical Devon oakwood, beside River Dart near Buckfastleigh. All year. Booklet available from National Trust shops and principal Shell garages in Devon and Cornwall.

48 SLAPTON LEY. From Slapton Bridge (SX 827444). All year, about 2½ km. Lakeside path, passing reed fringe, wooded and scrub-covered banks, and the open water of Slapton Ley (72 hectares). Flowers, insects, and birds especially good. Leaflets available at the boathouse.

49 STOKE WOODS, near Exeter. All year. Forest walk, sponsored by Exeter City Council and the Forestry Commission. Forestry and nature notes relative to locality at various points on walk. Start 176/928964. Guide from Exeter City Information Office, 18, Queen Street, Exeter, or from Forestry Commission, Flowers Hill, Brislington, Bristol, 4.

50 TROWLESWORTHY WARREN, on S.W. flank of Dartmoor; joins Cadover Bridge and is 5 km. N. of Plympton. All year. 2½ km. National Trust/Shell circular walk on open moors of Dartmoor, exploring traces of long history of man's occupation. Booklet available from National Trust shops and principal Shell garages in Devon and Cornwall.

51 YARNER WOOD NATIONAL NATURE RESERVE, Nr. Bovey Tracey (S.W. Region Nature Conservancy). 2½ km. Educational Nature Trail in association with Devon Schools Museum Service. Mixed woodland on eastern edge of Dartmoor. Starts from Yarrow Lodge nr. entrance to Reserve (175/787789). Booklet written primarily for teachers – available from Warden, Yarrow Lodge, Yarner, Bovey Tracey. (Tel.: Bovey Tracey 2330.)

52 YARNER WOOD NATIONAL NATURE RESERVE, Woodland Walk (S.W. Region Nature Conservancy) (175/787789). All year. 5 km. Extension to existing nature trail. Introduces the public to conservation management of woodlands, and work of the Nature Conservancy. Guide (free) from the Warden, Yarrow Lodge, Yarner Wood, Bovey Tracey.

DORSET

53 BROWNSEA ISLAND, Poole Harbour. Open 31st March–30th September. 2½ km. Sea, woodland and heathland birds; ornamental pheasants, peacocks. Starts Brownsea Island Quay. Leaflet available from shop on Quay. Organised by National Trust and Dorset Naturalists' Trust.

54 PUDDLETOWN FOREST WALK, Wareham Forest (178/743921). All year. 1½–5 km. Forest life in managed conifer wood. Starts 3 km. S. of Puddletown. Guide at site or from Forestry Commission, Flowers Hill, Brislington, Bristol, 4. (Tel.: 78311.)

55 SHIPSTAL (ARNE), Arne Nature Reserve, Wareham (R.S.P.B.). All year. 1¼ km. Start Reception Hut. Variety of trees and plants plus many species of woodland

birds and wildfowl. Guide obtainable from the Warden, Syldata, Arne, Wareham. Entrance fee. Half price to under seventeens.

56 STUDLAND HEATH NATIONAL NATURE RESERVE. (S.W. Region, Nature Conservancy.) Sea-shore and sand-dunes. Starts from car park outside Reserve (179/031835). Booklets and details from Warden, 3, Oxford Terrace, Cowlease Road, Swanage, Dorset, BH19 2QF.

57 STUDLAND HEATH NATIONAL NATURE RESERVE, Woodland Trail. (S.W. Region, Nature Conservancy). (SZ 032836.) Starts at car park. Birch woodland, developing from heathland. Dragonflies, mammals. Guide (free) from car park, or from Warden, as above.

58 WAREHAM FOREST WALK, Northport (178/905895). All year. 3½ km. Managed woods, heath, forest life and work. Starts 1½ km. from Wareham. Guide at site or from Forestry Commission, as above.

DURHAM

59 HAMSTERLEY FOREST PARK. 1½ km. W. of Hamsterley Village, nr. Witton le Wear (NZ 092315). Forest Drive. All year. 7 km. Quiet woodlands on Pennine foothills. Guide from Forestry Commission local office.

GLOUCESTERSHIRE

60 BIBLINS ADVENTURE TRAIL, Forest of Dean (SO 540153). All year, restricted use. 9½ km. Exacting walk-round area of great natural, geological and historical interest. Contact Biblins Adventure Centre, or Forestry Commission, Crown Office, Bank Street, Coleford, GL16 8BA, or Forestry Commission, Flowers Hill, Brislington, Bristol, 4. (Tel.: 78311.) Guide also available.

61 CANNOP PONDS, Forest of Dean (SO 607100). All year. 2 km. Plant and bird life in and around forest. Starts at B4226/B4234 crossroads. Guide in dispenser at Stone Works end of lake or Forestry Commission, Coleford, or Bristol as above.

62 CHRISTCHURCH, Forest of Dean. All year. 2½ or 5 km. Effect on Forest of Dean of deer, woodpeckers and fires; coal-mining and old iron-mines. Guide from Warden, Christchurch Camp Site or Forestry Commission, Coleford, or Bristol, as above.

63 CHURCHILL TRAIL, Forest of Dean. All year. 2½ or 4 km. Highly varied mixed woodland. Starts ½ km. from Parkend up Yorkley Road. Guide in dispenser nr. workshop or from Forestry Commission, Coleford, or Bristol, as above.

64 COOPER'S HILL LOCAL NATURE RESERVE (143/892143). 9½ km. S. of Cheltenham. Promontory of the Cotswolds overlooking Severn Vale. Woodland scarp slopes. Leaflet from County Planning Department, Shire Hall, Gloucester, GL1 2TN.

65 SPEECH HOUSE TRAIL, Forest of Dean (SO 620121). All year. 2½ or 4 km. Mixed woodland; deer, badgers, squirrels. Starts off B4226, 5 km. from Cinderford and Coleford. Guide at Speech House Hotel, or Forestry Commission, Coleford, or Bristol, as above.

66 SYMONDS YAT FOREST WALK, Forest of Dean (SO 562160). All year. 1½ or 4 km. Spectacular views of Wye Valley Gorge and Forest Garden, showing trees commercially grown in Forest of Dean. Starts at Log Cabin refreshment hut nr. Symonds Yat Rock. Guide from cabin or Forestry Commission, Coleford, or Bristol, as above.

HAMPSHIRE

67 BOLDERWOOD WOODLAND WALKS from which can be seen fine mature trees, wild deer and the forest of the past and future. From car parks and picnic areas (SU 243087) on by-road that runs from Lyndhurst via Emery Down and eventually N. to A31, Romsey–Ringwood road: 8 km. W. of Lyndhurst. Also Arboretum (SU 240080). Guide: Bolderwood Arboretum and Walks from Lyndhurst office or camping offices.

68 HENGISTBURY HEAD, Christchurch Harbour. All year. 1½ or 3 km. Grass, heath, oakwood, scrub, saltmarsh, archaeology, geology, birds. Starts from Ranger's cottage. Guide from Parks Department, Avenue Road, Bournemouth, and at trail.

69 OLD WINCHESTER HILL, nr. West Meon. (SU 62/647212.) All year. Chalk, grassland, vegetation and flora, yew woods, beech woods and regeneration of ash, etc., scrub species, Iron Age fort. Small exhibition in Reserve hut open to visitors at weekends (p.m.) April–September. Two Trails: White trail – 1½ km. (level ground); Red trail – 3 km. (steep slopes). Leaflets from dispensers at start of trail or from Warden, Mr. J. Kennard, Drocheneford, Mill Lane, Droxford, Southampton, SO13 1QS.

70 RHINEFIELD ORNAMENTAL DRIVE, New Forest (179/266057). All year. App. 2½ km. Collection of exotic coniferous trees. Starts 5 km. from Lyndhurst on A35 to Bournemouth. Guide from Forestry Commission, Queens House, Lyndhurst.

71 ROWHILL NATURE RESERVE, Aldershot. Interesting variety of habitat supporting broad selection of Britain's flora and fauna. All year. 1 hr. to 1½ hrs. The 20 hectares of ground extend from A325, Farnborough Road, at Heath End in W. to Weybourne Road at Parkland Grove in E. Guides can be purchased by callers at Heath End Nurseries, Farnborough Road, Heath End, Farnham, during business hours only. Weekdays, including Saturdays, 09.00–17.30; Sundays, 10.00–13.00.

HEREFORDSHIRE

72 BROCKHAMPTON WOODLAND WALK. 3 km. E. of Bromyard off Worcester Road – A44. Open all year. (*a*) A woodland walk: larch, beech, Douglas fir and very fine mature oakwoods (both pedunculate and sessile oaks), Wellingtonia and giant redwood. Birds include buzzard, raven, woodcock, nuthatch, pied flycatcher, coot and redstart. 1½ km. (*b*) Taking in the lake with mallard, coots, moorhen and little grebe (extra ¾ km.). Car parking in lay-by opp. Bringsty Post Office, 2 mins. from start of walk. Leaflet at entrance to walk and at Post Office.

73 DYMOCK FOREST WALK. W. on B4215 at Dymock (SO 677285). Oak and larch woods. Guide (*Queen's Wood*) from Forestry Commission, Bristol office, Flowers Hill, Brislington, Bristol, 4. (Tel.: 78311.)

74 HAUGH WOOD WALK, Hereford Forest (142/595365). All year. 1½–5 km. Mixed-age managed conifer woods; birds and forest life. Starts 8 km. from Hereford. Guide at site or from Forestry Commission, as above.

HERTFORDSHIRE

75 ASHRIDGE ESTATE, 5 km. N. of Berkhamsted. (National Trust.) All year. 1¼ or 2½ km. Beech, oak, sallow willow; deer, grey squirrels; woodcock. Starts at Bridgewater Monument off B4506 Northchurch to Ringshall road (SP 970131). Guide-book from local stationers or by post from the National Trust Area Office, Hughenden Manor, High Wycombe, Bucks.

76 HATFIELD FOREST. 5 km. E. of Bishop's Stortford. All year. 2 km. Managed by Essex Naturalists' Trust, trail starts at the Shell House, formerly a summerhouse used by the Houblon family who owned the forest from 1729 to 1923. Oaks, hornbeams and conifers. Wildlife, fallow deer, badgers, goldcrests and an occasional nightingale. Lakes contain tench and pike and are winter roosts for tufted duck and teal. No car park but cars can be driven to within a few metres of the start of trail. Leaflet available.

77 POTTERSCROUCH SCHOOL TRAIL, St. Albans (159/104046). 3 km. S.W. of St. Albans, off A414. All year. No dogs. Mixed coniferous and broadleaved plantations of varying ages. Guide from Chief Forester, Forest Lodge, Upper Icknield Way, Aston Clinton, Aylesbury, Bucks.

78 Tring Reservoirs, National Nature Reserve (SP 919142). All year. 2 km. Birds, especially wildfowl and waterside species. Marsh and water plants. Starts opposite Old Queen's Head Public House, Startops End, Tring. Guide available on Reserve at weekends, or from Regional Officer, The Nature Conservancy, S.E. Region, Church Street, Wye, Ashford, Kent.

HUNTINGDON AND PETERBOROUGH

79 HOLME FEN NATIONAL NATURE RESERVE, nr. Holm, Peterborough (134/200892). 1st June–31st October. 1½ km. Start Holme Lode Drove. Features of scientific interest. Mainly birch woodland and ornithological interest. Guides obtainable from Nature Conservancy Regional Office, Monks Wood Experimental Station, Abbots Ripton, Huntingdon. Dogs must be kept on a leash, fire risk in dry autumn. Entrance fee.

ISLE OF WIGHT

80 BRIGHSTONE FOREST. All year. 4 km. Mixed woodland, open downland, wonderful views of downs and coast, chalk grassland, associated birds and plants, barrows, and tumuli. Starting-point (420845). At car park off Brighstone–Calbourne road. Guide-booklet incorporating Parkhurst Walk, from local Forester, Ridget Lane, Mottistone, on trail, and/or from the Isle of Wight Tourist Board, as above.

81 BROOK. All year. 3 km. Varied countryside, trees, chalk-loving flowers, bird life, including kestrels. Greensand with lush growth of plants and ferns, many butterflies. Rhododendrons. Starting-point, Seely Hall. Guiding leaflets available from the Isle of Wight Tourist Board, as above (S.A.E.).

82 PARKHURST FOREST WALK. All year 5½ km. with shorter routes. Old Crown Woods dating back to Norman times. Enter first at Bulls Gate (off Forest Road) and drive up to parking area where walk starts. Guide Booklet, incorporating Brighstone trail, from office at Signal House and from Isle of Wight Tourist Board, as above.

83 RIVER MEDINA, Newport. All year. App. 5 km. Saltmarsh, varied trees and vegetation, swans, woodpeckers, kingfishers, cormorants, herons, greenshank, dunlin, etc. Starting-point, Newport Quay. Free car park at Coppins Bridge via Sea Street to Newport Quay. Leaflets from the Isle of Wight Tourist Board, as above (S.A.E.).

84 THE EASTERN YAR (576857). 3–5 km. N.W. of Sandown. All year. 6½ km. Sand and chalk downs. Starting-point, near old mill, signpost by road, pathway to left side of water, going upstream. Leaflet from Mr. O. H. Frazer, Mottistone Mill, Brighstone.

85 THE WESTERN YAR (354898). On bridle road F19 – left bank of river going south. All year. 10½ km. Chalk down ridge – large areas of saltings. Start at south end of Mill Road, footpath F1. Leaflet available from Mr. O. H. Frazer, Mottistone Mill, Brighstone.

86 SOUTH COAST WALK (491769). All year. 3½ km. Geological interest. Flowers and grasses, doves, jackdaws, wheatears, kestrels, skylarks, butterflies. Start car park above Blackgang. Leaflet available (no. 12) from the Isle of Wight Tourist Board, as above (S.A.E.).

KENT

87 BEDGEBURY (TQ 715336). Magnificent National Pinetum and fascinating series of Forest Plots, managed by the Forestry Commission Research Division. Open to the public without charge during daylight hours. Car park fee. Situated 8 km. (by road) N.W. of Hawkhurst, and 5 km. S. of Goudhurst. Best approach via London–Hastings road A21, to a point 24 km. S.E. of Tonbridge

(and 1½ km. W. of Flimwell crossroads), where a secondary road, signposted 'Bedgebury', diverges north to reach car park in 2½ km. *The Short Guide to Bedgebury Pinetum and Forest Plots* (H.M.S.O.), includes plans and recommended routes. A Forest Trail has been established near by.
88 HIGH ELMS WOODLAND WALK, Bromley. Country estate run by London Borough. Starts in High Elms Road, between Downe and Farnborough (Kent). Leaflet available from London Borough of Bromley.
89 KING'S WOOD FOREST TRAIL, Challock (TR 020503). A251 Ashford–Challock Road. Conifers and sweet chestnut coppice. Details from Forestry Commission.
90 WYE AND CRUNDALE DOWNS NATIONAL NATURE RESERVE, Wye, nr. Ashford (TR 077455). Open 20th April–30th August. Other times and school parties by arrangement. Chalk grassland and woodland, their associated plants, birds and mammals. ¾–1¼ km. Guide from Reserve Information Centre or from the Regional Office, The Nature Conservancy, S.E. Region, Church Street, Wye, Ashford.

LANCASHIRE

91 ARNSIDE KNOTT, 1½ km. S.W. of Arnside on Sauls Drive. Run by Arnside Parish Council on National Trust land. All year. Two routes, ¾ and 2 hours. Limestone, flora, fossils, red squirrels, lizards, birds, butterflies and moths. Guide available from Clerk to Arnside Parish Council and local retailers, or from National Trust Information Centre at Fell Foot, Newby Bridge.
92 BEACON FELL, Goosnaugh. All year. 2½ km. Guide to trail situated in Country Park embracing moorland and coniferous plantations. Guide obtainable from the Estates Department of the Lancashire County Council or from the Warden of the Park.
93 BROCK VALLEY, 5 km. E. of A6 at Catterall, 1½ km. W. of Beacon Fell Country Park, (SD 548431). All year. 1½ km. Running water, succession in old mill dams, woodland and geology. Guide (S.A.E.) from Mr. G. B. Stead, 48, Linden Avenue, Thornton Cleveleys, Blackpool.
94 CALDERSTONES PARK, off Menlove Avenue, Liverpool. All year. 1½ km. The trail shows how man and nature work together in a city park. Guide at start of trail or from Lancashire Naturalists' Trust, Willowmeade, Smithybrow Croft, Warrington, or from Publications Officer, City of Liverpool Museums, Liverpool, L3 8EN, or from Mansion House Café.
95 CLAIFE SHORE OF WINDERMERE (388959). All year. 3½ km. West shore of Windermere; aquatic insects, lake birds, fish. Natural oak woodland and larch plantation; bird life, forest trees. Car park ½ km. N. of Ferry House on shore of Windermere. Leaflet from all National Trust and National Park Information Centres, or from National Trust Area Office, Borrans Road, Ambleside, Westmorland.
96 EAVES WOOD, Silverdale. All year. 2½ km. Managed and natural woodland on limestone pavement; regeneration of trees including conifers. Bus or train from Lancaster. Enter wood by gate of 'Woodlands' (756465) or from Waterslack (754472). Guide from National Trust, 27, Springbank, Silverdale (Tel.: 420); Waterslack Farm; Lancaster Museum; local Post Office; National Trust and National Park Information Centres and National Trust Area Office, as above.
97 FORMBY POINT, Formby, nr. Southport. All year. 3 km. Pine woods and beach, along shore. Varied plant and animal communities. Guide from Squirrel Reserve Hut at entrance or from Miss P. Culshaw, Willowmeade, Smithybrow, Croft, Warrington, WA3 7BZ.
98 HOPWOOD MIDDLETON (SD 875084). All year. 3 km. Parkland and mixed woodland. Guide from Borough of Middleton Parks and Cemeteries Department, Town Hall, Middleton, nr. Manchester.
99 LYTHAM ST. ANNES NATURE RESERVE (SD 313305). All year. Guide to

fixed sand-dunes and dune slack flora and fauna. No fixed paths. Guide obtainable from Borough of Lytham St. Annes, Parks Department, 290, Clifton Drive South, Lytham St. Annes. School parties and specialist groups preferred.
100 RIDDING WOOD, Grizedale. All year. 1½–5 km. Managed wood and land for planting. Starts Forest Wild Life Centre half-way between Hawkshead and Satterthwaite, Furness. Guide from Forestry Commission, Dee Hills Park, Chester (Tel.: 24006), also from Forest Office, Grizedale, Ambleside, Westmorland.
101 SEA WOOD, Bardsea Country Park, Bardsea, nr. Ulverston (295737). All year. 1¼ km. Limestone, Deciduous woodland, with associated flora, birds and small mammals. Guide from County Estates Surveyor, Estates Dept., Winckley House, Winckley Square, Preston.
102 SMITHILLS, Bolton (118697). In grounds of Smithills Hall Ancient Monument, off Smithills Dean Road, Easter to 30th September. 1½ km. Geological interest. Broad-leaved woodland trees, good variety of woodland birds. Guide available from Custodian, Trailside Museum, Smithills Museum.
103 SPRING WOOD, Whalley (742362). All year. 1¼ km. Deciduous and coniferous trees, woodland flora. Woodland birds. Starts at car park or picnic site. Guide from County Estates Surveyor, Estates Dept., as above.
104 TARN HOWS, nr. Hawkshead. All year. 3 km. Viewpoint of great scenic beauty. Lakeland, mixed woodland, marsh flora, lakeside walk. Approach by B5285 Hawkshead–Coniston road, 1½ km. from turn off (330955). Car park at start of walk. Guide from all National Trust and National Park Information Centres, or from National Trust Area Office as above.
105 Woodland Trail, Towneley Park, Burnley. All year. 2½ km. Elm, beech, holly, yew, rhododendrons. Birdlife except April/May, September/October. Guide from Parks and Recreation Department, County Borough of Burnley, Rossendale Road, Burnley.

LEICESTERSHIRE

106 BRADGATE PARK, Newton Linford (522097). April–October. 1¼ km. Geological interest. Ancient oaks, exotic conifers, alders. Marsh plants. Heathland. Jackdaws, wagtails, water voles, fallow and red deer. Starts car park, Newton Linford. Guide from Department of Education, Leicester Museums, New Walk, Leicester.

LINCOLNSHIRE

107 GIBRALTAR POINT, Skegness. All year. 1¼ km. Saltmarsh, sand-dunes and shores; migrating birds in autumn. S. of Skegness at main car park of Gibraltar Point Nature Reserve. Leaflets from Information Centre at car park or Lincolnshire Trust, Manor House, Alford.

LONDON

108 CHILDREN'S CENTRE, British Museum (Natural History), Cromwell Road, SW7 5BD. All year. 1 hr. Indoor trails based on the museum collections in the public galleries, including plants and animals of woodland, farmland and hedgerow, pond and river, sea-shore, mountain, wildlife in danger, Africa, Australia, Polar regions. Tube to S. Kensington. Trail sheets for individual children available at Children's Centre 10.30–16.30 hours on Sat. and school holidays.
109 WALTHAM FOREST, London Borough of Waltham Forest (TQ 395910). All year. 3½ km. Great variety of trees, lake. 45 minutes from Oxford Circus. Bus 20A from Snaresbrook Station to Napier Arms. Starts from Oak Hill on A104. Printed guides (f/scp S.A.E.) from Mrs. K. Costar, Hon. Sec., British Naturalists' Association, Epping Forest Branch, 62, Woodstock Road, Walthamstow, London, E17 4BJ. Personal guides might be arranged for parties by contacting Mrs. Costar.

NORFOLK

110 EAST WRETHAM HEATH NATURE RESERVE, N. of Thetford. May–September, daily except Tuesdays 10.00–17.00 hours. 3¼ km. Heathland, meres, pinewoods with associated bird, mammal and plant life. Starts from the Warden's Office, near his house at N.E. corner of Reserve (TL 52/910882). Permit/Guide from Warden.

111 HICKLING BROAD NATIONAL NATURE RESERVE, N.E. of Norwich. April–end September, Wed. and Thurs., 10.00 and 14.00 hours. Water trail, large Broad, open reed and sedge beds, oak woodland with associated bird and plant life. 5 km., mainly by boat. Starts at Pleasure Boat Inn, Staithe. Car park adjacent. (TG 63/409226). Permit/Guide from Warden (Tel.: Hickling 276 between 08.00–09.00, 12.45–12.15, and after 19.00.)

112 HOLME NATURE RESERVE, N.E. of Hunstanton. April–September, daily except Tues. 10.00–17.00 hours. 3¼ km. Dunes, off-shore shingle spits, marshes and a lagoon of ornithological and botanical interest. Small natural history exhibition. Starts from 'The Firs' (Warden's House) or on Reserve (TF 53/705444). Permit/Guide from Warden.

113 HOVETON GREAT BROAD (part of Bure Marshes National Nature Reserve). (TG 318160). Early May–mid-Sept. Trail can only be reached by boat. NOT open on Sat. or Sun. mornings. ¾ km. Fen woodland, reed and sedge beds and broad not otherwise open to public view. Starts at bank of River Bure opposite entrance to Salhouse Broad, 4 km. downstream from Wroxham. Guide from Trail Warden.

114 BACTON WOOD, Wensum. Car park and Forest Walk in Bacton Woods, approached down by-road running S. from North Walsham–Bacton Road, B1150, 4 km. N.E. of North Walsham (TG 317313). Guide: Bacton Wood Forest Walk, Cambridge office.

115 SCOLT HEAD ISLAND, Scolt Head National Nature Reserve (TF 794464). By boat from Brancaster Staithe. May–August (incl.). 1¼ km. Flora of saltmarsh and dunes. Birds associated with these habitats and esp. tern colony. Shells, etc. of tide line. Guide from Nature Conservancy, Attingham Park, Shrewsbury, Shropshire.

NORTHAMPTONSHIRE

116 BURCHALLS WOOD FOREST TRAIL, Hazelborough Forest (146/658448). 2½ km. N.W. of Silverstone. From May–June onwards. 3¼ km. Forest of varying ages and types. Hardwoods and conifers. Woodland flora and fauna. Guide from site of District Office of the Forestry Commission, 6, Dern Gate, Northampton, NN1 1VB.

117 IRCHESTER COUNTRY PARK, nr. Wellingborough (SP 913660). On B570, ¾ km. from Irchester. All year. Two trails – 1 km and 2½ km. Woodlands planted on restored ironstone workings. Exposed quarry face. Meadow. Flora, birds and geological features. Guide from Warden's Office, or from Northamptonshire County Planning Dept., 9, Guildhall Road, Northampton (S.A.E.).

118 WAKERLEY FOREST TRAIL, Rockingham Forest (134/958990). 1½ km. W. of A43, 11 km. S.W. of Stamford, 14½ km. N.E. of Corby, towards Wakerley Village. Easter onwards. 1¼, 2 or 3¼ km. Forest of varying ages, with large variety of hardwoods and conifers. Guide from site or District Office of Forestry Commission, as above.

119 WYMERSLEY, nr. Northampton. All year. 2½ and 3 km. Forest walk, general woodland flora. Oak, lime and cherry trees. Special interest: ancient and historic oaks of Royal Forest. Starts from Forest Car Park and Picnic Site (GR 794518). Guide from Forestry Commission Office, at site of trail. Leaflet for teachers available.

NORTHUMBERLAND

120 EMMETHAUGH, Forest walk (NY 690872). Picnic site close to Kielder Castle. Information Centre and Forest Office, all at NY 632934 which lies 5½ km. further N.W. up Tynedale.

121 INNER FARNE, FARNE ISLANDS, off coast opposite Bamburgh. Reached by boat from Seahouses on mainland; visitors must make own arrangements for crossing. All year, weather permitting. Inner Farne is the breeding-ground for twenty species of birds. Wide variety of sea birds, notably eider duck, shag, guillemot, puffin, fulmar and terns. Also maritime plants. Landing fee. Leaflet and landing ticket available from National Trust Information Centre on pier at Seahouses and from the Trust's Wardens on the Island.

122 LEWISBURN, Kielder, North Tyne. All year. About 1½ km. Managed woodland and natural historical interest. Starts at Lewisburn, close to caravan and camping site (76/646904) on Bellingham–Kielder road – Bellingham 22 km. Kielder 5 km. Guide from Forestry Commission, Bellingham, Hexham; also from Warden, Kielder Forest (caravan and camping site), Lewisburn.

123 PLASHETTS, Forest Walk (693892). Up by-road N.E. of valley road, 6½ km. S.W. of Kielder Castle. Details from Forestry Commission, York Office.

124 KIELDER CASTLE Forest Trail (632934). Starts at car park below Kielder Castle. Guide from Forestry Commission, York Office.

125 ROTHBURY, Forest Trail (NZ 037997). Car park near Great Tosson on by-road, along S. side of River Coquet, 5 km. W. of Rothbury. Guide from Forestry Commission, York Office.

126 THRUNTON WOOD, Forest Trail (085098) 3¼ km. S. of Whittingham, which is 11 km. W. of Alnwick just W. of A697 Newcastle–Wooler road.

127 TYNEMOUTH, run by Tynemouth Village Association. All year. 6½ km. Starts Front Street. Historical associations, sands, rocks and pools. Leaflet available from Tynemouth Village Association, c/o St. Oswin's, 48, Front Street, Tynemouth, North Shields, NE30 4BX.

128 WALLINGTON HALL, 19 km. W. of Morpeth. All year. 3¼ km. Walk runs through parkland, past the Hall and on through mixed woodlands. Start at car park. Leaflet prepared in conjunction with Northumberland Wildlife Trust.

NOTTINGHAMSHIRE

129 ATTENBOROUGH. All year. 3¼ km. approx. Permits are required for certain photography and detailed study of the reserve. Large expanses of open water. Grassland. Islands. Interesting habitats for many kinds of plant life and birds. 5 km. from M1 motorway access point 25. Starts at car park (121/520343) nr. Attenborough station. Guide. Other publications. Enquiries Mr. A. Teather, 168, Long Lane, Attenborough. Observation Hide Key at above address or 166, Long Lane, Attenborough.

130 MAJOR OAK, Sherwood County Park. County Council in association with Nottinghamshire Trust for Nature Conservation. Open May to September. 2½ km. N. of Edwinstowe on B6034. Surviving areas of Robin Hood's Sherwood Forest. Undisturbed oak woodland. Guides available in Country Park car parks.

OXFORDSHIRE

131 BEACON HILL, Aston Rowant National Nature Reserve. (Nature Conservancy.) Open all year. 2½ km. Chalk grassland, flora, beechwood, insects, view. Small car park on Reserve (SU 41/732966). Guide at Display Centre along Trail.

132 QUEEN WOOD, Chiltern Forest (159/726956). 5 km. S.E. of Watlington. All year. No dogs. General interest, flora and fauna. School parties only. Guide from Forestry Commission, Cambridge Office, or Head Forester, 1, Forest Cottage, Christmas Common, Watlington.

SHROPSHIRE

133 EARL'S HILL, Pontesbury (SJ 411052). All year. 1½ km. Scree and rocky slopes, scrub, mixed woodland and stream. Park behind Shell garage, take second turn on left, follow footpath to Reserve gate. Guide from Shropshire Conservation Trust, Preston Montford Bridge, nr. Shrewsbury.

134 EDGE WOOD, Westhope, nr. Craven Arms (SO 480876). All year. ¾ km. Oak woodland on limestone. For car parking, see Guide from Shropshire Conservation Trust, as above.

135 FRANKWELL RIVERSIDE TRAIL, Shrewsbury (SJ 491131). All year. 1½ km. From public car park near Welsh Bridge. Riverside meadows and town streets. Information and guide from Car Park Attendant, Frankwell Car Park, Shrewsbury.

136 OLD RECTORY WOOD, Church Stretton (SO 451938). All year. ¾ km. Specimen trees, flowers, birds. Car parks in Church Stretton, ¾ km. walk up Burway Road, turn left after cattle grid. Guide from Shropshire Conservation Trust, as above.

137 PRESTON MONTFORD FIELD CENTRE, Montford Bridge, nr. Shrewsbury (SJ 432142). All year. ¾ km. Farmland, mixed scrub and river bank vegetation, animals and birds. Park at Field Centre with permission. Guide from Shropshire Conservation Trust, as above.

SOMERSET

138 ASHTON COURT ESTATE, Bristol. Woodlands, parklands and flatland. Woodpeckers, tree creeper, nuthatch and goldcrests. Wild flowers. Badgers and squirrels. Guide from City Museum, Queen's Road, Bristol, BS8 1RL.

139 AVON GORGE, Mendip Forest, Bristol. Car park in Leigh Woods, just W. of Bristol city and overlooking Avon Gorge. Three Forest Walks along forest road, running N.E. from stone arch beside A369. Viewpoints, Bristol–Portishead road, near Abbots Leigh (ST 552741). Guide: Avon Gorge Forest Walk at car park or from Forestry Commission.

140 BIDDLE COMBE, WELLS, Wells Natural History and Archaeological Society. All year. 4 km. Birds, plants, geology and topography. Starts from entrance to B.B.C. transmitter on Pen Hill. Guide from Hon. Curator, The Museum, Wells.

141 BLACK ROCK, head of Cheddar Gorge, 13 km. N.W. of Wells. All year. 2½ km. Starts on B3135 road at Black Rock Gate. Plantations, natural woodland, limestone screes, and rough downland and grazing. Managed by Somerset Trust for Nature Conservation. Leaflet from Reserve Officer, Southwell House, Trull, near Taunton.

142 CLOUTSHAM, nr. Porlock (902439). All year. 5 km. Woodland, moorland and river valley. Starts at Webber's Post on Dunkery Hill road. Guide from Exmoor National Park Information Centre, The Parade, Minehead. Car park at start, Organised by Somerset Trust for Nature Conservation.

143 EBBOR GORGE, National Nature Reserve, nr. Wells (S.W. Region Nature Conservancy). All year. Limestone woodland, dry gorge, screes unique to Mendip Hills, limestone grassland, magnificent scenery. Car park (165/522484) on edge of Reserve adjoining Deer Leap Road, nr. Wookey Hole. Path guide available from display centre situated just off car park. Details from Warden, East House, Wookey Hole. (Tel.: Wells 73773.)

144 NEROCHE FOREST TRAIL. All year. 3¼ km. Woodlands. By-road W. from Ilminster—Honiton Road A303, 5 km. W. of Broadway (177/274157). Guide from Forestry Commission, Flowers Hill, Brislington, Bristol, 4. (Tel.: 78311.)

145 NORTH HILL, Minehead. All year. 5 km. Bird Migration and man's effect on landscape of coastal woods and moors. Starts just W. of harbour (969473). Guide from Exmoor National Park Information Centre, The Parade, Minehead. Car park 90 metres before start of trail. Organised by Somerset Trust for Nature Conservation.

146 QUANTOCK FOREST TRAIL (164/173373). All year. 1½–5 km. Timber deer and other wildlife in managed woodlands. Guide at site or from Forestry Commission, as above.

STAFFORDSHIRE

147 CANNOCK CHASE FOREST TRAIL, Ladyhill (SK 018171) on by-road S. from Rugeley–Penkridge road, 2½ km. from Ladyhill. Wild-life, observation tower, pinewoods on heathy uplands.

148 COOMBES VALLEY RESERVE, nr. Leek. Access by permit or ring Warden at Leek 4017. Booklet. Visiting Sat., Sun., Tues. and Thurs., April–August. ¾ to 5½ km. Wooded valley above stream. Several hides available for watching. Kingfisher, dipper, sparrowhawks and pied flycatchers breed. Badgers common. Assemble at 11.00 hrs. or later at Warden's house at top of valley on road from Apesford to Basford. Six Oaks Farm, Bradnop, nr. Leek. Permits from Royal Society for the Protection of Birds, The Lodge, Sandy, Beds.

148a HAY HEAD, Walsall (131/041990). E. of Longwood Lane, 3¼ km. E. of Walsall. All year. 2 km. Follows course of long derelict late 18th century industrial canal arm leading to lime workings. Good variety of flora, mixed fauna and birds. Leaflet (S.A.E.) from Walsall Parks Department or any Walsall Library.

149 HAYWOOD WARREN OUTDOOR TRAIL, Cannock Chase, Staffordshire County Council. Off A513 Rugeley–Stafford road. All year. 5 km. Woodland, Conifer plantation, sandy heathland. Deer, animals and marsh and heath plants. Booklet from County Planning and Development Department, Staffordshire County Council, Martin Street, Stafford.

150 HAWKSMOOR NATURE RESERVE. 2½ km. N.E. of Cheadle. Open all year. Managed by Hawksmoor Local Management Committee. Bracken and heather-covered moorland, some forest. Forestry Commission has major tree-planting programme in the area. Trail passes a borehole, sand quarry and works which provide raw materials for a large variety of industries. (Three alternative walks: A: 4 km., B: 2½ km., C: 2½ km.) Parking for six cars at the start. Leaflet from Mr. P. L. Wilson, The Spinney, Greendale Oakamoor.

151 ILAM NATURE WALK. 7¼ km. N.W. of Ashbourne. Open Easter–October. 2 km. Managed by Staffordshire Nature Conservation Trust, a walk set in grounds of Ilam Hall in lower end of beautiful Manifold Valley. Valley rock of carboniferous limestone. Trees are largely introduced species which do not grow wild naturally in this area. Remains of Saxon Cross commemorating 11th century battle. Wild flowers. Nuthatches, green woodpeckers and willow warblers. Ilam car park. Leaflet from Ilam Tea Rooms and caravan site.

152 SEVEN SPRINGS OUTDOOR TRAIL, Cannock Chase, Staffordshire County Council. Off A513 Rugeley–Stafford road. All year. 1¼ km. Marsh spring plants, open woodland, bramble thickets and open ground. Booklet from County Planning and Development Department, as above.

153 SHERBROOK VALLEY, Cannock Chase. Starts Milford Common, on junction of A513 and Brocton road, 5 km. S.E. of Stafford. All year. 5 km. Pines, chestnut, grasses, and wild flowers. Blue tit, woodpecker, fallow deer and small animals. Leaflet from County Planning and Development Officer, Staffordshire County Council, Martin Street, Stafford.

154 ROUGH WOOD, Shortheath, Willenhall. Staffordshire Nature Conservation Trust. All year. 2 km. Woodland, open country and scrubland in former coal-mining and industrial area. Oaks and birches, hawthorn thickets, pools, bogs and marshes. Guide from County Borough of Walsall Parks Department, or from Hon. Secretary, Walsall Civic Society, 129, Lichfield Street, Walsall (S.A.E.).

SUFFOLK

155 KING'S FOREST WALK (TL 815715). Guide from Cambridge office, East England. Starts nr. West Stow village, just N. of Bury St. Edmunds–Mildenhall

road A1101. From village take by-road N. to Forest Office.

156 SANTON DOWNHAM FOREST WALK, Thetford Forest (825870). All year. 2½ km. Managed woodland, birds. Evidence of Stone, Bronze and Iron Age cultures have been found locally. Starts at Santon Downham Church, 5½ km. N.W. of Thetford. Guide from Head Forester, The District Office, Santon Downham, Brandon.

157 SOMERLEYTON HALL, nr. Lowestoft. Open Easter–31st May, Sun. and Thurs. 14.00–18.00 hours to 30th September, also on Tues. and Wed. 14.00–18.00 hours. Great variety of trees and shrubs, and associated animal life; pond, aviary, duck enclosure and maze. 1½ km. Somerleyton Hall lies 8 km. N.W. Lowestoft on B1074 and 11 km. from Great Yarmouth on A134. Admission fee. Reductions for parties. Prices include trail and maze. Leaflet from Estate Office, Somerleyton Hall. Free car park. No dogs.

158 SYCAMORE FARM, Swilland, Ipswich, East Suffolk. Managed by the Ipswich and District Natural History Society. Organised parties at all times by prior arrangement. All year. 1½ km. Modern arable farm managed so that maximum of wild-life can be held on farm, certain areas including ponds and hedges received special attention. 1½ km. Start at TM 200509. Car park TM 197507. Guide from New House, Sycamore Farm, as above.

SURREY

159 ABINGER FOREST TRAIL, Ranmore Common. 4 km. W. from Dorking to East Horsley (TQ 126501). Varied woodland, broad-leaved and conifer on crest of North Downs. Details from Forestry Commission.

160 BARFOLD COPSE RESERVE, nr. Haslemere. Access by permit only. Typical mixed woodland, birds. ¾ km. Guide, permits and full details from the Royal Society for the Protection of Birds, The Lodge, Sandy, Beds. (Tel.: Sandy 551.)

161 COULSDON DOWNS No. 1, Croydon (302572). Starts S. end of Farthing Downs off A23 at Coulsdon. All year. 5 km. Over Farthing Downs into Happy Valley. Archaeology, local history, chalk grassland, pond, mixed oak, wild cherry woodland, bluebells, beach and yew and associated flora and fauna. Car park. Seasonal guide-books from 'Welcome Tea Rooms' at Farthing Downs, or from Chief Officer of Parks, 19, South End, Croydon, CR0 1BE.

162 COULSDON DOWNS No. 2, Croydon (317568). Starts Fox Public House, Fox Lane off Coulsdon Road, B2030. All year. 4 km. Through Happy Valley and over Coulsdon Common. Oak woodland, yews, beech, rabbits, small mammals, chalk downland plants, chalk/flint quarries, heathland, birds, woodland and pond. Guides as above available from the Fox Public House during licensing hours or from the Chief Officer of Parks, as above.

163 THE GIBBET HILL NATURE TRAIL, E. of Hindhead village. Superb views embracing Chilterns beyond London basin round to South Downs. Surrey Naturalists' Trust. All year. 3¼ km. Car park. Leaflet from Hon. Sec., 7, London Road, and box on right-hand side of door into cafe in car park. Also from garage near car park.

164 GUILDFORD. All year. 6½ km. Varied woodland, pasture land, downland and ornamental garden. Diverse bird life. Leaflet free, available from Municipal Office, High Street, or from Guildford Public Library, North Street, or from Guildford Museum, Quarry Street.

165 PERROTT'S WOOD, Banstead. Run in collaboration with Surrey Naturalists' Trust. All year. 2½ km. Formerly grounds of Queen Elizabeth Hospital before being purchased by Banstead Urban District Council. Limes, hornbeam, firs, spruce, oak, rhododendron. Birdlife. Leaflets from Surrey Naturalists' Trust, Hon. Sec., 96a, Brighton Road, South Croydon, CR2 6AD.

166 THE PUNCH BOWL, E. of Hindhead village. All year. 4 km. Sandy soil, heath and gorse, with pine trees on higher ground and oaks on some of lower slopes,

managed by Surrey Naturalists' Trust, and Hindhead Local Management Committee of National Trust. Magnificent open countryside. Leaflet from the Hon. Sec., Hindhead Committee, 7, London Road, and box on right-hand side of door into café in car park. Also from garage near car park.

167 SELBORNE, nr. Alton, on B3006. All year. 1 hour. Famous associations with the naturalist Gilbert White. Chalk Hangar. Trees and grasses. Wild flowers, butterflies. Deer, voles, moles, and spotted woodpecker. Leaflet available from Alton Natural History Society, No. 2, Great Austin House, 90, Tilford Road, Farnham, Surrey.

SUSSEX

168 BLACKDOWN (SU 921309). All year. 2½ km. Heathland association, Scots pine and bushes, Forestry plantations. Limited bird life. Start car park on top of Black Down Hill. Leaflet from Haslemere Museum, local bookshop, and Hon. Sec., Black Down National Trust, Crosse Garden, Church Lane, Haslemere.

169 EAST HEAD, West Wittering. From 1st April. 2½ km. Beach and sand-dunes of promontory at entrance to Chichester Harbour. Dune reclamation, plants and birds of coast and mud-flats. Start at W. end of large car park behind beach W. of West Wittering. Leaflet from café or car park, or with S.A.E. from National Trust, Polesden Lacey, nr. Dorking, Surrey.

170 FRISTON FOREST. (*a*) Main Block. Forest Trail through plantations of pine and beech on South Downs, between Eastbourne and Seaford. Reached from B2105, running N. from Eastdean to Polegate (TV 526996). (*b*) Wilmington Block. Forest Trail, 5 km. Starts at TQ 558078, beside Abbots Wood, 11 km. N.W. of Eastbourne. Reached by A22, through Polegate, to point 3¼ km. N.; then W. towards Arlington.

171 GOODWOOD, Goodwood Estate, Chichester. 31st March–31st October (by appointment only). 1¼ km. Starts Trail Museum Hut. Variety of woodland. Designed with **blind** people in mind. Wildlife includes rabbits, squirrels and occasionally deer. Guide obtainable from Countryside Activities Manager, Estate Office, Goodwood House, Goodwood. Guide in Braille free of charge.

172 HORAM QUIET CORNER (576172), midway between Tunbridge Wells and Eastbourne on A267. Open Easter to end October. Chain of five lakes or hammer ponds, young plantations and open farmland. On edge of Wealden clays with old iron industry workings. Wide variety of wildlife. Well-written guide available on site or from Major M. R. R. Goulden, Horam Manor Estate, Heathfield. Free car park and toilets. Picnic area and refreshments available.

173 KINGLEY VALE, National Nature Reserve, West Stoke, Chichester. All year. 4 km. Chalk downland, yew woodland, and their associated plants and animals. Starts on footpath N. of West Stoke (824099), car park (824088). Guide from kiosk on site, or R. L. C. Williamson, The Nature Conservancy, Keeper's Cottage, West Dean Woods, Chichester.

174 LEONARDS FOREST, nr. Horsham. Forest Trail. All year. 3¼ km. Marlpost Wood, near Southwater, 8 km. S.W. of Horsham. Reached by leaving Horsham–Worthing road, A24, 6½ km. S. of Horsham and proceeding W. (signposted Christ's Hospital), then S. towards Dragon's Green (TQ 141255). Wide range of conifers and broad-leaved trees. Roe deer, and bird life. Free guide on trail.

175 MILL HILL. Open spring only. 1½ km. Open down land. Details from Mr. J. D. Ibbetson, Parks and Cemetery Superintendent, Buckingham Park, Upper Shoreham Road, Shoreham-by-Sea.

176 NAP WOOD, 6½ km. S. of Tunbridge Wells on A267. Arranged by Sussex Trust for Nature Conservation on central wealden oakwood leased to them for a Nature Reserve. Leaflet from STNC, Woods Mill, Henfield, and from the National Trust area office, as above.

177 SLINDON. 11 km. N. of Bognor, N. of A29 (SU 938106). Various forest

trails in young beechwoods and conifers on slopes of high South Downs: 1. Northwood Forest Trail; 2. Marden Forest Trail; 3. Selhurst Park Forest Trail. Details from Forestry Commission.

178 WARREN GLEN, Hastings Country Park, nr. Fairlight. April–October. 3¼ km. Start Fairlight quarry park. Trail leads through a disused quarry with excellent examples of rock exposures. Woodland includes oak, ash, sycamore and hazel. Varied wildlife. Guide obtainable from Hastings Parks Department, Alexandra Park, Hastings or the Information Bureau, White Rock, Hastings.

179 WEALD AND DOWNLAND OPEN AIR MUSEUM, Singleton, Chichester. Open 1100–1800 hours Easter week-end, then Sun. to 19th May, then Sat., Sun., Tues., Wed., Thurs., and Bank Holidays to 30th September, then 11.00–17.00 hours Wed. and Sun. to end October. ½ km. Start museum. Variety of woodland and bird species. Guides obtainable from the Souvenir Shop in the museum. Dogs must be on a leash. School parties must book in advance.

TEESSIDE

180 PRESTON PARK, Stockton. All year. ¾ km. Wooded areas, conservatory, museum and riverside attractions. Booklet at Park. Further information from Parks Manager, Sun Alliance House, 16/26, Albert Road, Middlesbrough.

181 STEWART PARK, Middlesbrough. All year. 1¼ km. Wooded park, conservatory, animal and bird compounds. Booklet at Park. (Car park.) Further information from Parks Manager, as above.

WARWICKSHIRE

182 ALVECOTE POOLS (120/252043). All year. ¾ km. Warwickshire Nature Conservation Trust. Small pools, colliery spoil heaps. Oak, birch, willows and alders. Wide variety of bird-life. Guide from Mr. G. A. Arnold, 257, Watling Street, Wilnecote, Tamworth, Staffs, B77 5BG.

183 EARLSWOOD NATURE, Solihull, Warwickshire (SP 104757). All year. 1½–5 km. A walk through mixed oakwood and lake shore, rich in bird-life. Guide from Museum and Art Gallery, Congreve Street, Birmingham, 3.

184 OVERSLEY WOOD, Birmingham (SP 105563). All year, by appointment only. Woodland and its management. Guide from Warwick County Museum Education Service.

185 ROUGH HILL WOOD, Studley (053637). ¾ km. W. of former Studley Station, off A448. All year. 1½ km. By appointment only. Oak woodland, plants and animals. Guide from the Conservation Officer, Landscape Section, Redditch Development Corporation. Plymouth Road, Redditch. (Tel.: 64200.)

186 STRATFORD-ON-AVON CANAL, Lapsworth to Lowsonford (SP 186710). All year. Canal and historical Guide from Warwick County Museum Education Service.

187 WHICHFORD WOOD (312346). Off A34 between Long Compton and Shipston on Stour. Closed Winter. 1½, 3 and 5 km. Mixed woodland in gently undulating country. Wildlife. Site of a Norman Castle and Iron Age fort. Details (S.A.E.) from Mr. F. A. Hewitt, Whitegates Farm, Armscote, Stratford-on-Avon.

WESTMORLAND

188 LOUGHRIGG FELL, Ambleside. Established by Charlotte Mason College and the National Trust. All year. Circular route of 4 km. Starts large public car park off Keswick Road in Ambleside. Open fell, pasture, small mixed woodland, riverside path. Guide from all National Trust and National Park Information outlets or from Bridge House Information Centre at start of walk.

189 SERPENTINE WOOD, Serpentine Road, Kendal. All year. 1½ km. Woods and verges on carboniferous limestone; trees, flowers, birds, geology, topography. Starts (512926) 1 km. W. of Kendal Town Hall, via All Hallows Lane and Beast Banks.

190 SKELGHYLL WOODS, Waterhead, Ambleside. All year. 2½ km. Deciduous and coniferous trees, varied ground flora; scenery (Jenkyns Crag viewpoint) and geology. Starts at junction A591/A593 (377031). Waterhead car park. Guide from all National Trust and National Park Information Centres or from the National Trust Area Office at Broadlands, Borrans Road, Ambleside.
191 WHITE MOSS COMMON. Ambleside. 1¼ km. All year. Lakeland, mixed woodland; stream banks, open fell, oak woods. Literary connections (Wordsworth). Geological structure. Natural regeneration. Rich bird-life. On main A591 Ambleside–Grasmere road 3 km. from Ambleside. Guide from National Trust and National Park Information Centres and National Trust Area Office as above.

WILTSHIRE

192 MARDEN NATURE TRAIL, between Calne and Chippenham. Open April to September. Up to 6½ km. Former railway track now private land beside River Marden between woods and meadows. Prolific natural vegetation, birds, small mammals. Guide from Calne and Chippenham R.D.C., Bewley House, Marshfield Road, Chippenham (or map and brief notes or free leaflet for school-parties from same address). Free list of things to look for issued with Guide.
193 POSTERN HILL WALK, Savernake Forest, Marlborough (SU 198682). All year. 1½–5 km. Birds and fungi in managed beech and oak woods and ancient ornamental broadleaf walks. Guide at site or from Forestry Commission, Flowers Hill, Brislington, Bristol, 4. (Tel.: 78311.)
194 WOODLAND PARK, Brokerswood, nr. Westbury (166/843524). All year. Eight trails. Length varies between ½ km. and 1½ km. Great variety of trees, wildlife, etc., natural history centre and museum. Courses held regularly on natural history and forestry subjects. Admittance fee (includes guides and natural history centre).

WORCESTERSHIRE

195 HADEN HILL, Cradley Heath, Warley. All year. 3 km. (short trail 1½ km.). Parkland, thirty varieties of trees, pondlife. River Stour – interesting historical setting. Starts Haden Hill House, off A459. Guide (free) from Warley Parks Department, Harry Mitchell Recreational Centre, Bloomfield, Smethwick, Warley.
196 LICKEY JUNIOR NATURE TRAIL, nr. Rednal, Birmingham. All year. 1½ km. Woodlands, shrubs and pools on acid hilltops and clay valleys. Starts right of toposcope in car park at Beacon Hill off B4096. Guide from Birmingham Parks Department, Auchinleck House, Five Ways, Birmingham, B15 1DS, or Information Department, Council House, Birmingham, B1 1BB.
197 RAVENSHILL WOODLAND RESERVE, Alfrick. 13 km. W. of Worcester (SO 740539). Open 1st March until end October. 2½ km. Managed by Worcestershire Nature Conservation Trust. Parking for eight cars at start. Entrance fee. Trail Guide with map and local flora, etc. available at Information Centre on site. A working woodland of varied character. Warblers, woodcock, badgers, orchids, Herb Paris. Two Trails ¾ km. (valley and pool with duck) and 2½ km. (Observation Tower and fine views of Malvern Hills and Severn Plain). Enquiries to Hon. Sec., High Wood, Alfrick, Worcester.
198 WYRE FOREST TRAILS. All year. 1½, 2½ and 4 km. Woodlands. Starts at Forester's Office nr. Duke William Inn, 5 km. W. of Bewdley on A456 (SO 750740). Guide from Forestry Commission, Flowers Hill, Brislington, Bristol, 4.

YORKSHIRE

199 AYSGARTH NATURE TRAIL (SE 011888). All year. 1½ km. Falls, flora and fauna. Leaflet from National Park Information Centre (Aysgarth) (summer months) or from Yorkshire Dales National Park Information Officer, or County Planning Officer, County Hall, Northallerton.

200 BISHOP WOOD, Selby (SE 555340). All year. Managed woodland and natural historical interest. Whole wood is open. 5 km. S.W. of Wistow on Sherburn in Elmet to Selby road. Minor road 1st fork left, straight across at next cross roads, travelling from Wistow. Guide from District Office, 1A, Grosvenor Terrace, York, YO1 4DB. Also from Forest Office, Bishop Wood, Wistow Common, Selby.

201 GRAVES TRAIL, Sheffield (34/898188). All year. ½ km. Woodland within public park with wide variety of natural history interest. Graves Park, Sheffield. Guide from Recreation, Museums and Libraries Departments, Sheffield Corporation.

202 JAY TRAIL, Riddlesden, Keighley. Keighley Naturalists' Society and Keighley Corporation. Up Bar Lane off main Keighley–Bradford road, to Scott Lane West, Riddlesden. All year. 3 km. complete circuit. Birds and animals, flowers. Illustrated booklet from Keighley Corporation, The Museum, Cliff Castle, or Keighley Naturalists' Society, 2, High Cote, Riddlesden, Keighley, BD20 5DQ.

203 MAY BECK FARM TRAIL (NZ 894024). 8 km. S. of Whitby. June–December. 6½ km. Start May Beck car park. Chance to observe traditional moorland farm. Glacial overflow channels and rock exposure in valley sides. Guide from Stone Cairn Dispenser in car park or by post from North York Moors National Park Information Service, County Hall, Northallerton. No dogs. Car park.

204 NEWTON DALE FOREST TRAIL. All year. 5 km. Managed woodland, historical interest, wildlife. Approach through villages Newton-upon-Rawcliffe and Stape, 13 km. N. of Pickering. Bear left over Stape Beck, follow country road, turn right over cattle grid (SE 92/75943). Guide from District Office, Forestry Commission, 42, Eastgate, Pickering.

205 NORTH DEAN, North Dean Wood, West Vale, Greetland, nr. Halifax. All year. Three trails, approx. 1½, 2½ and 3 km. Variety of bird-life and woodland on each trail. Start Clay House Park, West Vale, off A6026 or B6113. Guide from Trail Information Office, Clay House or from Elland Council Offices, Exley Lane, Elland.

206 RAVENSCAR NATURE TRAIL. 13 km. N. Scarborough. All year. 5 km. Geology, sea birds. Leaflet available at local cafés and shops or from County Planning Officer, County Hall, Northallerton (S.A.E.).

207 REGINALD FARRER, Clapham. Easter to end September. 5–8 km. Trees, flora, limestone scenery, show-cave. Leaflet (free) available at National Park Information Centre, Clapham or National Park Information Service, North Eastern Chambers, Station Square, Harrogate.

208 RIVELIN VALLEY, Sheffield (28/948713). All year. 3 km. River, associated woodland and disused dam showing various stages of recolonisation. Man's influence on flora and fauna of river valley. Bus 44, 47 and 54 or car. Guide from Recreation, Museums and Libraries Department, Sheffield Corporation.

209 SILPHO, Pickering Forests Trail. All year. 1½–5 km. Managed woods and land for planting. Starts on Hackness–Harwood Dale by-road, N.W. of Scarborough (93/965944). Guide from District Office, Forestry Commission, 42, Eastgate, Pickering.

210 SKIPWITH COMMON, No. 1 (SE 669378 or SE 642374). Nr. York. All year. 2½ or 3 km. Variety of trees and plants including Scots pine, birch, oak and willow. Wildlife includes fallow deer and over 100 species of birds have been recorded. Guide from Yorkshire Naturalists' Trust, 20, Castlegate, York, YO1 1RP.

211 SLURRING ROCK, Hepton. All year. 1½ hrs. Starts at the Lodge near the car park in Trust-owned Hardcastle Crags woodland. Woodlands, valley and clearings. Birdlife, small mammals. Bluebells in May. Guide from Hepton Rural District Council or from National Trust.

212 SNEVERDALE, Pickering Forests Trail. All year. 1½–5 km. Managed woods and land for planting. Starts nr. Dalby 1½ km. N. of Thornton-le-Dale (92/856883). Guide from District Office, Forestry Commission, Pickering, as above.

213 STRID WOOD, Bolton Abbey, Skipton, Yorkshire. All year. 3 km. Trail leads

through pleasant woodland and branch trails all converge at 'The Strid'. Natural vegetation with a variety of birds and small animals. For full details about guide contact, Leisure Managements Inc., 8, Minster Yard, York. Entrance fee.
214 SUTTON BANK, 8 km. E. of Thirsk. All year. 3 km. Flora and fauna. Wild duck. Leaflet available from Sutton Bank Car Park (summer months) or County Planning Officer, County Hall, Northallerton, or Yorkshire Naturalists' Trust, 4, Clifford Street, York (S.A.E.).
215 WYKEHAM, Pickering Forests Trail. All year. 1½–5 km. Managed woods and land for planting. Starts N. of Wykeham village, 8 km. S.W. of Scarborough (93/932884). Guide from District Office, Forestry Commission, Pickering, as above.

NORTHERN IRELAND

CO. ANTRIM

216 BALLYCASTLE FOREST, Ballycastle (D 117402). All year, 09.00–17.00. 1½ km. Starts at entrance gate to forest, 1¼ km. from the Diamond, Ballycastle. Access from Fairhill Street and track of former narrow-gauge railway. Owned by Department of Agriculture. General wildlife, hardwoods, local geology, soils and vegetation. Enquiries to Town Clerk, Ballycastle. (Tel.: 62225.)
217 GIANT'S CAUSEWAY. 14½ km. E. of Portrush, B146. Access by foot only from car park. All year. 5 km. Interpretation of famous geological monument. Organised by National Trust, Malone House, Barnett Demesne, Belfast, BT9 5PU, and the Ulster Museum, Belfast. Guide to area available from the National Trust as above.
218 PORTRUSH NATURE RESERVE, Portrush (C 286441). All year. Owned by Department of Development, Environmental Conservation Branch. Rock formations and marine fossils, trace of ammonites. Car park. Details from Department of Development, Stormont, Belfast, BT4 3SS. (Tel.: 68716.)
219 SHANE'S CASTLE NATURE RESERVE, 1 km. from Antrim on A6 to Randalstown (J 314387). RSPB managed. All year by appointment only, or Easter, and Weds. and weekends June–September without appointment. 3½ km. Trail borders Lough Neagh, with wintering wildfowl. Car park. Leaflet from O'Neill Estate Office, Shane's Castle (Tel.: Antrim 3380) or from Mr. B. W. Coburn, RSPB, 58, High Street, Newtownards, Co. Down. (Tel.: 3723.)
220 TARDREE FOREST, 8 km. E. of Connor on Kells/Parkgate road (J 184924). All year, 09.00–17.00 hours. 1½ km. Spruce, larch, pine and silver fir. Ground vegetation. Badgers, magpies, wood-pigeons and small woodland birds. Car park. Details from Forester, Tardree Forest, Kells, Ballymena. (Tel.: Kell 268.)
221 WHITEPARK BAY. 2½ km. W. of Ballintoy, 11 km. W. of Ballycastle on A2. All year. 1½ km. Devised by Route Naturalists Field Clubs. Vegetation types developed on sand and chalk. Geological features also displayed. Leaflet available from Miss M. E. Murphy, Coleraine High School for Girls, Coleraine, Co. Londonderry, or from the National Trust, as above.

CO. ARMAGH

222 OXFORD ISLAND (J 047616). Access from M1 Motorway at Lurgan interchange, take road to Lough Neagh. All year. 2½ km. Ground flora of the West and East shores, woody vegetation, regenerating alders, wildfowl. Car park. Enquiries to Craigavon Development Commission, Bachelor's Walk, Portadown. (Tel.: 34221.)

CO. DOWN

223 CASTLE PARK, Bangor (J 505814). From Main Street, Bangor, via Castle Park Avenue, opp. Railway Station. All year. 1½ km. Parkland, mature woodland, ponds with wildfowl collection, arboretum. Car park. Enquiries to Town Clerk, Town Hall, Bangor. (Tel.: 4371.) Leaflet available.

224 CASTLEWARD, 11 km. N.E. of Downpatrick, 2½ km. W. of Strangford on A25. Mouth of Lough Strangford. All year. (1½ km.) Mixed woodland, parkland and Lough Strangford shore. Identification display. Wildfowl collection. Starts from Stable Yard Public Car park. Self-guiding panels. Organised by the National Trust, as above. Guide to area available.
225 CRAWFORDSBURN, Crawfordsburn beach (J 468824). All year. ¾ km. Marine ecology, animals of rock pools and sandy shores. Car park. Details from Department of Development, as above.
226 MURLOUGH NATURE RESERVE, Dundrum (J 395342). 3 km. W. of Newcastle. All year. 3 km. Dune and shore ecology. Archaeology. Starts Twelve Arches Public Car park. Self-guiding panels. Organised by the National Trust, as above.

CO. FERMANAGH

227 CASTLECALDWELL FOREST, 8 km. E. of Belleek (H 007603). Managed by RSPB. All year 09.00–17.00 hours. 1¼–3 km. Mixed age, mixed species woodland. Also ecological display, and special shelter. Car park. Enquiries to Mr. Joe Magee, The White House, Lowerybane, Castlecaldwell. (Tel.: Belleek 328.)
228 CORREL GLEN FOREST, 6½ km. from Derrygonnelly (H 076545) Follow 'Forest Drive' signs – trail is opp. entrance to Lough Navar Forest Drive. All year 09.00–17.00 hours. ¾ km. Natural scrub woodland, and peat-covered moorland. Grey wagtail and dipper. Too arduous for elderly, care required when Sillies River in flood. Car park. Enquiries to Forester, Lough Navar Forest, Derrygonelly. (Tel.: 256.)

CO. LONDONDERRY

229 DOWNHILL GLEN (C 761354). 1½ km. W. of Castlerock on Coleraine–Limavady coast road A2. All year. 1½ km. General natural history and geology. Starts from Bishop's Gate Public Car park. Self-guiding panels. Organised by the National Trust, as above.
230 NESS WOOD, off A6 Londonderry–Dungiven road, or B69, Limavady–Claudy road at Loughermore (C 528117). All year. 3 km. Mixed woodland ecology and features of river development. Car park. Leaflet from Department of Development, Environment Conservation Branch, as above.

CO. TYRONE

231 DRUM MANOR FOREST PARK, 5 km. from Cookstown, off main Cookstown–Omagh road (H 767777). All year. 10.00–½ hour before sunset. 1¼ km. Woodlands of mixed coniferous and deciduous species including beech and ash. Heronry and small lake with wildfowl. Red squirrels. Car park. Enquiries to the Forester, Drumcairn Forest, Stewartstown, Dungannon P.O. (Tel.: Stewartstown 257.)
232 GORTIN FOREST PARK, 13 km. N. of Omagh, on Omagh–Gortin road (H 485820). All year. 10.00–½ hour before sunset. 1½ km. Dense conifer woodland and open moorland. Car park. Enquiries to Head Forester, Gortin Glen Forest, Lislap P.O., Omagh. (Tel.: Gortin 217.)
233 KILLETER FOREST, 13 km. W. of Killeter Village, follow signposting to Derg Lodge (H 080799). All year 09.00–17.00 hours. ¾ km. Scrub woodland and open moorland. Car park. Enquiries to the Forester, Killeter Forest, Castlederg. (Tel.: Castlederg 487.)

SCOTLAND

ABERDEENSHIRE

234 HAZLEHEAD MAJOR, Aberdeen (NJ 896055). Off A944 at Hazlehead traffic island. Daily during summer months. 5 km. Park, golf-course, woodland.

Booklet (free) from Parks and Recreation Department, St. Nicholas House, Aberdeen.

ARGYLL

235 CALADH CASTLE, Tighnabruaich (NR 999759). All year. 2 km. Steep paths with climbing. Larch, pine, oak, maples, spruce. Deer, wild goats and badgers. Steep paths in places; not suitable for those overtaxed by climbing. Car park. Guide from Forestry Commission, 20, Renfrew Street, Glasgow.

236 INVERINAN, Loch Awe (NN 001181). Off B845. All year. 2, 3, 3½, 7, 8 km. Managed woodland. Walks are intended to let older plantations be seen. Forest Centre illustrating wildlife of forest. Booklet from Forestry Commission, as above.

237 KILMUIR ARBORETUM AND FOREST PLOTS, Benmore, nr. Dunoon (NS 162823). All year. Takes 3 hrs. 10 mins. Extends from low ground nr. entrance to 300 m. on slopes of Cnoc ā Mhadaidh. Deciduous and coniferous. Many unusual trees. Car park. Guide from Forestry Commission, as above.

238 SIGNAL ROCK (NN 123564). Off A82, Glencoe. All year. 5½ km. Panoramic view from two knolls in floor of Glen. Deciduous and coniferous. Deer, otters and badgers. Car park. Guide from Forestry Commission, as above.

AYRSHIRE

239 CULZEAN COUNTRY PARK, Maybole. 17½ km. S. of Ayr on A719 or 8 km. from Maybole on B7023. March to October. ¾–1½ hrs. Guide at Country Park Information Centre, Culzean Castle, or from National Trust for Scotland, 5, Charlotte Square, Edinburgh, EH2 4DU. Please check details.

240 ENTERKINE WOOD WILDLIFE TRUST RESERVE, Annbank (426242). By appointment only. ¾ km. Badgers, birds, flowers, mammals of mixed woodland with stream. Entrance via gate on road between B744 and B730. Organised by Scottish Wildlife Trust. Guide from J. Lorrain-Smith, 22, Auchenbeg Crescent, Ayr. Please check details.

241 ROZELLE, Ayr (337192). ½ km. from Burns' Cottage. All year. ¾ km. from centre of Ayr on B7024. Birds, mammals and plants. Booklet from Director of Parks, 30, Miller Road, Ayr.

BUTE

242 LOCH FAD, Trail No. 1, Bute Museum. All year. 7 km. Level walk around loch with alternative walk over Barone Hill. Highland fault passes through loch. Alder, birch, general woodland, variety of duck on loch. Guide from Museum, Rothesay.

243 LOCH ASCOG, Trail No. 2, Bute Museum (NS 103634). All year. 1¼ hrs. Along shore road from Ascog Bay, then over hill to Rothesay. Geological interest. General wayside and sea-shore. Ducks. Guide from Museum, Rothesay.

244 ETTRICK BAY TO KILMICHAEL, Trail No. 3, Bute Museum (NS 035666 or NS 002685). All year. 8 or 16 km. A walk on a road beside the shore of Kilmichael. Geological interest. Great variety of hedgerow plants, shrub trees. Sea-shore birds, heron, eiderduck. Guide from Museum, Rothesay.

245 KINGARTH, Trail No. 4, Bute Museum (NS 091562). All year. 2–2½ hrs. General wayside marsh and sea-shore. Seabirds. Guide from Museum, Rothesay.

246 SOUTH END OF BUTE, Trail No. 5, Bute Museum (NS 105546). All year. 3 hrs. Fairly rough walk, sea-shore and grassy hill. Seabirds. Moorland plants. Guide from Museum, Rothesay.

247 BULL LOCH, Trail No. 7 (NS 026745). All year. 2–3 hrs. A rough walk with a certain amount of climbing. Oak woodland, and moorland with flowers. Seabirds and duck. Guide from Museum, Rothesay.

DUMFRIESSHIRE

248 AE FOREST WALK (NX 985895). 4 km. off Ae Bridge on A701. All year. $5\frac{1}{4}$ km. or $5\frac{1}{2}$ km. Afforestation, wildlife, views. Start and finish at Forest Office nr. Ae village. Booklet from Conservator, Greystone Park, Moffat Road, Dumfries.

DUNBARTONSHIRE

249 LOCH LOMOND PARK, BALLOCH. All year. $1\frac{1}{4}$–$1\frac{1}{2}$ km. Starts from main gate Nature Trail Information Hut. Specimen conifers, woodland and lochside flora, marsh and meadow grasses, wild birds. Guide from Supt's House, Balloch. Please check details.

EAST LOTHIAN

250 BARNS NESS (NT 716772). $5\frac{1}{2}$ km. S.E. of Dunbar off A1. All year. $\frac{3}{4}$ km. Geological trail across exposures of carboniferous rocks at low tide. Guide from Information Centres at North Berwick and Dunbar, and from County Buildings, Haddington.
251 DUNBAR (NT 678794). All year. $2\frac{3}{4}$ km. Starts at Dunbar rocks, W. of Harbour. Geology and shore life, written by local grammar school. Further details from the District Clerk, Town House, Dunbar.
252 PRESSMENNAN FOREST TRAIL (NT 617727). $2\frac{1}{2}$ km. S. of Stenton village. All year. 3 km. Forestry Commission plantation and lakeside estate woodland. Starts at Woodend, access track signposted. Leaflet from 'Honesty Box'.
253 YELLOWCRAIG (526855). 5 km. E. of North Berwick, off A198 at Dirleton. All year. $1\frac{1}{4}$ km. General trail through the old woodland, plantation bents, and dunes, geology and plants. Guide from Information Office, North Berwick, or County Buildings, Haddington.

EDINBURGH

254 HERMITAGE OF BRAID AND BLACKFORD HILL, Edinburgh. All year during park hours. $2\frac{1}{2}$–3 km. Vegetation, waterfowl and glaciation in woodland valley and hill scrub. Bus from city centre. Guide from Edinburgh Education Dept., St. Giles Street, or from Publicity Office, 1, Cockburn Street. Please check details.

FIFE

255 CRAIGHALL DEN, Ceres (NO 399108). $\frac{1}{2}$ km. W. of Ceres on Minor Road to Largs. All year. $2\frac{1}{2}$ km. Ancient track to Craighall Castle. Geographical and botanical interest. Heron and dipper and other birdlife. Car park. Leaflet from Ceres Post Office or Ceres Folk Museum, or (S.A.E.) from Scottish Wildlife Trust, 8, Dublin Street, Edinburgh, EH1 3PP.
256 DUNNIKIER PARK, Kirkcaldy (NE 277937). Starts at Dunnikier House. All year. $1\frac{1}{2}$ km. Woodland flora and fauna. Car park. Guide at Dunnikier Park or Kirkcaldy Museum or Parks Department, Town House, Kirkcaldy.
257 PITTENCRIEFF PARK, Dunfermline (NT 088873). All year. One hour. Rugged glen with trees, plants, insects, stream. Guide available at Park (Superintendent's Office or Museum), or from Carnegie Dunfermline Trust, Abbey Park House, Dunfermline.
258 RAVENSCRAIG PARK, Kirkcaldy (36/2992 NW) off A955. All year. $1\frac{1}{2}$ km. Woodland and coastal flora and fauna including exotic trees. Guide available at Ravenscraig Park or Kirkcaldy Museum or Parks Department, as above.

GLASGOW

259 GLASGOW NATURE TRAILS. The following trails are run by the Glasgow Parks Department: Dawsholm Park, Kelvingrove Park, Linn Park, Rosshall Park, and Springburn Park. $\frac{1}{2}$ km.–$2\frac{1}{2}$ km. Times and details should be checked with the Head Office, Parks Department, 50, John Street, Glasgow, C1.

INVERNESS-SHIRE

260 ACHLEAN, Cairngorms National Nature Reserve (NN 27/854976). Easter–mid-October. 3 km. Heather moorland, Scots pine, Deer observation tower. Rich animal and plant life. Car park. Guide from Achlean Croft. Please check details.
261 CRAIGELLACHIE, Aviemore (28/892122). Easter–September. 1½ km. Starts a few hundred metres W. of Aviemore Centre. Extensive natural birchwood at varying altitudes, with variety of plants, mammals, birds and insects. Guide from Centre. Please check details.
262 CULLODEN FOREST TRAIL (NH 718465). Starts at Smithton, 5 km. E. of Inverness on by-road off A96. All year. 3 km. Walk through tall woods, with historic associations with Battle of Culloden, 1746. Guide from Forestry Commission, 60, Church Street, Inverness. Please check details.
263 ISLE OF RHUM, Kinloch Glen (17/408990). Starts at head of Pier at Kinloch. All year. 5 or 6½ km. Moorland and woodland flora. Red deer, common and grey seals and otters. Day excursion boats from Mallaig in summer only. Guide from box at head of pier. Please check details.
264 ISLE OF RHUM, South Side (17/407991). Starts at head of pier at Kinloch. Summer. 2 km. each way. Coastal, woodland and moorland, flora, insect and bird life. Farmland and shelter belt plantations. Red deer and Rhum ponies. Excursion boats from Mallaig. Guide from box at head of pier. Please check details.
265 LOCH AN EILEIAN, Rothiemurchus (28/898084). Starting-point N. side of car park. Easter–September. 4 km. Freshwater loch surrounded by mature Scots pine, heather moors and wind-swept summits. Guide from shed at lime-kiln, nr. start of trail. Please check details.
266 QUEEN'S FOREST, Glenmore (43/976097). Starts at Glenmore camp site. All year. 5½, 6½, 7¼ km. Guide from Camp Warden or from Forestry Commission, as above. Please check details.

KINCARDINESHIRE

267 BANCHORY FOREST TRAIL (39/634945). Starts 5 km. along by-road running S.E. from Potarch on main Deeside Road, A93, 8 km. W. at Banchory. All year. 5¼ km. Views over forested hills and Dee valley to high Grampians. Guide from Forestry Commission, 6, Queen's Gate, Aberdeen.
268 CRATHES CASTLE, Banchory. 4 km. E. of Banchory. March to October. 2¾ km. Recent regeneration in woodlands, sand quarry, lake and stream. Guide from Castle. Organised by National Trust for Scotland, 5, Charlotte Square, Edinburgh, EH2 4DU.
269 ST. CYRUS NATIONAL NATURE RESERVE (NO 755648). Off A92 ¾ km. E. of St. Cyrus. All year. 4 km. Cliff, dunes and saltmarsh. Rich and varied plant-life changing in response to these alterations of the ground. Guide from Nature Conservancy, 12, Hope Terrace, Edinburgh, or from Tourist Information Centre, Town Buildings, Montrose.

KINROSS-SHIRE

270 LOCH LEVEN, Vane Farm. Off B9097, 3 km. from M90. All year (not Mon. or Fri.) 09.30 to 17.30 hours. 2½ km. Freshwater loch, rich farmland, rough grassland, open birch, mixed woodland. Winter wildfowl, trees, moorland ecology. Car park. Guide from Warden, Vane Farm; Royal Society for the Protection of Birds, Loch Leven Nature Centre, nr. Kinross, or The Lodge, Sandy, Bedfordshire.

KIRKCUDBRIGHTSHIRE

271 FLEET FOREST WALKS, Gatehouse-of-Fleet, Castle Douglas (NX 605563). Off A75, ¾ km. E. of Gatehouse-of-Fleet. All year. 1½, 2½ and 4 km. Deciduous and coniferous woodland. Flowering trees and shrubs. Birdlife and roe deer. Guide

from Forestry Commission, Greystone Park, Moffatt Road, Dumfries, or from 'Honesty Box' at start of trail.

LANARKSHIRE

272 ORBISTON GLEN, Bellshill (NS 7459). 1½ km. from M74, S.S.W. of Bellshill. All year. 1¾m. Wooded banks of South Calder Water, specimen trees, grasses, wild flowers. Pond with aquatic life. Historical, geological interest. Car park. Guide from Parks Superintendent, Council Chambers, Bellshill.

273 COREHOUSE NATURE RESERVE, Kirkfieldbank (NS 875420). Off A74 or A73, 3 km. from Lanark. Open 27th May and 30th September by permit only. 1½–3 km. Mixed woodland river trail. Great geological and botanical interest. Roe deer, badgers, otters. Car park. Guide from Secretary, Corehouse Nature Reserve, 18, Ladyacre Road, Lanark.

274 EAST KILBRIDE, Torrance House (NS 6552). Off A726, 2½ km. S.E. of town centre. All year. 1½ km. Deciduous trees, holly, rhododendron, Wild flowers. Deer, foxes, rabbits, badgers, sheep. Car park. Details from Director of Parks, Civic Centre, East Kilbride.

MIDLOTHIAN

275 MAN AND ALMONDELL, Entrance at South Lodge, East Calder. Artificial waterway in form of canal feeder. Woodland, birds, mammals, plants, geological interest. Booklet from Publications Officer, Midlothian County Council, George IV Bridge, Edinburgh. Please check details.

MORAY

276 MONAUGHTY FOREST, Torrieston (NJ 167591). On road to Pluscarden off B9010 6½ km. W. of Elgin. All year. 1½ and 3 km. General area of woodland with pines, spruce, larch and fir. Forest flora and fauna. For further details, contact Forestry Commission, 6, Queen's Gate, Aberdeen.

PEEBLESSHIRE

277 GLENTRESS FOREST TRAILS (62/284396). 3 km. E. of Peebles, on A72. All year. 7¾ km. Forestry, wildlife, plants and geology. Start and finish at car park. Booklet from dispenser at car park, or from Forestry Commission, Greystone Park, Moffat Road, Dumfries.

PERTHSHIRE

278 BEN LAWERS (NN 609379). Starts at car park, off A827. 4 km. N. of Loch Tay. All year. 2½–3 km. Mountain plants on burnside, grassland, bog and alpine zone. Raven, wagtail, wheatear, kestrel and buzzard. Leaflet from Trust Information Centre at car park, or from National Trust for Scotland, 5, Charlotte Square, Edinburgh, EH2 4DU.

279 BEN LAWERS MOUNTAIN TRAIL (NN 609379). Off A827, 4 km. N. of Loch Tay. All year. 5½ km. to summit – 11 km. return. Details as above – also geological interest. Guide as above, also 'Route to summit' sheet from National Trust for Scotland and Nature Conservancy.

280 BIRKS OF ABERFELDY (NN 855487). Off Crieff Road, A826, ½ km. S. of Aberfeldy. All year. 3½ km. Birch woodland, and mixed woodland. Botany, ornithology. Booklet prepared by the Scottish Wildlife Trust, available from Town Council, Municipal Chambers, Aberfeldy.

281 CRAIGVINEAN FOREST WALKS (018422). 1½ km. from A9 on B898. All year. 5¼, 1½ and 13 km. Wildlife, forestry and birds. Car park. Guide from Forestry Commission, 6, Queen's Gate, Aberdeen.

282 CRIEFF (NN 8587). Off A85 W. of Crieff. All year. 2½ km. Wooded banks of the River Turret and the lower slope of the Knock, a well-known local landmark.

Leaflet prepared by the Scottish Wildlife Trust, available from Crieff Hydro or Crieff Information Office, James Square, Crieff.

283 Drummond Hill Forest Trail, Kenmore, Aberfeldy. Forestry Commission. (NN 770449). Off A827, $\frac{3}{4}$ km. W. of Kenmore. All year. 5 km. Ascends main block of Forest to viewpoint overlooking Loch Tay and surrounding country. European larch and hardwoods. Roe deer, badgers, birdlife. Further details from Chief Forester, Dalerb, Loch Tay, Aberfeldy.

284 FASKALLY, Pitlochry. $\frac{3}{4}$ km. W. of Pitlochry on A9. All year. $2\frac{1}{2}$ km. Conifers and hardwoods. Birdlife and roe deer, otters. Car park. Guide available from local Forest Information Centre, or from Forestry Commission, as above.

285 KINDROGAN FIELD CENTRE TRAIL, Enochdhu, Strathardle (NO 055630). $1\frac{1}{2}$ km. off A924. All year. $1\frac{1}{2}$ km. Woodland, red squirrels, voles, mice and many kinds of birds. Starts at Field Centre garden, and follows path beside River Ardle. Car park. Guide from Warden, Kindrogan Field Centre, Enochdhu, Blairgowrie.

286 KINDROGAN HILL TRAIL, Enochdhu, Strathardle (NO 055630). $1\frac{1}{2}$ km. off A924. All year. 5 km. Woodland, forestry, moorland, many kinds of birds and magnificent Highland scenery. Starts at Kindrogan Field Centre. Car park. Guide from Warden, Kindrogan Field Centre, as above.

287 KINNOULL HILL, Perth (NO 134234). Starts at Lodge in Hatton Road – signposted from centre of Perth. All year. $1\frac{1}{2}$ km. Ecology and effects of man on hill, moor, wood and cliff. Roe deer, hares, voles, rabbits, red squirrels. Car park. Guide from Director of Parks and Recreation, Marshall Place, Perth.

288 LINN OF TUMMEL, Pitlochry. All year. $3\frac{1}{2}$ km. 20 hectares of lovely woodland on banks of Rivers Tummel and Garry. Booklet from Trust Information Centres at Dunkeld and Killiecrankie, or from the National Trust for Scotland, 5, Charlotte Square, Edinburgh, EH2 4DU.

289 QUEEN ELIZABETH FOREST PARK, Aberfoyle (NS 531987). Off A81, 3 km. S. of Aberfoyle. All year. Five walks: $2\frac{1}{2}$, 5, $9\frac{1}{2}$, 12 and 13 km. Starts at Cobleland Caravan Site. Forestry practice, local history and history of plantations and natural woodland. Booklet from Forestry Commission as above.

290 THE HERMITAGE, Dunkeld (NO 013423). B898, $\frac{1}{2}$ km. W. of Inver, $1\frac{1}{2}$ km. from Dunkeld. All year. $2\frac{1}{2}$ km. Woodland trail by River Braan. Pine and spruce, rhododendron and common woodland plants. Birdlife. Guide from Trust Information Centre at car park, and from National Trust for Scotland, as above.

291 TUMMEL FOREST WALKS, Pitlochry. 11 km. W. of Pitlochry. All year. 1–6 hrs. Conifers and broadleaves. Geological interest. Booklet from Forestry Commission, as above.

RENFREWSHIRE

292 MUIRSHIELS COUNTRY TRAIL, Lochloinnoch (NS 632315). $7\frac{1}{4}$ km. N.W. of Lochloinnoch. $\frac{1}{2}$–1 hr. Woodland, moorland, high viewpoint and waterfall. Theme based on Man in the Calder Valley. Starts at Information Centre. Guide from Park Ranger on site or from County Planning Office, 7, Glen Street, Paisley. Please check details.

293 PAISLEY GLEN (20/481608). Starts $\frac{3}{4}$ km. along Glenfield Road, Paisley, off B774. All year. 09.00 hours to dusk or 22.00, whichever is earlier. Partly established woodland with new and recent planting. Small reservoirs, burns, etc. Indigenous flora, associated with moorland area. Guide from Study Unit at Glen, or from the Director's Office.

ROSS AND CROMARTY

294 GLAS LEITRE, Beinn Eighe National Nature Reserve (NH 28/001649). Summer. 8 km. 4–5 hours. Pine forest on the shores of Loch Maree. Starts from car park on opposite side of road. Guide from container at car park adjoining picnic site. Please check details.

295 KNOCKAN CLIFF, nr. Elphin (NC 29/187091). Off A835, 19 km. N. of Ullapool. Easter–Summer. 1¼ km. each way. Cliff is of international geological importance. Plant life on lime-poor and lime-rich soils. Starts at view indicator on E. side of car park. Guide from Knockan Information Centre. Please check details.
296 SLATTADALE FOREST TRAIL (NG 887719). On Gairloch–Kinlochewe road A832 on shore of Loch Maree. All year. 1½ km. and Tollie Trail – 8 km. Wildlife, views and forestry. Car park. Guide from Forestry Commission, 60, Church Street, Inverness. Please check details.
297 TORRIDON. Mountain ranges 750 million years old. Red and roe deer, mountain goat, pine marten, golden eagle, peregrine falcon, sundews, butterwort, mountain sorrel, saxifrages. Information Centre. Self-guided walks organised by the National Trust for Scotland, 5, Charlotte Square, Edinburgh, EH2 4DU. Guide from Information Centre or from National Trust. Please check details.

STIRLINGSHIRE

298 ABBEY CRAIG, Stirling (NS 809956). Off A997, 2½ km. N. of Stirling. All year – winter 10.00 hours to dusk, summer 10.00 to 20.00 hours. Access route to Wallace Monument, with branch trails to public park and cliff top. Deciduous and coniferous, wildflowers. Squirrels and rabbits, roe deer. Car park. Guide from Tourist Centre, Town Clerk, Stirling.
299 INCHAILLOCH, Loch Lomond National Nature Reserve (NS 26/414906). All year. 4 km. Starts and finishes nr. pier at North Bay. Access by boat from Balmaha. Trail on island in Loch Lomond. Walk along woodland paths to viewpoints and historic sights. Guide from container on pier at North Bay. Please check details.

WIGTOWNSHIRE

300 KILSTURE FOREST WALK, Sorbie (NX 441485). 2½ km. N. of Sorbie on A746. All year. 1½ km. Broadleaves and conifer forest. Birds and beasts of field and forest. Car park. Guide from Forest Office or Forestry Commission, Greystone Park, Moffat Road, Dumfries.
301 LOCH TROOL WALK, Bargrennan, Newton Stewart (NX 400790). 5 km. W. of Glentrool Village. All year. 6½ km. Starts and finishes at Caldons Camp Site. Afforestation, wildlife, Bruce Memorial and views. Booklet from Warden or Forestry Commission, as above.
302 NEWTON STEWART FOREST TRAILS, Larg Hill, Bruntis Lochs and Stroan Bridge (NX 452646). S.E. of Newton Stewart on A75, All year. 3½, 7 and 5¼ km. resp. Guides from Forestry Commission, as above.

WALES

ANGLESEY

303 HENDAI FOREST TRAIL (SH 404635). All year. 1½ km. Starts Newborough Forest Car Park. Forests planted to protect sand-dunes from erosion. Medieval houses exposed by blown sand. Guide from Forest Information caravan at car park or from Forest Warden, Gwydyr Uchaf, Llanrwst, Caerns. Forestry Commission.
304 NEWBOROUGH FOREST TRAIL. 1¼ km. Describes coastal vegetation and bird life, and the measures taken by Forestry Commission to stabilise sand-dunes to make possible the planting of trees. Guide from the Nature Conservancy, Penrhos Road, Bangor, Caernarvonshire.
305 PENRHOS. Starts near A5 where Stanley Embankment meets Holy Island. The pathway was laid by Anglesey Aluminium Ltd., and forms the course of nature trail established by the Company in response to European Conservation Year. Leaflet available from Anglesey Aluminium Ltd., Caegan, Holyhead.
306 SOUTH STACK. Birds and flowers. Open mid-May to end-July. A guided

walk down the steps to the lighthouse. Leaflets from South Stack café and Anglesey Tourist Association Centres.
307 YNYS LLANDDWYN NATURE RESERVE, Newborough Warren (SH 393635). Leaflet available describing features of interest of Reserve and footpaths in area. Car parks. Guide from Nature Conservancy, Penrhos Road, Bangor, Caernarvonshire. Written permit required to visit parts other than footpaths.

BRECONSHIRE

308 BRECON PRIORY GROVES (SO/045290) Spring–Autumn. $2\frac{3}{4}$ km. Beech and mixed woodland with related flora and some geological interest. Starts from A438 in Brecon, near junction with B4520. Parking in Brecon near by. Guide from National Park Information Centre, 6, Glamorgan Street.
309 TAF FECHAN FOREST (SO 043162). All year. $1\frac{1}{2}$ km. Starts from Owl Grove Picnic Place $\frac{3}{4}$ km. N. of Taf Fechan Reservoir on Pont Sticill/Talybont road. Flat riverside walk in forest amid foothills of Brecon Beacons. Guide from Forestry Commission, Churchill House, Churchill Way, Cardiff, or from 'Honesty Box' at start, or National Park Information Centres. (Forestry Commission.)
310 TALYBONT FOREST (SO 061171). All year. $\frac{1}{2}$ to $2\frac{1}{2}$ km. A series of four woodland and waterfall walks on saddle under Brecon Beacons between reservoir valleys of Taf Fechan and Talybont. Start from car parks at saddle or Pont Blaeny-glyn. 8 km. N. of Pont Sticill on Pont Sticill/Talybont road. Guide from local forest office or Forestry Commission, Churchill House, Cardiff, or National Park Information Centres. (Forestry Commission.)

CAERNARVONSHIRE

311 BEDDGELERT FOREST TRAIL (SH 578492). All year. $1\frac{1}{2}$ km. Forest and mountain scene. Starts from Forest Camp Site 3 km. N.W. Beddgelert Village, A487. Guide from Camp Warden or from Forest Warden, Gwydyr Uchaf, Llanrwst, or from Forestry Commission, Churchill House, Churchill Way, Cardiff, CF1 4TU.
312 CWM IDWAL. All year. $2\frac{1}{2}$ km. Classic area for study of biology, land use, glaciation in Snowdonia and geomorphology. Take path from A5 at Ogwen Cottage (SH 649604). Guide from the Nature Conservancy, Penrhos Road, Bangor.
313 CWM-Y-LLAN, Snowdon. All year. 4 km. Features of biological, geological and historical interest, land use of upland sheepwalk. Bethania, Nant Gwynant at SH 628505. Car park. Guide from the Nature Conservancy, as above.
314 GREAT ORME, Llandudno. Starts by Happy Valley café. All year. 8 km. Sheltered valley, woodland and heath, cliff and shore, bare rock and cultivated land. Wild flowers, butterflies and moths. Booklet from Llandudno Urban District Council.
315 GWERNGOF UCHAF, Capel Curig. On A5 London–Holyhead road, nr. Llyn Ogwen. All year. $1\frac{1}{2}$ km. Open mountain area with climb of 60 m. Designed to demonstrate the working of a hill farm in rough country as well as drawing attention to geology and botany of area. Car park. Self-guiding plaques.
316 GWYDYR FOREST TRAIL (SH 756576). Above Ugly House, A5, 5 km. W. of Betws-y-Coed. All year. 5 km. Mountain forest and river scene. Guide from Forest Warden, Gwydyr Uchaf, Llanrwst. (Forestry Commission.)
317 LADY MARY'S WALK (SH 790610). $1\frac{1}{2}$ km. Forest Exhibition Gwydyr Uchaf above Gwydyr Castle. Regeneration of mature forest in mountain landscape. Guide from Forest Warden, Gwydyr Uchaf (see Gwydyr). (Forestry Commission.)
318 THE MINERS' TRACK, Snowdon. All year. 3 km. Features biological, geological and historical interest. Views of Snowdon summit. Starts from Pen-y-Pass car park nr. Llanberis at SH 647556. Guide from the Nature Conservancy, as above.
319 WALKS IN GWYDYR FOREST. Ten walks based on Betws-y-Coed. $1\frac{1}{4}$ to

8½ km. Forest, mountain, river and lake; wildlife and local history. Illustrated guide-book from Forest Warden, Gwydyr Uchaf (see Gwydyr) or from local shops and hotels. (Forestry Commission.)

CARDIGANSHIRE

320 DEVIL'S BRIDGE (Coed Rheidol). All year. ¾ km. The owners, Crest Hotel Ltd., charge a fee for entry to trail (Jacob's Ladder footpath). Historical, geological and biological features of well-known Rheidol Gorge below Devil's Bridge, adjacent to National Nature Reserve. Many steps. Starts at Hafod Arms Hotel Kiosk (SN 742771). Guide from Kiosk at roadside or from Hafod Arms Hotel.

321 DOVEY ESTUARY. All year. 1¼ km. Aspects of sand-dune ecology. Starts at Ynyslas Dunes Information Kiosk (SN 608942). Guide from Nature Conservancy Information Kiosk at Ynyslas Dunes, or the Regional Officer, Plas Gogerddan, Aberystwyth. (Tel.: Bow Street 551.)

322 RHEIDOL FOREST WALK, Gogerddan (SN 633837) 5 km. N. of Aberystwyth off A4159. All year. 1¼ km. Forest and woodland. No guide. (Forestry Commission.)

323 TALIESIN FOREST WALK, Tyn-y-Garth (SN 692945). All year. Forest of unique charm between Aberystwyth and Machynlleth along A487 road. No guide, but plaques on site. Signpost 'Artists Valley'. Forestry Commission, Churchill House, Churchill Way, Cardiff, CF1 4TU.

324 YSTWYTH FOREST WALK, Aberystwyth (SN 694716). All year. 3 km. Forest and gorge scenery. 16 km. S. of Aberystwyth on by-road linking B4340 and Pontrhydygroes. No guide. Forestry Commission as above.

CARMARTHENSHIRE

325 ROMAN GOLD MINES, Dolaucothi. All year. 1½, 5 and 8 km. The Roman Workings at Dolaucothi constitute possibly the finest preserved example of a Roman gold-mine with its aqueduct systems in Europe. Three separate nature trails have been constructed by the National Trust. Information Boards with illustrative materials are sited at key points. Guide available on site or from County Museum, Quay Street, Carmarthen.

DENBIGHSHIRE

326 MOEL FAMAU FOREST TRAIL, Coed Clwyd (SJ 171611). Open all year. 5 km. Woods and open valley. Starts at car park at Coed Clwyd 2½ km. E. of Ruthin. Detailed guide from District Forest Office, Forestry Commission, Park Road, Ruthin. Leaflet from 'Honesty Box' at car park. (Denbighshire, Flintshire Education Committee jointly with Forestry Commission.)

327 PWLLYCROCHAN WOODS, Colwyn Bay (SH 845785). All year. 1½ km. Mixed woodland rich in flora and fauna. Owned by Borough Council. ¾ km. from Town Centre. Leaflet from Public Library, Colwyn Bay.

328 TAN-Y-CUT WOOD, Froncysyllte (SJ 281411). All year. Wood and birds, wild flowers. On A5 by Shropshire Union Canal. Leaflet from Wrexham Rural District Council, Wrexham.

329 WORLD'S END, Llangollen (SJ 232478). June–August. 1½ km. Approached from Llangollen via Panorama Walk and Minera via B5426. Forest (Forestry Commission) and moorland. Shell/County Trust Trail. Leaflet from North Wales National Trust, Llys Gwynedd, Ffordd Gwynedd, Bangor, Caernarvonshire or Forestry Commission, Oswestry.

FLINTSHIRE

330 BISHOPSWOOD, Prestatyn (SJ 068814). All year. 3 km. Bird life, archaeological and geological interest. Organised by Prestatyn Urban District Council. Further details from Council or from North Wales Tourism Council, Civic Centre, Colwyn Bay, Denbighshire.

331 BUCKLEY TOWN (SJ 279645). Starts at Hawkesbury Community Centre, just off Liverpool Road. All year. 7¼ km. Trail covers local history and industrial archaeology. Guide available from District Council Offices and Flintshire County Council, Shire Hall, Mold.
332 EWLOE CASTLE, Deeside (SJ 292670). Starts from A55. All year. 2½ km. Woodland, open farm land, river valley features and historic ruins of Ewloe Castle. Guide available from District Council Offices and Flintshire County Council, as above.
333 HOLYWELL TOWN (SJ 195764). Starts from Pen-y-Maes Estate. All year. 5 km. Covers a small wooded river valley with features of river erosion; Basingwerk Abbey, a ruined Monastery which dates from the 12th century; industrial features, and the legendary holy well from which the town derives its name. Guide available from the District Council Offices and Flintshire County Council, as above.
334 LEETE, Loggerheads (SJ 198626). Starts from A494 Mold to Ruthin road. All year. 2 km. Features geology, river erosion and plant life of a limestone area; also industrial archaeology; the famous Leetes, water channels associated with corn mills and lead mines. Guide available from Flintshire County Council, as above.
335 LEETE, Rhydymwyn (SJ 207649). Starts in Rhydymwyn village, off A541 Mold–Denbigh road. All year. 6 km. Many features similar to trail above. Limestone gorge features, limestone quarry with fossils. Good variety of trees, wild flowers, etc. Guide available from District Council and Flintshire County Council, as above.

GLAMORGAN

336 CARDIFF CITY COUNCIL PARKS DEPARTMENT has drawn up a series of nature trails and walks: Nature trails for Bute Park, Caerphilly Common and the Wenallt. Walks for Cefn On, Nant Fawr, Rumney, Taff Valley and Llandaff. Details and brochures from Parks Department, Wedal Road, Roath Park, Cardiff.
337 OXWICH NATIONAL NATURE RESERVE, Gower (SS 502865). All year. ¾ km. Sand trail. Aspects of sand-dune ecology. Car park. Guide from Nature Conservancy, Gower Countryside Centre, The Old School Room, Oxwich.
338 RHOSSILI, GOWER COAST NATIONAL NATURE RESERVE (SS 414881). 24 km. W. of Swansea. All year. 5 km. Cliff-top walk starting and finishing at Rhossili car park. Limestone flora. Fulmars, petrels, guillemots and razorbills. Also an Iron Age village and medieval open field system. Guide from Nature Conservancy, Gower Countryside Centre, as above.
339 TAIR ONEN FOREST TRAIL, Bonvilston (ST 031768). All year. 1½ or 3 km. Start from Hensol Woods Picnic Place, ½ km. N. of Welsh St. Donats on Welsh St. Donats/Ystrad Owen road. Coniferous and broadleaved forest. Guide from Forestry Commission, Churchill House, Churchill Way, Cardiff, CF1 4TY, or from 'Honesty Box' at start.

MERIONETH

340 CEFN ISAF FARM TRAIL, Llanbedr. All year. 3 km. Working of typical Welsh hill-farm. Starts nr. Salem Chapel. Guided by plaques.
341 COED LLYN MAIR, Coedydd Maentwrog National Nature Reserve, Vale of Ffestiniog. Open all year, although certain pictorial signs must be removed in winter. ¾ km. Scenic views (lake Llyn Mair), woodland, ravine and many mosses. Starts from Tan-y-Bwlch Station on Ffestiniog railway (SH 650416); or from car park on B4410 (SH 651414). Guide from the Nature Conservancy, Penrhos Road, Bangor, Caerns., or from Tan-y-Bwlch Station.
342 DOLGEFEILIAU FOREST TRAILS, Coed-y-Brenin, Dolgellau (SH 721269). All year. 3, 2½ and ¾ km. Mountain, forest and river scene. Starts Dolgefeiliau picnic site 13 km. N. Dolgellau, A487. Guide from Forest Warden, Massgwm Centre, Ganllnyd, Dolgellau or from 'Honesty Box' at start. (Forestry Commission.)

343 FARCHYNYS WOODLANDS AND ESTUARY TRAIL, Bontddu (116/659183). All year. 1½ km. Starts ¾ km. W. of Bontddu village on A496. Guided by plaques by Merioneth Planning Authority.
344 NANTCOL, Llanbedr. All year. ¾ km. Riverside walk. Starts from car park and camping site. Guided by plaques.
345 PRECIPICE WALK, Dolgellau. All year. 5 km. Woodland, meadows, lake and sheepwalk. Starts 4½ km. along Llanfachreth Road. Signposted by Merioneth Park Planning Authority.
346 TANYCOED FOREST TRAIL, nr. Machynlleth (SH 755054). All year. 3 km. Mountain and forest scene. Arboretum. Starts Tan-y-Coed picnic site 6½ km. N. of Machynlleth on A487. Guide from Forest Office, Ceinws Camp, Machynlleth, Mont., or from Forest Warden, Maesgwm Centre, Ganllwyd, or from 'Honesty Box' at start. (Forestry Commission.)
347 TYN-Y-GROES FOREST TRAIL, Coed-y-Brenin, Dolgellau (SH 730233). All year. 3 km. Mountain and Forest. Starts Tyn-y-Groes picnic site 9½ km. N. Dolgellau, A487. Guide from Forest Warden, Maesgwm Centre, Ganllwyd, Dolgellau or from 'Honesty Box' at start. (Forestry Commission.)

MONMOUTHSHIRE

348 EBBW FOREST (ST 237959). All year. 3 km. Mainly coniferous but bisected by remnants of broad-leaved trees and shrubs along stream. Scenic walks. Start from car park E. of Abercarn on Newport–Brynmawr road, A467. (Forestry Commission.)
349 GRAY HILL COUNTRYSIDE TRAIL, Wentwood Forest (ST 428939). Car park and leaflet dispenser at Wentwood Reservoir Picnic Site (Monmouthshire County Council). All year. Oak coppice, heathland and forestry plantations. Archaeological interest and views over Severn Estuary.
350 MYNYDD DU FOREST, Black Mountains (SO 266252). All year. 2½ and 3 km. Start at Ffawyddog Wood Picnic Place 9½ km. N.E. of Crickhowell off Llanthony road. Planted forest, ground flora on rides. Mountain scenery and species. Guide from 'Honesty Box' at start or Forestry Commission, Churchill House, Churchill Way, Cardiff, or National Park Information Centres. (Forestry Commission.)
351 ST. MARY'S VALE, Sugar Loaf (SO 284162). All year. 3 km. Oak, beech, alder woods on National Trust land. Leaflet from National Park Information Centre, Monk Street, Abergavenny.
352 TINTERN FOREST, Chapel Hill and Barbadoes (ST 525970). All year. 2½ and 3 km. Start from car park at old 'Tintern Saw Mills' near Royal George Hotel, Tintern. Maturing broad-leaved and coniferous woodlands with views of Wye Valley. Guide from Forestry Commission, Cardiff as above, or from Forest Office and 'Honesty Box' at start. (Forestry Commission.)
353 WYNDCLIFFE, St. Arvans, nr. Chepstow (ST 523973). All year. Mixed woodland, ground flora, famous view over River Wye. Car park. A Monmouthshire Naturalists' Trust/Nature Conservancy Trail. Leaflet dispenser at start of trail.

MONTGOMERYSHIRE

354 HAFREN FOREST TRAILS (SN 857870). 11 km. W. of Llanidloes. Source of River Severn. 1¼, 5 and 9½ km. Moorland and forest scene, wildlife. Starts Rhyd-y-Bennwch, signpost Old Hall from Llanidloes. Guide from 'Honesty Box' at start or from District Forest Office, County Office, Llandrindod Wells. (Forestry Commission.)
355 HAFREN FOREST (SN 857871). All year. ¾ km. Starts from car park/picnic site. Riverside walk. Guide from Forestry Commission, Victoria House, Victoria Terrace, Aberystwyth.
356 LLYN CLYWEDOG. Lakeside walk. Starts near car park/viewing area. Picnic site. Leaflets available along walk. Nest boxes.

PEMBROKESHIRE

357 DALE PENINSULA (811058). All year. 9½ km. Geology, landscape, history of Milford Haven and Dale peninsula (St. Ann's Head). Starts at Griffin Inn, Dale. Guide from local shops, Dale Fort Field Centre, Haverfordwest, or Pembrokeshire Countryside Unit, Broad Haven, Haverfordwest.

358 MARLOES SANDS. 21 km. S.W. of Haverfordwest. All year. 4 km. Starts and finishes at Marloes Sands Car Park. Selenium and old red sandstone cliffs, with spectacular coastal scenery. Ravens and choughs, grey seals, reed-buntings and curlews. Guide from West Wales Naturalists' Trust, Victoria Place, Haverfordwest.

359 SLEBECH FOREST, nr. Minwear (SN 054141). Easter–October. 3 km. Starts from car park along by-road running S.W. from A40 at Canaston Bridge. Views over wooded estuary of Eastern Cleddau river in Pembrokeshire Coast National Park. Guide from local Forest Office or Forestry Commission, Churchill House, Churchill Way, Cardiff, or National Park Information Centres. (Forestry Commission.)

LONG-DISTANCE TRAILS

ISLE OF WIGHT

360 BEMBRIDGE TRAIL, Shide, nr. Newport (505881) to Bembridge Windmill (640875). All year. Approx. 24 km. South side of chalk downs, some forestry, fine views, marshland in east. Parking in St. George's Lane. Guide from County Surveyor, Isle of Wight County Council, County Hall, Newport, Isle of Wight.

361 COASTAL PATH AROUND THE ISLAND. All year. Approx. 90 km. altogether. At present can only be walked in sections. Varied characteristics, downland cliffs to estuarine areas, urban areas, woodland, downland and farmland. Guide from County Surveyor, as above.

362 HAMSTEAD TRAIL, Hamstead Ledge, nr. Yarmouth (405920) to Brook (385836). All year. Approx. 13 km. Saltings at Newtown, agricultural land, then on to downs. Starting-point Hamstead Lodge, nr. Yarmouth. Guide from the County Surveyor, as above.

363 NUNWELL TRAIL, Oakfield, Ryde (596919) to Lake Common (587839). All year. Approx. 16 km. Mixed country, crossing main spine of downlands, then water meadows. Guide from the County Surveyor, as above.

364 SHEPHERDS TRAIL, Whitcombe Cross (487874) to Atherfield (451800). All year. Approx. 16 km. High ground, views, associated plants and birds. Guide from the County Surveyor, as above.

365 STENBURY TRAIL, Week Down, Ventnor (545772), to Blackwater, Newport. All year. Approx. 16 km. River valley and downlands. Starting-point Whitwell Road. Guide from the County Surveyor, as above.

366 TENNYSON TRAIL, Carisbrooke (482881) to Alum Bay (301847). All year. Approx. 24 km. Downland, marine views, forest. Tennyson monument. Tumuli. Starting-point, Nodgham Lane, Carisbrooke. Guide from the County Surveyor, as above.

367 WORSLEY TRAIL, Brighstone (432843) to St. Blasius Church, Shanklin (579805). All year. Approx. 24 km. Pine forest and high countryside. Starting-point, Brighstone Forest car park off Brighstone–Calbourne road. Guide from the County Surveyor, as above.

SURREY

368 DOWNLAND RAMBLES, Croydon. Starting-points in Coulsdon (299583), Old Coulsdon – (209583), Purley – (315614) and Whyteleafe – (34586). All year. Car park. Three circular walks intertwined to offer variations. The routes run through many beautiful parts of the North Downs using footpaths, bridle-paths,

commons and public open spaces. The guide gives local history and nature notes and is available from Chief Officer of Parks, as above.

369 WOODLAND RAMBLE, Croydon. Starting-point, Conduit Lane, Coombe Road, Croydon (345643). All year. 21 km. circular walk (shorter walks suggested in Guide). The route takes one through eight of the best woods in South London. Car park. Guide containing local history and nature notes, available from Chief Officer of Parks, 19, South End, Croydon, CR0 1BE.

YORKSHIRE

370 SHEFFIELD – Round Walk. All year. 16 km. A clearly signposted walk in the S. and S.W. districts of Sheffield, passing through 400 hectares of parkland, woodland and riverside public open space. Starting-point, Endcliffe Park; end of walk Graves Park. Bus services to City Centre available at 9 points on route of walk. Map included in Guide from Recreation, Museums and Libraries Departments, Sheffield Corporation.

MOTOR TRAILS

ENGLAND

LINCOLNSHIRE

371 FENLAND TOUR. April and May. Guide to conservation areas round Spalding, for use by motorists; available from Springfields Centre in Spalding or Lincolnshire Trust for Nature Conservation, The Manor House, Alford.

SCOTLAND

372 ATHOLL WAY MOTOR TRAIL, Blair Atholl. All year. 32 km. Road from Blair Atholl to Dunkeld. Conifers, plants, historic interest. Guide from Blair Castle, or Trust Information Centres at Dunkeld, Killiecrankie and Ben Lawers, or from National Trust for Scotland as above.

373 INVERPOLLY MOTOR TRAIL (NC 29/187088). All year. 80 km. Starts and finishes at Knockan Information Centre on A835, 22½ km. N. of Ullapool. Through the mountainous Coigach and Assynt districts of Wester Ross and Sutherland. Guide from Knockan Information Centre.

ISLE OF BUTE

374 MOTORISTS' TRAIL, Trail No. 6 (NS 106654). All year. 50–55 km. (1½–2½ hrs.) Designed for motorist driving around island. General woodland and seashore. Sea and shore birds. Guide from Museum, Rothesay.

11 FORESTRY COMMISSION PROPERTIES AND FOREST TRAILS

The Forestry Commission are very helpful. Visits to their forests (see Figs. 3:5–3:8) can be arranged by writing to the Conservator of Forests in the area you wish to visit.

Address of Conservators of Forests

NORTH-WEST ENGLAND Dee Hills' Park, Chester, CH3 5AT (0244 24006): Cumberland, Westmorland, Lancashire, part of Yorkshire (Lune and Ribble Valleys), Cheshire, Shropshire, Staffordshire, Warwickshire, Leicestershire, Nottinghamshire and Derbyshire.

NORTH-EAST ENGLAND 12 Grosvenor Terrace, York, YO3 7BD (0904 20221): Northumberland, Durham, Yorkshire (except Lune and Ribble Valleys).

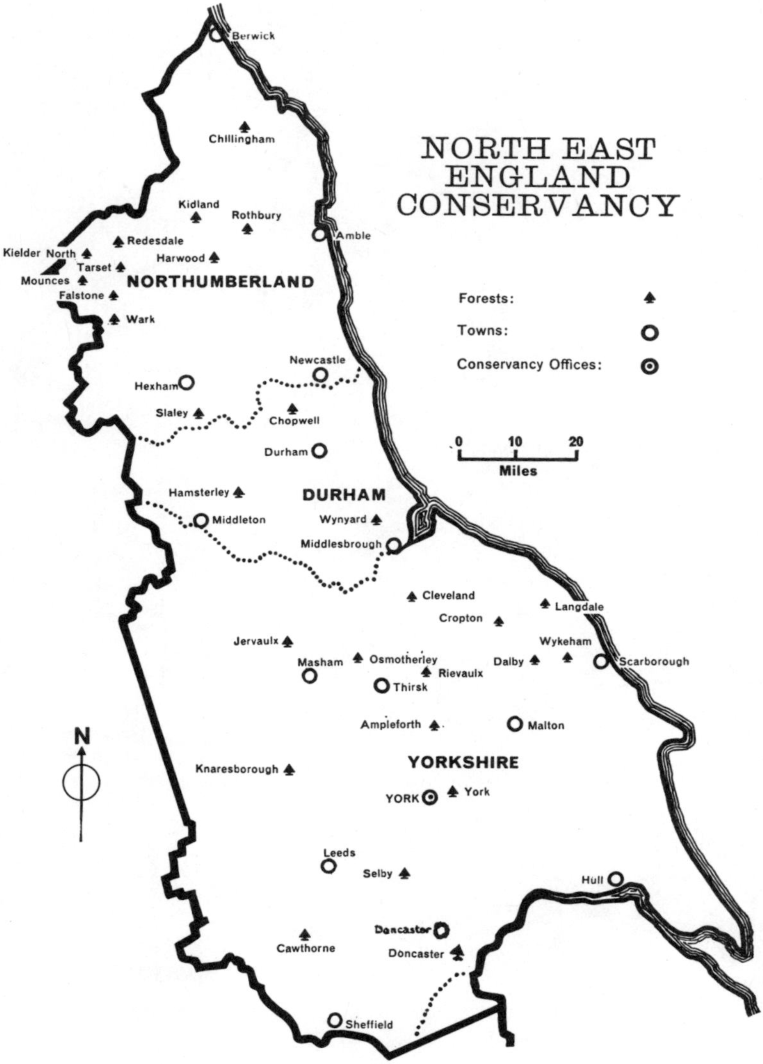

3:5 The Forestry Commission forests and Conservancy regions of Northern England.

3:6 The Forestry Commission forests and Conservancy regions of East and South-East England.

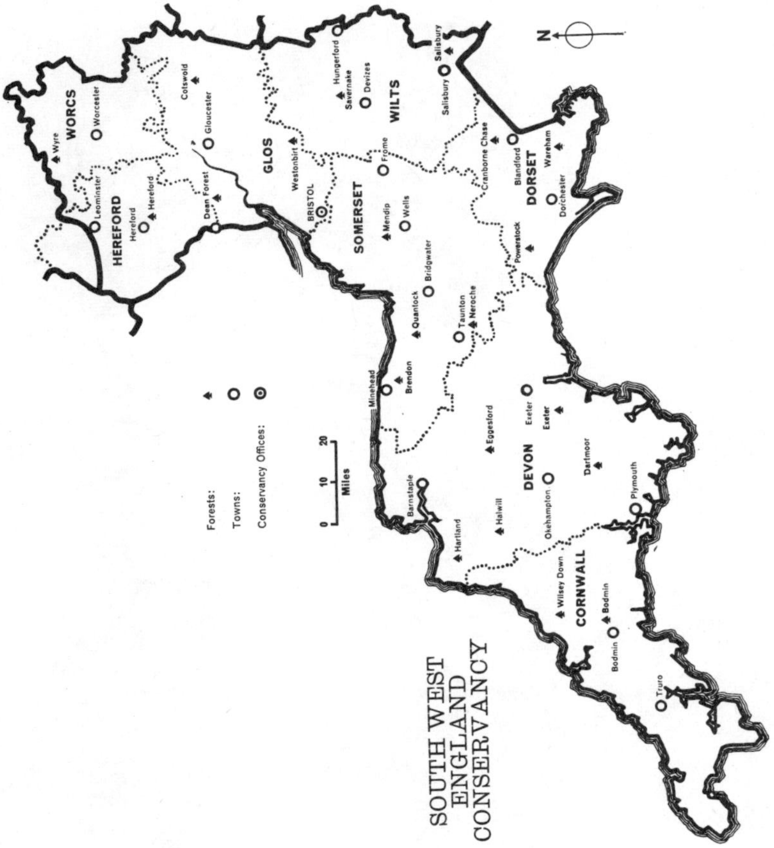

3:7 The Forestry Commission forests and Conservancy region of South-West England.

3 : 8 The Forestry Commission forests and Conservancy regions of Wales.

3:9 The Forestry Commission forests and Conservancy regions of North-West England.

EAST ENGLAND Brooklands Avenue, Cambridge, CB2 2DY (0223 54495): Lincolnshire, Rutland, Norfolk, Cambridgeshire, Northamptonshire, Bedfordshire, Oxfordshire, Buckinghamshire, Hertfordshire, Essex, Suffolk and Huntingdonshire.
SOUTH-EAST ENGLAND and NEW FOREST The Queen's House, Lyndhurst, Hants., SO4 7NH (0421-28 2801): Berkshire, London, Middlesex, Kent, Sussex, Surrey and Hampshire (New Forest and Isle of Wight), East Dorset.
SOUTH-WEST ENGLAND Flowers Hill, Brislington, Bristol, B54 5JY (0272 78311): Herefordshire, Gloucestershire, Wiltshire, Dorset (except east), Worcestershire, Somerset, Devon and Cornwall, Forest of Dean.
NORTH SCOTLAND 21, Church Street, Inverness (0463 32811): Caithness, Sutherland, Ross and Cromarty, Inverness, north-west Argyll, Nairn (except north-east), Moray (south), Orkney, Shetland.
EAST SCOTLAND 6, Queen's Gate, Aberdeen, AB9 2NQ (0224 33361): Nairn (north-east), Moray (north), Banff, Aberdeen, Kincardine, Angus, Kinross, Fife (except south-west), north-east Perth.
SOUTH SCOTLAND Greystone Park, Moffat Road, Dumfries, DG1 1NP (0387 2425): Midlothian, East Lothian, Berwick, Roxburgh, Selkirk, Peebles, Dumfries, Kircudbright, Wigtown, south Ayrshire, south-east Lanarkshire.
WEST SCOTLAND 20, Renfrew Street, Glasgow, G2 3BG (041-332 7261): Argyll (except north-west), south and west Perth, Stirling, Dunbarton, Renfrew, Clackmannan, south-west Fife, north Ayrshire, north-west Lanarkshire, West Lothian, Bute.
NORTH WALES Victoria House, Victoria Terrace, Aberystwyth, SY23 2DA (0970 2367): Anglesey, Caernarvon, Denbigh, Flint, Merioneth, Montgomery, Radnor, Cardigan (except south).
SOUTH WALES Churchill House, Churchill Way, Cardiff, CF1 4TU (0222 40661): Pembroke, Carmarthen, Brecknock, Glamorgan, Monmouth, south Cardigan.

The Forestry Commission will also help schools to establish a school forest and may provide up to 100 young trees for planting in school grounds or playing fields. Smaller numbers for pot raising can also be supplied. Applications should be made to the local Conservator.

Ben Reid & Co. Ltd., Pinewood Park, Countesswell Road, Aberdeen, supply tree seeds in small quantities for school use.

Some schools may find it difficult to visit a Forestry Commission woodland. The Royal Forestry Society of England and Wales, 102, High Street, Tring, Herts. will, wherever possible, arrange for school parties to have conducted tours of private woods close at hand. Any school wishing to make such a visit should contact the Secretary of the Society.

The Arboretum, Westonbirt, nr. Tetbury, Gloucestershire, is open to the public between 10 a.m. and 8 p.m. All rides and avenues are signposted and specimens labelled.

Guided tours can be provided at the National Pinetum, Bedgebury, Goudhurst, Cranbrook, Kent, on weekdays if good notice is given.

Much useful free literature is available from the Publications Officer, Forestry Commission, 25 Savile Row, London, WIX 2AY. This includes *Britain's New Forests*, *Forestry in England*, *Forestry in Wales*, *Forestry in Scotland*, *Forestry and the Town School*, *Starting a School Forest*.

Other books can be obtained from Government Bookshop, Mail Orders, P.O. Box 569, London S.E.1, including guides to the Forest Parks and Areas of Public Access.

Glen Trool, Argyll, Queen Elizabeth Forest Park Guide, Forests of North East Scotland, North Yorkshire Forests, Snowdonia, East Anglian Forests, Glamorgan Forests, Glenmore Forest Park, Glentress, Kilmuir Arboretum (Argyll), New Forest, Westonbirt Arboretum, Dean Forest and Wye Valley, Bedgebury Pinetum, Forests of Central and Southern Scotland, The New Forests of Dartmoor, Drumtochty, are the guides which are available at present.

Slides and Film Strips

A large number of film strips on forests and forestry activity are available from the following sources in addition to The Slide Centre Ltd., Portman House, 17 Brodrick Rd., London, S.W.17.

'Trees of Britain' – 22 frames, colour, Educational Productions, Bradford Road, East Ardsley, Wakefield, WF3 2JN.

'The Woodlands' – Colour, E.P.

'Flowering Trees' – 28 frames, colour, E.P. Illustrates the foliage and fruits of sycamore, maple, lime, wild cherry, rowan, horse chestnut.

'Coniferous Trees' – 33 frames, colour, E.P. Foliage and cones of Scots pine, European larch, Norway and Sitka spruce, noble fir, Sequoia, etc.

'Studies of Common Trees' – colour, parts 1 and 2, 35–31 frames – Common Ground, 41, Cadogan Gardens, London, S.W.3.

'Trees in the Landscape' – coloured, parts 1 and 2, 36 frames each part. 'Unicorn Head'. Orders to John King Ltd., Bond Street, Brighton, Sussex.

'The Life History of the Pine' – 26 frames, colour, E.P.

'The Forester' – colour, E.P.

Films

School Forestry activities are shown in the film 'School Forestry', a 16 mm. film which can be borrowed free of charge from the Forestry Commission (Book early.)

'Twilight Forest' – 27 mins., colour, Unilever Film Library, Unilever Ltd., Blackfriars, London, E.C.4.

'The Woodlands' – 16 mm. sound, 20 mins., E.F.V.A., Paxton Place, London, S.E.27. Geology, flora and fauna of some woodland areas.

'The Spruce Bog' – 23 mins. Central Film Library. An essay in ecology. How a spruce bog is formed.

'Wild Highlands', colour, sound, 21 mins. Films Officer, British Transport Film Library, Melbury House, Melbury Terrace, London, N.W.1. It shows the abundance of wild life in the Ardnamurchan Peninsula, Argyll.

Wall Charts

The following Wall Charts are useful:

Wealth from the Forests. Pictorial Charts Unit, 153, Uxbridge Road, London, W.7. Conditions governing the growth of a tree and articles produced from timber.

'Coniferous Forests'. Pictorial Charts Units. Timber Industry in Canada and uses to which the world timber is put. Drawings of Canadian trees and animals.

'Tree Posters' – larch, oak, beech, horse chestnut, elm, ash. T. Gerrard and Co. Ltd., 46A–48, Pentonville Road, London, N.1.

'British Trees' – Summer identification. Winter identification. Educational Productions Ltd., East Ardsley, Wakefield, Yorks. or Royal Forestry Society of England and Wales, 49, Russell Square, London, W.C.1.

Useful information on forestry is also available from the addresses below:

(*a*) Royal Forestry Society of England and Wales and Northern Ireland, 102 High Street, Tring, Herts.

(*b*) Royal Scottish Forestry Society, 7 Albyn Place, Edinburgh, 2.

(*c*) Timber Growers' Organisation (For England and Wales), 35 Belgrave Square, London, S.W.1.

(*d*) Scottish Woodland Owners Association Ltd., 6, Chester Street, Edinburgh, EH3 7RD.

(*e*) Society of Foresters of Great Britain at: Forestry Commission, Greystone Park, Moffat Road, Dumfries, Scotland.

(*f*) Commonwealth Forestry Association at: Royal Commonwealth Society, Northumberland Avenue, London, W.C.2.

(*g*) Commonwealth Forestry Bureau at: Commonwealth Forestry Institute, South Parks Road, Oxford.

(*h*) Forest Tree Seed Association of England and Wales, 25 Savile Row, London, W.1.

(*i*) Scottish Forest Tree Seed Association, 25 Drumsheugh Gardens, Edinburgh, 3.

(*k*) Forest Products Research Laboratory, Princes Risborough, Buckinghamshire.

12 VISITS TO QUARRIES AND GEOLOGICAL SITES

Details of the main rock exposures in an area are given in the Geological Survey memoirs of the 1″ sheet area. Lists of these are given in the Geological Survey Handbooks on the Regional Geology of Great Britain.

The following handbooks are available:

England and Wales

London and Thames Valley
Central England
East Yorkshire and Lincolnshire
The Wealden District
The Welsh Borderland
South-West England
Hampshire Basin and adjoining areas
East Anglia and adjoining areas
South Wales
North Wales
The Pennines and adjacent areas
Bristol and Gloucester District
Northern England

Scotland

Grampian Highlands
Northern Highlands
South of Scotland
Midland Valley of Scotland
Tertiary Volcanic Districts

These and lists of the 1″ Geological Sheet memoirs in print are available from Her Majesty's Stationery Office, P.O. Box 569, London S.E.1

A list of 'Miscellaneous Mines in Great Britain' is issued by the Ministry of Power, Thames House South, Millbank, London S.W.1.

A Directory of British Fossiliferous Sites is available from Palaeontological Society, Burlington House, London, W.1.

The Geologists' Association published a series of Geological Guides which show the main points of geological interest in an area. These are available from Scientific Anglian Bookshop, 30 St. Benedict's Street, Norwich, NOR 24J.

GUIDES

No. 1 'Geology of the Area around Birmingham' 1971
No. 2 'The Lake District' 1970
No. 3 'Geology around the University Towns: the Oxford District' 1973
No. 4 'Malvern Hills' 1971
No. 5 'Silurian Inliers of the South-Eastern Welsh Borderland' 1967
No. 6 'Geology around the University Towns: Liverpool' 1965
No. 7 'The Area Around Manchester' 1970
No. 8 'The Area around Stoke-on-Trent' 1958
No. 10 'The North Coast of Cornwall from Bude to Tintagel' 1970
No. 11 'Geology around the University Towns: Hull' 1962
No. 12 'The Estuarine Region of Suffolk and Essex' 1973
No. 13 'The Isle of Skye' 1969
No. 16 'Geology around the University Towns: The Cardiff District' 1971
No. 17 'Geology around the University Towns: Swansea, South Wales' 1969
No. 18 'Geology around the University Towns: North-East Ireland, The Belfast Area' 1958
No. 20 'The Isle of Mull' 1969
No. 22 'The Dorset Coast from Poole to the Chesil Beach' 1969
No. 24 'Central Weald: Hastings Beds' 1958
No. 25 'The Isle of Wight' 1972
No. 26 'The Peak District' 1972
No. 27 'Geology of some Classic Areas: South Shropshire' 1968
No. 28 'Geology of Snowdonia' 1968
No. 30a 'The London Region (North of the Thames)' 1967
No. 30b 'The London Region (South of the Thames)' 1967
No. 31 'North-East Scotland: The Dalradian' 1960
No. 32 'Isle of Arran' 1969
No. 34 'Geology of the Yorkshire Coast' 1968
No. 35 'Moine Schists and Lewisian Gneisses around Mallaig' 1964
No. 37 'Cheviot Hills' 1965

13 FIELD CENTRES FOR STUDY AWAY FROM THE HOME DISTRICT

The Field Studies Council, 9 Devereux Court, Strand, London, W.C.2, runs a series of Field Studies Centres; but the cost is fairly high and they are more suitable for older pupils.

The Youth Hostels Association, Trevelyan House, St. Albans has now equipped some of its hostels with fieldwork facilities and these provide excellent cheap accommodation. Fig 3:10 shows the main hostels and those with fieldwork facilities in England and Wales. In Scotland there is one centre at Garth in Perthshire, which is equipped for field studies. It has all kinds of interesting habitats near by with the exception of the sea-shore.

Many Scottish hostels do not provide cooked meals; but they are excellent for adventure holidays.

Among other hostels suitable for field study are Melrose in the Borders, Stirling, Rowardennan and Carbisdale.

The Scottish Y.H.A. has its headquarters at 7 Glebe Crescent, Stirling.
Northern Ireland Y.H.A., 28 Bedford St., Belfast, N. Ireland.
An Oige (Irish Y.H.A.), 39 Mountjoy Square, Dublin, Ireland.

The Youth Hostels Association (St. Albans) publish two useful booklets, free of charge: *Youth Hostels for School Journey Parties*, *Youth Hostles for Field Studies.*

Field study broadsheets are also available for most hostels mentioned in these publications.

Booking for the school journey parties should be made through the warden at the appropriate hostel. Children aged 9 and upwards travelling as a school journey party can use youth hostels without necessarily being members of the Y.H.A. provided they are under the care of responsible bodies who are themselves, members. To ensure proper supervision one leader of the same sex is required for every 15 children. It may be possible for school parties to have the use of a room for classwork. Youth Hostels are not available for school parties who merely wish to tour the country by motor coach, although a coach can be used to take the party to the hostel.

Below is a specimen itinerary.

The north Yorkshire moors and coast

Visiting hostels at Saltburn, Whitby, Boggle Hole, Wheeldale, Westerdale, Helmsley and Malton.

The possibilities of this unspoilt region are inexhaustible. Whatever the nature of the project there is ample opportunity for study at first hand. The contrast in structure and land use between the moors and the vale of Pickering; the involved course worn for itself by the Esk in its journey to the sea, and on the coast itself, the unrivalled exposures of blue Lias and other rocks of the Jurassic series – all suggest a diversity of geographical, biological and other studies. To the traditional occupations of farming, fishing, boat building and mineral working, are now added the extensive

3:10 Centres in the British Isles belonging to the Holiday Fellowship, Youth Hostel Association and Methodist Youth Camps.

SUMMARY TABLE OF THE Y.H.A. FIELD STUDY CENTRES

		High Close	Hawkshead	Bradda Head	Bryn Gwynant	Lledr Valley	Llangollen	Golant	Instow	Crowcombe	Swanage	Slimbridge	Duntisbourne	Charlbury	Streatley	Kemsing	Blaxhall	Sheringham	Hartington	Eyam	Grinton Lodge	Boggle Hole	Saltburn	Rock Hall
Human	History		■	■		■	■	■					■	■	■	■	■		■	■	■	■	■	■
	Architecture		■					■		■			■	■	■	■	■	■	■	■	■		■	■
	Pre-History		■	■		■	■	■			■		■		■	■			■	■	■	■	■	
	Settlement	■	■	■	■	■	■	■	■	■	■	■	■	■	■	■	■	■	■	■	■	■	■	■
	Land Use	■	■	■	■	■	■	■	■	■	■	■	■	■	■	■	■	■	■	■	■	■	■	■
Plant and Animal Habitats: Coastal	Sandy shores			■				■	■	■	■							■				■	■	■
	Muddy shores							■	■	■	■	■					■							■
	Rock/rock pools			■				■	■	■	■											■	■	■
	Dunes								■		■							■					■	■
	Saltmarsh							■	■		■	■					■	■						
	Estuarine				■			■	■		■	■					■	■					■	
	Sea birds			■				■									■	■					■	■
Plant and Animal Habitats: Fresh-water	Rivers	■	■		■	■	■	■	■			■	■	■	■	■		■	■	■	■			
	Lakes	■	■		■	■	■								■									
	Streams	■	■	■	■	■	■	■	■	■	■		■	■	■	■	■		■	■	■	■	■	■
	Ponds		■							■	■	■		■	■	■			■					
Plant and Animal Habitats: Land Vegetation	Moorland or Heath			■	■	■		■	■	■	■					■	■	■	■	■	■	■	■	■
	Rough pasture	■	■	■	■	■	■	■	■						■				■	■	■		■	■
	Calcicolous plants				■						■		■		■	■			■	■	■			
	Deciduous woods	■	■		■	■	■	■	■	■	■	■	■	■	■	■	■	■	■	■	■		■	
	Coniferous woods	■	■		■	■	■	■		■					■		■		■	■				
Geomorphology	Land form/structure	■	■	■	■	■	■	■	■	■	■	■	■	■	■	■			■	■	■	■	■	■
	Coastal formation			■				■	■	■	■						■	■				■	■	■
	Drainage	■	■	■	■	■		■	■	■	■	■	■	■	■	■	■		■	■	■	■		
	Glaciation	■	■	■	■	■	■										■	■			■	■	■	
Geology	Igneous Rocks	■	■	■	■	■		■											■	■			■	■
	Mineral veins	■	■	■	■	■		■											■	■	■	■	■	
Geology: Sedimentary Rocks – Tertiary and Recent	Pleistocene	■	■	■	■	■						■	■	■		■	■	■			■	■		■
	Pliocene															■	■	■						
	Oligocene																							
	Eocene										■				■	■	■							
Geology: Sedimentary Rocks – Cretaceous	Chalk										■				■	■	■	■						
	Gault & Upper Greensand										■				■	■								
	Lower Greensand										■				■	■								
	Wealden										■					■								
Geology: Sedimentary Rocks – Jurassic	Purbeck Beds										■													
	Portland Beds										■				■									
	Kimmeridge Clay										■				■									
	Oxford Clay													■	■									
	Oolite									■	■	■	■	■								■	■	
	Lias									■		■	■	■								■	■	
Geology: Sedimentary Rocks – New Red	Triassic									■									■					
	Permian									■														
Geology: Sedimentary Rocks – Carboniferous	Coal																		■					■
	Millstone Grit																		■	■	■			
	Culm						■		■															
	Limestone			■			■		■										■	■	■			■
Geology: Sedimentary Rocks – Lower Palaeozoic	Old Red Sandstone			■					■	■														
	Devonian							■		■														
	Silurian	■	■				■					■												
	Ordovician				■	■																		
	Cambrian			■	■	■																		
	Pre-Cambrian																							

planting operations of the Forestry Commission over large areas of the moors.

The place-names – Celtic, Norse, Danish, Swedish, French – hint at many elements which have shaped its history and the area is rich in historical buildings and ancient monuments. The barrows of Bronze Age settlers are seen on every high point on the moors, and one of the few exposed stretches of paved Roman road lies within a stone's throw of Wheeldale hostel.

The large areas of open country provide opportunity for practice in map reading and use of the compass.

Film Strip

The Youth Hostels Association produce the following film strip.
'Learning on Location'

Slides Available from The Slide Centre, Portman House, 17 Brodrick Road, London, S.W.17.

Films 16 mm. films are available on hire from the Y.H.A.

'Off the Beaten Track.' Colour. 20 mins.
'Going to the Hills.' B/W. 17 mins.
'Hostellers.' Colour. 24 mins.
'Leading in the Hills.' Colour. 15 mins.
'Youth Hostelling in Norway.' Colour. 12 mins.
'Survival in the Hills.' Colour. 18 mins.

The Holiday Fellowship, Home Centres Division, 142 Great North Way, Hendon, London, N.W.4 also allow parties to use their adult guest houses in the off-peak period between October and Whitsuntide, excluding Bank Holiday weekends. These provide excellent accommodation at a great variety of country, mountain and seaside places (Fig. 3:10). They also have Youth Guest Houses at Hythe, Malhamdale, Newlands, Snowdon, and the Wye Valley; and Youth Camps at Devil's Bridge, and Staithes. The cost for these youth camps varies according to the place and season.

Methodist Youth Camps have centres at Mundesley-on-Sea, Norfolk and Totland Bay, Isle of Wight. These provide good, cheap accommodation in areas of great environmental interest. Further information can be obtained from Rev. Norman Valley, Mundesley-on-Sea, Norwich, NOR 33Y, Norfolk.

Many local authorities have their own field study centres which are extremely valuable. A list of these centres is available from the Geographical Association, Administrative Secretary, 343, Fulwood Road, Sheffield, S10 3BP. The schools in the authorities' areas are notified of the facilities and conditions of use of the centres.

The Country-wide Holidays Association have centres which can be made available to school parties. Full details are obtainable from the Secretary, The Country-wide Holidays Association, Birch Heys, Cromwell Range, Manchester, M14 6HU.

The Centres are at:

Ambleside	Filey	Perranporth
Barmouth	Fowey	Porlock
Barton-on-Sea	Grasmere	Ramsey
Borrowdale	Hope	Rhu
Cromer	Kinfauns	Shanklin
Dawlish	Llanfairfechan	Westward Ho
Eskdale	Onich	Whitby

14 FIELD TRIPS ABROAD

Many children now travel abroad with a school party and observations of much value can be made. Location is a factor that must be taken into consideration for it is extremely difficult to do fieldwork without a good knowledge of the language. Visits to a country where English is almost universal, like Norway or Holland, are very useful; but where English is not commonly spoken, a working vocabulary should be gone over in class before the trip. It is necessary to give the pupils a detailed itinerary. Follow-up work at school should be done after the holiday.

Youth Hostels offer very cheap accommodation. For planning a youth hostel tour abroad the following booklets are needed. They are available from the Y.H.A. (Services) Ltd., 29, John Adam Street, London, WC2N 6JE.

The International Youth Hostel Handbook, Vol. 1 contains details of hostels in Europe, the Near East and North Africa.

The International Youth Hostel Handbook, Vol. 2 contains details of hostels in Australasia, America and Asia.

Youth Hosteller's Guide to Europe – This is a guide to the main tourist areas of Europe.

The *Y.H.A. Continental Travel Key*. This contains the practical current information about passports and money regulations, rail and boat fares, and timetables. Available in February each year.

The Youth Hostel Association also run a Travel Service from 29, John Adam Street, London, WC2N 6JE.

Passports or a group passport can be obtained for a party from:

London: Passport Office, Clive House, 70, Petty France, London, SW1H 9HD.

Belfast: Foreign and Commonwealth Office Passport Agency, 1st Floor, Marlborough House, 30, Victoria Street, Belfast, BT1 3LY.

Glasgow: Passport Office, 1st Floor, Empire House, 131, West Nile Street, Glasgow, G1 2RY.

Liverpool: Passport Office, 5th Floor, India Buildings, Water Street, Liverpool, L2 0QZ.

Newport: Passport Office, Olympia House, Upper Dock Street, Newport (Mon.), NPT 1XA.

Peterborough: Passport Office, Westwood, Peterborough, PE3 6TG.

The main tourist agents can arrange reasonably priced tours; but it is wise to use only a well recommended tourist agent.

The Central Bureau for Educational Visits and Exchanges, 43, Dorset Street, London, W.1 provides facilities for group and individual exchange with most European countries. They link schools for correspondence exchanges, for exchanges of documentation and for visits. Correspondence is extremely useful in the language classes. Documentation interchange can cause a whole variety of projects arranged on a class to class or club to club basis depending on the activities of the schools concerned:

(1) Magazines, scrap-books, tape recordings and photographs can be exchanged.

(2) The Historical and Geographical Societies can continue to exchange project work.

(3) Art and Photographic Societies can exchange technical documentation and specimens of work.

(4) Sporting event descriptions can be arranged by post.

Visits are the most important conclusion of such contacts; but apart from normal visits they may be arranged for special project purposes.

(i) A school orchestra may travel abroad.

(ii) Athletics or sports teams may travel abroad.

Advice on travel arrangements can be given by the Central Bureau.

15 EDUCATIONAL CRUISES

Since April 1961 the British India Steam Navigation Company Ltd., 1 Aldgate, London, E.C.3 has been organising educational cruises in N.W. Europe, the Baltic, the Mediterranean and N.W. Africa in three vessels, specially converted for the purpose. The cruises vary in duration from ten to fifteen days. A resident Director of Education organises a full programme while the ship is at sea. Party leaders are given classrooms for work with their own parties, and preparatory lectures are given in the assembly hall. Conducted shore excursions are arranged at each port. The cost for dormitory accommodation varies depending on the nature of the cruise. Useful information for party leaders is contained in two booklets provided by the British India Steam Navigation Company; *Information for Party Leaders* deals with booking procedure and all the relevant details pertaining to educational cruises; *Notes for the Guidance of Party Leaders* gives suggestions for pre-cruise study and follow-up work.

A description of such a voyage is given in *We Go in a Ship* by S. L. Corbridge. (Harrap.)

16 AIR FLIGHTS

Charter flights are being made increasingly by school children. They give a new view of the landscape and unrealised relationships become clear particularly if the flight can be over a familiar area. One school took the children for a 15-minute flight over the school area and the children had a tremendous thrill at seeing their own home from the air (Fig. 3:11). The patterns of roads, houses, railways and factories stand out much more clearly from the air and a flight over a rural district shows up the pattern of land use (Fig. 3:12). Historical remnants, hill forts (Fig. 3:13) and, under certain conditions, crop marks, and physical features like escarpments (Fig. 3:14) and dry valleys become clearer.

There are five steps in the organising of a school flight. After getting the permission of the head and the local authority and the enthusiasm of the children for the flight, the charter flight should be arranged with the nearest charter company, the route, arrangements for a visit of the airport buildings, and arrangements for postponement of the flight in case of bad weather, should be finalised. The parents are circulated giving details of the flight, cost and aims, and asking for a signature saying that they want their child to accompany the flight. A verifying meeting held at the school for the parents and the children would enable many of the fears of the parents to be allayed.

The flight might be part of a topic on transport or local geography and history. Much work can be done with the class on the history and methods of flight, on navigation, on plotting and mapping the route. Many charter flights are in 36-seater Dakotas and it is difficult to enable everyone to see out of the windows so that a change of places at certain intervals is needed. The flights are normally at about 1,525 m. or more, at a speed of about 150 knots so that picking up of landmarks is rather difficult. Each child, or pair of children, should have a map, preferably an air map of a 1/250,000 scale (the detail of the one-inch map is too confusing) with the route clearly marked on it. If possible the route of the flight should be followed on the ground and the landmarks pointed out. Air photographs of significant points could be examined (see Chapter 4). Children liable to suffer from air sickness should take the necessary precautions.

During the flight many children will want to take photographs. To do this a rather fast film, Kodak Tri-X and Verichrome or Ilford HP3 and HPS is needed, and if colour is being used an ultra-violet filter is recommended. The light reading should be taken on the ground and adjustments made if the weather changes on the flight. A fairly fast shutter speed should be used, at least 1/125 but preferably 1/250. The camera should be held as steady as possible close to the window, but without being leaned on the window. These photographs make an important contribution to the after-flight discussion and work.

After the flight, maps can be drawn and descriptions, sketches and photographs of the landscape produced. There is scope for models, flight logs, friezes and wall charts.

In *Geography*, January 1966, there is an account of such a school flight: Brearley, D. *The Use of Charter Flights in the Teaching of Geography.*

Teaching material on flights is available as follows:

Film Strips

'Behind the Scenes of an Airline.' Educational Productions.
'Air Routes of the World.' (Several). Educational Productions.

Slides

'World Aerospace.' Five sets from The Slide Centre, Portman House, 17 Brodrick Road, London, S.W.17.

Books

Allward, M. *Aircraft.* Ward Lock.
King, C. *Airports.* Blackie.
Preston, D. R. and Stewart, D. A. *Civil Aviation.* Methuen.
Wymer, N. *Behind the Scenes at London Airport.* Dent.
Allward, M. *London's Airports.* Ian Allan.
Pattle, R. J. *Aircraft.* Bodley Head.

Other Visual Materials

Japan Airlines Co. Ltd., 8 Hanover Street, London, W.1. Free brochures and posters; films on loan.

Air Ministry, Adastral House, Theobalds Road, London, W.C.1. Free booklet on planes.

British European Airways, 103 Wigmore Street, London, W.C.1. A book *About your Flight.*

Pan American World Airways, 193 Piccadilly, London, W.1. Free booklet on planes, and magazines.

Qantas Air Lines Ltd., 57 Piccadilly, London, W.1. Free booklet and magazine.

Education Officer, Aer Lingus, P.O. Box 179, 9 Lower Abbey Street, Dublin, Eire. Pictures of airports, planes, timetables, maps.

3:11 The centre of Birmingham from the air showing the Bull Ring, New Street Station and the Inner Ring Road

3:12 The Chew Valley, near Bristol, showing field patterns. The fields are larger in the top part of the picture. Large regular fields indicate recent (i.e. 19th century) enclosures. Small irregular fields indicate early enclosure.

3:13 Maiden Castle, an Iron Age fort

3:14 Wenlock Edge, Shropshire. The sharper escarpments are formed of Wenlock and Aymestry limestone.

17 NATIONAL PARKS, AREAS OF OUTSTANDING NATURAL BEAUTY, LONG-DISTANCE FOOTPATHS

These parks are part of our heritage and a study of one of them could bring home to the children the importance of these open spaces. They would realise that the parks are parts of the country (Fig. 3:15) where the natural beauty of the area is being preserved. The land is not nationalised and the designation 'National Park' confers no right of access on the public.

Users of National Parks – walkers, climbers and picnickers – should always remember that the farmers' fields are, and will remain, as private in the National Parks as elsewhere.

The park planning authorities negotiate additional access to open country.

Other areas, mostly smaller and perhaps less spectacular than National Parks, have been designated as Areas of Outstanding Natural Beauty. Unlike National Parks they have no special administrative arrangements, but designation strengthens the hands of the local planning authorities in resisting any development likely to impair the quality of the landscape.

Eight long-distance footpaths, one of which is also a bridleway, have been established.

NATIONAL PARKS

	Area (Sq. Miles)	Area (Hectares)
Peak District	542	140,378
Lake District	866	224,294
Snowdonia	845	218,855
Dartmoor	365	94,535
Pembrokeshire Coast	225	58,275
North York Moors	553	143,227
Yorkshire Dales	680	176,120
Exmoor	265	68,635
Northumberland	398	103,082
Brecon Beacons	515	133,385

AREAS OF OUTSTANDING NATURAL BEAUTY

	Area (Sq. Miles)	Area (Hectares)
Gower	73	18,907
Quantock Hills	38	9,842
Lleyn	60	15,540
Surrey Hills	160	41,440
Dorset	400	103,600
Northumberland Coast	50	12,950
Cannock Chase	26	6,734
Shropshire Hills	300	77,700
Malvern Hills	40	10,360
Cornwall	360	93,240

3:15 National Parks, Areas of Outstanding Natural Beauty, Long-Distance Footpaths.

North Devon	66	17,094
South Devon	128	33,152
East Hampshire	151	39,109
East Devon	103	26,677
Isle of Wight	73	18,907
Forest of Bowland	310	80,290
Chichester Harbour	29	7,511
Solway Coast	41	10,619
Chilterns	309	80,031
Sussex Downs	379	98,161
Cotswolds	582	150,738
Anglesey	83	21,497
South Hampshire Coast	30	7,770
Norfolk Coast	174	45,066
Kent Downs	326	84,434
Sussex Coast and Heaths	151	39,109
Dedham Vale	22	5,698
Wye Valley	125	32,375
Mendip Hills	78	20,202
North Wessex Downs	676	175,084
Arnside and Silverdale	29	7,511
Lincolnshire Wolds	216	55,944

LONG-DISTANCE FOOTPATHS AND BRIDLEWAYS

	Length (Miles)	Length (Kilometres)
Pennine Way	250	402
Pembrokeshire Coast Path	167	269
Offa's Dyke Path	168	270
South Downs Way	80	129
South-West Peninsula Coast Path		
Cornwall, North	135	217
Cornwall, South	133	214
Devon, South	93	150
Somerset and North Devon	82	132
Dorset	72	116
Cleveland Way	93	150
North Downs Way	141	227
Ridgeway Path	85	137

Information and publicity material is obtainable from The Countryside Commission, 1, Cambridge Gate, London, NW1 4JY.

Guide books to : Brecon Beacons, Dartmoor, Exmoor, Lake District, Northumberland, North York Moors, Peak District, Pembrokeshire Coast, Snowdonia and Yorkshire Dales National Parks are available from Her Majesty's Stationery Office, P.O. Box 569, London, S.E.1 (for Mail Orders).

Detailed information about individual parks may be obtained from the park planning authorities or by visiting the Information Centres named below, which generally will be open to help you on weekdays and Saturdays during the summer months. There are also mobile centres in most of the parks.

BRECON BEACONS National Park Joint Advisory Committee, County Hall, Brecon.
Information Centres at: Abergavenny – 2, Lower Monk Street; Brecon – 6, Glamorgan Street; Llandovery – 8, Broad Street.
DARTMOOR National Park Committee, County Hall, Topsham Road, Exeter.
Information Centre at: Two Bridges (caravan) – near Princetown.
EXMOOR National Park Joint Advisory Committee, County Hall, Taunton.
Information Centres at: Combe Martin (caravan) – The Beach Car Park; Lynton – Lyn and Exmoor Museum, Market Street; Minehead – Market House, The Parade.
LAKE DISTRICT Planning Board, County Hall, Kendal.
Information Centres at: Ambleside – The Old Court House, Church Street; Bowness (caravan) – The Glebe; Keswick – Moot Hall; Waterhead (caravan) – Ambleside; Windermere – District Bank House, High Street.
NORTHUMBERLAND – The Countryside and National Park Planning Committee, County Hall, Newcastle upon Tyne.
Information Centres at: Byrness – 9, Otterburn Green, Byrness, Otterburn; Ingram – The Old School House; Once Brewed – Military Road, Bardon Mill, Hexham.
NORTH YORK MOORS National Park Planning Committee, County Hall, Northallerton.
PEAK PARK Planning Board, Aldern House, Baslow Road, Bakewell.
Information Centres at: Bakewell – The Market Hall, Bridge Street; Buxton – St. Ann's Well, The Crescent; Castleton – Castle Street; Edale – Field Head.
PEMBROKESHIRE National Park Committee, County Offices, Haverfordwest.
Information Centres at: Fishguard – Town Hall; Haverfordwest – County Museum; Pembroke – Drill Hall, Main Street; St. David's – City Hall; Tenby – The Norton.
SNOWDONIA Park Joint Advisory Committee, County Offices, Penarlag, Dolgellau.
Information Centres at: Aberdyfi – The Wharf; Bala – Old British School, High Street; Blaenau Ffestiniog – Queen's Bridge; Dolgellau – Bridge End; Harlech (caravan) – adjoining Morfa Stores, Beach Road; Llanberis – Craig Afon, Snowdon Road; Llanrwst – Glan-y-Borth.
YORKSHIRE DALES National Park Joint Advisory Committee, County Hall, Wakefield.
Information Centres at: (North Riding) Aysgarth Falls, Leyburn; (West Riding) Clapham (via Lancaster) – Reading Room; Malham (caravan) – The Car Park.

In three of the National Parks special types of Information Centres have been set up, namely:

1. Brecon Beacons: The Mountain Centre, Libanus, Cae Harn.
2. Lake District: National Park Centre, Brockhole, Windermere.
3. Pembrokeshire: Countryside Unit, Broad Haven.

Slides of many of these areas are available from The Slide Centre, 17 Brodrick Road, London, S.W.17.

4 Fieldwork: Techniques and Recording

Accurate recording of the observations made on the field visits is essential; but on preliminary visits the children may not feel the need for recording. On later visits it is important that they do so. Much discussion will take place between the children and the teacher and by posing the right question the children will be made to think more about a problem or observed phenomena. The observations must be made permanent either by tape recording, written recording, graphical representation, i.e. photographs, maps, or by preserving collected specimens. The actual methods used will depend on the topic.

1 TAPE RECORDING

The tape recorder has numerous uses in the classroom, for making school broadcasts, for slide show commentaries, speech training, language training, and recording music; but it can be most useful for making a permanent record. These records are of four main types: interviews, environmental sounds, direct recording and producing tapes for exchange. For these purposes a battery portable is best (see p. 114.) Full instructions for operating it are given with the recorder.

(a) Taped interviews

For a good interview the questions should be thought out beforehand. They should be direct but polite and should enable a complete picture to be formed. A farm visit makes an excellent subject for a tape recording. If authentic sounds can be recorded they can be spliced into the tape later. Similar interviews can be made on visits to the fire station, to the docks or a factory.

(b) Environmental sounds

These sounds can easily be recorded in urban environments, e.g. the noises of towns: motor vehicles, trains, fire engines, factory hooters, factory machinery. Bird song recording benefits from some kind of parabolic reflector into the middle of which the microphone is fitted. (Fig. 4: 2) This reflector can be set up in the school garden or near the bird table and directed towards the bird that is singing.

For help in identifying birds the following records produced by E.M.I. Ltd. are valuable.

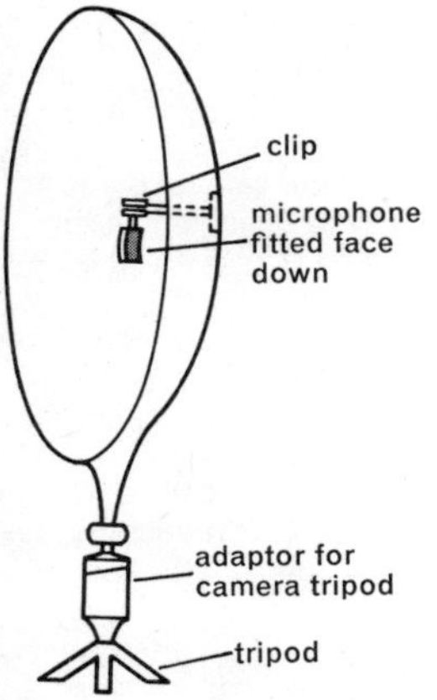

4:1 A parabolic reflector.
4:2 A home-made parobolic reflector in use in Norway.

Bird Recognition – An Aural Index: Victor C. Lewis.

Each set of three records is available in a presentation box with an attractive cover, together with informative booklet written by Victor C. Lewis, who recorded this bird vocabulary. Each set is sold as a complete unit; records cannot be purchased separately.

Volume 1 – Birds of the farm and garden:
Record nos. 7EG 8923/4/5.

SONG THRUSH – Three calls: two songs
BLACKBIRD – Five calls: two songs
ROBIN – Three calls: two songs
DUNNOCK – One call: two songs
SPOTTED FLYCATCHER – One call: one song
GOLDFINCH – Four calls: two songs
GREENFINCH – Five calls: four songs
CHAFFINCH – Three calls: three songs
BULLFINCH – One call: one song
WREN – Two calls: one song
SWALLOW – Three calls: three songs
HOUSE MARTIN – One call: two songs
SAND MARTIN – Two calls: one song
SWIFT – Calls and 'scream'
PIED WAGTAIL – Call only
YELLOW WAGTAIL – Call only

Volume 2 – Birds of heaths, commons, fields and hedgerows:
Record nos. 7EG 8926/7/8.

SKYLARK – Two calls: two songs
WOOD LARK – One call: two songs
TREE PIPIT – One call: two songs
MEADOW PIPIT – Two calls: one song
RED-BACKED SHRIKE – Call only
DARTFORD WARBLER – Two calls: one song
WHINCHAT – Two calls: one song
STONECHAT – Call only
LINNET – Four calls: two songs
GRASSHOPPER WARBLER – One call: One song
NIGHTJAR – Three calls: one song
WHITETHROAT – Five calls: five songs
LESSER WHITETHROAT – One call: four songs
YELLOW BUNTING – Two calls: two songs
CORN BUNTING – One call: one song
CIRL BUNTING – Two calls: one song

Volume 3 – Woodland, copse and 'wet habitat' birds:
Record nos. 7EG 8929/30/31

BLACKCAP – Three calls: two songs
GARDEN WARBLER – Three calls: two songs
WILLOW WARBLER – One call: three songs
WOOD WARBLER – Two calls: two songs
CHIFFCHAFF – Two calls: three songs
NIGHTINGALE – Three calls: one song
MISTLE THRUSH – Two calls: one song
NUTHATCH – Five calls
GOLDCREST – One call: two songs
REDSTART – Two calls: one song
PIED FLYCATCHER – Two calls: one song
SEDGE WARBLER – Two calls: one song
REED WARBLER – One call: three songs
REED BUNTING – One call: one song
MARSH WARBLER – Three calls: two songs.

A Tapestry of British Bird Song
Record no. CLP 1723
A fascinating journey in sound through different bird habitats – from dawn chorus to dusk concert. Commentary written and spoken by Victor C. Lewis. A leaflet giving a general introduction to the language of birds, and notes on each of the species heard, is provided free with this record.

DAWN CHORUS: ROOKS AND STARLINGS: SKYLARK: PHEASANT: TAWNY OWL: CANADA GEESE: CUCKOOS (male and female): WOOD PIGEON: GREEN WOODPECKER: PARTRIDGE: JAYS: BLACKBIRD (alarm): SONG THRUSH: ROBIN: BLACKBIRD: HOUSE MARTINS: SWALLOWS: PIED FLYCATCHER: REDSTART: GARDEN WARBLER: BLACKCAP: CHIFF-CHAFF: WOOD WARBLER: GREENFINCH: CHAFFINCH: WREN: HEDGE SPARROW: GREAT WHITETHROAT: LESSER WHITETHROAT: TURTLE DOVE: GOLDCREST: NUTHATCH: GREEN SPOTTED WOODPECKER: WILLOW WARBLER: QUAIL: LAPWINGS: CORN BUNTING: CARRION CROW: YELLOW BUNTING: REED BUNTING: WOODLARK: TREE PIPIT: MEADOW PIPIT: HERONS AND YOUNG: MANDARIN DUCK: SEDGE WARBLER: REED WARBLER: MARSH WARBLER: WHINCHAT: DARTFORD WARBLER: LINNET: CURLEWS: SWIFTS: SAND MARTINS: NIGHTINGALE PLUS CHORUS: GRASS/HEDGE WARBLER: NIGHTJAR:

Songs of British Birds
Ludwig Koch recorded these bird songs, which are published in collaboration with the B.B.C. An illustrated booklet is available with these records.

Record no. 1: ref. 7EG 8315
Gardens and parks – BLACKBIRD: SONG THRUSH: ROBIN: GREAT TIT: BLUE TIT: CHAFFINCH: GREENFINCH.
Birds of the Woodlands – CHIFFCHAFF: WILLOW WARBLER: GREEN WOOD-PECKER: BLACKCAP: GARDEN WARBLER: GREATER SPOTTED WOOD-PECKER.

Record no. 2: ref. 7 EG 8316
Fields and hedgerows – SKYLARK: MEADOW PIPIT: GOLDFINCH: WHITE-THROAT: WOODLARK: DUNNOCK: CORN BUNTING.
Riverside and marshland – REED WARBLER: SEDGE WARBLER: MARSH WARBLER: GRASSHOPPER WARBLER: REED BUNTING: MOORHEN: COOT.

Wildfowl Calling
Record no. 7EG 8764
Peter Scott provides the commentary.

WHITE-FRONTED GEESE: WILDFOWL MEDLEY: TRUMPETER SWAN: BLACK-NECKED SWAN: NE-NE: BAR-HEADED GOOSE: ANDEAN GOOSE: CEREOPSIS: CANADA GEESE: MEDLEY OF DUCK CALLS: MALLARD: RUDDY SHELDUCK: RADJAH SHELDUCK: COMMON EIDER: LONG-TAILED DUCK: BARTRAM'S GOLDENEYE: RED-BILLED WHISTLING DUCK: CHILE WIDGEON: EUROPEAN WIDGEON: WHITE-BACKED DUCK: GARGANEY: BERWICK SWAN.

The Slide Centre, Portman House, 17 Brodrick Rd., London, S.W.17, produce a series of slides of birds and animals and a record to go with them.

The Royal Society for the Protection of Birds, The Lodge, Sandy, Bedfordshire produce bird song records including a series 'Listen – the Birds': 7" 33⅓ r.p.m. double-sided records. 18 records available.

Record 501 – BLACKBIRD: SONG THRUSH: MISTLE THRUSH: GOLDEN ORIOLE: ROBIN: CUCKOO: NUTHATCH: WOOD PIGEON: JAY.

Record 502 – GARDEN WARBLER: BLACKCAP: WREN: WOOD WARBLER: CHIFFCHAFF: FIRECREST: GOLDCREST: COAL TIT: MARSH TIT: GREAT TIT.

Record 503 – NIGHTINGALE: WILLOW WARBLER: WHITETHROAT: ICTERINE WARBLER: GREAT REED WARBLER: REED WARBLER: MARSH WARBLER: GRASSHOPPER WARBLER.

Record 504 – TAWNY OWL: LITTLE OWL: SCOPS OWL: LONG-EARED OWL: BARN OWL: WRYNECK: GREEN WOODPECKER: GREY-HEADED WOODPECKER: GREATER SPOTTED WOODPECKER: BLACK WOODPECKER.

Record 505 – SKYLARK: WOODLARK: TREE PIPIT: HOOPOE: REDSTART: BLACK REDSTART: SWALLOW: SAND MARTIN.

Record 506 – STARLING: PIED FLYCATCHER: SERIN: RED-BACKED SHRIKE: WHINCHAT: REED BUNTING: NIGHTJAR: TURTLE DOVE.

Record 507 – DUNNOCK: HOUSE SPARROW: TREE SPARROW: GREEN-FINCH: GOLDFINCH: CHAFFINCH: LESSER REDPOLL: LINNET: TWITE: CORN BUNTING: YELLOWHAMMER.

Record 508 – COMMON SANDPIPER: SNIPE: WOODCOCK: GOLDEN PLOVER: CURLEW: LAPWING: OYSTER CATCHER: REDSHANK: WADER CHORUS.

Record 509 – SEABIRD COLONY: HERRING GULL: LESSER BLACK-BACKED GULL: GREAT BLACK-BACKED GULL: COMMON GULL: BLACK-HEADED GULL: COMMON TERN: ROCK PIPIT: MEADOW PIPIT: CHORUS OF GULLS.

Record 510 – MALLARD: GADWALL: SHOVELLER: TEAL: WIDGEON: POCHARD: SHELDUCK: CANADA GOOSE: MUTE SWAN: WHOOPER SWAN: LITTLE GREBE: RED-THROATED DIVER.

Record 511 – RED GROUSE: BLACKCOCK: DUNLIN: WHEATEAR: STONE-CHAT: RING OUZEL: SPOTTED FLYCATCHER: PIED WAGTAIL: YELLOW WAGTAIL: GREY WAGTAIL: CORNCRAKE.

Record 512 – SWIFT: HOUSE MARTIN: BLUE TITS: TREE CREEPER: CARRION CROW: ROOK: JACKDAW: MAGPIE: KITTIWAKE: SANDWICH TERNS.

Record 513 – GREAT SKUA: ARCTIC SKUA: ARCTIC TERN: LITTLE TERN: BLACK GUILLEMOT: MANX SHEARWATER: FULMAR: CORMORANT: SHAG.

Record 514 – SEDGE WARBLER: BEARDED TIT: HERON: BITTERN: RED-NECKED PHALAROPE: WATER RAIL: MOORHEN: COOT: BLACK-TAILED GODWIT: BAR-TAILED GODWIT.

Record 515 – BUZZARD: OSPREY: PEREGRINE: SHORT-EARED OWL: SHORE LARK: QUAIL: PTARMIGAN: BLACK GROUSE: PARTRIDGE: PHEASANT.

Record 516 – GREY PLOVER: DOTTEREL: RINGED PLOVER: WHIMBREL: TURNSTONE: SPOTTED REDSHANK: GREENSHANK: KNOT: SANDERLING.

Record 517 – STOCK DOVE: COLLARED DOVE: CUCKOO: LESSER SPOTTED WOODPECKER: WAXWING: CROSSBILL: FIELDFARE: RAVEN: HOODED CROW: CHOUGH.

Record 518 – LESSER WHITETHROAT: CRESTED TIT: MARSH TIT: LONG-TAILED TIT: NUTHATCH: CORN BUNTING: REDPOLL: BULLFINCH.

Apart from bird song, animal noises, mainly farm animals, and natural phenomena like the wind, running rivers, the waves on the sea can be recorded.

(c) Direct recording

The tape recorder can be used directly to record information in exactly the same way as a written record.

One record of land use mapping is thus:

'July 30th, A. 456, proceeding north-east from Blakebrook: field one, pasture; field two, arable: wheat; field three, pasture; etc.'

These tapes can be edited either by splicing or by re-recording on to a second tape recorder. When trying to synchronise a tape with a film it is necessary to have a more or less soundproof room for the recording. Reasonable results have been obtained by projecting the film through a window into the sound room, where the recording is taking place.

(d) Tape exchanges

Tapes giving information about the local school area could be exchanged with schools in other parts of the country and abroad. *The Teachers World* has a tape exchange scheme. The embassy of another country might be able to put you in touch with a school willing to make exchanges. The Central Bureau for Educational Visits (see Chapter 3) can arrange contacts in Europe for exchanging correspondence and tapes.

World Wide Tape Talk, 35, The Gardens, Harrow, Middlesex, provides individual contacts for tape recordings.

Tape Recorders For this recording a simple portable tape recorder is best. The Philips, transistor portable is very easy to use and gives acceptable results. Other useful and fairly cheap recorders are listed below:

The Philips Cassette recorder uses cassettes giving 60 minutes of recording.

Sony tape recorders available from Denham and Morley Ltd., 453 Caledonian Road, London, N.7.

National tape recorders. Available from Unamec Ltd., United Africa House, Blackfriars Road, London, S.E.1

Sanyo Reporter. Available from Sanyo Service & Sales, Ludgate House, Ludgate Circus, London, E.C.4.

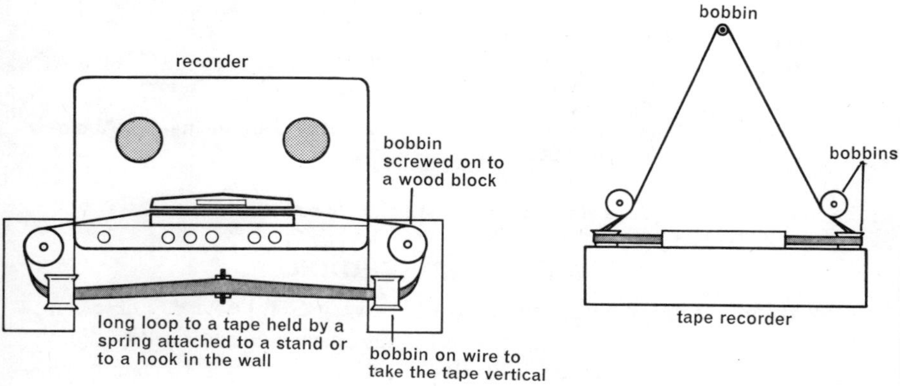

4:3 A simple adaptation for a continuous loop of tape.

For other classroom uses it may be better to have a more robust mains model.

Tape Loops An interesting use of a tape recorder is to make a tape loop to emphasise some point or perhaps to use it with a small number of slides, as part of an individual teaching aid. The tape must be kept taut so that it does not get tangled. One way of doing this is shown in Fig. 4:3.

Tapes Tapes in normal use are of four main types – standard, long-play, double-play and triple-play. The standard and long-play tapes are most suitable for school work because they are more robust than the other types of tape. P.V.C. tape is more expensive than acetate; but the record is permanent.

Tapes should be kept in boxes and away from extremes of heat and cold. They should be labelled clearly by writing on the leader, by sticking labels on the spools and by labelling the boxes.

Tape Recording tape is produced by:

E.M.I. Tape Ltd., Hayes, Middlesex.
Scotch Magnetic Tape, Minnesota Mining and Manufacturing Co. Ltd., 3M House, Wigmore Street, London, W.1.
Kodak Standard Play; Dept. 70, Kodak House, Kingsway, London, W.C.2.
Agfa-Gevaert Ltd., Great West Road, Brentford, Middlesex.
Synchrotape, Adastra Electronics Ltd., Unit 22, Cricklewood Trading Estate, Claremont Road, London, N.W.2.

Cheaper tape is available from:
Leda Tapes (D), 43, Elizabeth Avenue, London, N.1.
H.J. Enterprises (Dept. TR), 7, Masons Avenue, Wealdstone, Middlesex.

Tapes can be made into records. 7″ 45 r.p.m. record or 10″ L.P. 12″ L.P. These are made by Deroy Sound Services, Deroy, Hawk Street, Carnforth, Lancs.

Books

Barsley, M. *Tape Recording.*
Hack, R. *The Tape Editing Guide.* Focal Press, 1961.
Barsley, M. *Tape Recording.* Michael Joseph.
Hack, R. *The Tape Editing Guide.* Focal Press, 1961.
Weston, J. *The Tape Recorder in the Classroom.* National Committee for Audio-visual Aids in Education, 1968.

Magazines

Sound and Picture Tape Recording, Anglia Echo Newspapers Ltd.

2 WRITTEN RECORDING

For recording in the field, a work board is a very useful device. These can be made of plywood or hardboard and should have a pocket fixed to them for holding pencils (Fig. 4:4). A plastic bag is necessary for keeping the contents dry. The recording paper should be made into a pad with a stapler so that there is an adequate supply of lined and plain paper. Since these field records are to be re-organised at school it is important that they should be readily translatable so that a well laid out record is kept.

These records may take the form of a description, a direct record, a census, or a record of an interview. The description of the place of observation, date, companions, and weather at the time should be recorded.

A Description of a visit

Here is a typical record of a visit to a colliery.

October 11th: visit to a colliery.

'The colliery buildings were grouped at the end of the main roadway. Towering above the assembly of lamp-house, offices, canteen, and workshops was the new pit-head gear, a giant wheel held in a huge concrete frame. There was a long low office building built of bricks

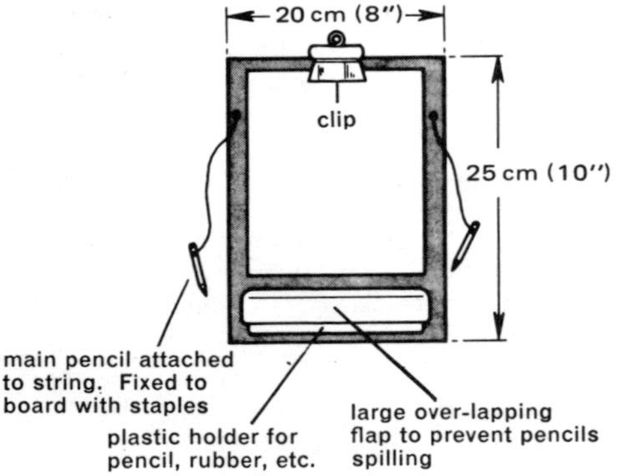

4:4 Fieldwork work board.

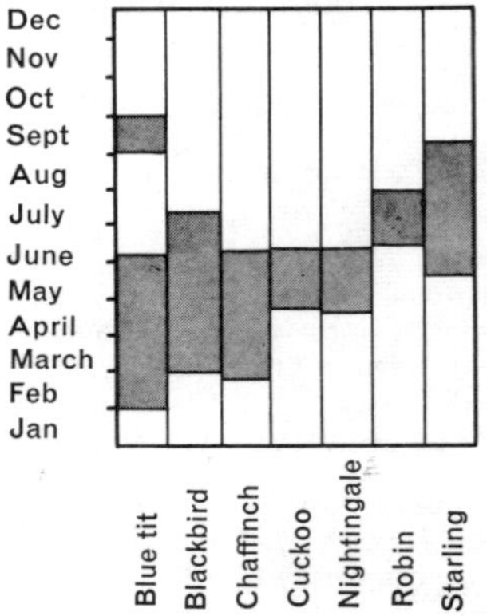

4:5 Histogram showing the months when different species of bird sing.

with a flat concrete roof. The lamp-house was larger; but was again brick built with a flat roof. In all there were ten different buildings around the pit-head.'

B The direct record The direct record is a note of an observation e.g. (1)

'June 13th, 1967, on the north side of the road – Rosebay Willow Herb. Two plants were 3′ 2″ (96 cm.) high, one was 3′ 3″ (99 cm.) high, one was 2′ 6″ (76 cm.) high, and the last one was 3′ 6″ (1·07 m.) high.'

Details of whether the plant was in bud, in flower, or in seed should be noted.

e.g. (2)

'May 25th, 1967. A group of ten swallows flying from the south-west, weather fine, wind light, force 2.'

C Census record method The census record method is easier to follow and makes sure that the children are aware of the important things that need recording. Varied forms of census can be used to suit the subject. Here are a series of examples.

1. BIRDS These can be observed from the classroom or out of doors. Birds may be attracted if a bird table is built and a water supply provided. A regular supply of food should be left and if possible the provision of food should go on throughout the holidays for the birds become conditioned to coming to the table. Lack of reinforcement leads to loss of conditioning so you may have to start all over again after the vacation. Many experiments can be carried out by providing different foods and seeing which birds eat which particular food. This can be recorded as shown in Fig. 4:6. A similar record can be made of the species of bird eating the different foods and visiting the bird table. A simple record of the number of birds can be taken at set intervals of time. 'Head counts' can also be taken on any walk or outing. Be adaptable, if a squirrel steals the food from the bird table change the study to one of food preferences in squirrels. Nest records can be made of the number of visits a bird makes to the nest and the reasons for the journey, whether the nest is being built or the young fed. This observation is helped by clearing some of the twigs from around the nest. A data sheet for each nest will be required. The season of bird song is also of significance. The songs can be recorded on a monthly basis (Fig. 4:8) and the final results plotted into a histogram (Fig. 4:5). Bird migration is also easily checked (Fig. 4:7).

If you intend to go in for bird recording in a really expert way and to send up your recorded observations to the nearest ornithological group or to the

Date 1st May, 1973

Time	Food: Nuts	Fat	Seed	Meat	Bread
9.00– 9.30					
9.30–10.00					
10.00–10.30					
10.30–11.00					
11.00–11.30					
11.30–12.00					
12.30– 1.00					
1.00– 1.30					
1.30– 2.00					
2.00– 2.30					
2.30– 3.00					
3.30– 4.00					
4.00– 4.30					
4.30– 5.00					

4:6 A census table to record the number of birds visiting a bird table and taking various foods.

Bird	1st seen	Last seen
Blackcap		
Fieldfare	Autumn (Oct. 1st)	
House Martin		
Nightjar	May 16th	
Nuthatch	May 16th	
Pied Wagtail	May 16th	
Redwing	May 16th	
Sanderling	May 16th	
Lesser Whitethroat	April 17th	
Greater Whitethroat	April 19th	
Marsh Warbler		
Swallow		
Swift		

4:7 Record of migrating birds.

Month June, 1973

Bird	Date of Call
Blue Tit	1, 2
Blackbird	1, 2, 3, 4, 5, 6, 7, 8, 9, 10, 11, 12, 13, 14, 15, 16, 17, 18, 19, 20, 21, 22, 23, 24, 25, 26, 27, 28, 29, 30
Chaffinch	1, 2, 3, 4, 5, 6, 7, 8, 9, 10
Cuckoo	1, 2, 3, 4, 5, 6, 7, 8, 9
Nightingale	1, 2, 3, 4, 5, 6, 7
Robin	1, 2, 3, 4, 5, 6, 7, 8, 9, 10, 11, 12, 13, 14, 15, 16, 17, 18, 19, 20
Starling	

4:8 Monthly record of the date of bird song

British Trust for Ornithology, you will use a recording card which is obtainable from The British Trust for Ornithology, Beech Grove, Station Road, Tring, Herts, or from The Royal Society for the Protection of Birds, The Lodge, Sandy, Bedfordshire.

Several other bird study activities are listed below:

(i) *A record of flight* could be made with large birds by observing the time when a bird beats its wings, glides with wings open, glides with wings closed (Fig. 4:9). A most interesting comparison can be made between the various bird flight patterns.

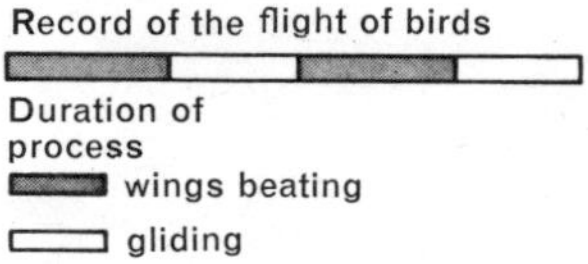

4:9 A simple way of recording bird flight.

(ii) *Bird pellets* reveal an astonishing array of material which can be sorted by soaking in water, separating the contents with a setting needle. The contents can then be mounted. Only a few birds, e.g. the owl, produce bird pellets.

(iii) *Nesting* boxes can be made (Fig. 4:10, 11a, b, c). The Royal Society for the Protection of Birds, The Lodge, Sandy, Bedfordshire, also sell nest boxes; roofed table; seed hopper and a food basket.

(iv) *Nests* can be collected at the end of the season. The landowner's permission should be asked. The nest can be mounted on a frame.

(v) *Eggs* should not be collected by children, but observations of the eggs, their shape and colour, can be made.

4:10 The Do-it-Yourself Nestbox.

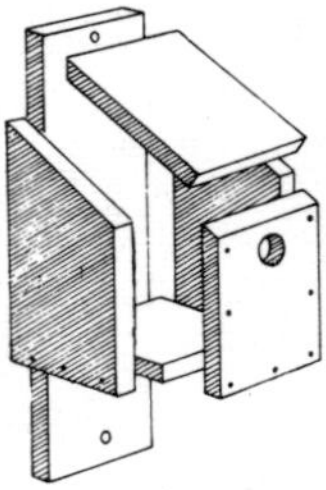

4:11d Assembly of the Nesting Box

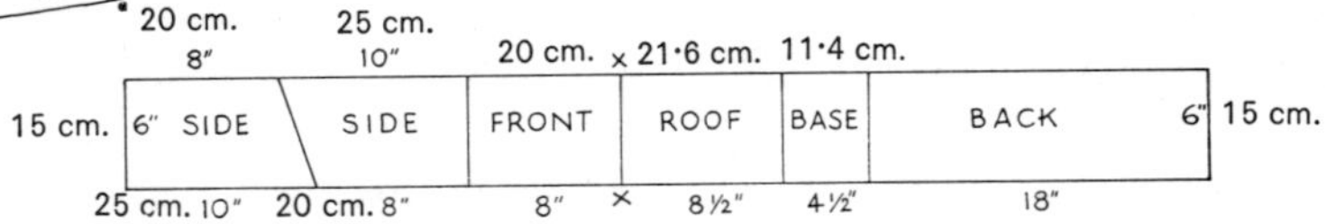

4:11a Measuring the pieces of wood.

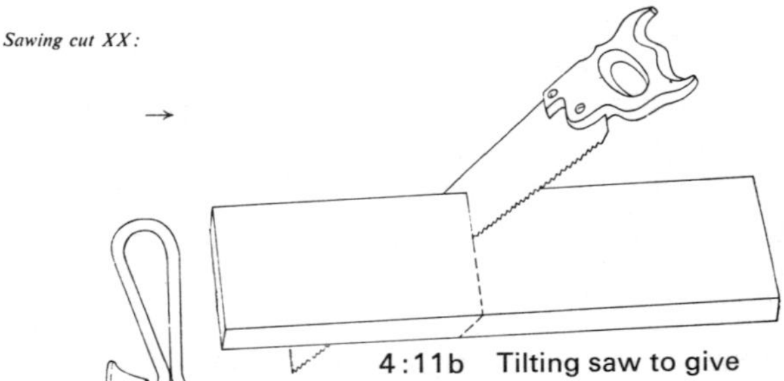

4:11b Tilting saw to give sloping edges

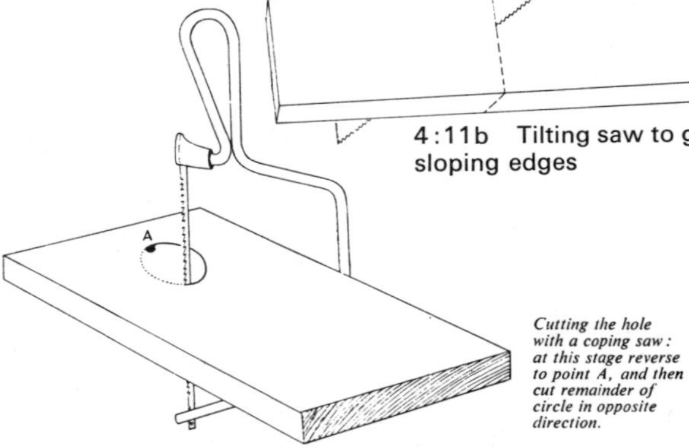

4:11c Cutting the hole with a coping saw.

(vi) *Photographs* of birds on the bird table can be taken. The camera should be set up in the room facing the bird table. A rapid exposure (see later) should be used and the observer should remain partially hidden and then operate the camera by a remote control cable. If a telescopic lens is available it should be used, but photographs taken on a simple camera can be enlarged to show the birds more clearly.

D.I.Y. Nestbox

This nestbox has been specially designed for schoolchildren; it is so easy to make and requires so few tools that schools without woodwork instructors or workshops should have no difficulty. It will attract hole-nesting birds such as Blue Tits, Great Tits, Tree Sparrows and Nuthatches.

Materials required: a 15 cm. (6″) × 1·8 cm. (¾″) unplaned board approximately 1·5 m. long (4′ 9″), two dozen 4 cm. (1½″) nails, a few tacks and a 15 cm. (6″) × 5 cm. (2″) strip of rubber, waterproof canvas or leather. Softwood is adequate: cedar is probably best as it lasts well, but ordinary deal or pine is cheaper and can be treated to prevent rot.

Cutting the pieces Cut the board in lengths as shown in Fig. 4:11a. The slopes of the two Sides are formed by the one diagonal cut. The width of the Base is 4½″ (11·4 cm.) for exactly ¾″ (1·3 cm.)-thick wood (i.e. 6″ (15 cm.) minus two thicknesses of wood). The exact length of the Back does not matter. Tilting the saw sideways slightly (see Fig. 4:11b) when making the cut between the Front and the Roof (cut XX) provides a sloping top edge for the Front and a sloping back edge for the Roof.

Making the hole The hole should be 1⅛″ (2·8 cm.) in diameter (draw around a 10p piece) with its top 1″ (2·5 cm.) down from the top of the Front. There are several ways of cutting the hole but, for the amateur without an electric drill or a hand-brace and suitable bit, I would personally recommend using this coping saw method:

Make a small hole just inside the circle. Remove the blade from the coping saw, push it through the hole and then fit it back on to the saw. Cut around the edge of the circle as far as you can until stopped by the frame of the saw hitting the wood; then reverse back to the starting hole, unhitch the blade from the saw, remove it from the wood and put it back facing the other way, and then cut round in the other direction to complete the circle.

Alternative methods are: using a fret-saw (but blades break easily in thick wood), using a hand-hole saw, enlarging a small hole with a round file, or sawing the Front in two and cutting out with a knife or file then glueing together.

Assembly Nail together in this order: one Side to the Back, then Base, the other Side, Front. Before nailing the Front, lay the Roof in position to make sure that the Front does not project too high. (See Fig. 4:11d.)

For a hinge use a 6″ × 2″ (15 × 5 cm.) strip of thick rubber, waterproof canvas or leather, nailed (preferably with copper tacks) to the Back and Roof. Although this will need renewing occasionally, it cannot rust up and it also provides a waterproof join. Fix little hooks or clips at both sides of the Roof to hold it down (brass 'side-hooks' are best).

Treating the wood To make softwood last several seasons, treat it with wood preservative – on the outside only.

The D.I.Y. nestbox notes are based on an article from Bird Life, *the magazine of the Young Ornithologists' Club. This national club for children provides information, organises outings and holiday courses, runs projects suitable for schools, and has a special School Group Membership. Details from: Y.O.C., The Lodge, Sandy, Bedfordshire. It is organised by the R.S.P.B.*

Bird Books

Benson, S. V. *The Observer's Book of Birds.* F. Warne, 1960.
Campbell, B. *Birds in Colour.* Blandford, 1973.
Coward, T. A. *The Birds of the British Isles and their Eggs* (3 volumes). F. Warne 1969 (very well written and illustrated).
Daglish, E. F. *Name This Bird.* Aldine publications.
Evans, G. *The Observer's Book of Birds' Eggs.* F. Warne, 1954.
Fitter, R. S. R. *The Pocket Guide to British Birds.* Collins, 1966.
Ford, R. L. E. *Eggs and Nests of British Birds.* A. & C. Black.
Grabianski, J. *Birds.* Dent.
Hall, C. A. *A Pocket Book of Birds' Eggs and Nests.* A. & C. Black (well illustrated).
Holland, J. *Bird Spotting.* Blandford.
Joy, N. H. *How to Know British Birds.* H. F. & G. Witherby.
Kerrod, R. *Birds.* F. Watts.
Reade, W. & Hosking, E. *Nesting Birds, Eggs and Fledglings.* Blandford.
Singer, A. *Book of Birds in Colour.* Hamlyn.
Vevers, G. *Birds and Their Nests.* Bodley Head.
Westell, W. P. *British Nesting Birds.* Dent.
Willett, W. *Birds of Britain.* A. & C. Black. 1951.

Wall Charts

Large wall charts of birds are available from the R.S.P.B. (Royal Society for the Protection of Birds). Small wall charts and postcards of birds are also available.

2. ROAD TRANSPORT A very simple census to make is one of the traffic, using a form (Fig. 4: 12). With younger children it is advisable to station them in a safe place – a school playground, a patch of enclosed ground, or some friend's front garden. The census should be split into ¼-hour intervals and taken throughout the day. Information about kind of vehicle, registration number for place of origin, cargo carried, name of firm if a lorry or van, and the number of passengers, should all be noted. The task of recording should be split because it is impossible for one child to get all the information required. Forms of census are shown in Figs. 4: 12, 13, 14, and the results have been mapped in Figs. 4:15, 16. In counting, the five-barred gate method is easy (Fig. 4:12).

It is possible to work out the speed of the vehicle by placing two children along a road in sight of each other with a stopwatch, at a measured distance apart; half a mile (or 1 km.) is convenient. When the vehicle passes the first child, the stopwatch is started; when it passes the second child he raises his hand and the watch is stopped (Fig. 4:16). It is useful to have two children at the recording end. The distance between the two children should be measured with a car mileometer, a clicker wheel, or it can be measured on a large scale map.

The registration numbers and letters of vehicles are listed in the A.A. Handbook. When recording the numbers only the last two letters are required, e.g. CTA 678 becomes TA (Lancashire) for recording purposes. 158 AXL becomes XL (London). Date letters after the registration numbers can also be collected, e.g. KWP 932J is 1971. The country of origin of cars can also be recorded. Foreign cars will be most commonly recorded in the holiday period and in the holiday areas.

Slides and *film loops* have been prepared for this subject by The Slide Centre, Portman House, 17 Brodrick Road, London, S.W.17.

4:12 Census form for general traffic.

Time	Buses	Cars	Lorries	Vans	Bicycles M/cycles	Pedestrians
9.00–9.15	III	卌 卌 卌 II	卌 III	卌 卌 卌 I	II	卌 卌 卌 卌
9.15–9.30						
9.30–9.45 etc.						

This incorporates the five barred gate method of counting.

4:13 Census of vehicle registration numbers from which information as shown in the map at 4:17 can be built up.

Time	Buses	Cars	Lorries	Vans	M/cycles
9.00–9.15	AKN 203H GUC 941L	UK 7011J GWK 45D VGH 102 JAC 848D PUG 128E RK 8496K URR 489H	KJH 574C CBY 490H	EHX 453H APT 630K	FGK 45F
		etc.	etc.	etc.	etc.

Note: *The registration marks shown in this example do not relate to actual vehicles.*

4:14 Census of cargoes carried in lorries or vans.

Time	Lorries	Vans
9.00–9.15	Timber Steel rods Concrete Generator Petrol	Groceries Furniture Greengrocery Milk Carpets Garden supplies
	etc.	etc.

Note: *In the case of cars and buses a similar count can be taken, relating to passengers as opposed to cargoes.*

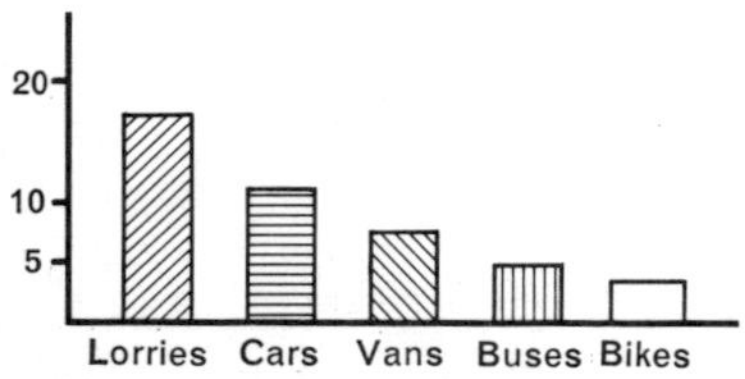

4:15 Histogram of kinds of vehicles passing the census point.

Vehicle	Time on stop watch	Speed in m.p.h.
1	1·0 mins.	30
2	2·0 mins.	15
3		
4		
5		
6		
7		
8		
9		
10		
11		

4:16 Recording the speed of vehicles (over a measured half-mile).

D Record of an interview As with the tape-recorded interview the project should be discussed with the children and a series of questions produced. The information obtained from an iron works visit is described below as an example.

The questions asked were:

(i) Why was the factory established here? (ii) Where do the materials come from? (iii) How are the materials transported? (iv) What are the main products? (v) Where are they sent? (vi) How are they transported? (vii) Describe the factory and its site.

Barrow Ironworks was started in 1859. The factory was built on a spacious site at Hindpool where there was space for slag tipping and expansion. The site faced Walney Channel from which cooling water was obtained. The factory was built after negotiations had been completed for

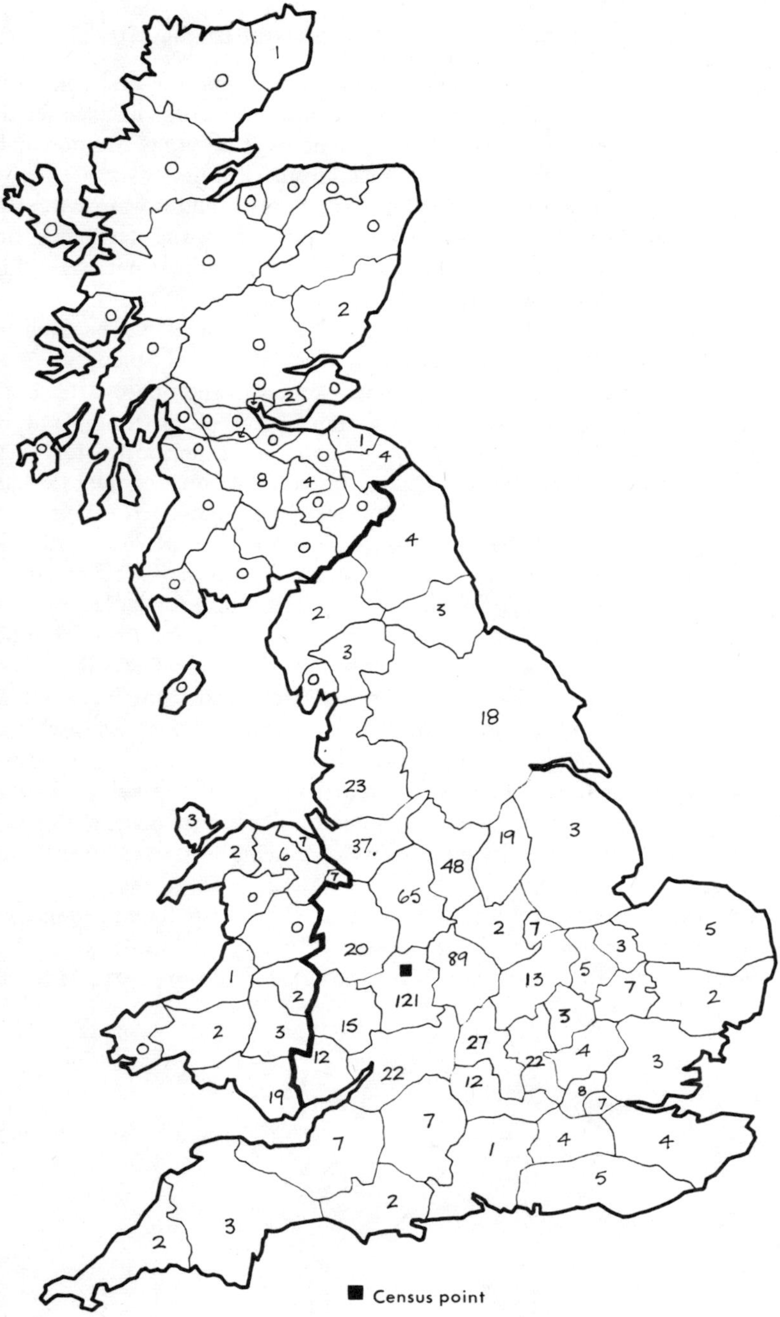

4:17 Map showing origin and number of vehicles passing Mustow Green crossroads in a two-hour period.

the railway link to the Durham coalfield from where the best coke could easily be obtained. The richness of the local haematite balanced the disadvantage of the high cost of coke at Barrow. Limestone was obtainable from Stainton Quarry and moulding sand from Yarlside.

From the port there was still some export of ore, and it was used for the export of pig iron. The next step was the building of the steel works on a site next to the iron works designed to use the pig iron while it was still hot to make re-smelting unnecessary.

As the local haematite was worked out all the iron ore had to be imported. This ore, mainly haematite, came from West Africa and Spain. Scrap was used at the rate of 200 tons (203 tonnes) a month, and one-quarter of this came in the form of metal turnings from Vickers-Armstrongs. The rest was mainly steel turning scrap from Preston and Southport. Most of the limestone came from Stainton Quarry by rail. The bulk of the coke came from Yorkshire because this coke, improved by the addition of Welsh slack, was 29*s.* (£1.45) a ton cheaper than the Durham coke. Barnsley, Royston, Manners Main and Hemsworth, were the main sources. Some 457 tonnes of coal a year were used for locomotives. Firebricks for ladles, of which normally 152–203 tonnes a year were consumed, came from Bonneybridge and Sheffield, while refractory bricks came from Backworth (Newcastle-upon-Tyne). Oil which was brought by road from Heysham was used at the rate of 500 tons (507 tonnes) a year and was used for steam raising. The cooling water for the blast furnaces came from near-by Walney Channel; but seawater corroded the pipes and valves, and the pipes were blocked by sand and sea animals. There were plans to use purer water from four boreholes at Ainslie St. drawing water from the Bunter Sandstone.

The main products were haematite iron for casting. The production of pig iron varied from 147,600 tonnes in 1959 to 411,985 in 1956, and the average labour force was 700. Of this production of some 203,208 tonnes,

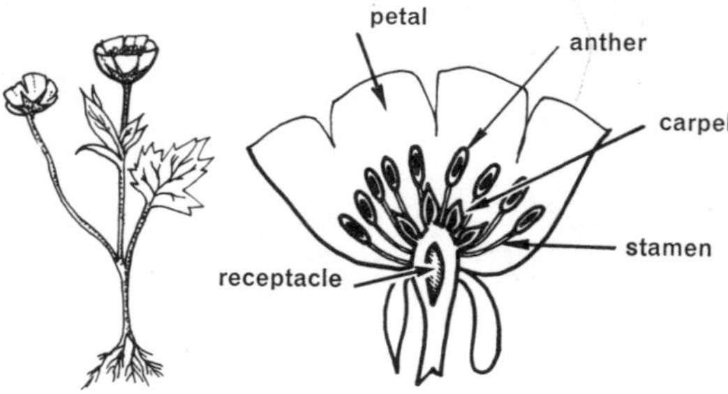

4:18 Child's sketch of a flower.

15% went to the steel works, 15% to ingot mould foundries, 20% to car manufacture and allied foundries, and 30% to textile and allied foundries.

The car and allied foundries were in the Birmingham area, the textile users in the Bradford and Leeds district, the Nottingham and Leicestershire district, and the Manchester, Preston and Blackpool district. The main steel foundries were in the North Staffordshire district and the Barrow district. The haematite pig-iron market was steadily declining because alloys were made which took the place of metals produced from haematite pig iron and large users of this pig iron were now producing their own. In 1963 the Millom Ironworks bought out the Barrow works and it was closed down.

3 GRAPHICAL METHODS

Sketches

Drawing is a most important method of recording, especially when reinforced by prints, rubbings and photographs. Sketching encourages close observation and develops sketching skill. Moreover it obviates the necessity for collecting specimens that may be rare. Sketching needs considerable practice and not all pupils can sketch. They should be encouraged and helped as far as possible; but if a child cannot sketch it will be better to let this child use some different medium. The labelling of the sketches is of considerable value. For record purposes notes should be made of the date of sketching, the scale, the subject, the locality, as precise as possible, and the weather at the time.

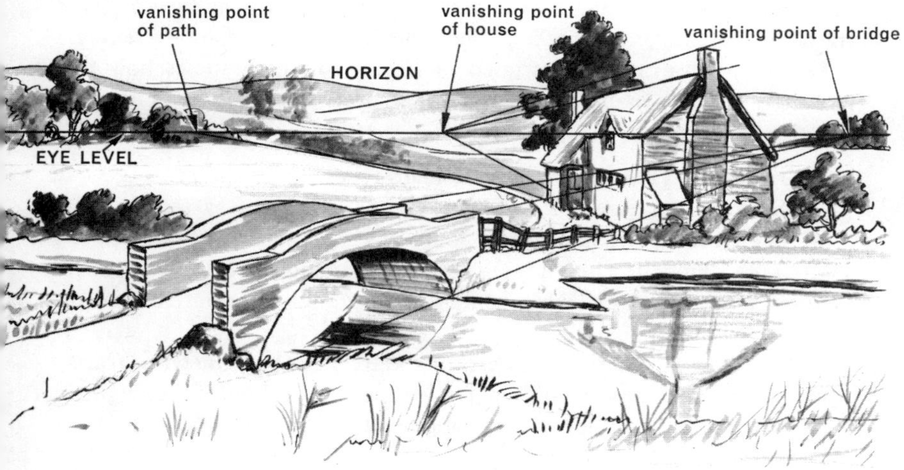

4:19 Details of a landscape sketch.

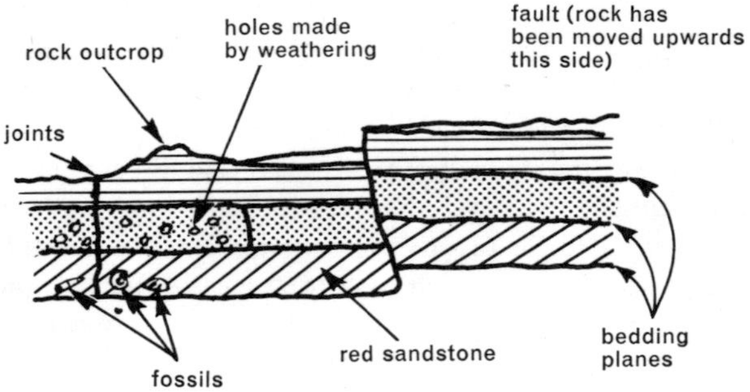

4 : 20 Sketch of a rock outcrop.

4 : 21 Tree sketches and silhouettes.

If possible the sketches should be made to scale – preferably to natural scale. Fig. 4:18 shows a typical child's sketch of a flower. Flowers, trees, insects, houses, road signs, rock exposures, landscapes can all be well illustrated by sketches or by drawing. They should be coloured appropriately.

Landscape drawing is illustrated in Fig. 4:19 which shows how the picture is drawn to natural size and how perspective is produced. Fig. 4:20 shows a rock exposure.

Tree Sketches These can be of four main types.

(*a*) Sketch of the tree in summer, e.g. Fig. 4:21

(*b*) Sketch of the tree in winter, e.g. Fig. 4:21.

(*c*) Tree silhouette (Fig. 4:21) can be drawn and filled in with pencil shading, crayon or paint. They can also be torn out of coloured or black paper.

(*d*) Sketches can be made of parts of the tree, the buds, flowers, fruits, twigs, trunk, etc. These should be painted the exact colour of the original. This is extremely valuable for observation and recognition.

Building Type Sketches Sketches of buildings of significance are fairly easy to draw.

Paintings and photographs

Old paintings and photographs of the locality can be used to compare the present with the past. Many of these pictures are available in museums and a comparison with a view from a similar viewpoint today can be most instructive.

TAKING PHOTOGRAPHS

Photographs are an easy way of obtaining a good record. Children should be encouraged to take photographs, to develop the film and make prints. We must point out however, that at first the results may not be very good. If a small number of prints is required it is better to send the films to a laboratory like Paragon Photographic Services, Brighton, which is efficient and comparatively cheap. However, photography is so fascinating that we would suggest that printing and developing should be encouraged where possible.

A simple camera, like the Kodak Brownie or Instamatic camera, makes an excellent recording instrument for a child (Fig. 4:22). It takes roll film

4 : 22 The main types of cameras.

which can easily be processed and from which satisfactory prints can be made by contact printing. The use of 35 mm. cameras means that the black and white photographs must be enlarged. This necessitates more expensive equipment, enlargers, etc. 35 mm. cameras are excellent for colour photographs which are processed by the makers. As the children become more skilled they can use a half frame camera which takes 72 photographs on a 35 mm. colour film and is therefore very economical. Reflex cameras are excellent particularly for close-up photographs for the picture can be completely composed in the viewfinder. For very close-up photographs special lenses or extension tubes are needed or, alternatively, it is possible to enlarge the significant part of the photograph.

Composing the picture

The first rule of all photography is to think before you 'click'. By moving the viewpoint up (by standing on a fence or a tree) or down (by kneeling or stooping) or by moving it to the left or right, a much better record can be made. Backgrounds are very important and should be as plain as possible.

Lighting must be good so that the objects can be clearly seen; choice of light adds much to the picture. Pictures taken in the middle of the day tend to be flat and uninteresting. Morning and evening when the sun is low in the sky are the best times for landscape photography.

The composition of the picture should be one in which the landscape is divided into thirds from left to right so that there is no one object standing like a sentinel in the centre. Horizontally, one-third of the photograph should be sky (Fig. 4:23). Later experimentation can show the best methods

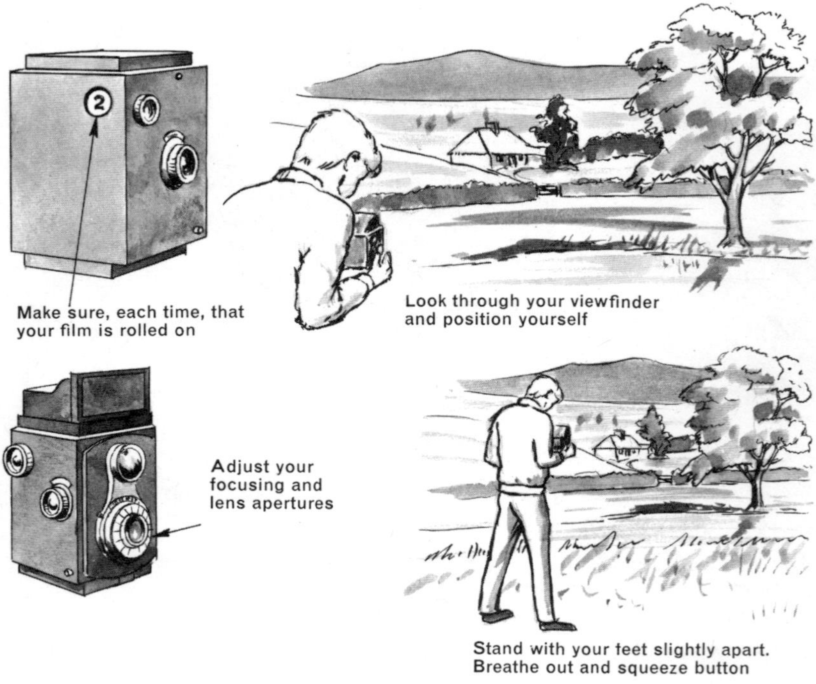

4 : 23 How to take a photograph.

for special subjects. When photographing buildings it is sometimes difficult to get far enough away. Without special lenses the easiest way is to photograph the building in sections from left to right; but if the building is tall it is difficult to include all of it without tilting the camera. Sometimes a high viewpoint – from a house across the road – creates a satisfactory picture. The inclusion of an interesting foreground also helps. Landscapes can be usefully framed by trees or a rock pillar. It is important to be near enough to the scene to cut out all the unwanted parts of the picture. In landscapes, or when scale is important, a person, or implement (e.g. a geological hammer, or a ruler) should be included in the photograph. This makes the scale quite clear.

Loading the camera

Loading the camera should be done in the shade according to the directions given with the camera. Before loading, any dust in the back of the camera should be removed. Normal black and white films for usual purposes are Ilford FP3 or HP3, or Kodak Verichrome. Colour films are of two main types – reversal film mainly for producing transparencies or negative film from which colour prints are produced. These are Kodacolor, or Kodachrome II, Ilford colour or Agfa CT 18, all reversal films, and Agfa CN 17 (negative film).

Exposure

On simple cameras the exposure is set, and for a beginner it is wise to treat a more complex camera as a simple one by setting the aperture at F 11 and the time at 1/100. For colour photographs an exposure meter is necessary if there is to be no wasted film.

Lens hoods are helpful when photographing in strong sunlight so that no sun rays shine directly into the camera lens.

Processing

Some kind of darkroom is necessary; but a store room or cupboard is adequate. A source of electricity is necessary for a darkroom light to facilitate exposing the print.

Developing the film (Figs. 4:24, 4:25)

Equipment needed:

A developing tank – made by Paterson or Johnson.

Developer. This is in liquid or powder form. Proprietary developers are produced by the main photographic chemical producers, e.g. Johnsons, Kodak.

Fixer – Johnsons (Fixadon), Kodak.

Two measuring cylinders and mixing beakers.

4:24 Equipment for developing a film.

A thermometer.
A stirring rod.
A source of heat for heating the developer and fixer.
A source of water.
Plastic clothes pegs and weights for hanging up the film.
A timer, watch or an alarm clock.

The film is loaded into the tank in the *darkroom*. For roll film this necessitates the removal of the backing paper. It is an excellent idea to practise loading the tank in daylight with an old film. The film is fed into the spiral and this is rotated until all the film is loaded. This spiral is then placed in the tank and the cap replaced. The developer is then mixed with the correct

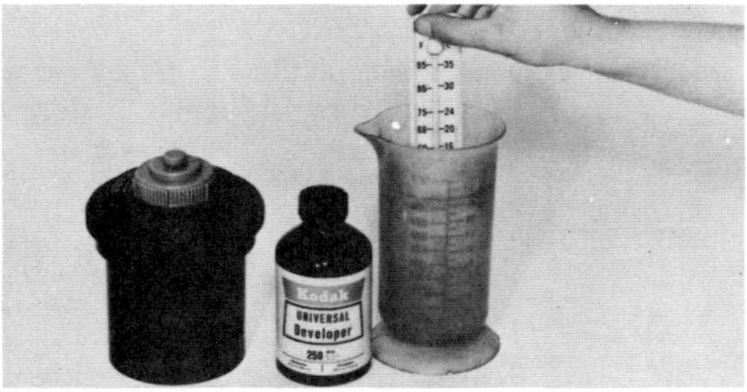

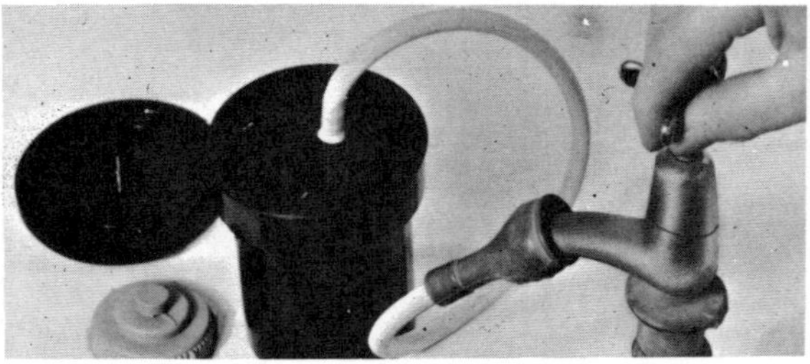

4:25 Washing the film. The hose is attached to the tap and water pours into the tank.

amount of water and heated up to the correct temperature – normally 20° C (68° F). It can be heated by standing it in a bowl of hot water until the required temperature is reached. Having ascertained the correct time for development the clock is started, the developer poured into the tank and occasionally agitated by using the rod in the centre of the spiral. After the correct time has elapsed the developer is poured down the sink or into a storage bottle for use later. The film must then be rinsed before the fixer which has already been mixed is added to the tank. Time is not so critical in this case; but it is better to give it too long rather than too little time. After fixing, the film is washed. This can be done in the tank or by putting the spiral containing the film into the sink. After washing, the film is taken from the spiral and hung up to dry, with plastic clothes pegs, in a room where there is not too much dust in the air. A weight should be put on the

4:26a This first dish contains the developer, the second is a water wash and the third dish is the fixer.

4:26b A measuring cylinder, thermometer, dish, timer, stirring rod and masking frame.

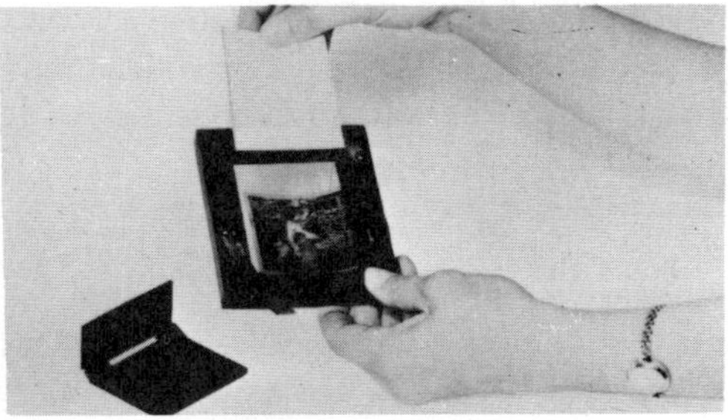

4:26c Printing frame.

end of the film. While the film is drying, all the equipment should be thoroughly washed.

Printing (Fig. 4:26 a, b, c)

(i) *Contact*

Requirements:

Printing paper, e.g. Kodak Bromide paper. This paper must be kept wrapped.

A darkroom.

Developer – (Johnsons '468', Kodak, etc.)

Fixer (Johnsons Acid Fixer, Kodak.)

Printing frame with a mask.

A safelight – (made out of a cocoa tin with a dark yellow filter).

A timer.

Three developing dishes (for developer, water, fixer).

One light for exposure.

Print tweezers.

The negative and printing paper are placed together in the printing frame with the negative on top. The light source should be a 40–60 watt bulb at 2 ft. (61 cm.) from the printing frame. The time of exposure is found by trial and error using test strips. Light negatives need less light, dark negatives more light. From 5 to 10 seconds is a normal exposure.

The print is then put into the developer emulsion side up and is immersed for 45 to 60 seconds. (The temperature of the developer should be ascertained from the leaflet supplied with the developer.)

The dish should be gently rocked so that the liquid moves over the print. If it is left too long the print will show a yellow stain on the white parts and if too short a time elapses the dark parts will look bleak.

The print should then be lifted by the corner with tweezers to avoid finger printing, the solution allowed to drain off, then placed in the water, then in the fixer. It is helpful to push the print into the fixer with a glass rod. The prints can be washed in the light in the sink. They are best washed in running water. They should then be allowed to drain and dry.

(ii) *For enlarging*, the process is the same except that an enlarger is used. (Fig. 4:27). The negative is fed into the negative carrier and the picture focused on to the paper below. The focusing is done before the paper is inserted on the base board. The enlarger lamp is then switched on for the requisite time and the print developed as before.

With care excellent results can be obtained.

Cinephotography also provides an excellent record especially where it is necessary to record movement. Useful 8 mm. films can be made showing fieldwork techniques. These can be converted and used in the cassette loop-film projector. Children of this age group can easily work a simple cine camera.

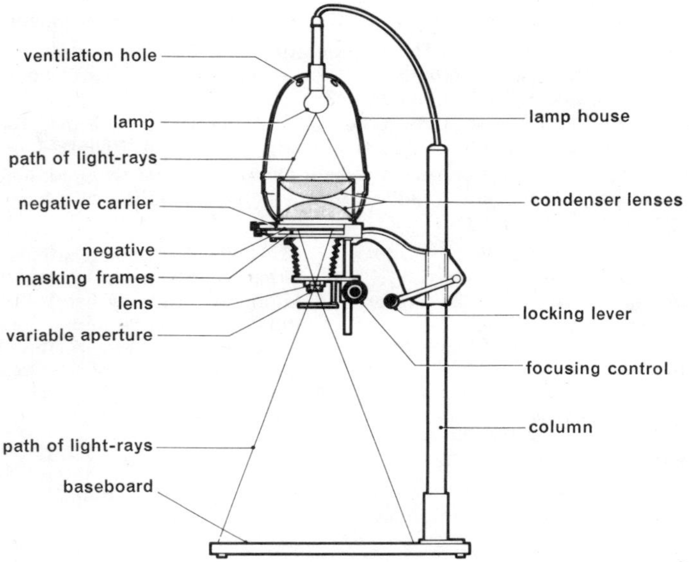

4:27 An enlarger

Books

Catling, G. *Better Photography*. Kay and Ward.
Chambers, E. J. *Light and Photography for Young Experimenters*. Bell.
Corey, D. *The Camera*. Ladybird.
Emanuel, W. D. *All-in-One Camera Book*. Focal Press.
Gottlieb, W. P. *Photography*. Dobson.
Lindner, G. *Photography*. Burke.

SOURCES OF PHOTOGRAPHS

Photographs are useful for discussing topics not easily seen by other means. Museum postcards are extremely valuable and many useful photographs can be obtained from the museums (see Chapter 3).

Historical buildings – National Buildings Record, Fielden House, Great College Street, London, S.W.1.
Local newspapers and from Central Office of Information, Government Building, 3 Bromyard Avenue, Acton, London, W.3.
Wales – Central Office of Information, 42 Park Place, Cardiff.
Radio Times Hulton Picture Library, 35 Marylebone High Street, London, W.1.
The Director, Geological Survey and Museum, Exhibition Road, South Kensington, London, S.W.7.

The Director, Natural History Museum, London, S.W.7.
The Director, Science Museum, London, S.W.7.

Air Photographs present a unique view of the country. They are obtainable from:

(*a*) For England and Wales, The Air Photographs Officer.

(*b*) For Scotland, Air Photographs Officer, Scottish Development Department, York Buildings, Queen Street, Edinburgh, 2.

(*c*) For Northern Ireland, Deputy Keeper of Public Records, Public Records Office of Northern Ireland, Law Courts Building, May Street, Belfast, 1.

When ordering details of the area for which photographs are required, map grid numbers etc. should be sent. In addition many commercial firms also provide air photographs of specific objects.

1 Aerofilms and Aero-Pictorial Ltd., 4 Albemarle Street, London, S.W.1.
2 Fairey Air Surveys Ltd., 24 Bruton Street, London, W.1.
3 B.K.S. Air Surveys Ltd., Cleeve Road, Leatherhead, Surrey.
4 Meridian Airmaps Ltd., Commerce Way, Lancing, Sussex.
5 Kemp Air Surveys Ltd., Southampton Airport, Southampton.
18, Nechell's House, Dartmouth St., Birmingham.
6 Lithograve (Birmingham) Ltd., Air and Commercial Photographers, Unit
7 Air-Views, Att. Mr. Martin, Manchester Airport, Ringway, Cheshire.
8 Plan Air, 2 North-east Circus Place, Edinburgh, 3.

The Ordnance Survey, Air Photo-Cover Section, Romsey Road, Maybush, Southampton also provide photographs.

Maps

Maps are the basic tool for all recording. Many children today see maps in use from their early days, on television, in newspapers, and most commonly during the weekend outings in the car.

Using large-scale maps in project work soon familiarises the children with them. For children without this knowledge a start can be made by drawing a map of the classroom. A large outline, perhaps 6′ × 6′ (1·8 m. ×

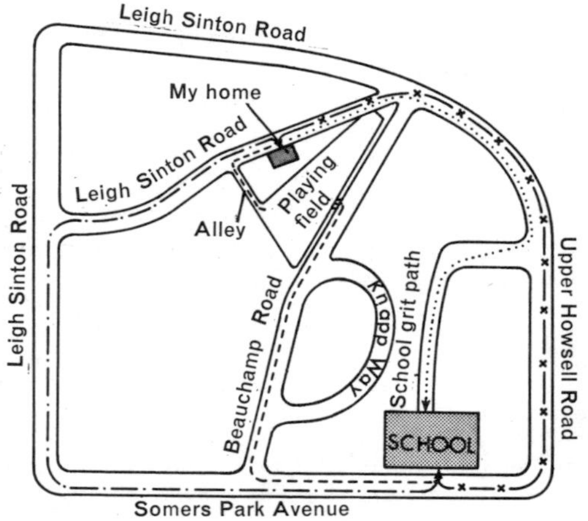

4 : 28 Map showing the routes to school.

1·8 m.), should be prepared by the teacher on squared paper and then the details, desk, cupboards, etc., can be chalked in by the children. At first these can be put in using building blocks, tins of convenient blocks of wood. This can be followed by giving children duplicated maps of the classroom on which they can mark desks, routes to the door, windows, cupboards, etc. Measurement of the room with tapes, pacing or spans, follows and the map can be drawn to scale. From this there is a progression from maps of rooms at home, a map of the school (Fig. 4:28) and maps of the neighbourhood. The street can be paced out and this data plotted on a map.

During the making of these maps the problem of conventional signs will arise. At first, children will draw three-dimensional symbols; but with discussion they will soon realise the significance of symbols as seen from above. The transition from these to the Ordnance Survey symbols is a straightforward one. By using a really large-scale plan-type map these symbols become self-evident.

ORDNANCE SURVEY MAPS

Ordnance Survey maps are being metricated starting with the 1″ to the mile, which becomes 2 cm. to the kilometre (1¼″ = 1 mile). Further information available from Ordnance Survey, Southampton address. The 1/1250 map (Fig. 4:29) is best for school use and it may be possible to have this enlarged by a photo-copying firm to a size of 1/500. This map shows all details and they can be easily identified on the ground. In an urban area a useful exercise is the mapping of where the children live or the kind of shops in the main street, the public buildings, the children's routes to school, the trees in park or playground, their position, height and type.

As the children get older there is a natural transition to the 1/2500, the 1/10,560 map, the 2½″ map, and finally to the 1″ and ¼″ maps (Fig. 4:30, 31). These maps are most useful in planning journeys across the British Isles and France, in the planning of holiday journeys, and for use in planning and following the route of the school journeys.

Contours seem difficult for the younger children but to see a child of 9 looking at the ground on a sloping hill and comparing it with the contour lines makes one realise how easy they are to see. Demonstrations of contours can be clearly made using a model of an island in a glass tank, filling it up to specific levels and marking the levels on the contour map. They should be seen from above by the children so that the circular patterns of the contours can be clearly seen. Contours cut out of cardboard to build up a contour model also demonstrate this. The measuring of valley profiles helps children to understand contours.

The maps mentioned are obtainable from the Ordnance Survey, Southampton, at a discount of 25% on large-scale maps and of 33⅓% on the maps of a scale under three miles to the inch. Detailed plans of the large scale maps of the school area are obtainable from the Ordnance Survey.

The 1″ geological survey maps are useful for local studies. These are of three types, showing drift, solid or both solid and drift deposits. The drift maps are generally the most useful. Fig. 4:32 shows the 1″ geological maps that are available at present. The older 1″ geological maps may be available in the local library.

For coalfield areas 6″ maps are available. For special areas it is also possible to get photostats of the 6″ maps of the area from the Director, the Geological Museum, Kensington, London, S.W.7. The memoirs for these

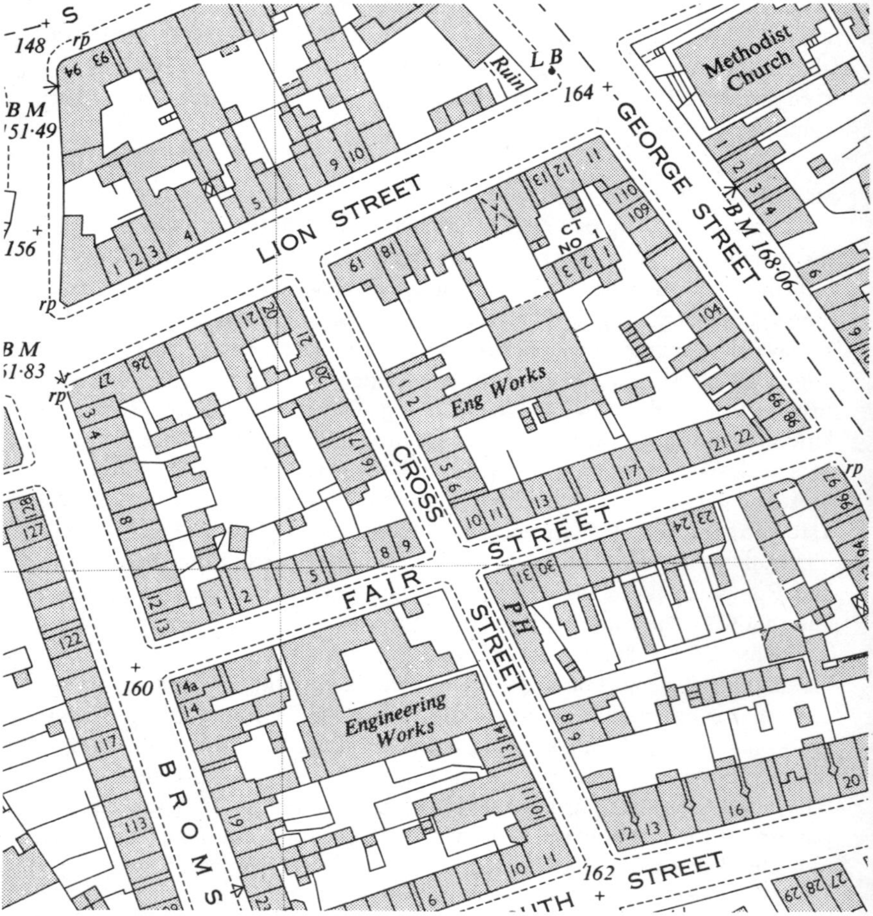

4 : 29 Part of a 1/1250 Map. These maps show much detail and are excellent for children to plot on.

1″ sheets also provide much local information for the teacher. These geological maps are available from the Ordnance Survey, Southampton.

The soil survey sheets are also obtainable from the Ordnance Survey.

SOIL SURVEY MAPS

England and Wales
3rd Edition Sheets (1 : 63 360)

Blackpool	(66)	Aberystwyth	(163)
Leeds	(70)	Church Stretton	(166)
Southport	(74)	Llanilar	(178)
Preston	(75)	Cambridge	(188)
Formby	(83)	Aylesbury	(238)
Beaumaris	(94)	Abingdon	(253)
Rhyl	(95)	Bridgend	(261/2)
Bangor	(106)	Cardiff	(263)
Denbigh	(107)	Reading	(268)
Derby	(125)	Weston-super-Mare	(279)
Wem	(138)	Wells	(280)
Melton Mowbray	(142)	Glastonbury	(296)

3rd Edition Sheets (1 : 63 360) Land Use Capability Maps, Melton Mowbray (142)
Composite Sheets (1 : 63 360)
Anglesey (93, 105 and parts of 92, 94, 106, 118, 119).
Pwllheli (parts of 105, 117, 118, 133, 134).
Exeter and Newton Abbott (325 and 330).
Composite Sheets (1 : 25 000)

Romney Marsh
Selsey Bill
Bognor Regis
Worthing
Chichester

Breckland Forest Sheet 1 (Swaffham)
Breckland Forest Sheet 2 (Brandon)
Breckland Forest Sheet 3 (Thetford)

Outline Edition (1 : 25 000)
Soil Maps

SE 60 (Armthorpe)
SE 74 (Barnby Moor)
TG 13/14 (Banningham and Sheringham)
TM 49 (Beccles North)
ST 65 (Crewe West)

Exmoor Forest Sheets (Parts of 73/74, 83/84)
TQ 59 (Harold Hill)
SO 53 (Hereford South)
SD 58 (Sedgwick)
SK 17 (Tideswell)
SE 65 (York East)

Scotland: 3rd Edition Sheets

Jedburgh (17)
Morebattle (18)
Kilmarnock (22 and part of 21)
Kelso (25)
Berwick-upon-Tweed (26)
Peterhead and Fraserburgh (87 and 96)

Forfar (57)
Inverurie (76)
Aberdeen (77)
Huntly (86)
Elgin (95)
Banff (96)

The published memoirs are listed below:

PUBLICATIONS OF THE SOIL SURVEY OF GREAT BRITAIN

The following are obtainable from the Soil Survey, Rothamsted Experimental Station, Harpenden, Herts, or from Edward Stanford Ltd., 12/14, Long Acre, London, W.C.2.

BULLETINS OF THE SOIL SURVEY OF GREAT BRITAIN

Soils of the Middle Teign Valley District of Devon by B. Clayden (with map)

The Soils of the West Midlands by D. Mackney and C. P. Burnham (with map)

Soils of the West Sussex Coastal Plain by J. M. Hodgson (with 4 maps); (without maps)

Soils of Romney Marsh by R. D. Green (with map)

Soils of Lancashire by B. R. Hall and C. J. Folland (with map)

MEMOIRS OF THE SOIL SURVEY OF ENGLAND AND WALES

The Soils of the Wem District of Shropshire (Sheet 138) by E. Crompton and D. A. Osmond (with map)

The Soils of the Glastonbury District of Somerset (Sheet 296) by B. W. Avery (with map)

The County of Anglesey – Soils and Agriculture (Sheets 93, 105 and parts of 92, 94, 106, 118 and 119) by E. Roberts (with map)

The Soils and Land Use of the District around Rhyl and *Denbigh* (Sheets 95 and 107) by D. F. Ball

The Soils and Land Use of the District around Bangor and Beaumaris (Sheets 94 and 106) by D. F. Ball

The Soils and Land Use of the District around Aylesbury and Hemel Hempstead (Sheet 238) by B. W. Avery (with map)

The Soils of the Mendip District of Somerset (Sheets 279 and 280) by D. C. Findlay (with 2 maps)

The Soils of the District around Cambridge (Sheet 188) by C. A. H. Hodge and R. S. Seale (with map)

The Soils and Land Use of the District north of Derby (Sheet 125) by E. M. Bridges (with map)

The Soils of the Church Stretton District of Shropshire (Sheet 166) by D. Mackney and C. P. Burnham (with 2 maps)

Soils of the Preston District of Lancashire (Sheet 75) by E. Crompton (with map)

Soils of the South-west Lancashire Coastal Plain (Sheets 74 and 83) by B. R. Hall and C. J. Folland (with 2 maps)

Soils of the Reading District (Sheet 268) by R. A. Jarvis (with map)

Soils of the Leeds District (Sheet 70) by A. Crompton and B. Matthews (with map)

Soils of North Cardiganshire (Sheets 163 and 178) by C. C. Rudeforth (with 2 maps)

QUARTER-INCH MAPS OF GREAT BRITAIN

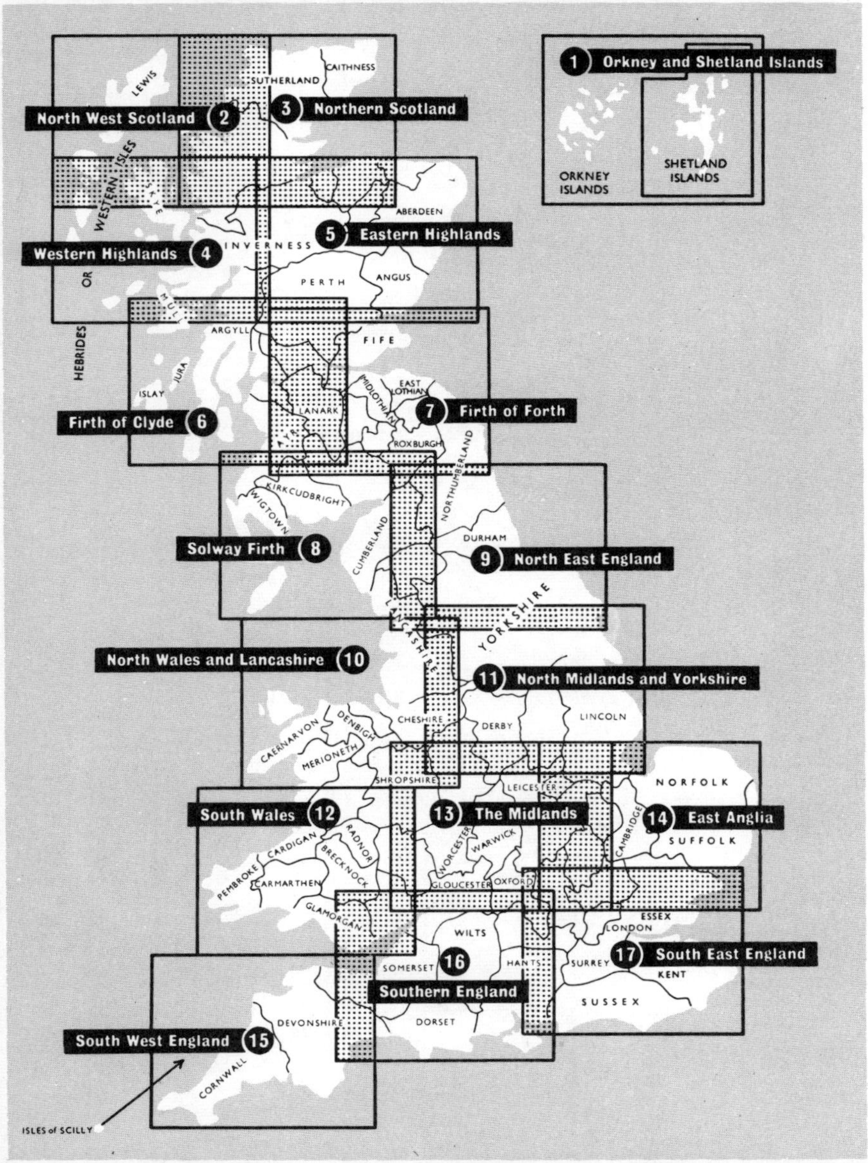

These maps are obtainable from Ordnance Survey Agents and all good booksellers

4 : 30 Key to the Quarter-Inch Maps of Great Britain.

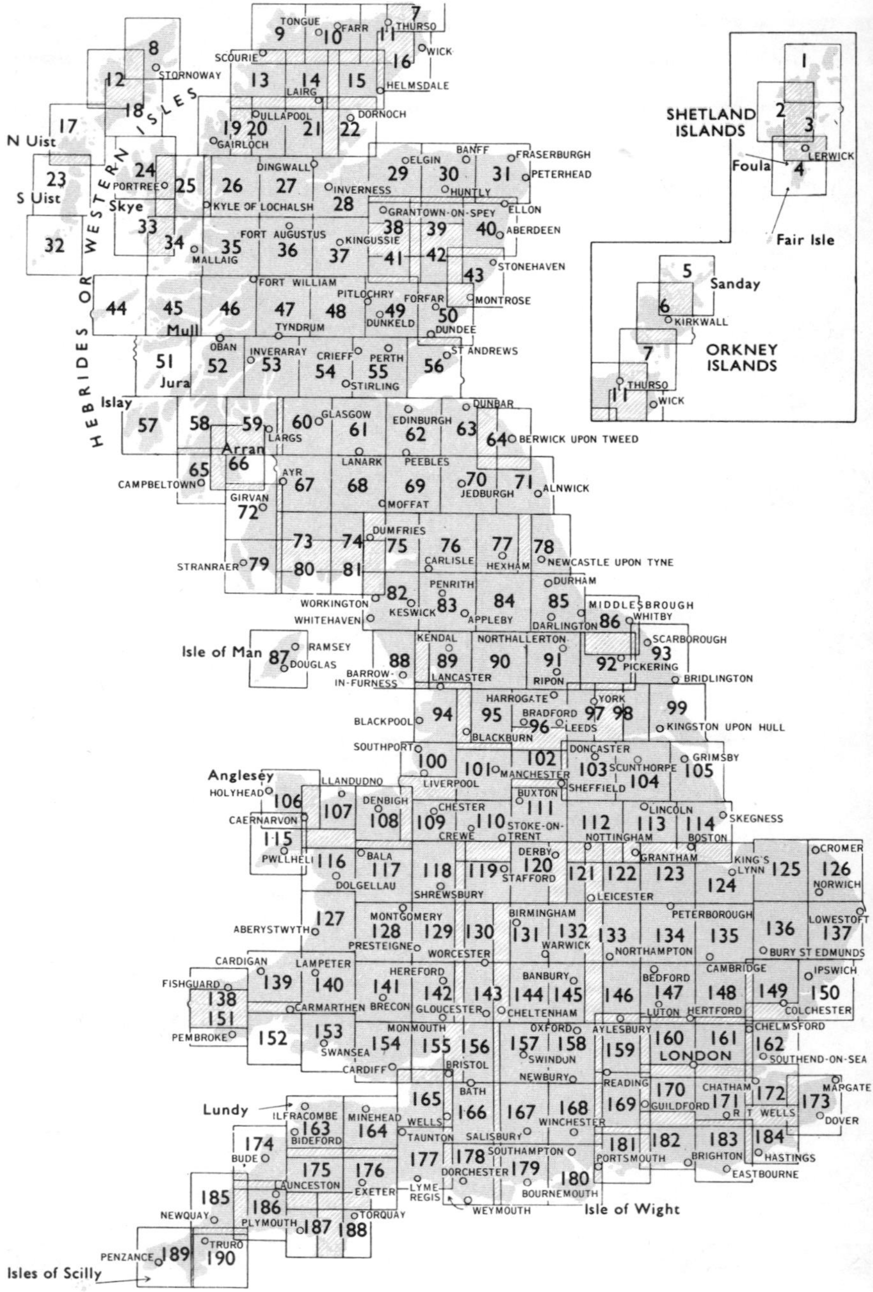

4 : 31 Key to the One-Inch Ordnance Survey Maps of Great Britain.

INDEX TO THE
ONE-INCH AND QUARTER-INCH
GEOLOGICAL MAPS of ENGLAND and WALES

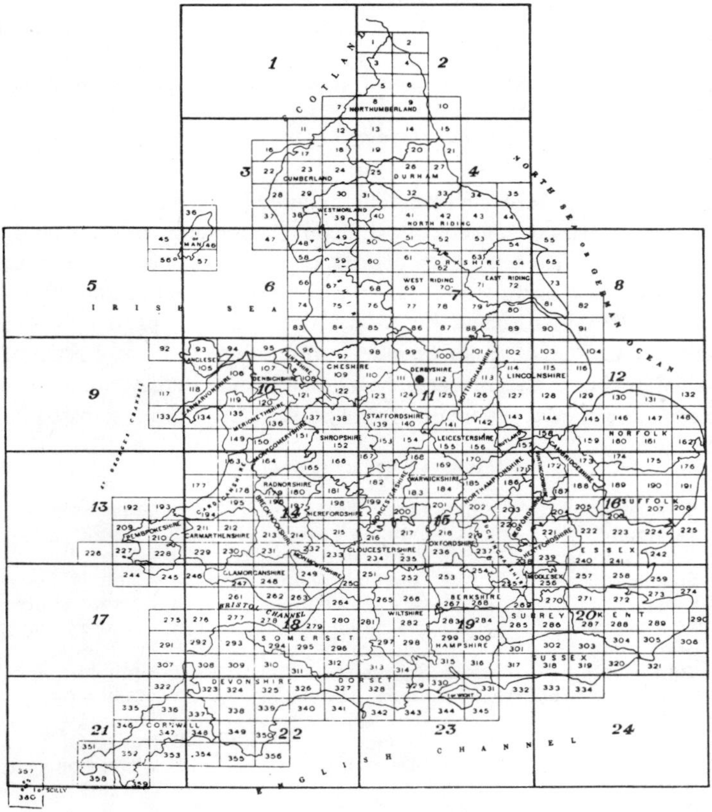

4 : 32 Key to the Geological Survey Maps that are available.

The following are obtainable from H.M.S.O., T. Nelson and Sons, 18, Dalkeith Road, Edinburgh, EH16 5BJ.

Memoirs of the Soil Survey of Scotland:

The Soils of the Country round Banff, Huntly and Turriff. (Sheets 86 and 96) by R. Glentworth (with 2 maps)

The Soils of the Country round Jedburgh and Morebattle (Sheets 17 and 18) by J. W. Muir (with 2 maps)

The Soils of the Country round Kilmarnock (Sheet 22 and part of 21) by B. D Mitchell and R. A. Jarvis (with map)

The Soils of the Country round Kelso and Lauder (Sheets 25 and 26) by J. M. Ragg (with 2 maps)

The Soils round Aberdeen, Inverurie and Fraserburgh. (Sheets 76, 77, 87 and 97) by R. Glentworth and J. W. Muir (with 3 maps)

The Soils of the Country round Haddington and Eyemouth. (Sheets 33, 34 and part 41.)

LAND UTILISATION MAPS showing the detailed land use are also available. The older 1″ series is now out of print; but the memoirs of these land utilisation surveys written for each county and entitled 'The Land of Britain Series' are most useful for local studies. The Second Land Utilisation Survey of Britain directed by Miss Alice Coleman of King's College, London, WC2R 2LS, is an excellent production. It is on a scale of two and a half inches to the mile and shows the land use in fifty-four categories. The available sheets, obtainable from Edward Stanford, are listed below:

ENGLAND AND WALES

13 St. Austell
44 Yarmouth (I. of Wight)
45 Shanklin
50 Exeter
56 Bournemouth
77 Brighton
91 Southampton
110 Winchester (South)
118 Dungeness
138 Folkestone
140 Lynton
158 Dover
160 Cheddar
174 Deal
175 Llantwit Major
176 Barry
187 Croydon
193 Bridgend
194 Cardiff West
205 South London
206 Bexley
207 Gravesend
210 Port Eynon
211 Port Talbot
212 Ogmore Valley
213 Pontypridd
214 Newport (Mon.)
224 City of London
225 East London
226 Basildon
227 Southend on Sea
230 Llanelly South
231 Swansea
232 Rhondda
233 Mountain Ash
235 Chepstow
244 London North
249 Milford Haven
252 Llanelly North
253 Pontadawe
254 Hirwaun
255 Merthyr Tydfil
263 Thame
271 Haverfordwest
274 Pontyberem
278 Abergavenny
279 Monmouth
281 Gloucester
287 Harpenden
310 Luton
333 Ampthill
355 Bedford South
376 Bedford (North)
388 Presteigne
397 Kimbolton
425 Aberystwyth
442 Thetford
448 Newtown
452 Wolverhampton (South)
454 Nuneaton
461 Methwold
464 Loddon
465 Lowestoft
487 Cader Idris
515 Stafford
525 Fakenham
558 Stoke on Trent
570 Pneygros
571 Capel Curig
572 Pentrefoelas

573 Ruthin
586 Caernarvon
587 Bethesda
589 Denbigh
620 Llanerchymedd
637 Wallasea (Liverpool)
640 Manchester
654 Doncaster
655 Hatfield Moors
666 Hemsworth
667 Thorne
675 Duibury
676 Castleford
677 Goole
679 Kingston-upon-Hull
687 Leeds
688 Sherburn-in-Elmet
689 Selby
698 Tadcaster
699 Elvington
708 York West
709 York East
713 Lancaster
719 Barton-le-Willows
723 Dalton-in-Furness
724 Grange-over-Sands
730 Malton
742 Kirkby Moorside
753 Rosedale
793 Spennymoor
794 The Hartlepools
801 Durham City
815 Tyneside
820 Whitley Bay
825 Blyth
838 Coldstream

SCOTLAND

S138 Dunfermline

The Land Use Survey Handbook by Alice Coleman outlines the procedure of the survey and is a useful handbook for Land Utilisation Surveys.

HISTORICAL MAPS

The Ordnance Survey publish a series of archaeological and historical maps which contain much information to be used in the study of the history of the region. These are:

Britain in the Dark Ages – New edition, 1 sheet, 16 miles to one inch.
Ancient Britain – two sheets, scale 10 miles to one inch, showing the more important relics.
Roman Britain – single sheet, 16 miles to one inch. Shows Britain from A.D. 43 to A.D. 410.
Monastic Britain – two sheets. Britain from the conquest to 1539.
Southern Britain in the Iron Age – 10 miles to one inch. Britain south of a line from Scarborough to the Isle of Man during the half millennium before the Roman conquest.
Hadrian's Wall – This shows the whole wall. Scale 2 inches to one mile.
Antonine Wall – Scale 2½ inches to one mile.

The Royal Geographical Society, Kensington Gore, London, S.W.7, with Bartholomew & Son Ltd. produce a series of *JOHN BLAEU'S* county maps dating from the seventeenth century. These maps are as follows:

JOHN BLAEU'S ENGLISH COUNTY MAPS.

Sheets available:

Cambridge
Cheshire
Cornwall
Cumberland
Essex
Hampshire
Hertfordshire
Kent
Lancashire
Middlesex
Norfolk
Oxford
Surrey
Sussex
Warwickshire and Worcestershire
Yorkshire

Size 61 X 45 cm.

The British Museum, London, W.C.1, publish litho-offset prints of Saxton's county maps as follows:

Map of England and Wales – 1579
Caernarvonshire and Anglesey (an Elizabethan map of Snowdonia) – 1578
Cheshire – 1577
Cornwall – 1576
Cumberland and Westmorland (an Elizabethan map of the Lake District) – 1576
Denbighshire and Flintshire (one map) – 1577
Derbyshire – 1577
Devonshire – 1575
Durham – 1576
Dorset – 1575
Essex – 1576
Glamorganshire – 1578
Gloucestershire – 1577
Hampshire – 1575
Hertfordshire – 1577
Herefordshire – 1577
Kent, Surrey, Sussex and Middlesex (one map) – 1575
Lancashire – 1577
Lincolnshire and Nottinghamshire (one map) – 1576
Monmouthshire – 1577
Montgomeryshire and Merionethshire (one map) – 1578
Norfolk (an Elizabethan map of the Broads) – 1574
Northamptonshire, Bedfordshire, Cambridgeshire, Huntingdonshire and Rutland (one map) – 1576
Northumberland – 1576
Oxfordshire, Buckinghamshire and Berkshire (one map) – 1574
Pembrokeshire – 1578
Radnorshire, Brecknockshire, Cardiganshire and Carmarthenshire (one map) – 1578
Shropshire – 1577 (51 cm. × 63 cm.)
Somerset – 1575
Staffordshire – 1577
Suffolk – 1575
Warwickshire and Leicestershire (one map) – 1576
Wiltshire – 1576
Worcestershire – 1577

Average size of the above maps is 20″ × 24¾″.

Yorkshire – 1577 25″ × 33″ (63 cm. × 84 cm.)

Ireland by Baptista Boazio, 1599 22¾″ × 35¾″ (58 cm. × 91 cm.) litho-offset in six colours.

Orders should be addressed to the Director (Publications), The British Museum, London, W.C.1.

Photo-copies of the Speed County maps of England can be obtained from the British Museum.

In the eighteenth and nineteenth century many maps were made for private subscribers and some of these are often available in the local library (Fig. 4:33). The first edition maps of the One-Inch Ordnance Survey are being reprinted by David and Charles, South Devon House, Newton

Abbot, Devon. Of great importance for the local study are the private estate maps often on a very large scale. These are sometimes in county records or in private collections. The enclosure maps of the late eighteenth and early nineteenth centuries and the tithe maps of 1841 show a wealth of detailed information. These are often available in the library or in county records offices.

Plans for turnpikes, canals, and railways are common and are to be found at the County Record Office.

FOREIGN MAPS A list of large-scale foreign maps for an extension of local studies are obtainable from Messrs. E. Stanford Ltd., 12–14 Long Acre, London, W.C.2.

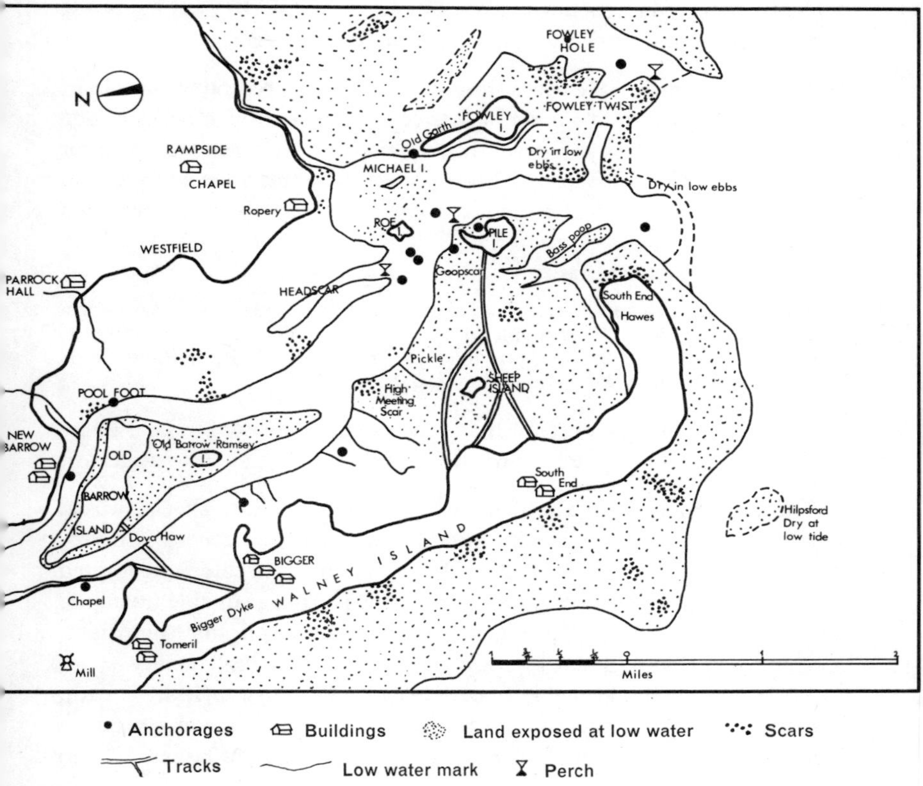

4 : 33 A map of the Pile of Foudrey 1737, Barrow-in-Furness. This map was paid for by private subscription. 1 mile = 1·6 km. approx.

STREET PLANS These are produced by most local authorities and can serve as a base map for plotting data, e.g. bus routes, traffic flows, etc. The scales, often about 3 inches (7·5 cm.) to the mile, are generally too small for plotting buildings.

FIELD SURVEY MAPS For many types of fieldwork the children need a base map. These can be duplicated in the following ways.

A. *Composition or Clay Trays* The map to be reproduced is drawn in special ink upon a sheet of hard paper. When dry it is evenly pressed face downward upon the composition of clay and then carefully removed. The ink impression will then be clearly seen on the composition or clay. Copies are then taken off one at a time, by gently and evenly pressing a sheet of paper over the tray and removing quickly.

The Crusader Manufacturing Co. Ltd., Crusader Works, Walthamstow, London, E.17 produce a hectograph copier in foolscap size.

B. *Spirit Duplicator* These are simple to use and can reproduce in colour. The map is drawn on to a piece of master copy paper which has a carbon sheet of the requisite colour beneath it. A biro or a hard pencil is used for the drawing. This master copy is then put on to the machine and the map is transferred on to paper. About 200 copies can be obtained from one master copy.

Among those available are:

'Banda', from Block and Anderson Ltd., Banda House, Cambridge Grove, Hammersmith, London, W.6. 'Fordigraph' from Fordigraph Office Mechanization Ltd., Ofrex House, Stephen Street, London, W.1. 'Roneosprite', from Roneo Ltd., Roneo House, Finsbury Market, London, E.C.2.

Both the composition duplicator and the spirit duplicator can be used by children but one would hesitate to allow children to use an ink duplicator.

C. *The Ink Duplicator* The maps can be traced on to a special waxed stencil and the machine does the rest. Drawing on the stencils is a very skilled job for the stencil easily tears. If a large number of copies are wanted it is worthwhile having an electronic stencil made from a suitable tracing or photo-copy. These stencils are made by the main duplicator companies, i.e. Gestetner, Roneo. These reproductions are of a very high quality.

Ink duplicators are available from: *Gestetner Duplicators* (B.S.O.) Ltd., Gestetner House, 210 Euston Road, London, N.W.1. They also produce map outlines – Duroprint. Also from *Roneo Ltd.*, 53/65 Whitfield Street, London, W.1

D. *Modern Photo-copiers* can also produce stencils for the spirit duplicator. With the liquid type of copier the process is the 'carborapid' process, while with the dry type of copiers the carbon master is produced by an 'infra-red' process. The master copy is then used on the duplicator in the usual way. There is a wide range of photo-copiers produced today. The dry copiers are probably most convenient, but one must make sure that the machine will take copies from books.

Main suppliers include:

Block and Anderson Ltd., Banda House, Cambridge Grove, Hammersmith, London, W.6.
Contoura Photocopying Ltd., 83, Cromwell Road, London, S.W.7.
Gestetner Ltd., Tottenham, London, N.17.
Roneo Ltd., Finsbury Market, London, E.C.2.
Smith-Corona Ltd., Smith-Corona House, 248–250 Tottenham Court Road, London, W.1.

Photo-copying at school If only a small number of copies are wanted photo-copies will be useful. Many libraries offer a photo-copying service.

Photo-copying can be done quite easily at home by the following method.

Equipment needed:

2 pieces of glass approx. 45 × 45 cm. (18″ × 18″) (or as large as any original copy).
Reflex paper negative.
Reflex paper positive.
Photographic developer.
Photographic fixer.
Two developing dishes.
One 100 watt lamp with a tin can lampshade.

The copy with the reflex paper face down is put between the sheets of glass. They are exposed for approximately 10–15 seconds with a 100 watt lamp 60 cm. (2 ft.) from the glass sandwich (Fig. 4:34). Then the reflex paper is put face to face with the negative paper and this is exposed for 45–60 seconds. The print is then developed in the usual way. Copies can be made from single sheets or from books in this way.

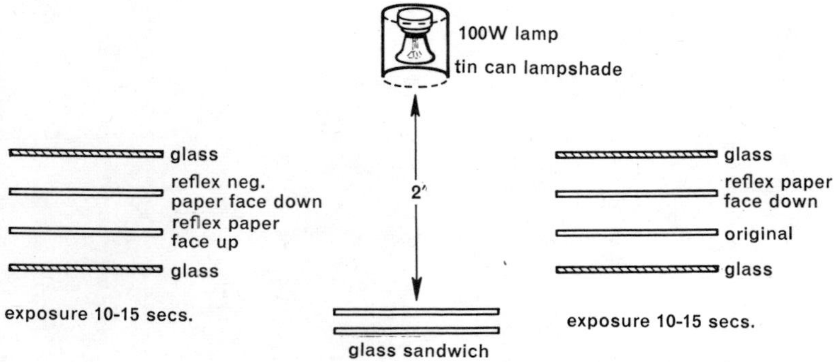

4 : 34 The arrangement of glass and photographic paper for reflex copying.

ENLARGING MAPS Maps can be laboriously copied by hand, by the squares method or with a pantograph; but an easy way of enlarging is to use an epidiascope which will enlarge the picture to any size. The enlarged image is thrown on to a piece of paper and then one traces the outline.

SURVEYING AND MEASURING

Surveying the school field or playground can be done in two ways.

1. To survey a field we need: a measuring tool, tape, chain or clicker wheel. Marker poles or high jump stands for marking corners. An instrument for measuring right angles. This can be a cross staff (Fig. 4:35), a prismatic compass (Fig. 4:36) or a large hardboard right-angle triangle cut on the 3, 4, 5 principle (Fig. 4:37).

If the area to be surveyed is regular, it can be done by constructing two triangles (Fig. 4:38). It is a matter of surveying the sides of the triangles and the perpendiculars. Before starting the survey mark the corners of the triangles with high jump stands or marker poles. Start from *A* and with the measuring tape, chain or clicker wheel measure the side of the triangle *AC*, then measure *CB*. From *B* measure the distance to the point *E* where the perpendicular *CE* is measured. This is done by using the cross staff. Two boys are needed for this to look through the sights of the cross staff on to the markers at *B* and *C*. The cross staff is moved until both points can be seen at once. The angle is then a right-angle. A marker is placed at this point *E* and the distance *EC* measured. Measure *EA* and then measure the

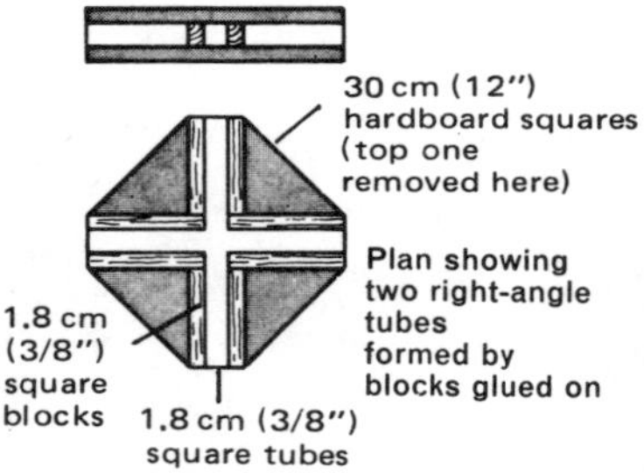

4 : 35 A surveyor's cross for setting large right angles.

4 : 36 Using a prismatic compass.

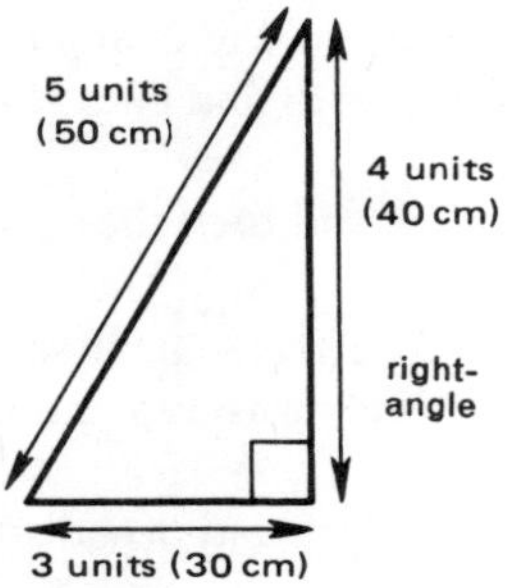

4 : 37 A hardboard triangle on the 3, 4, 5 principle.

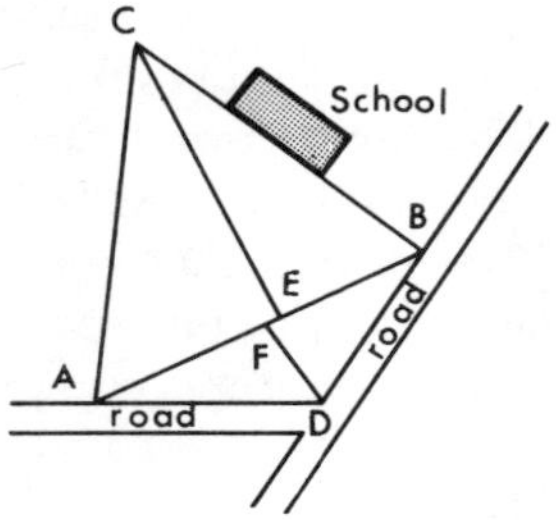

4 : 38 Layout of triangle for a survey of a regular field.

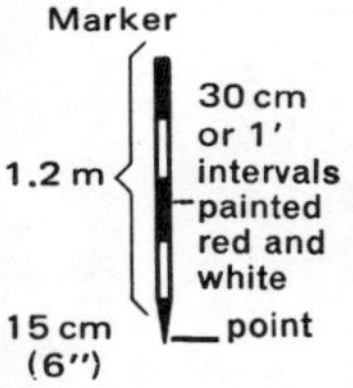

other sides *AD*, *BD*, and the perpendicular *DF*, in the same way. To draw the plan use graph paper. Draw *AB* to scale and at point *E* (to scale) construct a right-angle using a protractor and draw perpendicular *CE*. The distances *AC* and *CB* should be equal in scale to the distances measured. Construct perpendicular *FP* and sides *AD* and *BD*.

If however the boundaries are irregular (Fig. 4:39) it is necessary to mark out a triangle (*ABC* in the sketch), to measure the sides and angles of the triangle, and then to measure the distances of these triangle sides from the boundaries. These are called *offsets*. These offsets are measured by placing a marker post at the point where the offset reaches the boundary (i.e. point *FP*). Offsets are perpendicular to the side of the triangle and are measured with the cross staff sighted on to marker *A* and *FP*. After the offsets are measured, the lengths of the sides of the triangle are measured with a tape and the angles measured by using a prismatic compass. Sight

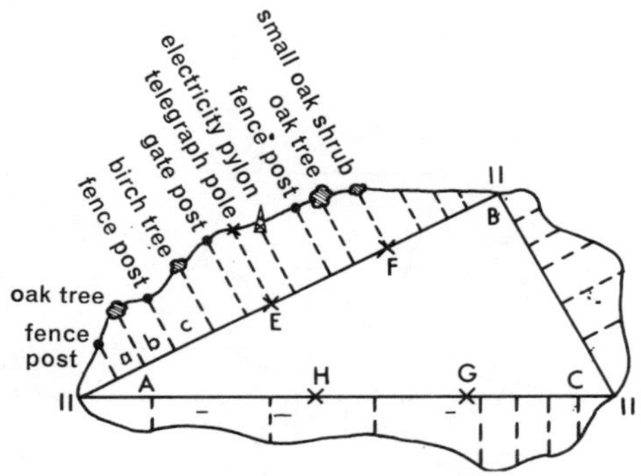

4 : 39 Layout for a survey of an irregular field.

from *A* to *C* and note the angle (e.g. 90°); measure from *A* to *B* and note the reading 61°. The bearings from *B* to *C*, *B* to *A*, *C* to *B* and *C* to *A* are measured in the same way.

The measurements can be plotted in the field book and then the survey is drawn to scale on squared paper.

2. The offset method is simple for an area which has a rectangular shape (Fig. 4:40). The procedure is as before. The line *AB* is measured and the offsets are measured at right angles to *AB* as before.

These survey methods can be used for areas of waste ground, woodlands and river terraces.

Offset	*Distance*	
	Point *F*	
Small oak shrub	10·67 m. (35 ft.)	
Oak tree	6·10 m. (20 ft.)	
Fence post	10·67 m. (35 ft.)	
Electricity pylon	13·72 m. (45 ft.)	
Telegraph pole	15·24 m. (50 ft.)	Total distance between offsets 170·68 m. (560 ft.)
Gate post	10·67 m. (35 ft.)	
To birch tree	15·24 m. (50 ft.)	
To fence post	6.10 m. (20 ft.)	Distance between the offsets
To oak tree	10·67 m. (35 ft.)	
To fence post 35 ft.	7·62 m. (25 ft.)	
	Point *A*	

Transect from *A* to *B*

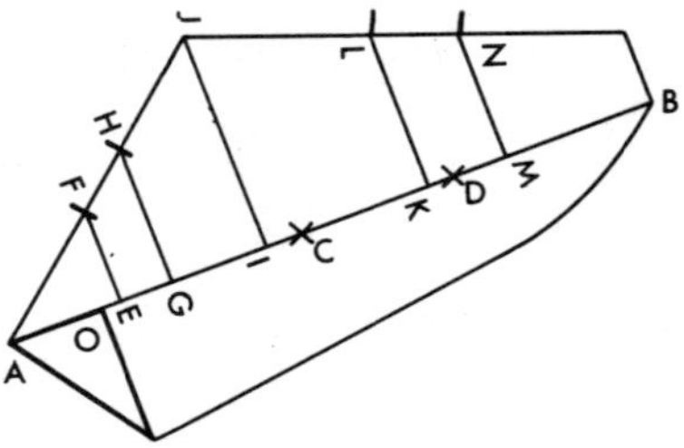

4 : 40 Measuring offsets. The offsets are measured from line AB.

Compass traverses can be made of surveys along linear routes. Some means of measurement, e.g. tape, clicker wheel, pacing, or a prismatic compass are needed.

In our diagram a distance is paced along the road from point *A* (50 paces). At this point a compass sight is taken on to a suitable object, the telegraph pole (295°). The position of each point is fixed by sighting it from two points, the distance between which is measured by pacing (Fig. 4:41). At each change of direction in the road further sightings are taken. From the field book the route can be plotted with a ruler and protractor.

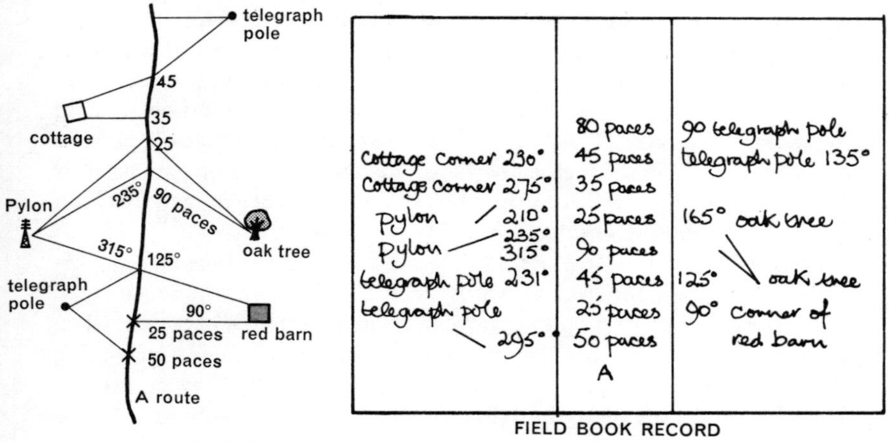

4 : 41 A compass traverse and field book record.

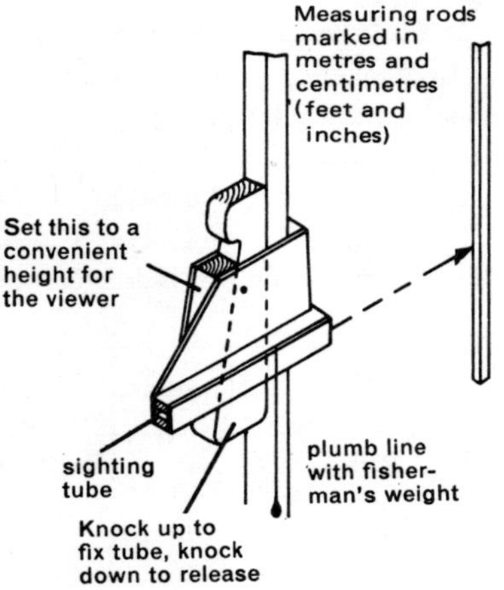

4 : 42 Making a surveyor's level.

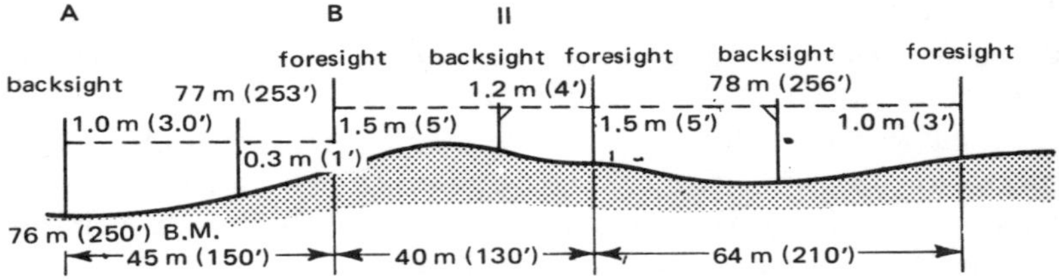

4 : 43 Surveying the height of the ground.

Levelling Transects across river valleys or along river profiles can be made using a measuring instrument, and a levelling instrument – a measuring staff. This level is described in Fig. 4:42. To make a transect (Fig. 4:43) requires three children, one to read through the level, another to see that the plumb-bob is vertical by observing from the side, and one to hold the staff to sight on to. The height of the first point is known either because it is a spot height or a bench mark (bench marks are found on gate posts or on stones thus ⩚) and are marked on the 25″ map. Bench mark lists can be obtained from the Ordnance Survey.

A sight taken backwards, i.e. in this case to the left is known as a *backsight* whereas the sight taken forwards, i.e. to the right, is the *foresight*.

The instrument is set up at a convenient point (*I*) and a backsight taken on to the staff at station *A* 76 m. (250 ft.) This backsight is 1 m. (3 ft.), and means that the height of the instrument is 76 + 1 = 77 m. (250 + 3, i.e. 253 ft.) This figure is written in the appropriate column. On the same line is written the height of the station 76 m. (250 ft.) and the distance, *O*. The staff is then moved on equal distance beyond the instrument to *B*, and a foresight, 0·3 m. (1 ft.), is taken. The distance between the two points is entered. The foresight is subtracted from the height of the instrument and this is the reduced level. The instrument is then moved beyond the staff station and a backsight is taken, 1·5 m. (5 ft.). Since this is the same staff station as the last foresight, the backsight figure is placed on the same line. The new height is found by adding the backsight to the reduced level of the place where the staff is held; the result is 78·2 m. (257 ft.).

The procedure is then continued until the whole transect is completed.

Backsight	Foresight	Height of Instrument	Reduced level	Distance	Remarks
3·0		253·0	250	0	Bench mark
5·0	1·0	257·0	252	150	
5·0	4·0	258·0	253	130	
	3·0		255		

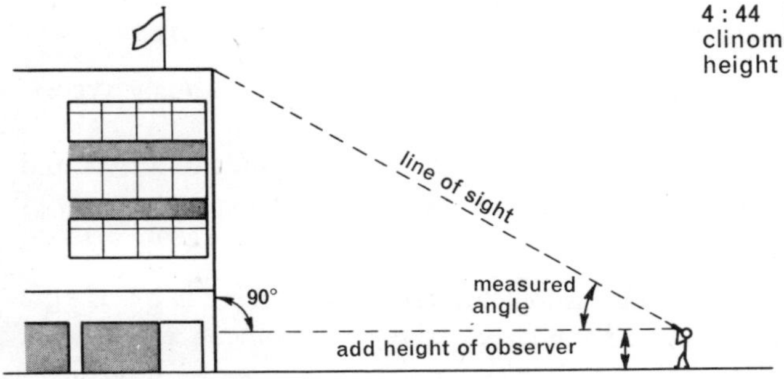

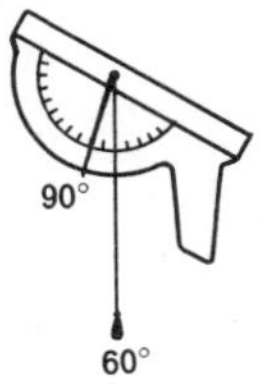

4 : 44 Using a clinometer to find the height of a building.

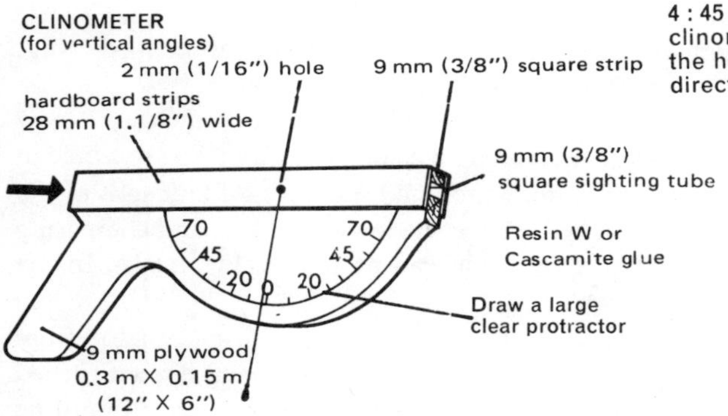

4 : 45 Making a clinometer to measure the height of a tree directly.

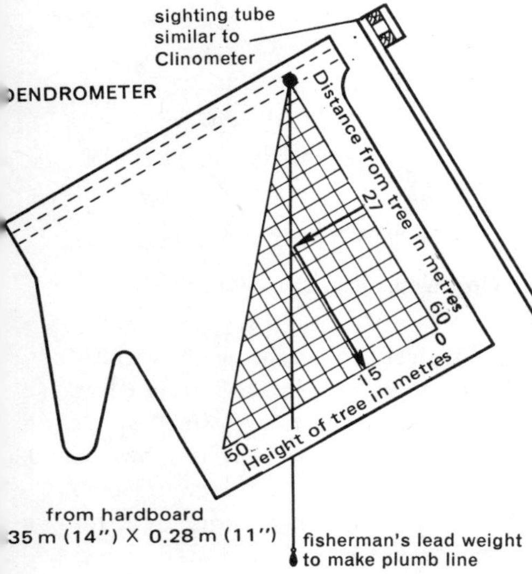

4 : 46 Making a dendrometer.

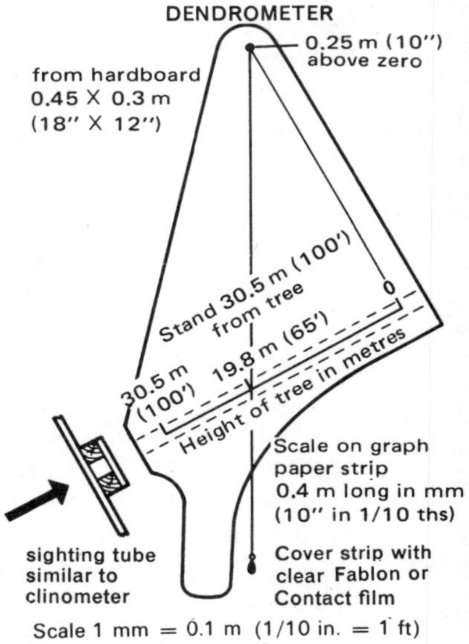

4 : 47 A dendrometer. This is used standing 30·5 m. (100 feet) from the tree.

These transects can be completed by adding information about vegetation, soil, rocks, slope, land use, buildings, etc.

A profile up a river valley can be made as part of a study of a river and this could be tied up with nature of the river bed, geology, rate of flow of the river and vegetation, etc.

Heights of buildings can be measured in various ways. One is by using a clinometer (Fig. 4:44). The method of making a clinometer is shown in Fig. 4:45. The height of the building can be found by making a scale drawing or the clinometer can be so made (Fig. 4:46) so that the height is read off from the instrument.

For the measurement of tree height the dendrometer can be made (Fig. 4:47).

Clinometers can also be used for measuring the angle of slopes.

The height of trees can be measured on a sunny day by sticking a pole in the ground near the tree to be measured and measuring the length of the shadow. By measuring the length of the shadow of the tree and comparing it with that of the pole, the tree height can be found (Fig. 4:48). In the example the tree is 8 m. high.

Height of trees can be obtained by a boy walking a distance away from the tree and sighting the height with a pencil. The pencil is then turned sideways and at the tree another boy moves in or out as directed until he comes to a spot equal to the height of the tree. Mark this with a peg or stone and measure the distance to the tree.

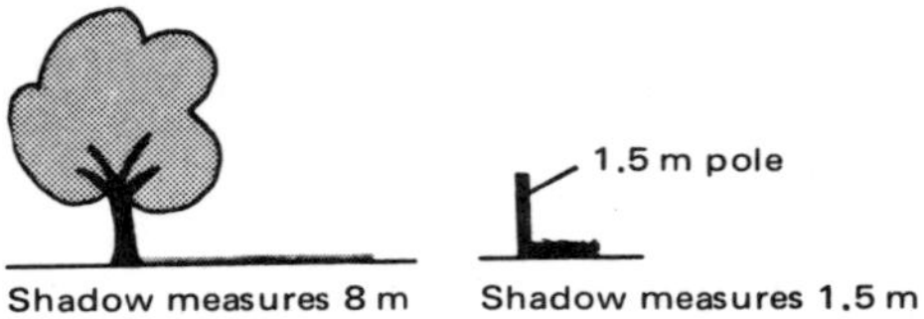

4 : 48 Finding the height of a tree by the shadow method.

Width of streams Part of a river study involves the measuring of its width. If there is a convenient bridge the distance can be measured easily either by measuring the distance across the bridge or if the river is small a rope can be carried across and measured. A more complex way is shown in (Fig. 4:49). Start measuring at a point opposite the landmark and pace along the river bank placing a stick *D* at a measured distance from the starting-point. Pace out the same distance beyond *D*. Turn at right angles (this can be measured as described earlier) and walk away from the river until point *D* is in line with the landmark.

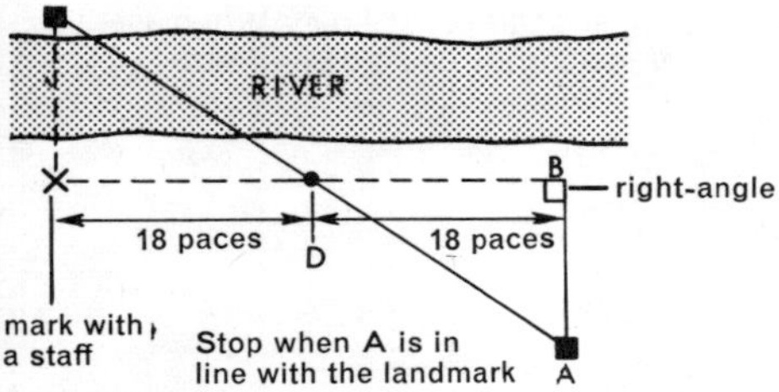

4:49 Finding the width of a stream: the similar triangle method.

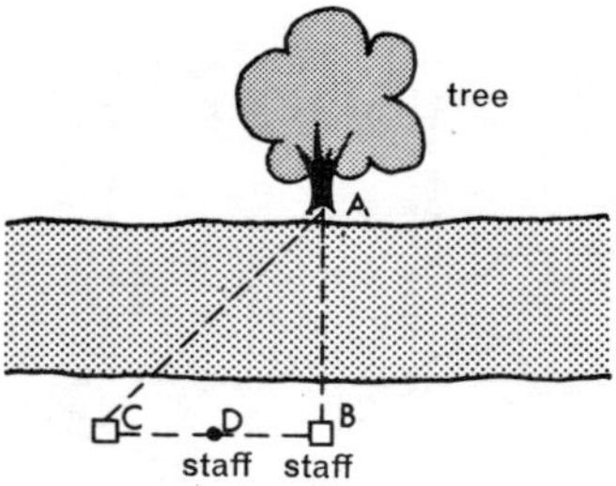

4 : 50 Finding the width of a stream: 45° set square method.

A 45° set square of the hardboard type can be used to find the width of a stream (Fig. 4:50). At right angles to the landmark *A* place a staff *B*. Walk along the river back from *B* and mark another point *D* with a staff between the points *B* and *C*. Set up the 45° triangle horizontally at a point *C* where points *D* and *B* are seen in line with one side of the triangle by one observer and point *A* can be seen by another observer. The distance *BC* is equal to the width of the river.

The depth of a stream can be measured at a bridge by marking a series of intervals along the parapet and sounding the depth of the water at each point with a plumb-line. The line should have a weight on the end and coloured ribbons to mark the depths.

Another way is to have a rope to which a marked stick is tied at right angles (Fig. 4:51). Another rope with tapes at intervals is tied from bank to bank. A boy stands at each end of the rope with the staff and this is dunked into the water while the depth is noted by a third boy. The staff is then pulled across to the next mark and the process repeated. If the end of the stick is hollowed out and fitted with a circular collar, stones from the bottom of the river can be collected in grease or wax contained in this collar.

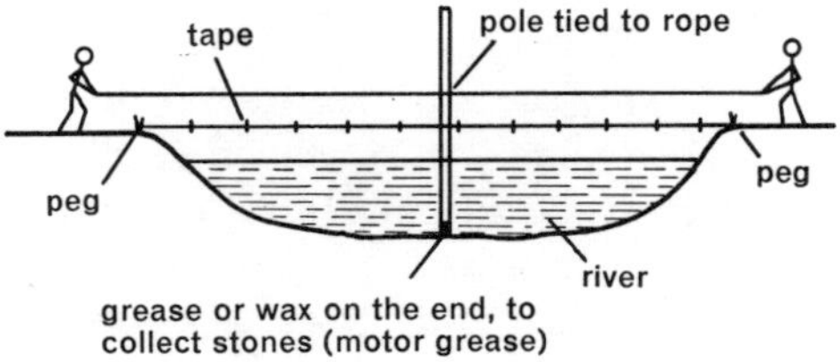

4:51 Measuring the depth of a stream and sampling the bottom.

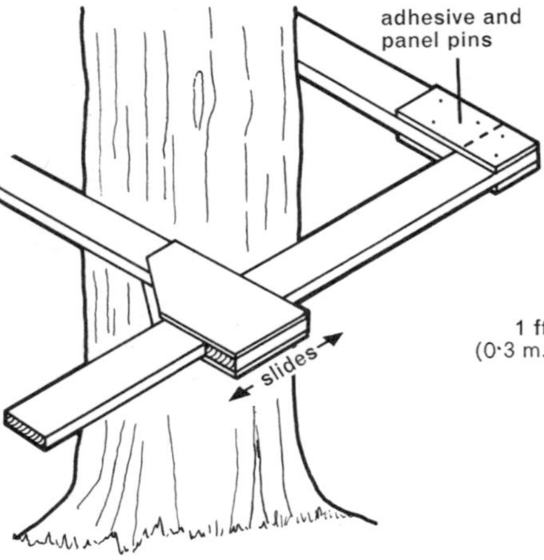

4:52 This diagram shows the construction of callipers. When used, these should be held in a horizontal position.

4 : 53 A simple quadrat.

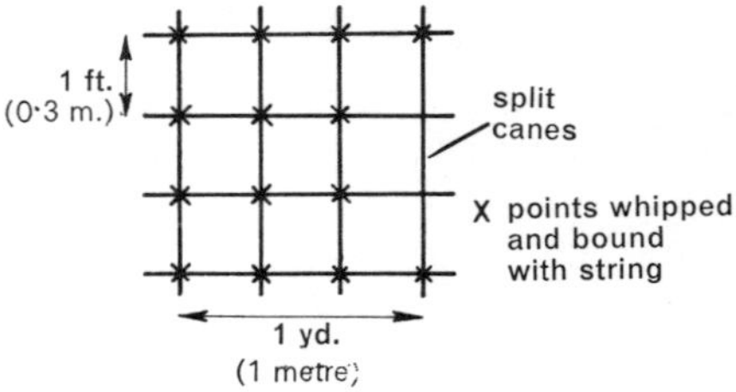

Girth of trees These can be measured either directly with a tape around or with callipers. Fig. 4:52 shows how these can be made.

METHODS OF SURVEY When carrying out a survey of some type it may be possible to investigate and if necessary map the whole area, as for example with a village; but if some larger area is to be covered it will be necessary to sample the area in some way by choosing the area to be studied either by deliberate selection, e.g. in a town where a sample may be made of an old historic part, of a new modern housing estate, of a high-class residential area, of a factory area, or by random sampling.

Transects are an excellent way of making samples. They are especially useful for the following purposes.

Town studies A transect can be made by pacing the distances along a street and noting the kinds of houses and shops on each side of the road. The house-types can be plotted on a 25″ map. Similar transects can be made of villages or other streets in the town.

Rural areas Transects can be made of land use, vegetation types, soils, physical features, etc. These transects may be surveyed as described in the earlier section or simply paced or measured with a tape.

Quadrat frames For studies of vegetation detailed studies can be made by using a simple quadrat frame, made of string and counting the number of species in each square (Fig. 4:53). The plants in the quadrat can be marked by use of the initial of the plant or a symbol, e.g. RW—Rosebay Willow Herb or Ұ =Rosebay Willow Herb.

Biological studies Transects are especially useful for biological studies. They may be of the belt or line type (Fig. 4:54). The belt transect covers

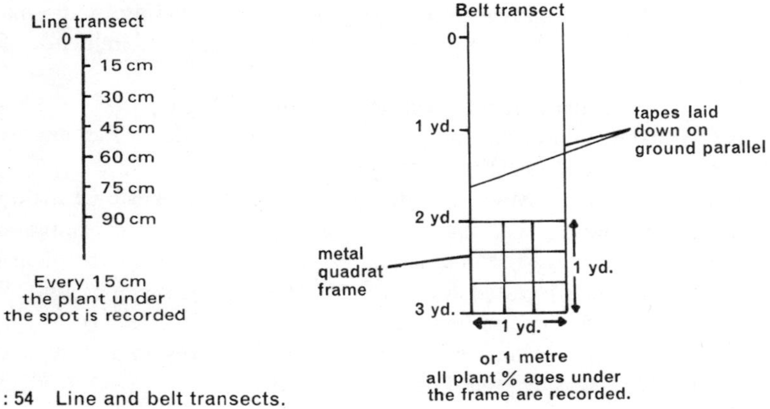

4 : 54 Line and belt transects.

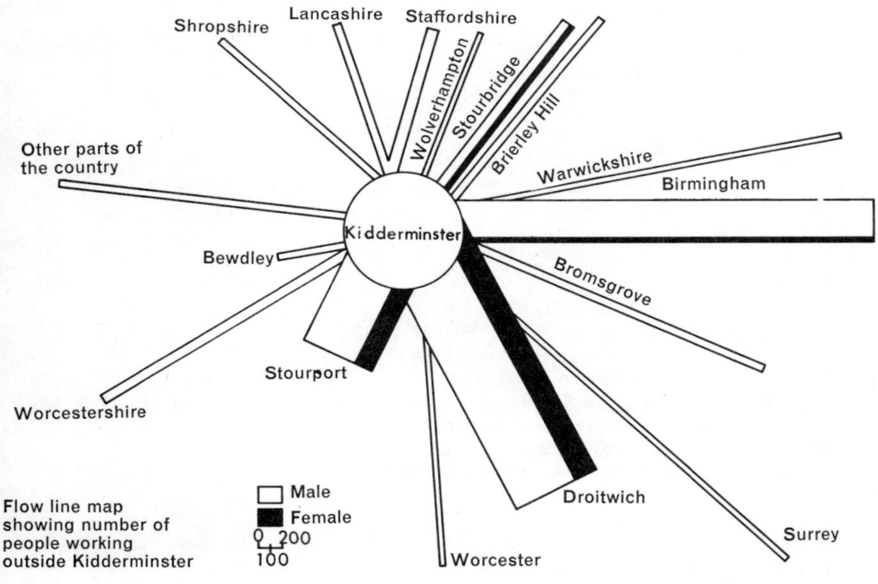

4 : 55 Flow map showing where the men and women work who live in Kidderminster and work outside the borough. The width of the line is proportional to the number.

a belt of given width, e.g. 1 metre or 1 yard that is measured along a line. The line transect is simple measurement as shown in Fig. 4:54.

Children's maps Much of the information obtained from these environmental studies can be mapped directly on to an outline map (especially a

25″ map). This is a simple process of colouring or shading in the map, e.g. house-types, land use, building uses, shops, sphere of influence of a town.

Other ways of mapping information are also useful.

1 *Flow maps* These are maps showing flow of goods, traffic, imports; exports, population, etc. (Fig. 4:55).

2 *Statistical maps* Much information can be put on maps by using dots or histogram blocks, e.g. these could show the number of employees employed in factories; the population by villages in an area; the plant or tree vegetation of a forested area, of fields or pieces of waste ground. Pie graphs (Fig. 4: 56) can also be used.

In this diagram the total of the commodity is expressed as 100% and therefore each 1% is measured by 3.6° of the circle.

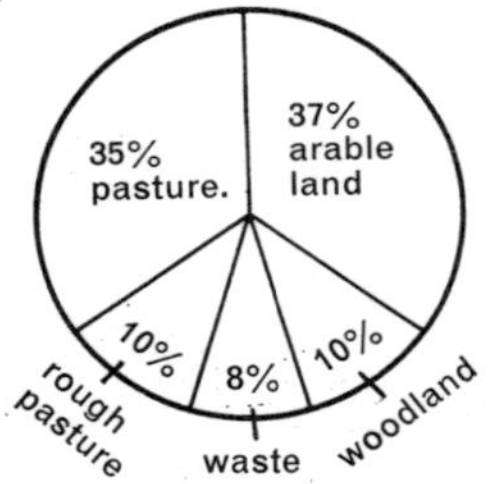

4 : 56 A pie graph: The land use of a parish.

Useful books:

Barker, R. S. *Maps.* Bodley Head.
Birch, T. W. *Maps.* Ward Lock Educational. 1963.
Debenham, F. *Map Making.* Blackie. 1963.
Hart, T. *Mapmaking.* Kaye and Ward.
Higgins, A. L. *Elementary Surveying.* Longman. 1970.
Gagg, J. C. *Maps and Symbols.* Blackwell.
Matkin, R. B. *Your Book of Maps and Map Reading.* Faber.
Purton, R. W. *Maps and Mapmaking.* Muller.

Slides of maps available from The Slide Centre, 17 Brodrick Road, London, S.W.17.

Rubbings and prints

(A) BRASS RUBBINGS Church brasses are of historic importance for they give a good picture of the costume of the period and focus on an individual of some importance whose history it may be possible to trace. Fig. 4:57 shows a typical brass rubbing.

Materials needed are a sheet of detail paper, black crayon or a heel-ball, a soft duster, weights or sticking paper for fixing the paper.

4:57 The brass of John Fortey Woolman.

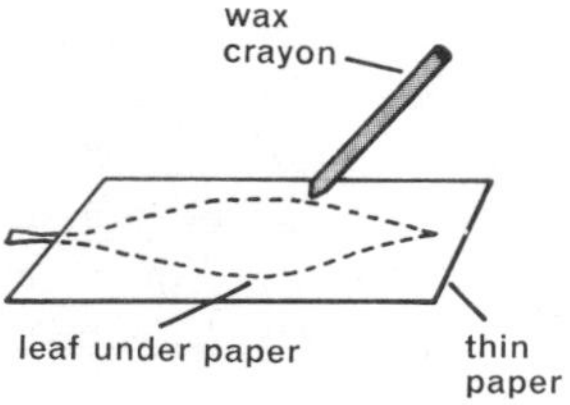

4 : 58 A leaf rubbing.

When the permission of the vicar has been obtained, dust the brass carefully, lay the paper over the brass and begin rubbing so that the paper does not slip. Apply the crayon in even strokes and do not lift the paper until the rubbing is finished. Do not go over the edges of the paper.

Another way of making rubbings is to rub them with white crayon and then to stain the whole rubbing with a black stain to pick out the lines. A useful stain is Dryad Ebony Stain, available from Dryads Ltd., of Leicester. After completion the rubbing can be mounted.

Books: Morris, M. *Brass Rubbing*, Studio Vista.
Gittings, Clare. *Brasses and Brass Rubbing*, Blandford.

(B) BARK RUBBINGS This is best done in pairs. Thin white paper is placed on the tree trunk and then while one pupil holds the paper the other covers the paper with firm even strokes of the heel-ball or cobblers' wax (obtainable from Woolworths or shoe-repair shops). The covering should be even enough to show up the pattern of the bark. The name of the tree and date of the rubbing should be written at the bottom of the sheet, and a line indicating the vertical should be drawn. These rubbings can be mounted on black paper at school.

Wax resist methods can be used by rubbing the paper over with a candle. Then the sheet is painted over with the same colour as the original bark and the raised part of the bark or twig remains colourless.

(C) BRICK AND BOND RUBBINGS Similar methods can be used to make records of the textures of building materials, e.g. stone, pebble dash. The various bonds of bricks can be recorded in the same way.

(D) LEAF PRINTS (Fig. 4:58) There are many ways of making leaf prints and some of them can be done at school. Details can be found in the section on 'Plants in the Classroom' in Chapter 7.

Plaster casts

These are especially useful for animal tracks, leaves, twigs and fruits. The main requirements are a supply of plaster of Paris, cardboard, a metal surround tin, a supply of water in a bottle, a mixing bowl and spoon, a tin of Vaseline, a cleansing rag, some wrapping material, newspaper, and a haversack or satchel for carrying the cast.

To make a plaster cast the track to be cast is surrounded by a strip of cardboard, that has been greased. An ice-cream carton with the bottom removed makes a useful surround. It has the advantage of being ready-waxed. The success of the cast is in making the plaster of the right consistency when it is added to the water and stirred. The plaster should be poured gently over the print and allowed to set for half an hour. Remove the surround, clean, trim and sandpaper the cast. The print should be varnished and the name and date of collecting should be painted or scratched on the back.

Casts can also be made of leaves by first pressing them into clay.

4 COLLECTING

Children should be discouraged from collecting plants and animals, since it is so important to conserve our natural flora and fauna. Many rare plants have been destroyed by careless collecting in the past. If the teacher considers some collection of plants essential, then it is suggested that only those which are extremely common and those that grow as weeds on cultivated land should be used.

It is suggested that observation, recording, sketching and photography *in situ* should largely take the place of collecting. Where collecting is mentioned in the pages that follow, it should be carried out with great care and with regard to conservation needs.

Useful Books:

Ary, S. and Gregory, M. *The Oxford Book of Wild Flowers.* O.U.P.
Carey, M. C. and Fitchew, D. *Wild Flowers at a Glance.* Dent.
Christiansen, M. *The Pocket Encyclopaedia of Wild Flowers.* Blandford.
Hall, C. A. *A Pocket Book of British Wild Flowers.* A. & C. Black.
Hutchinson. *British Wild Flowers.* Penguin.
Kosch, A. *Wild Flowers.* Burke.
Macleod, R. D. *Key to the Names of British Plants.* Pitman. 1952.
Nicholson, B. E. *The Oxford Book of Garden Flowers.* O.U.P. 1970.
Philipson, W. R. *Wild Flowers.* A. & C. Black. 1950.
Ross, A. *Wild Flowers in Britain.* Blackwell.
Scott, T. H. and Stokoe, W. J. *Wild Flowers of the Wayside and Woodland.* Warne.
Stokoe, W. J. *The Observer's Book of Wild Flowers.* Warne. 1956.

Ferns and grasses Can be collected in the same way as flowers although a large box and slightly larger presses may be necessary.

Useful books include:
Groves, J. *Grasses,* Parts I, II, III. School Natural Science Society (pamphlets). 1972.
Rose, F. *Observer's Book of Grasses, Sedges and Rushes.* Warne.
Step, E. *Wayside and Woodland Ferns.* Warne. 1965.
Stokoe, W. J. *The Observer's Book of Ferns.* Warne. 1961.
Taylor, P. *British Ferns and Mosses.* Eyre and Spottiswoode. 1960.

Cultivated flowers, fruits and vegetables

Gardens and flower shops provide an opportunity for the study of flowers in an urban environment. This could also lead to a geographical study of the places where many of the shop flowers are grown and how they are transported. The history of the flowers makes an excellent study. The greengrocer's shop similarly provides a study of fruits and vegetables.

TYPES OF FRUIT AND VEGETABLES IN A GREENGROCER'S SHOP

Type	*The parts that we use*
Potatoes	Stem tubers
Artichokes	Stem tubers
Onions	Bulb
Carrots	Swollen-tap roots
Turnips	Swollen-tap roots
Cabbages	Large vegetative buds
Cauliflowers	Large inflorescences
Brussels Sprouts	Swollen buds
Peas	Seeds
Tomatoes	Fruits (True berries)
Gooseberries	True berries
Blackberries	Compound drupes
Apples and Pears	False fruits (pomes)
Nuts	Single-seeded dry fruits

Mosses and Lichens These are collected and are dried and transferred to envelopes, all of which must be clearly labelled. Lichens will keep if dried well.

Fungi Fungi can be collected; but they are very difficult to preserve and should be drawn, painted or photographed, as soon after collection as possible. Spore prints are interesting. Cut through the stalk (stipe) close to the head and place the head down on white paper, gill side down (Fig. 4:59).

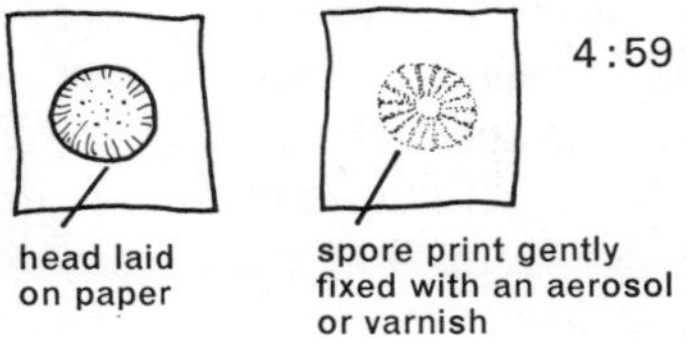

4:59 A spore print.

Fungi can also be grown in natural or artificial media (see Chapter 7 on Living Things).

Book: Hvass, *Mushrooms and Toadstools in Colour*, Blandford.

Trees Collect twigs with buds, leaves with flowers and leaves with fruits. Some flowers are very difficult to press; but the fruits can either be dried and stored in a box, or they can be stored in moss and then planted in the spring. Some of these will germinate and others will not.

The making of plaster casts is discussed earlier.

Skeleton leaves can be collected, sometimes ready rotted. Otherwise they can be made by processing ripe leaves. The leaves should be allowed to stand in water in which cabbage has been rotted. When they are well rotted they should be crushed with chloride of lime, dried between blotting paper and glued on to black paper. They can also be produced chemically by submerging them in boiling water for one or two minutes and then transferring them to a strong solution of potassium permanganate. After two hours the specimens can be removed, bleached and mounted.

The girth, height, flowering habits and amount of growth of trees can be studied season by season. The trees in the local park can be plotted on a map. A short step takes the children to a study of different kinds of timbers and their world-wide history and distribution.

The school forestry project is one way of tackling this problem (see Chapter 3).

Some recommended books are:

Darlington, A. *The World of a Tree.* Faber.
Hadfield, M. *Your Book of Trees.* Faber.
Hall, C. A. and Jay, B. A. *British Trees* ('Young Naturalists' Series). Black. 1951.
Kosch, A. *Trees.* Burke.
Lemmon, R. S. *Trees.* Muller. 1963.
Lister, G. *Conifers* ('School Natural Science' Series). Heffer. 1972.
Prime, C. T. and Deacock, R. J. *Trees and Shrubs.* Heffer. 1970.
Schwartz, A. *Bark.* Thames and Hudson. 1956.
Shepherd, W. *Let's Look at Trees.* Muller. 1964.
Step, E. and Edlin, H. *Wayside and Woodland Trees.* Warne. 1964.
Stokoe, W. J. *The Observer's Book of Trees.* Warne. 1961.
Wood, J. B. *Growing and Studying Trees.* Blandford. 1966.

Pond or river study

It would be as well to start this study in early April and continue at frequent intervals through May and June. The study is very worthwhile for all ages in the Primary School and should provide stimulus for worthwhile work in other subjects as well as Natural Science.

Teachers should select from the account given below, material suitable to the age and ability of the children. The need for good class control during a study of this kind is obvious. Students on teaching practice should ensure that the class teacher is in attendance when the fieldwork is being undertaken.

First visit

This should be well organised and planned. The teacher should have previewed the area and 'sampled' it so that the commoner plants and animals are known.

The class should be encouraged to take with them note and sketch books and prominent features of the locality should be recorded by the children on the spot. Flowers, fruits, seeds, twigs and bark rubbings should be collected. In this context, discourage wholesale collection of plants; there is no merit in bulk and the countryside could easily be denuded of plants by over-eager children. A lesson on 'Nature Conservation' prior to a visit would not be out of place.

Dipping in the pond or stream at this time of year may be unproductive but should be undertaken; however frog spawn may well be found. All animals found in water can be taken back to the classroom and kept in very large jam jars or fish tanks. Keep the water-level low in order to give as large a surface to volume ratio as possible. Do not over-stock your aquaria. Keep tanks in a cool but fairly light place; the main danger is over-heating. The cardinal rule with animals in classroom is *if we cannot get it to feed it is returned.* Just two or three of each kind of animal is quite enough.

Classroom work

If the visit has been well planned it should be successful and the children will be stimulated to go further. All material collected should, if possible, be identified by *the children* and a good selection of suitable books is therefore essential (see bibliographies). The teacher only gives help with identification when the child is in difficulty. Direct, guide, assist but *let the children find out.*

Things to do immediately and again following later visits.

(1) Identify.

(2) Draw, paint, sketch, trees, flowers, fish, insects, etc.

(3) Bark rubbings.

(4) Find out how animals live in, on and near water, feeding, breathing, reproducing, enemies, etc., etc.

(5) Food chains.

(6) Temperature of water compared with land – take readings regularly.

Some plants may not be in flower and therefore may be difficult to identify. If they are removed with a clump of earth and placed in a plastic bag they can be replanted in an old sink or plastic bowl and identified as they flower. Try to recreate in the sink the conditions under which the plants were living.

Treatment of material

Plants

Flowers may be pressed and it is good practice to press also the leaves and roots. These are aids to identification. They can be placed on grey or white card and covered with transparent Fablon. Try to arrange them, prior to pressing, so that the flowers and leaves are shown to best advantage. Each card should be labelled with the name of the plant, the date of collection, the place of collection and with any other interesting observation, e.g. 'only a few plants in flower on this day'.

A chart or diary should be started as a long-term project which will demonstrate the life cycle of the plants in your district for that particular year.

The pressings may later be assembled in a book or wall chart form as part of the display on the study.

This is unique as every area will differ slightly from elsewhere – also each year will be different. If this is done for several years then one can easily check such statements as 'late spring', 'early summer' from the behaviour of the flora and fauna in your area.

Pond animals

Have one child of a group in charge. Keep a chart by the tank on which dates of feeding – not too often – are recorded. The water from the pond is better than tap water for 'topping up'.

Daphnia and cyclops (water 'fleas') are the best foods for many fish. They can be collected readily from ponds by butter muslin nets and will provide really excellent diet. As they remain alive until eaten they do not foul the water.

Many pond animals are carnivorous, e.g. dragonfly nymphs, diving beetles and their nymphs. They will eat the rest of the animals in the tank. Children can consult reference books to find out the diet of animals and segregate as necessary. Read about the life cycles and encourage organisms to breed by providing correct conditions. Sticklebacks will breed fairly readily in a classroom tank.

Animals should be observed, drawn regularly and changes noted. Behaviour should be recorded. Questions can be set, e.g. How does a pond skater walk on water? This provides a wonderful introduction to the study of surface tension with older juniors. What happens if we put a pond skater on clean water in a jam jar and add some detergent to the water? Can razor blades float on water? Why does a diving beetle come to the surface?

Why are gnat larvae lying on the surface? Remove some to clean water in a jam jar. Cover surface with thin film of oil. What happens? Why? (Malaria and control of mosquito.)

There are many possible lines of development in this field.

Amphibia, e.g. frogs, toads and newts

There is an excellent chapter on their care in Maxwell Knight's *Frogs, Toads and Newts of the British Isles* (Brockhampton Press, 1962).

Do not keep too many tadpoles. Maxwell Knight recommends 6–7 per tank. Very young tadpoles can be fed on crushed lettuce. Older tadpoles can be removed into a pie dish and fed on worms for twenty minutes. This prevents uneaten worms from fouling the tank.

Toad tadpoles tend to be blacker and smaller than the 'furry-golden' frog tadpoles of the same age.

Keeping sticklebacks in an aquarium is another possibility.

Related projects

1 Mapping the pond or river.

Its position in relation to the school, village, etc., should be shown. Older juniors may make a quantitative survey of the area. A 25″ or 50″ map should be obtained and enlarged if necessary so that the position of individual trees, bushes, etc. around the pond can be shown.

2 Uses of pond or stream.

Uses of the pond or river both today and in the past. Children glean information from parents, aged villagers, old books, etc. Flooding, freezing, drownings are subjects likely to arise.

3 Trout streams.

Investigation might be made into prices paid for fishing rights and the habits of trout. Start trout-breeding which is relatively straightforward if running tap-water can be made available.

Later visits

Ideas and interests quickened in preliminary visit will be followed-up by the children. Sometimes the children will be working in a group united in a common goal. Some children will perhaps be working alone at a unique interest.

Give the children a purpose to their work. You may well have an exhibition for the whole school to see. All the class should be able to see the work done by individuals so that the exhibition provides a time when all relevant material can be assembled.

Other topics

(1) What is the bottom of the pond or stream made of? Collect samples either by hand or by a lead pipe which has one end blocked and smeared with Vaseline. Try to identify any stones found.

(2) Plot the depth of the pond or river. If it is small and shallow it can be waded but push a stick in before you enter as many ponds have very thick mud bottoms.

With muddy ponds, their depth can be shown by 'dunking' (Fig. 4:65).

(3) Speed of flow of rivers should be recorded. This can be done by dropping in soft drink cans and timing the flow over a given distance (speed in knots; 1 knot—1 nautical mile, i.e. 1,830 m. (2,000 yds.) per hour). Is the speed the same over the whole of the river or is it faster near banks?

(4) Nature of bottom – bedrock or drift.

(5) Form and nature of the sides, i.e. undercutting or deposition.

(6) Classification of plants and animals found. A very useful School Natural Science Society pamphlet on this is available.

Many forms found will be larvae of insects. If properly fed and given the correct conditions these will turn into imagos. Small tanks with a few or even individual species are preferable to large tanks for some carnivores, e.g. Dytiscus.

(7) If plenty of clay is available in school fix up your own 'river' with a bend, place small corks and note flow around bend. This work leads on to a simple study of river erosion.

Tips on techniques

1 Keep children quiet on pond or river side; otherwise you will catch very little.

2 Collect pond weeds with drag. These will yield much on placing in water in classroom.

3 Scrape bottom to collect bottom dwellers.

4 Small rotten tree branches often have large colonies of Hydra which are not obvious until the branch is re-immersed in water.

5 Do not waste time trying to catch large fish – they will not survive in a classroom anyway.

Books for classroom:
Ainsworth, R. *By Pond and Stream.* Heinemann.
Allen, G. and Denslow, J. *Freshwater Animals.* O.U.P.
Clegg, J., ed. *Pond and Stream Life.* Blandford, 1973.
Clegg, J. *Freshwater Life of British Isles.* Warne. 1965.
Clegg, J. *Observer's Book of Pond Life.* Warne. 1967
Engelhardt, W. and Merxmuller, H. *Pond Life.* Burke.
Wong, H. and Vessel, M. *Pond Life.* Addison-Wesley.

Books for teacher:
Macfadyen, A. *Animal Ecology.* Pitman, 1970.
Mellanby, H. *Animal Life in Fresh Water.* Methuen, 1963.

Useful equipment
Honey jars (screw-tops)
Large tins with lids and string handles
1 collecting net (old chip basket lined with muslin and fitted to brush handle)

Seaweeds Zoning of seaweeds is excellent evidence of the importance of biological adjustments to the site.

Equipment needed: haversack or old basket; screw-top jars; sharp knife; a supply of polythene bags; piece of zinc 28 × 23 cm. (11″ × 9″); supply of muslin washed to remove the lint; paint brushes; setting needle.

The seaweeds should be carefully collected and put with a date slip into bags. When a number have been collected they should be washed in a bowl of sea water and placed in a second bowl. To mount take paper or white card, lay it on the zinc and gently submerge it in a third bowl with the paper uppermost. When the arrangement is complete, lift and tilt the plate. To press put 6 sheets of blotting paper on the pressing board, and add one sheet of mounting paper continuing until all the specimens are inserted. Then press for six hours and change the paper. (Some weeds rot in fresh water; therefore they should be washed in sea water.)

Book: Dickinson, C. I. *British Seaweeds*. Eyre and Spottiswoode. 1963.

Animals from the fishmonger's shop

For urban children the fishmonger's slab presents a whole array of fish and other animals. Rabbits and hares are mammals. Many birds may appear such as hens, cockerels, turkeys, ducks and geese, pheasants, partridges and grouse, when they are in season. Deep sea fish of many kinds appear – plaice, sole, cod, eels, halibut, mackerel and others. Oysters, whelks and cockles are molluscs, while crabs, lobsters, prawns and shrimps are members of the crustacea.

Collecting shells Shell collecting needs a scoop, preferably oblong with a rounded end, tins, glass-tubes, forceps, cotton wool, old flour bags and a pond net. Shell creatures can be killed by dropping them into hot water. Univalve shells can be cleaned with a pin and the shell should be washed and dried. If it is not possible to remove all the animal the shell should be sealed with sealing wax. Shells can be sectioned either by rubbing on a file for coarse shells or on sandpaper for the less robust shells.

Books:
Barrett, J. and Yonge, C. M. *Pocket Guide to the Seashore*. Collins. 1951.
Evans, I. O., ed. *Observer's Book of Sea and Seashore*. Warne.
Jackman, L. *Exploring the Seashore*. Evans.
Kosch, A. *Seashore*. Burke.

Marshall, N. B. *Ocean Life in Colour.* Blandford. 1973.
Yonge, C. M. *The Sea Shore* ('New Naturalist' Series). Collins. 1949.
Vevers, G. *Seashore Life in Colour.* Blandford. 1969.

Mammals For the urban environment, the main animals that can be observed are the domestic ones, dogs and cats, the animals that can be reared in school (see Chapter 7), or farm animals, birds, cows, sheep, goats, pigs, horses. In rural environments it is possible to investigate them on a more detailed scale. Many tracks can be found. These may be food tracks, foot tracks, droppings or the homes of these animals.

Food tracks may be skeletons of cones of the Scots Pine left by squirrels, hazel nuts opened by a field mouse, or snail shells broken by a song thrush. Individual animals and birds have characteristic foods and ways of eating their food.

Tracks are collected by making them into plaster casts or by making life size drawings.

The homes of the animals can be discovered, mapped and observed. Great skill is needed however to photograph these animals. A visit to a museum where these animals are preserved could be used to develop a mammal project.

The smaller mammals can be trapped by setting mammal traps in the hedgerows. The Longworth Mammal Trap is excellent (Fig. 4:60). The traps must be visited at least once a day so that no animal is in the trap too long.

4:60 A Longworth Mammal Trap.

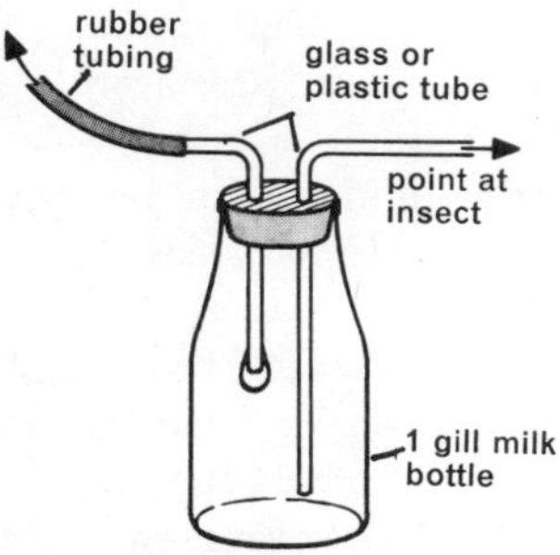

4:61 A Pooter. Breath is drawn in through the rubber tubing and the insect is drawn into the bowl.

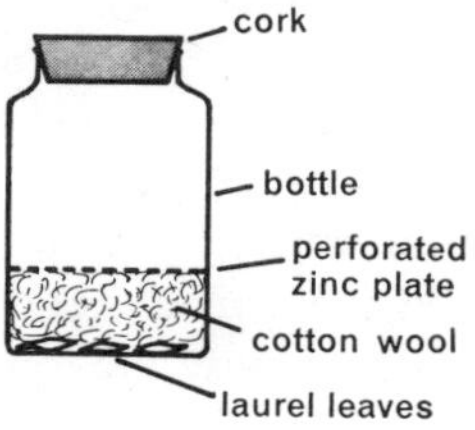

4:62 A killing jar.

Books:
Branley, F. M. *Big Tracks, Little Tracks.* Black.
Carrington, R. *The Mammals.* Time-Life.
Ford, R. *British Wild Animals.* Black.
Keeling, C. H. *Meet the Mammals.* Harrap.
Lawrence, M. J. and Brown, R. W. *Mammals of Britain: Their Tracks, Trails and Signs.* Blandford. 1973 (revised edition).
Lemmon, R. S. *Big Cats.* Muller. 1963. (A very good detailed account of tracks.)
Osmond, E. *Animals in Great Britain.* Four Square Books.
Pike, O. G. *Wild Animals in Britain.* Macmillan. 1950.
Ross, A. *Tracking Animals.* Blackwell.
Seton, E. T. *Animal Tracks and Hunter Signs.* Ward. 1960.
Stehli, C. and Brohmer, P. *Mammals and Animals.* Burke.
Stephen, D. ed. *Mammals.* Collins.
Williamson, M. *Mammals.* F. Watts.

Insects Requirements are a glass-bottomed pill box, or tobacco tin, walking stick for beating, forceps, nets, a pooter (Fig. 4:61), a newspaper or beating tray. Insects can be collected at night by sugaring trees. Choose a rough-barked tree, such as elm, oak, poplar, silver birch. Sweeping in thick herbage will collect a large number of specimens. Ponds, clumps of grass, moss, decaying vegetation all afford a large yield of insects. Small insects are picked up with a pooter. They can also be found by lifting stones, old logs, cow dung or the bodies of dead birds and animals. The stones should be replaced, so that the natural environment is not disturbed. Insects can be caught by beating bushes on to a newspaper. When caught, the specimens should be placed in a collecting jar (Fig. 4:62) containing ethyl acetate and carbon tetrachloride.

When dead the insects should be placed in a paper envelope made with typing paper or newspaper. A date is put on the flap. The insect can then be set at home. An excellent way of preserving insects is to kill them with ethyl acetate and preserve them in alcohol or formalin. Formalin is very cheap and is obtainable from chemists. This should be made into a 4% solution. If this is kept in an airtight jar the insects will keep for ever.

Pupae can also be collected and killed by being dropped in hot water (this water should be just off the boil). After drying in blotting paper they can be stored in cork-lined airtight cases containing naphthalene flakes. Some of the pupae should be allowed to hatch.

Jam jars set in the bushes at frequent intervals make excellent traps. A statistical count could be made of the catch in each jar and information obtained about the times of the day when these insects are most active.

Moths and butterflies can be caught in nets and killed and set in the same way.

Books:
Allen, G. and Denslow, J. *Insects and Other Small Animals.* O.U.P.
Clegg, J. *Insects.* Muller.
Daglish, E. F. *Name This Insect.* Dent.
Dibb, J. R. *Field Book of Beetles.* A. Brown & Son.
Gillespie, T. H. *Our Friends the Spiders.* Chatto.
Hirons, M. J. *Insects of Farm and Garden.* Blandford Press. 1966.
Hyde, C. *British Insects.* Black.
Hyde, G. E. *British Insects.* A. & C. Black.
Ladyman, P. *Ladybird, Butterfly and Earwig* ('Stand and Stare' Series). Methuen.
Linnsen, E. and Newman, L. H. *Observer's Book of Common Insects and Spiders.*
Prior, M. *Insects.* Black.
Riley, N. *Insects in Colour.* Blandford, 1973.
Sandars, E. *An Insect book for the Pocket.* O.U.P.
Savoury, T. H. *Spiders.* Muller. 1965.
Sherman, J. *Insects.* Dobson.
Warnicke, G. *Butterflies.* Burke.
Williamson, M. *Insects and Spiders.* F. Watts.

Soils Soils can be collected by using a soil auger (the light screw type) available from Baird and Tatlock Ltd., Freshwater Rd., Chadwell Heath, Essex. Soil sections can also be dug out with a spade and put in a bag or tin. It is important not to disturb the sequence of the soils and careful notes should be taken of the colour and depth of the layers. It is possible to preserve a soil profile by using a piece of spouting from an old building and wrapping the profile around with plastic or Sellotape. A series of profiles could be preserved in this way. A soil monolith or profile can be made by sticking the parts of the profile on to a flat piece of board.

The acidity of the soil should be taken either with litmus paper or a pH kit (obtainable from B.D.H. Ltd., Poole, Dorset). The soil is mixed with barium sulphate and distilled water to which the indicator is added. The soil then changes colour and the colour is matched against the colour chart. The vegetation of the soil should be described.

Back at school, different kinds of soil could be collected with their characteristic vegetation, together with an analysis of the soil, colour, texture, pH, etc. This leads to a series of experiments on plant nurture with different fertilisers.

A very useful reference book for children is *Soils* by G. A. Perry (Blandford Press).

Rocks and fossils Equipment needed is a geological map showing the varying strata, a rucksack and newspaper – or, better, bags in which to collect the specimens. The names of the specimen, location and date should be marked on the bag or paper and also written on a separate piece of paper which is included in the wrapping. A blank paper pad should be taken and a geological hammer and chisel are very useful. If the fossil is very large a return journey should be made, taking a crowbar. Many good fossils are obtained from the scree material at the base of a cliff particularly in spring after the winter weathering has brought down fresh falls of rock. A stiff clothes brush is useful for cleaning away rock dust and shellac can be used to harden soft material. If the specimens are damp they should be wrapped in waterproof wrapping. A pocket knife is used for testing hardness of rocks. A hand lens helps to identify the rocks and dropper bottles (plastic ones are safest) are obtainable from A. R. Horwell Ltd., 17 Cricklewood Broadway, London, N.W.2. These hold the weak hydrochloric acid which is used for testing of calcareous rock. Photographs make a good record and should be taken if possible.

On returning to school the fossils should be carefully cleaned by using a wire brush and a hammer and chisel or a penknife. Limestone can be dissolved with a solution of 15% acetic acid or 10% formic acid. Great care should be taken that all the fossil is not dissolved away. If the fossils break they can be joined with Durafix P.V.A. glue.

Fossil sites locations are discussed in Chapter 3, while the main groups of common fossils are illustrated in Fig. 4:63. At school model landscapes of the bygone geological eras can be constructed.

Rocks Rocks are of three main types, volcanic, sedimentary and metamorphic. To identify them a fresh face should be broken with a hammer and note taken of the colour and arrangement of the minerals. The following characteristics can be observed.

1 Hardness This is measured by MOH's Scale of Hardness (see over).
2 Colour
3 Texture – gritty, sandy, clayey, etc.
4 Smell
5 Taste – Rock salt is easily identified in this way
6 Strength
7 Weight
8 Characteristics of the rock when heated
9 Shape

MOH'S SCALE OF HARDNESS

Hardness	Reference mineral	Remarks
1	Talc	Can be scratched by the finger nail
2	Gypsum	
3	Calcite	Can be scratched by a brass pin or copper coin
4	Fluorspar	Easily scratched by a knife
5	Apatite	Scratched with difficulty by a knife
6	Orthoclase	Easily scratched by file
7	Quartz	Scratched with difficulty by a file
8	Topaz	All minerals harder than 6 will scratch glass
9	Corundum	
10	Diamond	

The reference material (rock type) is drawn across a fresh face of the rock to be tested and if a scratch is visible the unknown is softer than the reference material.
Crystalline rocks are often igneous. The table below shows the characteristic groups.

Igneous Rocks

Group and Texture	*Chemical Composition*	
Volcanic (Glassy)	*Acid*	*Basic*
	Ryholite	Basalt Tachylite
Intrusive Large crystals in a fine matrix	Felsite Porphyry	Dolerite
Plutonic Large crystals	Granite	Gabbro

Sedimentary Rocks are generally in layers (stratified) and consist of particles of other rocks transported and laid down by wind, water or ice.
Metamorphic Rocks are those that have been changed by heat and pressure. This either changes the mineral form, as in the creation of mica, or presses the rocks into new planes of cleavage (breakage) or into layers (foliation).

The study of the evolution of life throughout Geological Time can be studied. A simplified Geological Table is given on p. 176.

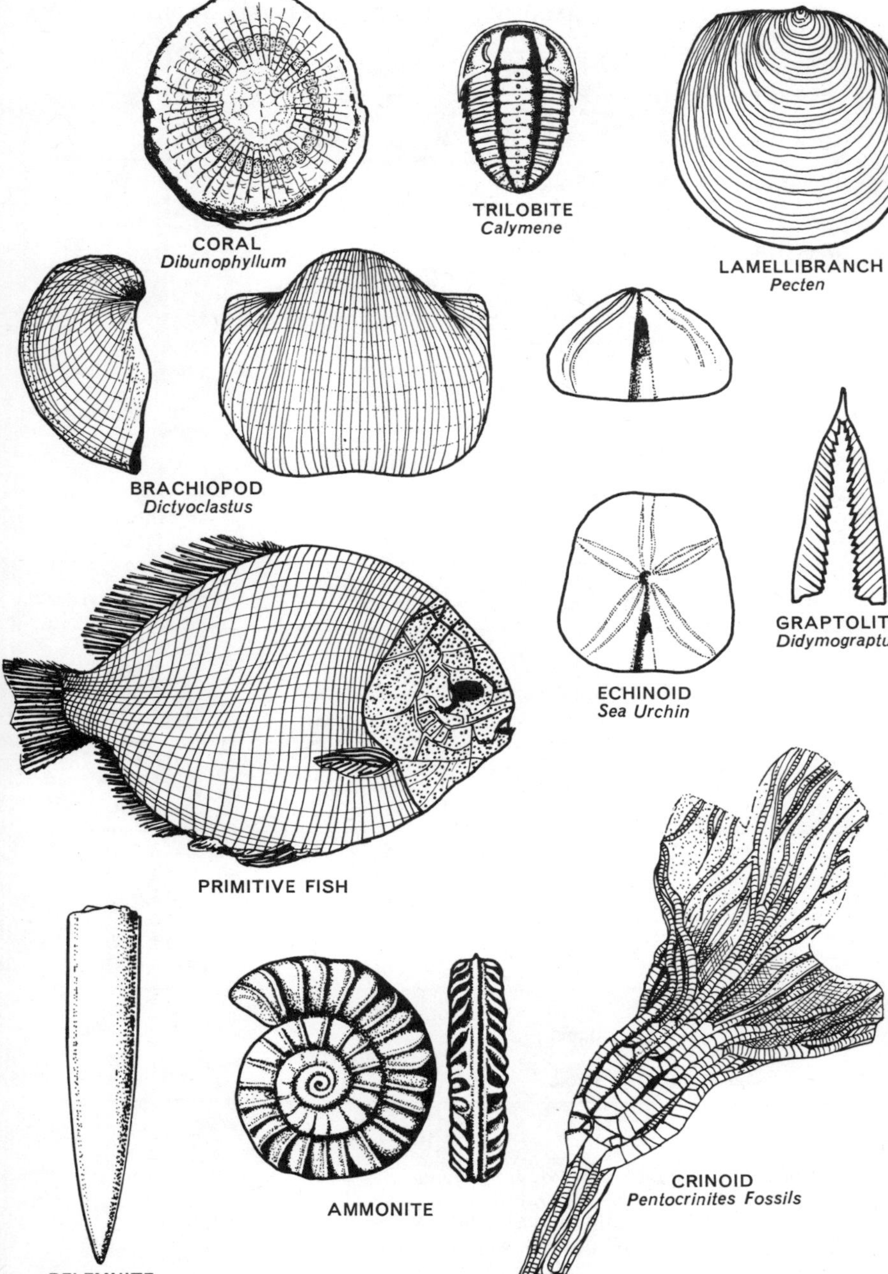

4:63 Some common fossils.

Metamorphic Rocks	
Strong Cleavage	Very fine grained – *Slate* Much flaky Mica on cleavage – *Phyllite*
Foliation well marked	Folia thin and wavy – SCHIST Folia coarse – GNEISS
Massive and compact	Hardness 3 to 3·5, Effervesces with acid – *Marble* Hard, does not effervesce with acid – *Quartzite*

THE GEOLOGICAL TIME SCALE

Age in millions of years	*Era*	*Period*	*Thickness in Metres*
1	Quaternary	Pleistocene and Holocene	1,800
11	Caeno-zoic	Pliocene	4,500
25		Miocene	6,500
40		Oligocene	8,000
70		Eocene	13,000
135	Mesozoic	Cretaceous	15,500
180		Jurassic	13,500
255		Triassic	9,000
270	Palaeo-zoic	Permian	6,000
350		Carboniferous	14,000
400		Devonian	11,500
440		Silurian	10,500
500		Ordovician	12,000
600		Cambrian	13,000
	Proter-ozoic	Pre-Cambrian	
4,500	Azoic		

Books

Kirkaldy, J. F. *Minerals and Rocks in Colour.* Blandford. 1973 (latest edn.)
Kirkaldy, J. F. *Fossils in Colour.* Blandford (revised ed. 1970.)
Pearl, R. M. *Introduction to the Mineral Kingdom.* Blandford. 1966.
Swinnerton, H. H. *Fossils* ('New Naturalist' Series). Collins. 1970.
British Museum *Palaeozoic Fossils.* H.M.S.O.
British Museum *Mesozoic Fossils.* H.M.S.O.
British Museum *Caenozoic Fossils.* H.M.S.O.

A simple key to Sedimentary Rocks

	Rock consists of individual grains Siliceous or sandy	Effervesces with hydro-chloric acid *Calcareous*	Earthy smell when breathed on *Clayey*
Pebbles in a fine matrix	Pebbles angular – BRECCIA Pebbles rounded – CONGLOMERATE		Pebbles angular – BOULDER CLAY
Grains comparatively uniform	Grains rounded – SANDSTONE Grains angular – GRIT	Grains round – COLITIC LIME-STONE	
Compact individual grains scarcely visible – FLINT		Soft and friable - CHALK. Harder with calcite visible – LIMESTONE Plastic in water – CLAY Non plastic in water – FULLER'S EARTH Laminated and can be split into thin leaves – SHALE. Contains quartzose silt – MUDSTONE. Contains clay and is friable – MARL. As above but consolidated – MARLSTONE	

If carbonaceous the rocks are some type of coal. If friable and earthy it is *PEAT*, if black – *COAL*.

Children's books

Crosby, P. *Rock Collecting.* Muller.
Dalby, D. H. *Instructions to Young Geologists.* Museum Press. 1957.
Evans, I. O. *The Observer's Book of Geology.* Warne.
Forbes, D. *British Fossils.* A. & C. Black. 1961.
Podendorf, I. *The Junior True Book of Rocks and Minerals.* Muller.
Science on the March, Unit 3. *The Weather and the Earth.* Longmans.
Zim, H. S. and Schaffer, P. R. *Rocks and Minerals.* Paul Hamlyn. 1971.

Samples of rocks and fossils can be bought from E. J. Arnold & Sons Ltd., Butterley Street, Leeds, 10. More sophisticated collections can be obtained from: Gregory Bottley & Co., 30, Old Church Street, Chelsea, London, S.W.3.; R. F. D. Parkinson, Doulting, Shepton Mallet, Somerset.

Wall Charts

A Chart of Fossils is obtainable from Shell Petroleum Co., Shell Centre, London, S.E.1.

Film Strips

A useful film strip on Fossils is produced by Common Ground, 41, Cadogan Gardens, London, S.W.3, entitled 'Introduction to Palaeontology'.

5 Classroom: Development and Display

CLASS RECORDS

The types of record that the children make will depend upon the topic under consideration. For slow, retarded or very young children and for some specific topics a verbal report may be enough.

Verbal reports

It is to be expected that children will wish to communicate their findings almost immediately verbally to the other members of the group. This should be allowed. If one discovers something, one wishes to communicate one's findings. If it is exciting this means immediate communication. Remember Archimedes in his bath! The children should be explorers. Much of the thrill of exploring is relating it afterwards; hence the popularity of travel books.

With a class working on a particular topic a time should be set aside for 'report-back' sessions. During these sessions the teams are encouraged to evaluate their progress, to plan ahead and to inform the whole class. Each team member will normally contribute something, not necessarily every time, but periodically. Do not press really shy children too hard; when they have been excited by a topic they will need no encouragement to report. If the impetus is being taken out of a project by over-frequent reporting-back, the latter can be held over until later.

Written records

1 *The note-book – class or individual* If a group of children have been working on the various aspects of, say autumn, they can draw and record their findings on paper, and this can be put together in a large book or folder for this topic. It is sometimes preferable with older children for them to make up their own book on one aspect of the topic.

A group of pupils may be researching into temperature changes. Does the air temperature change at the same rate as the temperature of a pond? (Or a large bath of water outside?) Graphs may be drawn, further reading and further experiments undertaken. The booklet that results from this activity should be placed in a classroom library. The class library in this context is indeed true to name for it will become a library containing books produced by the children. Each of these books should carry a simple bibliography.

Written records also include labelling collected specimens. This should be undertaken by the children. When a specimen is collected in the field a numbered tag should be affixed. In the field note-book the following information should be given about the specimen:

Number	*Collected by*	*Date*
17	F. Smith	1/7/73
Name	*Condition*	*Identified by*
(Unknown)	In bud? flowering? in seed?	Miss Smith

Habitat – In patch of grass by main road.

When an experiment is undertaken notes of the experimental procedure are important. Children should be encouraged to write up their experimental work in the form of notes. These are not to be so rigid as to need the sub-headings *Experiment*, *Apparatus*, etc. It should be explained that others may wish to follow along the path they have trodden. Those following must be given directions so that the way is clear. We should therefore record several things in our reports, such as *why* we are doing something. This will usually be in the form of a problem, e.g. 'To find out whether 170 gm. of cotton wool squashed together keeps water hotter longer than 170 gm. of cotton wool fluffed out?, We must record *what we did*, *what we found out* and see if our question is answered.

Example

'We had two tin cans of different sizes (look at the drawing). John put a

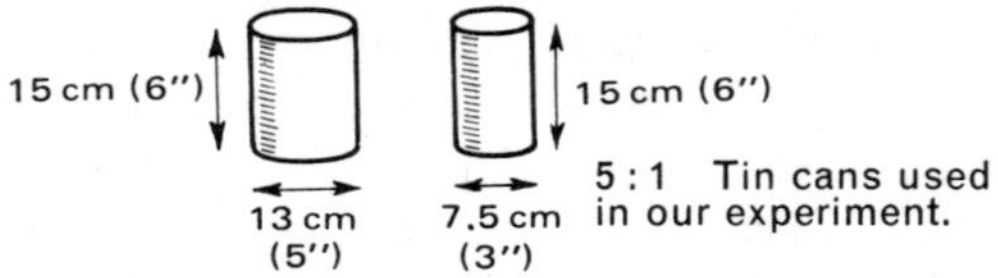

milk bottle in the smaller can and I stuffed in 170 gm. of cotton wool. I held the bottle in the other can and John put in 170 gm. of fluffy cotton wool. We got some hot water in the kettle and poured it into a milk bottle until it was up to the line we marked. John poured it into the bottle in the little can – we used a funnel. Then we poured water from the kettle into the milk bottle again up to the mark. This was poured into the big can bottle. I put a thermometer into each bottle and we looked at the temperature. It was 61° C. for each bottle.

'We looked at the temperature in each bottle every five minutes at first. Here is what we saw:

	Fluffy Cotton Wool	*Squashed Cotton Wool*
1	61° C.	61° C.
2	59° C.	58½° C.
3	58½° C.	57½° C.
4	58° C.	57° C.

'After this we looked at them every twenty minutes.

5	54° C.	52° C.
6	52° C.	50° C.

'We saw that the fluffy cotton wool kept the water hotter. We think that fluffy cotton wool has more air in it and the air keeps the warmth in it.'

Some Ideas For More Work Compare the following for heat retention:
(*a*) Feathers – squashed feathers and fluffy feathers.
(*b*) Foam plastic squashed, and foam plastic normal.
(*c*) From the barber's – squashed hair and fluffy hair.

The following can then be investigated: Insulation of roofs, pipes, bursts. Vacuum flasks. This work leads on to graphs.

Graphical methods

(*a*) *The Column Graph,* best shown by a diagram.

Pictogramic form

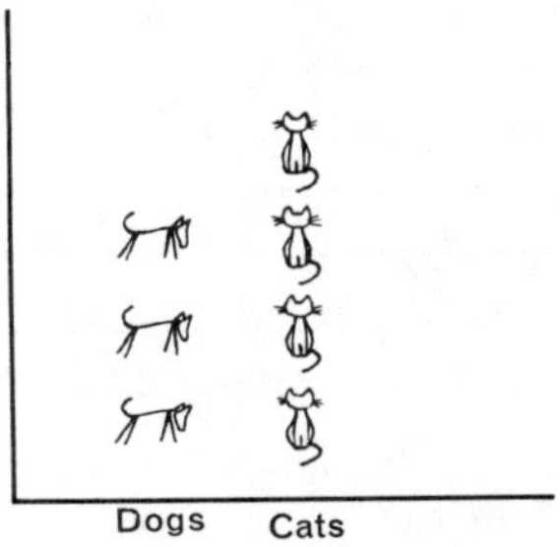

5 : 2 Column graph (pictogram) showing 'Class pets'.

The animals could be drawn on to match boxes for very young children. It is important that the match boxes are the same size. Older children will use a key and have different coloured squares (all the same size) to indicate the types and numbers of pets. It should be obvious from the graph which is the most common pet.

(*b*) *Bar line graph*
With older children who have experienced the above technique, there is no need to have a wide column. The column can shrink to just a line.

In the above case the information presented on the graph is discrete or non-continuous. There is no link between the dogs and the cats; they are separate entities. In some cases there will be a continuous distribution, e.g. the increase in weight of the baby gerbils (see 'Animals' in Chapter 7, p. 259) as they grow older. They will not be weighed every day, but say every Monday morning before feeding. It is quite obvious that the animal has been putting on weight during the intervening week. In this case the column graph can be used, but the columns are placed adjacent to one another.

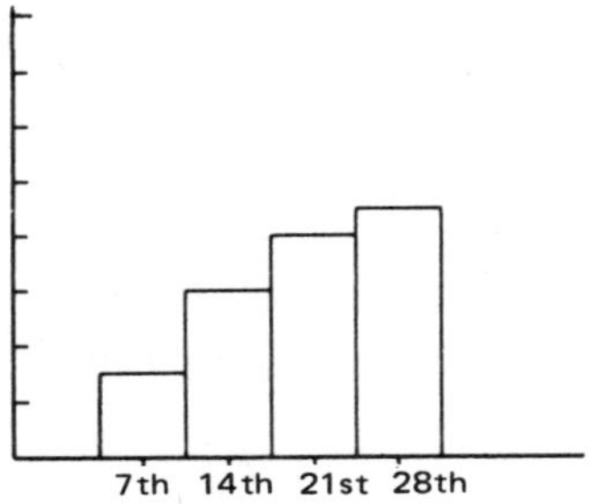

5 : 3 Histogram showing increase in weight of gerbils.

This is known as a *Histogram.*

This recording leads on to the problems of averaging. If the whole family of 6 are weighed in the same box on the same balance at the same time is it better than weighing one for recording purposes? Why? What is the *average* increase in weight? There is often a runt (a slower one to develop) and a more advanced. How much do they depart from the average? Would a human mother want her baby to be weighed as an 'average'? Would the Government want to know every baby's weight? (This by the way, leads on to sampling – which can be discussed here.)

Sampling

Children were interested in the number of plantains on a large school lawn. It was decided it would be impractical to count each one. How could the approximate total be found? It was decided that selected squares could be observed and the numbers in these squares counted. 1 metre squares were marked out with bamboo canes. How could the places be chosen at random? It was decided to toss a cricket ball over the shoulder and make the square where it landed. (This technique is really unsatisfactory for statistical sampling of vegetation but is adequate at this level.) Within each square metre a white cardboard circle was placed over each plantain to ease the counting. The area of the lawn was known and it was decided to take as a sample one-tenth of the total number of square metres. By multiplying the total plantains obtained, the average total for the lawn was obtained. Interest was expressed in the variations in numbers within the 1 square metre frames (quadrats) and these were plotted on the graph. Interest arose in the total number that would have been indicated if the lowest 'yield' per quadrat or if the highest 'yield' had been taken.

Graph of Numbers of Sample

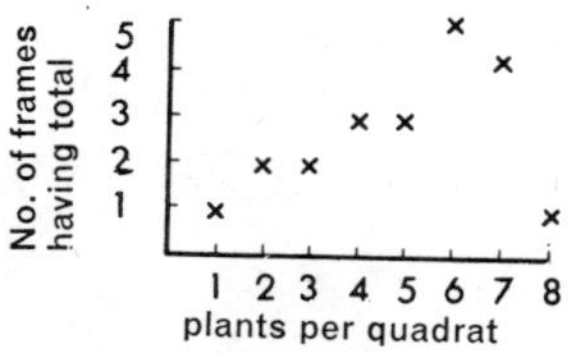

5 : 4 Graph showing the number of plantains in each frame (quadrat).

It will readily be appreciated that this graph work becomes more 'graphic' if the environment is used for material and that if the need for graphs arises spontaneously out of a topic approach – a real topic, not the 'Postal Service' studied from afar. I have a feeling that the 'Travels of a Penny' on which we were brought up have been replaced with the 'Journey of a Letter'. My point is that experience is a good stimulus for writing.

(*c*) *Pie Graphs*

These are sometimes used in books as a neat way of showing the distribution of, say, water in the world. They tend to be inaccurate and unsuitable for recording accurately-obtained results. They have however a visual appeal.

Construction

Divide the percentages of the data items into 360 degrees.

$$\frac{50}{100} \text{ of } 360 = \tfrac{1}{2} \times 360 = 180$$

Measure off the angles obtained with a protractor in the centre of a circle and draw radii.

Model making

(*a*) *Clay*

Clay can be purchased, but it can also be dug up. It is much more worthwhile if you can find the clay to use for your models. They may be fired in a simple kiln (Fig. 5:5).

Leave spaces between the bricks for air to enter. Fill the inside with sawdust and pots and light the sawdust at the top. The base can be on bricks or soil – do not set it up on a tar-macadam playground!

Firing in kiln

Do not make your models larger than 7·5 cm. diameter and they should not be more than 2–2·5 cm. thick. If they are solid then push knitting needles into them to make holes. Allow the clay one week to dry in a warm classroom.

(*b*) '*New-style*' *clay*

Margros Multiplas too, is an interesting medium for making models, for moulding, casting and printing. It sets hard when immersed in water at

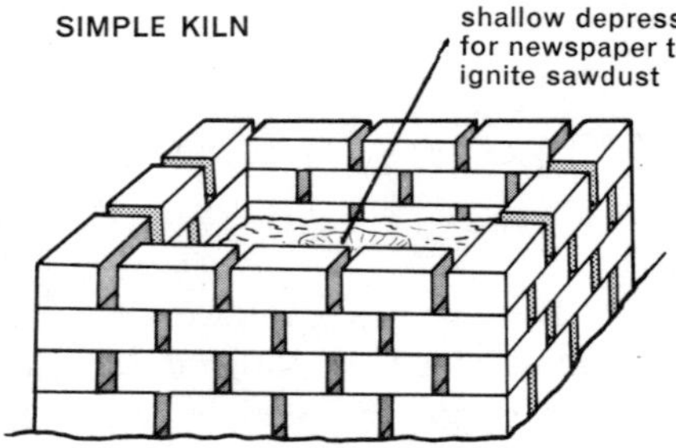

5 : 5 Simple kiln for use in schools.

100° C. Details from Margros Ltd., Monument Way West, Woking, Surrey.

(*c*) *Plasticine*

There is really no need to mention this old favourite. Its uses are numerous, for model harbours, houses and many other purposes.

(*d*) *Playdoh*

A relatively new material produced by Meccano. It has many advantages for the younger child. It is non-toxic, and can be eaten without ill-effect. It is very plastic, and if kept in its airtight tin, it can actually be extruded – which demonstrates how many plastic articles in everyday use are made. A simple machine is available 'The Fun Machine' for making standard shapes and could be useful for say, model brick-making. It sets very hard if left out for some time and this is obviously most useful on occasions, e.g. when permanent bricks are required. It disintegrates in water and cannot be used for holding water in model locks, etc.

(*e*) *Milk straws*

Milk straws can be used for model making and are particularly valuable for mathematical shapes, pyramids and the like. The straws are held together with short pieces of pipe cleaner, bent to the required angle and pushed into the straws.

(*f*) *Balsa*

Balsa wood is cheap, readily obtainable and easily worked. With suitable glues, excellent models can be made of many structures – house frames, bridges, etc. Many boys will be aero-modellers and would welcome the opportunity for model construction. These models are static things and are often things of great beauty, reflecting hours of patient work. Would it be heresy to suggest that a quickly-made model to show a particularly interesting feature is more valuable?

(*g*) *Plaster casts*

Useful for pieces of twigs, leaves, tracks of animals, copies of fossils, etc.

Equipment: Plaster of Paris (Dental quality is best), jug of water, mixing bowl, spoon, knife, Vaseline, newspaper, sheet of glass or cellulose acetate or thick polythene, water colours and poster paint, paint brush, and clear varnish and brush (optional).

Method: Place newspaper on the bench or table and on it place the glass sheet or alternative. Using the jam jar as a rolling pin, roll out the sheet of Plasticine to about 1·5 cm. thick of a size sufficient to take the object to be cast. Lightly smear the surface with Vaseline. Place the material upon the Plasticine and half embed it by rolling with the jam jar. Trim down the Plasticine to a suitable size and shape. Build a wall of Plasticine say 2 to 2·5 cm. high around the Plasticine base ensuring that the joints are smooth and without cracks.

Pour water into the mixing bowl and sprinkle plaster powder into the water until it just comes to the water surface. Mix the plaster and water to form a pourable creamy paste. Add the paste to the mould, pouring carefully but quickly in a steady stream starting from the edge of the mould and allowing the paste to flow around into the depressions driving out the air as it travels. Aim for a finished thickness of about 1·5 cm.

When the plaster is *quite* dry (next day?) peel away the walls of the mould and gently lever up the plaster cast. If the cast is not dry it will crack. The raised part of the mould should now be painted, comparing it with the original material, so that as near as possible to the original colours are reproduced.

When making plaster casts of footprints out of doors you will not require the Plasticine base and the plaster can be poured directly into the print, the surrounding walls being made of strong, but pliable cardboard fastened in a circle by paper clips. The plaster cast of the footprints are obviously negatives.

(*h*) *Scale models*

Most of the materials mentioned would be very suitable for making a scale model of a particularly interesting area. Plaster has been used for making a model dockyard, but Plasticine has been found to be more satisfactory. The material was modelled to scale from 6″ or 25″ Ordnance Survey maps, enlarged if necessary. The model was set out on a large butcher's tray (it could have been a polythene lined box). The docks were filled with water and lock gates were made out of glass slides. Demonstration of the tide going out of the river was shown by siphoning off water from the river. Importance of high tide to ships wishing to get into the graving dock was demonstrated.

(i) Relief models

The older children in our group will be familiar with maps and their uses. They will find it difficult to relate the contours on the map to the physical features of the landscape on the ground. It is a help to construct relief models to show how contours reflect surface configuration.

These models make a vital contribution to any study of a locality. A simple method is to take an Ordnance Survey map 1/25,000 and trace out each contour on to tracing paper. The contours can be enlarged if necessary by use of an epidiascope or by the squares technique.

Each contour can be transferred to a sheet of hardboard and cut out with a fine-tooth saw. The cut-out shapes are stuck together with Copydex and plaster of Paris is used to smooth out the edge so that the slope flows. A technique, still in its infancy, is to transfer the contours to expanded polystyrene ceiling tiles. In this case the cutting out may be done with a hot wire. This produces a very light model.

A less precise technique is to model the relief of the area in fine mesh wire-netting using papier mâché or plaster of Paris for infilling.

No matter which technique is used, the relief model should be mounted on a strong base and the model painted to show outstanding features such as settlements, woodlands, rivers, etc.

(j) Working models

Hints on the construction of simple working models to demonstrate principles or for experiments will be found in the topic sections of the book. Meccano produce some excellent kits for working model construction. There are two types:

(1) A plastic kit, made out of large pieces which younger children can handle and which make very effective models.

(2) The metal Meccano. Most boys will be familiar with these kits. Even if they have never purchased them they will have coveted them in model-shop windows. Although these kits are not cheap they will last for a very long time and the number of working models that can be constructed from one set is enormous. Particularly impressive is the 'Site Engineer's Construction Kit' and the purchase of just one set in a school would be a real investment. (It's good to make do with beer-bottle tops for gears, but it's marvellous to have a really good working model demonstration to make understanding science a really painless process!)

Full details of the range are available from: Meccano Ltd., Binns Road, Liverpool, 13.

Meccano Ltd. point out that they will supply schools directly at a discount of approximately 20% on retail prices, provided they receive the order on official paper and that the parts supplied are for educational purposes only and are not for resale.

Bilofix, available at trade terms from Bilo Toys Ltd., Richard Leys, Kettering, Northants, also provide a building set. The pieces are made out of close grain beech wood. A host of models can be made and the wood has a wonderful feel. Younger children will particularly enjoy Bilofix, but owing to the absence, as yet, of gear wheels, etc. its use for making working models is limited.

Photographic records (see p. 129).

Silhouettes

These can be most useful as 'snap' aids to identification. Birds have characteristic shapes in flight, and by constructing silhouettes there is a real aid to identification. In World War II silhouettes of aircraft were one of the training aids for aircraft spotters. Incidentally, a silhouette of say a swan in flight viewed the opposite way is similar to a bird of prey.

Move such a model in one direction and young poultry chicks ignore it; move it the other way and they crouch.

Silhouettes are also useful for tree shapes, bridge types, townscapes. They can be linked with work in Art by using cork sheet, or thin plastic foam for the silhouette and then mounting it on painted polystyrene tiles. These tiles are now very cheap and can be used in many ways in the classroom.

Rubbings

Methods of making these are dealt with in Chapter 4, p. 160.

Diagrams and drawings (**sketches**)

No one wants to make a fetish of wonderful drawings. On the other hand, a skill in drawing can be acquired through training, and this involves lots of practice. It also is very time-consuming. We are aware that very young children have not the muscular co-ordination and finesse necessary to produce good drawings but they should be encouraged to do their best. The purpose of a drawing in Environmental Studies is to show something accurately. This means that if say, a twig is drawn it should be exactly like the original. If the drawing is tinted then the tints should be the colour of the twig. If a drawing of something is inaccurate then it is pointless, and a diagram will serve better. There appears to be some confusion between drawings and diagrams. Diagrams must be accurate but they need not be things of great beauty involving delicate shading, etc. Diagrams should show clearly the salient features of an object and should not be too time-consuming.

5 : 6 The difference between a drawing and a diagram.

The diagram and drawing of a buttercup show clearly the differences. The need in the classroom for good drawings and diagrams is based on the fact that to produce them you need skill in observation. The drawing or diagram produced indicates to the teacher the skill of the child in really looking at the object. Really 'seeing' is very important and the teacher should take pains to train children to look at things. It does need training for we all look at many things without really seeing them.

Sketches are quite different; these are used to give a general impression of an object or scene. If, for example, one is walking around a town looking at the various bridges, one would not expect children to produce a diagram or drawing of each. One would expect a sketch which should show the main features.

Displays

A. NATURE TABLE

There is in many classrooms an area more or less separate from the remainder, which is called the 'Nature Table'. In other classrooms this may be termed the 'Discovery Table' or the 'Investigation Table'. The latter two names perhaps reflect the impact that physical science has made on the schools and the idea of investigation or discovery. The secondary schools manage without such areas perhaps because they seem too unsophisticated or perhaps because laboratories are not expected to have them. We feel this is wrong. Laboratories all too often become places of danger where touching, tasting and sniffing of objects are forbidden. It is appreciated that there are dangerous, even lethal, materials in laboratories and these should not be available to children except under careful supervision, but the taboo is too often all-embracing. Is there not a case for a side bench area with interesting material upon it that can be played with,

5 : 7 Sketch of bridge showing general features.

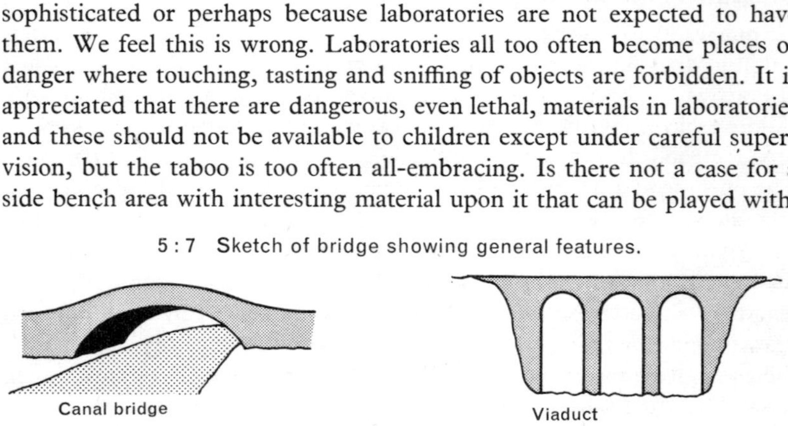

sorted out, viewed? Visit an exhibition or museum. Where are the crowds? They are working the models, fiddling with those instruments. People pay to look through telescopes and play with pin tables. Let us have, wherever possible, material that children can handle themselves. Children should be made to feel at home in a laboratory. Is this heresy? (The really dangerous chemicals, the really valuable equipment should be stored out of the way.) By feeling 'at home' we mean relaxed. A good home does not allow hooliganism or extreme permissiveness. The relaxed atmosphere develops through mutual trust and understanding. Perhaps the young teacher would do well, initially, to err on the side of rigidity or restriction rather than permissiveness until the class learn through their group probings that he is fair, just and competent. By the same token the teacher will have to get to know his class. Has it ever been printed – it has often been said – 'You can always relax your discipline, but it is difficult to tighten up'? This is good advice for the young teacher.

The name 'Nature' persists, and why not? The terms 'discovery', and 'investigation' are just expressions showing how a good Nature table should be used. However, it does not matter what it is called. Some teachers, some classes, may feel insulted by 'Nature'! Choose as you will! The important thing is to have a good table. How do you recognise a good table, when you see it? You don't really, you recognise a good one when you see how it is used! The neat, well laid, carefully arranged 'area' may be arid and sterile; no one may look at it except the proud teacher. Nature areas are not for teachers, or visiting inspectors and organisers – they are for children. The good 'area' will be stimulating to the children. If set up properly by the teacher it will foster interest, it will demand attention, provoke investigation, require consideration. It can be used by the teacher to stimulate an interest in an area of study the teacher wishes the children to follow. Too often we drag the children along the path of a project. The Nature table can show them a glimpse of the trail and make them really want to tread the path. Do not be afraid of following your own hobby-horse, if you have one. When one visits an exhibition of children working in science and sees some marvellous work on materials, cosmetics, computers, birds, fish and other things, enquire further, talk to the teacher concerned; his background is textiles, cosmetics, mathematics or he is a keen ornithologist or fisherman. The teacher with a really interesting hobby is half-way there with children, provided of course the hobby is suitable for children to study! The table should stimulate children – not them all – that is impossible – but the majority.

It should lead them on, it should provoke questions in the children – questions that demand answers. The answers should not be given, but a means of finding the answers should be suggested. Teachers should not be expected to know all the answers; perhaps they should know some of the sensible questions that need asking! We believe that teachers should learn with and from children whenever it is necessary or possible. To travel along on an investigation with children, stimulating them towards the sensible questions to ask themselves about the problem being faced, is the attitude to adopt. An experiment is nothing but a question asked of Nature. It is important that the correct question is asked; otherwise the answer will be meaningless. Hence the care needed in experiment design in advanced work. To reduce variables to the one under experiment is vital. Teachers are often afraid to reveal their ignorance to children. Why? There are so many areas of knowledge where the teacher is more than competent that to show ignorance of an aspect is to admit to being human. Surely we want children to think of us as humans rather than gods!

Physical considerations

Many schools lack if not the table space, the display space near to the table. Suitable display space can be made from pegboard in dimensions to suit your own table. If the Nature table is actually a table then the space beneath it may be used. It can be fitted with shelves which will support jars, cans, etc. for collecting in the field. The front and sides of the table may be curtained or pegboard used to give further display space, either for specimens brought in, or for books useful for the topic under consideration.

A portable wooden surround to fit the dimensions of the natural table is a useful piece of equipment. If the space enclosed is fitted with strong plastic sheet then, if appropriate to the study in hand, clumps of living material may be brought in.

Cover the plastic either with peat or soil, to a depth of 5 or 6 cm., then plant in clumps of material. This is very useful if the topic is a pond or lake. The centre of the display could be a plastic sandwich tray approximately 30 × 45 × 7 cm. from Woolworths. Around the tray, which would contain a few representative animals and plants of the pond, could be kept clumps of vegetation from the pond side. If clumps are brought back to the classroom with soil and roots in plastic bags the plants will survive in classroom for many days if watered well. They may be returned to the pond side on

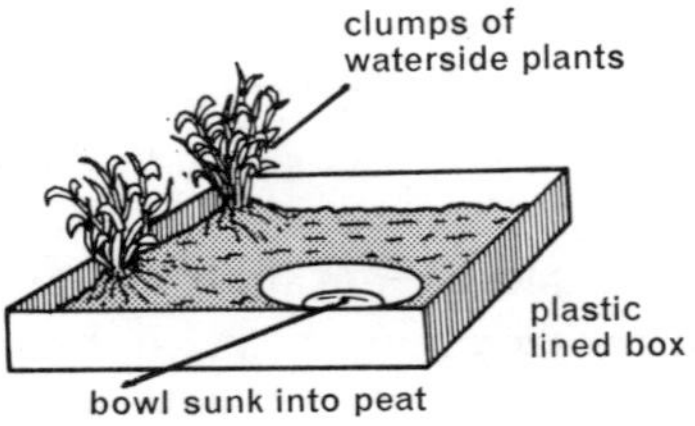

5 : 8 A plastic lined box for living plants.

5 : 9 A wooden block used as a tube and label support.

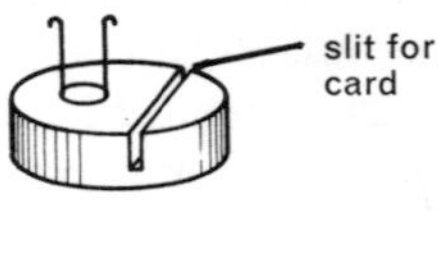

completion of the display. Obviously no one would advocate collecting clumps of Early Purple Orchids but there is a need for habitat collections.

Containers for Display

Test tubes make excellent receptacles for display of individual plant specimens but 'Haliborange' bottles are cheaper. The bottles can be fastened directly to the pegboard by a Terry clip fitting obtainable from good hardware stores.

Simple tube supporters can be made out of wooden blocks bored to take the tube and with a cut slit for the cardboard bearing the name of the specimen (Fig. 5:9).

Egg boxes are useful for holding containers. Cut holes in the projecting parts and insert small bottles or test tubes. Do not use large tubes. Small 'Squeezy' bottles are useful for displaying large plants but fittings to support them on pegboards are comparatively expensive.

Many of the small plastic bottles holding shampoos, etc. have ridges near the top and base. If these are used, wires pushed through the pegboard and around the container at the top and near the base will be sufficient to hold them on the board. Useful label holders are golf tees. Paste the label on to the broad end and stick the tee through the hole in the board.

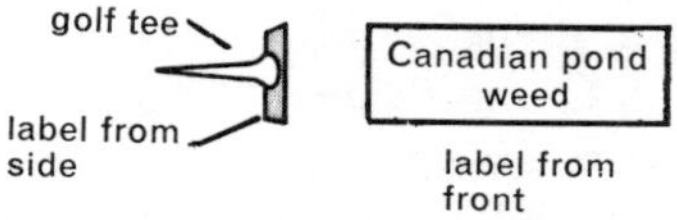

5 : 10 A golf-tee label holder.

Ink-well carriers are useful for transporting display plants if small bottles are used in place of the ink wells.

Displaying growing plants

The old idea of jam jars lined with blotting paper and with seed squashed between glass and paper takes a lot of beating. Use either sphagnum moss to push out blotting paper to the side or use a wad of newspaper. One disadvantage of this method is that with many plants the roots grow rapidly and then get wrapped around in a layer on the base of jam jar preventing measurements. To overcome this use a large 'growth measuring tube'.

Growth measuring tube

Use thick cellulose acetate sheet (reclaimed) available from Ians Ltd., Calls Buildings, Quayside, Newcastle-upon-Tyne, or Polyglaze from hardware stores is suitable. Cut a strip 45 × 10 cm., roll into a tube. Fasten tube by a paper clip at each end and seal along joint with Sellotape. Line the tube with blotting paper, push newspaper inside the blotting paper to hold it firm against the sides. Drop one or two seeds down between the blotting

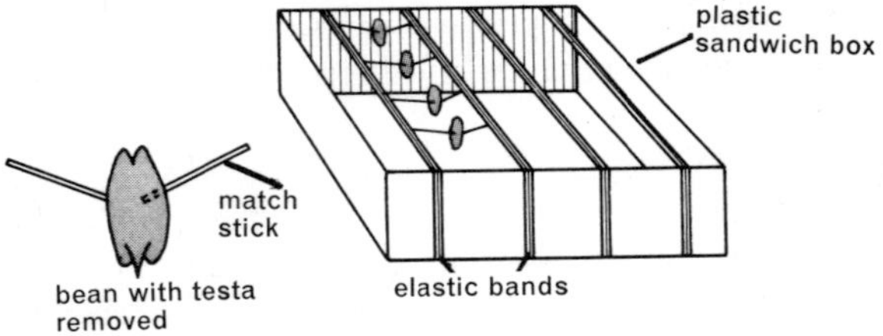

5 : 11 A sandwich box germination container.

paper and the glass – a knitting needle facilitates the operation. Immerse the tube in a jam jar half full of water. Growth of shoots and roots can readily be recorded.

Bulbs, e.g. onion, crocus, can be supported over water in ink bottles by using plastic net (Tygan, Netlon). The roots will pass out through the net and into the water. Change the water regularly.

A simple way of seeing how large seeds germinate

Soak seeds overnight then carefully remove the testa or seed coat. Set up as shown in the diagram.

Add water to the box so that the bottom of the seeds are just covered. If a sandwich box is used then different seeds can be aligned parallel to each other, e.g. Broad beans, French beans, Runner beans. For other methods for living material – see 'Living Things' – Chapter 7.

No one would advocate that the table should always be in use for living materials. There are times in the year when this is most difficult. The table may reflect the topic under consideration at the time. If for example 'Water' is being considered one would expect to find such items as:

1 Taps, ball valves, plumber's force pumps (borrowed or begged from a plumber).
2 Models of filter beds – with dirty water to filter!
3 Experiments on evaporation – with instructions.
4 Demonstrations of obtaining fresh water from salty water.
5 Methods of determining density, with equipment.

Too much – maybe, but children working on different aspects of the topic will want their model to be on show. At times the display board may be used to hang interesting wall charts, diagrams, books useful for the study. It should have a visual appeal and should above all be used. You must expect water to be splashed about, so cover labels and instructions with transparent plastic or polythene.

B. CHEMICAL GARDENS

An attractive display can be made which demonstrates the scientific principle of osmosis and which might be a stimulus for art.

A large screw-top preserving jar is required. Into this is poured the contents of a tin of water-glass solution (Sodium silicate, obtainable from a chemist). The jar is topped up with water, ten times the quantity of water-glass. Distilled water is preferable if it can be obtained. Shake well so that the resulting solution is a thin slightly viscous liquid. Drop into the solution a few crystals from the following salts:

Cobalt Nitrate – Dark blue growths.
Copper Sulphate – (Poison) Blue-green growths.
Ferric Chloride – green growth.
Ferrous Sulphate – browny-yellow growth.
Manganese Chloride – rose-pink growth.

The growths – actually tubes – will reach heights of 5–6 centimetres in the bottle. The actual method of growth is fascinating to watch.

If children are undertaking this technique they must wash their hands thoroughly afterwards. Obviously they must be warned about NOT tasting chemicals.

C. CLASS MUSEUMS

The Nature table is a museum – a museum of living things. It is a museum of working models, of demonstrations, of experiments. There is a place for museums of dead materials or non-living materials. Children pass through a phase of collection and acquisitiveness. They will treasure objects, stones, skulls and bones that they have found on walks. No one would advocate keeping an area set on one side for the permanent display of unchanging material. Museums arrange special displays to stimulate interest and we should follow this example. Suppose a child has brought in a bone that he has found. The teacher can discuss its size, shape and perhaps hazard a guess where it has come from. It is very helpful if a box of bones can be produced to augment the single display. One obtains bones by collecting them! Or by asking children over the year to bring them in and keeping them together in the 'bone box'. The same holds good for other materials – minerals and rocks, different metals. It is useful to paste inside the box lid a list of books (held by school library, or local library) which are useful background reading at the children's level.

Some children will have their own museums at home. These may range from the usual stamp collection, through regimental badges and insignia to pressed flower collections. These amateur enthusiasts should be encouraged to bring in their collections and to talk about them. I am always amazed by the knowledge that most unlikely children have when they are fired by the collecting habit. I have taught a 12-year-old who could discuss cacti with experts. They usually like to talk about their hobbies, so foster this idea.

You will tend to forget what you have in those numerous cardboard boxes. They may be labelled on the outside but often they hold too much for this technique. A simple card index is the answer. A small box which will hold several dozen cards is required. There is a card for each box number and on each card is a list of the box contents. It is then an easy matter to add or delete from the cards as more material is collected or as material is discarded!

Displays of dead pressed plants are discussed on p. 166. Details of displaying insects may be found on p. 171. It is emphasised that museums in the classroom should be temporary and as soon as the specimens have stopped stimulating children they should be returned to their storage boxes.

Some special methods for material

(i) *Museum jars*

Only a few schools will wish to preserve and mount material in museum jars. The old glass museum jar has been largely replaced by the perspex jar and these are not fragile. As this is a relatively specialised field readers are referred to the leaflet 'Perspex in the Laboratory', available free from T. Gerrard and Co. Ltd., Worthing Road, East Preston, Littlehampton, Sussex, or 'Cell Mounts' from P. K. Dutt Ltd., Clan Works, Howard Road, Bromley, Kent.

(ii) *Embedding resins*

Cemar F.R. 264 – obtainable from Griffin and George, Frederick Street, Birmingham, 1. This technique has advantages over museum jars. It produces the specimen embedded in a block of transparent resin. The blocks are virtually unbreakable and the objects, e.g. butterfly, moss, etc. are displayed in a most attractive way. Full instructions are supplied with the kits.

(iii) *Geological specimens.* See Chapter 4, p. 173.

Services in the classroom (Does not apply to schools with Laboratories)

Water supply

Where there is a tap in the classroom the availability of water is no problem and teachers whenever possible should try to get a sink and tap fitted. This is difficult! There are now available large plastic containers with taps which are used for caravans and camping and these may be purchased fairly cheaply. A free source of plastic containers is a good wine shop. Many wine stores are selling 'British' and other wines from bulk and they have throw-away plastic containers which will hold several litres of water. If these can be obtained they are most useful. Large plastic bottles are also useful for carrying back pond water.

Gas supply

The majority of classrooms are not supplied with town gas. With the children we have in mind certain experiments will require a heat source. With younger juniors a kettle of hot water from the staff room may suffice but a stronger heat source is often required when working with older children. There are several possibilities open. None should be used without supervision.

Spirit burners are sold by Woolworths and are useful but can be rather unstable. A spirit heater can be made out of an ink bottle. Punch a hole in the cap; a metal tube may be soldered to this, but it is not essential. Make a wick out of bundles of cotton string, thread through the hole into the bottom of bottle, leaving five or six centimetres to spare in the base. Part fill the bottle with methylated spirits, allow time for the wick to soak up the liquid. How does it do it?

Camping gas burners may be purchased from hardware stores, as may Calor gas and many schools where town gas is unavailable are finding Calor gas of great value.

6 Seasonal Patterns of the Environment

Many features of the environment can be studied at almost any period of the year, but for the aspects of the work which are often regarded as natural science there may be optimum conditions at certain seasons. Even in these times of increasing urbanisation of our land, it is wise for children to appreciate the patterns of the seasons and the rhythms of life and death. Although a 'hard and fast' syllabus for these studies is to be deprecated, yet it is useful to plan ahead in outline. To help in this, the following approximate calendar of events in nature may be useful.

SOME FEATURES OF THE YEARLY PATTERN IN NATURE

JANUARY

Animals

Some lambs may be seen with their ewes on farms.
Some animals such as dormice, hedgehogs, bats, snakes and frogs in hibernation.
Very little bird 'song', except for robins, rooks, starlings and sparrows. Many birds will visit bird tables for food.
In snow or mud, tracking of birds and other animals may be possible.
Most insects resting in larval or pupal stages.

Plants

Plants in flower may include winter aconites, snowdrops, birch (catkins), alder (catkins), gorse.
Deciduous trees can be studied in their leafless state. Sketches and plaster casts of twigs can be made, together with bark rubbings.
The winter condition of herbaceous biennials and perennials (roots, corms, bulbs, tubers) can also be examined.
Evergreen shrubs and trees, including most of the conifers.

Natural phenomena

Possibly snow crystals and flakes.
Frost and its action.
Ice and its properties; icicles.
Winter storms and floods; effect of flooded land on winter cereals.

FEBRUARY

Animals

Increasing numbers of lambs seen on farms.
Hibernating animals may awake for short time in any mild spell.
Squirrels begin building breeding nest (drey).
Frogs may begin to spawn.
Bird song from blackbird, thrush, chaffinch, robin, wren and yellowhammer.
Lapwings can be seen in the fields and species of wading birds in estuaries, flooded gravel pits and sewage farms.
Rooks begin to build nests, and many bird species begin 'courting displays'.

Plants

Several species of plants in flower in woodland and in gardens, e.g. lesser celandine, snowdrop, crocus. These early flowering plants usually have underground food storage organs.

Elsewhere, the coltsfoot and barren strawberry may be found in bloom.

Honeysuckle, elder and ferns in sheltered places begin to unfold their leaves.

Natural phenomena

Changeable climatic conditions may give hail, rain, snow, ice, gale-force winds, frost, sunshine, mist and fog. This is a good time to carry out weather studies and keep weather records. Photographs help, too, in recording weather conditions.

Long nights give opportunities for study of moon and stars.

February outdoor and classroom work

Look out for and record any wild animals, including any known hibernators.

Learn to recognise birds by their plumage, gait, flight and song.

Record any bird mating displays and early building of nests.

Identify and record any water birds seen, including waders.

Record any newly-born animals on farms.

Continue winter tree shape recognition, and make a collection of bark rubbings and sketches of twigs.

Record any trees seen to be in flower, including the catkin-bearers. Why do these trees carry flowers so early in the year?

Make a list, with dates, when species of herbaceous plants first seen in bloom.

Studies of weather, soil and astronomy can be carried out.

MARCH

Animals

Young animals are usually plentiful on farms at this time.

In the wild, young foxes and badgers may be seen; if any rabbits have escaped myxomatosis, they will probably have produced young also.

Watch out for the 'mad March' hares leaping wildly about in the fields.

Hedgehogs, dormice and bats may not yet have moved out of hibernation.

Frogs and toads have moved to the water for breeding, and their spawn is usually easy to find in ditches and shallow ponds.

Birds of many species are busy with courtship displays, mating, nest-building and egg-laying. Bird songs are loud and plentiful.

As earthworms move up nearer the soil surface, moles are increasingly active and many molehills appear particularly on the lighter soils.

Among insects on the move, look out for Brimstone, Small White, Red Admiral and Peacock butterflies which have emerged from the pupal stage.

Plants

Species in bloom will include dog's mercury, ground ivy, wood anemone, wood violet and marsh marigold.

In the garden, daffodils, narcissi, hyacinths, crocuses and aubretia are in bloom.

As winter jasmine fades, forsythia becomes very colourful and almond trees begin to flower.

Some trees show swelling buds, and the horse chestnut is an obvious one to observe. The yellow catkins of the common sallow or 'pussy willow' and the white flowers of the blackthorn are common in hedge and copse.

March outdoor and classroom work

Observe, record and sketch the stages of the opening of tree buds.

Simple experiments to show the upward movement of sap in plants (see Chapter 7).

Seed germination tests and experiments (see Chapter 7).

Record woodland plants in flower.

Sowing of seeds in pots, boxes and out of doors.

Growth of bulbs and corms.
Recording of bird song.
Observation of birds collecting nesting materials. Path of the sun in the sky and the lengthening day.
Planets and stars.

APRIL

Animals

The animals which hibernate are now seen on the move again.
Squirrels are now producing young in their dreys, and both field voles and water voles are breeding at this time.
Newt eggs may be found wrapped in the leaves of water plants.
The cuckoo and other summer migrants have now reached this country, and nesting and brooding of eggs continues. Bird song is again plentiful this month, probably at its peak.
More butterflies including the Large White, the Orange Tip and the Red Admiral are commonly seen. Other insects increase in number and both blackfly, greenfly and their destroyers, the ladybirds, can be found in the garden.

Plants

Among wild flowers, look out for wild arum, greater stitchwort, dog violet, bluebell, red dead nettle, white dead nettle, wood sorrel, wood anemone, lady's smock, cow parsley, germander speedwell and greater celandine among others. In damp places, you may find the horsetail (Equisetum) showing its cone-shaped fruiting structures.
In the garden, flowering plants include saxifrage, alyssum, aubretia and arabis.
Many trees are now unfolding their leaves.

April outdoor and classroom work

Record flowers in bloom in various habitats.
Pond-dipping and collection of aquatic life for classroom aquaria.
Further experiments with seeds.
Recording of songs of birds.
Sketches of way in which leaves of trees and shrubs unfold.
Growing of annuals from seeds and observation of life cycle stages.

MAY

Animals

Observe and record feeding and care of young in various bird species.
Tadpoles of frogs, toads and newts are developing. Insects, including species of butterflies and moths, are more numerous. Queen wasps have come out of hiding and may be seen on rotten wood collecting material for nest construction.
Bird song tends to decrease near the end of the month.

Plants

Fruit trees in the garden and some wild trees such as elder, hawthorn, gean (wild cherry) and guelder rose can be seen in flower.
Woodland plants in flower include wood sanicle and woodruff. In meadowland buttercups are common and ox-eye daisies make a splash of white. In ponds, the water crowfoot is usually in bloom.

May outdoor and classroom work

Record changes in flowering species in woodland, meadow and other habitats.
Watch and record tadpole development.
The blossoms of garden and wild trees and shrubs are worth sketching or painting.
How plants are protected – spines, prickles, thorns, stinging hairs, etc.
Experiments to illustrate the general activities of plants, e.g. absorption of water, transpiration, photosynthesis.
Studies of life histories of some flowerless plants.

JUNE

Animals

Caterpillars are prominent and many species can be found.

In the pond one can now find many aquatic organisms, some as larvae and some in adult form. If a school nature study pond is stocked with dragonfly larvae, it may be possible for children this month to see the adult dragonfly emerge from its nymph stage on water weeds.

Young birds are common, and summer visitors such as the house martin, swallow and swift are busy building nests and brooding their young.

Plants

Many plants are now in bloom in a variety of habitats, particularly meadows and fields, hedgerows, chalkland and as weeds in the garden.

Rootstocks, tubers and bulbs of plant receive surplus food for storage.

June outdoor and classroom work

Ecological work recording interdependence of plants, animals, soils and weather.

Pond-dipping and stocking of several small aquaria in classroom and plastic or fibre-glass pond in school grounds. Watch development of the various larvae.

Bird identification studies.

Animal (including bird) behaviour – movements, defence and attack, food-getting and eating, home-building, relationships with others of same species, care of the young, mimicry, etc.

The path of the sun; length of day and temperature rise and fall.

JULY

Animals

Watch out for the various species of butterflies, ants and snails.

Bird song is scarce.

Young birds having left the nest, may still be fed by parents.

Plants

Many plants are now producing seeds, and these have various methods of dispersal. There are still some plants in flower. Thistles, toad flax, knapweed, silverweed, hop trefoil, grasses, rose bay willow herb, harebell, ragwort, yellow flag iris and water mint may all be found.

July outdoor and classroom work

Collect fruits and make sketches of the adaptations for dispersal of seeds.

Record plants still in flower in various habitats.

Collect, dry, label and store seeds from garden and the wild for use next spring.

Watch various flowers for certain periods of time and record the visits of insects.

Look out for the swarming of ants, and make a record of what you see happening. Refer to books for more details of the ants' behaviour.

AUGUST

Encourage children to continue observing and recording during the holiday period.

Animals

Birds such as lapwings, jays, magpies, blackbirds, sparrows and starlings may be heard but, apart from the robin, very few sing in a melodious way. Cuckoos, house martins and swifts prepare to move away southwards. Large numbers of starlings and sparrows may be seen together.

Hares and possibly rabbits may be seen leaving the corn as it is harvested.

Toads and frogs have left the ponds after breeding.

Plants

Many farm crops are harvested; others such as main crop potatoes, swedes, sugar beet are left to continue growth.

Wild fruits are common in woodland and hedgerow. Rose hips, the haws of the hawthorn, privet fruits, elderberries, sloes, blackberries can all be found. Early apples and pears are gathered.

Near the end of the month some leaves begin to take on their autumn colours.

Fungi appear in the woods late in the month.

August outdoor work

Collect, group and sketch wild fruits from the hedgerow.

Record birds preparing for migration.

If at the seaside try to identify creatures and plants of the seashore, sand-dunes and rocky pools. Shells and various types of small pebbles are worth collecting for display in school later.

SEPTEMBER

Animals

Many birds are migrating, and other animals are collecting and storing food. Flocks of rooks and starlings are common, while large groups of sparrows can be seen feeding on the ears of grain not yet harvested.

Spiders are commonly seen while insects are dying off or are sheltering for the winter in the larval or pupal stage.

Plants

This is an excellent month for the study of fungi.

Many plants are preparing for leaf-fall and wonderful colours can be seen in leaves such as maple, lime, beech, bramble, hawthorn, and in fruits of privet, elder, blackthorn, dog rose, yew, hawthorn and spindle.

A few plants such as ivy, hedge woundwort, knapweed, white dead nettle, yarrow and gorse may still be in flower.

September outdoor and classroom work

Collection, grouping, labelling and sketching of autumn leaves and fruits. Seed dispersal methods displayed.

Recording preparations of animal life for the winter ahead.

Collecting and listing flowering plants.

Making a 'fungi garden'.

Study of food storage organs of plants.

Observations of rising and setting sun, shortening days and decreasing temperature, linking these observations with plant and animal behaviour.

OCTOBER

Many features mentioned for September also apply to October.

Animals

Certain animals such as the dormouse, snake, toad, frog and the queen wasp move into hibernation quarters. On ivy flowers, Tortoise-shell and Peacock butterflies may be found.

Spider webs are common on plants and on fine days the gossamer floats in the air.

Squirrels are still busy collecting and hiding supplies of food. Chaffinches may be seen in flocks and fieldfares arrive in this country. They may be seen feeding on rowan, yew and other fruits.

The rut of fallow deer begins this month.

Plants

Many fungi can be found, e.g. gas-tar fungus (*Tricholoma sulphureum*) in woods; red-milk fungus (*Lactarius deliciosus*) in pine woods; fly agaric fungus (*Amanita muscaria*) near birch trees; red emetic fungus (*Russula emetica*) in beech woods; honey agaric fungus (*Armillaria mellea*) on stumps and trees; common helvel fungus (*Helvella crispa*) on sandy banks and tufted yellow club fungus (*Clavaria fusiformis*) in woods.

The leaves of the beech turn brown and sloes, hazel nuts, horse chestnuts and sweet chestnuts are ripe.
Maple and sycamore seeds can be seen blowing in the wind.
On oak trees notice the marble galls caused by the gall wasps *Cynips kollari.*

October outdoor and classroom work
Fungi can be collected and toadstool 'gardens' made in containers in the classroom. Emphasise the poisonous qualities of many fungi.
Bird tables can be bought or made, and placed in view of the classroom. Observation and recording can be made of the food preferences of different species which visit the table.
Collections of fruits (fleshy and dry) can be displayed in the classroom; encourage children to find out how these are linked with animal feeding (including man).
Try to find the larvae or pupae of insects in rotten trunks, in the leaf litter under trees or in garden soil. How do they manage to survive in this form?

NOVEMBER

Animals
Hedgehogs may still be seen in mild weather. Bats also still take the air on mild evenings. The singing birds include the song thrush, the mistle thrush, the wren, the robin and the hedge sparrow.
Wood pigeons can be seen in large flocks, often feeding on any brassicas in the fields. Goldcrests and greenfinches are sometimes seen.

Plants
Leaves of many trees show attractive autumn tints early in the month. Leaf-fall continues fairly fast particularly in stormy weather.
You may find a few wild plants such as chickweed, daisy and red dead nettle still in bloom.
Some lichens, e.g. green cup lichen (*Cladonia pyxadita*) and reindeer-moss lichen (*Cladonia spp.*) can be found.
Fungi are less frequent but look out for white ear fungus (*Hygrophorus virgineus*), cloudy cap fungus (*Clitocyba nebularis*), silver leaf fungus (*Stereum purpureum*) and candle-snuff fungus (*Xylaria hypoxylon*).
Examine germander speedwell plants to find the woolly gall caused by a fly, *Perissia veronicae.*

November outdoor and classroom work
An exhibition of materials collected earlier in the year. Simple showcases and boxes can be made.
This is a good time for studying soils, the weather, common rock samples and fruits and vegetables seen at the greengrocer's shop.
Observations and recordings of birds visiting the bird tables should be kept.
Winter work on trees as suggested in Chapter 7 may be carried out.

DECEMBER

Animals
There is little animal activity this month, but foxes, stoats and weasels may be seen searching for food.
Most birds are silent but the nuthatch and the great tit may be heard.
Titmice may be observed breaking open oak marble galls to feed on the larvae inside.
Moles, on the move for food, throw up molehills in fields and in gardens.

Plants
A few plants may be found in flower, e.g. gorse, shepherd's purse, groundsel, Christmas rose (in gardens).
Holly berries give a bright colour to the hedgerow.

This is a good time to search for and collect mosses such as purple-fruited heath moss (*Ceratodon purpureus*), triangular-leaved feather-moss (*Hylocomium triquetrum*), wavy hair moss (*Atrichum undulatum*) and red-stemmed feather-moss (*Pleurozium schreberi*).
Among the fungi to be seen are: velvet-stemmed agaric (*Collybia velutipes*), sulphur-tuft toadstool (*Hypholoma fasciculare*), brown stypic fungus (*Panus stypticus*), scarlet elf-cup fungus (*Sarcoscypha coccinea*), witch's-butter fungus (*Tremella mesenterica*), common zoned bracket fungus (*Polystictus versicolor*) and yellow-leather fungus (*Stereum hirsutum*). Most of the above will be found on old stumps or dead branches.

December outdoor and classroom work
A collection of mosses makes an attractive 'moss-garden' if kept moist.
Studies of evergreen shrubs and trees. Plants associated with Christmas.
Similar indoor work to that suggested for November can be carried out this month.
This is also a good time for star studies on clear evenings, as darkness soon falls.

Slides & Nature Calendar available from The Slide Centre, Portman House, 17 Brodrick Road, London, S.W.17.

SOME FEATURES OF THE YEARLY PATTERN IN FARMING

On arable farms the year begins again as soon as harvest is completed, so for convenience a calendar may be set out to begin with October and to finish in September.

By using a geographical reference book of British climatic statistics, or by reference to local weather recording stations, it is possible to obtain for each month average figures for rainfall, hours of sunshine and temperature. These will vary obviously according to the location of the farms which are studied. By using a good quality diary, the amount of daylight and darkness in the middle of each month can be found by reference to 'lighting up' and 'lights out' times.

The enterprises on a farm may vary considerably. Some farms may have only one main enterprise, for example, a dairy herd while others may have several, for example – arable crops for sale; sheep for fat lambs; a pig unit – all on the one farm.

The farm calendar that follows is intended as a rough guide to activities on farms in southern England. Remember that weather, soil conditions and altitude can all affect the time at which farm operations can be carried out.

FARM CALENDAR

OCTOBER

Arable: ploughing of any land cleared of crops.
- (*a*) Cereals: prepare tilth and sow winter oats and winter wheat.
- (*b*) Root crops: lift the mangold crop and clamp or store under cover; lifting of sugar beet.
- (*c*) Potatoes: complete lifting and store in clamps or sheds.
- (*d*) Other crops: sow winter beans.

Livestock: lowland ewes are put to the ram; amounts of winter food available are checked.

General: machines and equipment not needed through the winter are checked, oiled, greased and stored.

NOVEMBER

Arable: ploughing continues whenever possible; farmyard manure spread for ploughing in; lime spread on ploughed land, if necessary.
(*a*) Cereals: wheat sowing continues.
(*b*) Root crops: continue harvesting mangolds and sugar beet.
(*c*) Potatoes; set up seed potatoes in trays for chitting (sprouting).
Grassland: slow-acting fertiliser such as basic slag spread on pastures.
Livestock: (*a*) Dairy cattle: dairy herd brought in for winter; strongest heifers can be inseminated.
(*b*) Sheep: silage may be fed to in-lamb ewes.
General: cleaning of drains and ditches to avoid flooding.

DECEMBER

Arable: manure spreading and ploughing continue as weather permits.
(*a*) Cereals: last of winter wheat should now be in the soil.
(*b*) Root crops: continue lifting sugar beet; despatch to factory as permitted.
(*c*) Potatoes: inspect clamps or store for diseased tubers.
Livestock: (*a*) Sheep: prepare lambing pens; feed ewes well.
(*b*) Others: fat stock and poultry sent to Christmas markets: artificial light may be used in laying houses if desired.
General: hedging and ditching can be done; exposed water pipes should be lagged.

JANUARY

Arable: continue manure carting and spreading in frosty weather; complete ploughing if possible.
(*a*) Root crops: feed mangolds to stock as required.
(*b*) Potatoes: grade and sell some from store; seed of late varieties can be set up for chitting.
Grassland: harrow out matted grasses in permanent pastures and apply lime or fertilisers. On leys apply fertiliser, mainly nitrogenous.
Livestock: (*a*) Dairy herd: mate or inseminate cows as they come on heat.
(*b*) Sheep: pregnant ewes kept on high quality food; lambing begins.
General: Mend farm roads; check condition of gates and fences; laying of hedges, overhaul tractors and machinery.

FEBRUARY

Arable: if weather is suitable, land prepared for cereals.
(*a*) Cereals; sow spring varieties if weather and soil conditions allow.
(*b*) Root crops: continue to feed mangolds as required.
(*c*) Potatoes: continue to grade and sell from store.
(*d*) Other crops: spring beans and cereal-legume mixtures can be sown.
Grassland: continue harrowing old grassland, and apply nitrogenous fertilisers as needed.
Livestock: (*a*) Dairy herd: still housed indoors; milk yield tends to fall.
(*b*) Beef cattle: any animals out-wintered in the fields should have extra rations taken to them.
(*c*) Sheep: lambing continues.
(*d*) Pigs: make sure that any new litters are protected from chills.
General: hedging and ditching are continued; overhaul any machinery not yet dealt with; if day-old chicks are not bought in, then eggs should be incubated this month on the farm.

MARCH

Arable: seed bed prepared for cereals, using cultivators, harrows and rolls, as appropriate. Clean fields infested with couch grass.

(*a*) Cereals: sow spring cereals; autumn-sown corn can be harrowed to destroy weeds and dressed with fertiliser (mainly nitrogenous).

(*b*) Root crops: mangold seed can be sown: clear away the remains of last year's mangold storage clamps.

(*c*) Potatoes: grade and sell from store; prepare land and plant any early varieties.

(*d*) Fodder crops: sow peas and beans.

(*e*) Other crops: sow cereal-legume mixtures.

Grassland: harrow and roll old pastures; dress or spray ley grasses with nitrogenous fertiliser.

Livestock: provide shelter against cold winds for young lambs; treat cattle against warble fly attack. Dairy herd can be allowed for short periods on 'early-bite' leys.

APRIL

Arable: (*a*) Cereals: roll autumn cereals after frosty weather to firm the roots; continue harrowing to destroy weeds among autumn sown cereals; continue sowing of spring cereals. Oats and barley may be undersown with grasses and clover for leys.

(*b*) Root crops: sow mangolds and sugar beet.

(*c*) Potatoes: plant main crop varieties.

(*d*) Fodder crops: sow kale; spray peas to control weeds.

Grassland: control the grazing carefully by electric fencing or paddocks; harrow over used leys to spread droppings.

Livestock: (*a*) Dairy herd: cattle now out on leys or pasture; feed roughage before they go out to avoid digestive disorders arising from fresh grass.

(*b*) Sheep: tails of lambs docked; male lambs castrated.

General: silos prepared for silage making; sheep-shearing equipment checked.

MAY

Arable: (*a*) Cereals: finish applications of nitrogen; spray with selective weed killer for weed control.

(*b*) Rootcrops: continue inter-row cultivation (steerage hoes) to control weeds; begin singling of crops mechanically or by hand; swede seed is sown; complete sowing of mangolds and sugar beet.

(*c*) Potatoes: continue inter-row cultivations to kill weeds.

Grassland: ley grass is cut for silage and for grass-drying; apply nitrogenous fertiliser to aftermath; spray permanent pasture to kill perennial weeds.

Livestock: (*a*) Dairy herd: milk production is at a very high level; continue to control grazing of grassland carefully.

(*b*) Sheep: shearing takes place; some fat lambs available for sale; watch for foot-rot occurring in ewes, making them lame.

General: clean out the buildings where the cattle have been housed for the winter.

JUNE

Arable: (*a*) Root crops: turnip seed is sown; weeding and thinning of other root crops continue; control black aphis attacks on mangolds and sugar beet.

(*b*) Other crops: any crops other than grasses and clovers, intended for silage-making can be cut.

Grassland: hay-making is in full swing; apply nitrogen to remains of crop to encourage second growth.

Livestock: (*a*) Dairy herd: plenty of grass available; milk yield still high.
(*b*) Sheep; sheep may be shorn; fly 'strike' by bluebottle flies is common; lambs weaned and ewes put on to poorer pasture.

JULY

Arable: (*a*) Cereals: harvesting of autumn sown cereals begins.
(*b*) Potatoes: spraying against potato blight may be necessary.
Grassland: hay-making continues; silage-making using second crop of grass; further nitrogen may be applied after cutting of hay to extend grazing season.
Livestock: sheep: dipping may be done to control parasites.
General: overhaul harvest machinery early in the month.

AUGUST

Arable: plough pastures for re-seeding and cultivate stubble fields as soon as corn is cleared; the latter action encourages the growth of weeds which will later be ploughed in and killed.
(*a*) Cereals: harvesting is in full swing, given good weather conditions; combine-harvested grain must be dried in grain drier.
(*b*) Potatoes: control outbreaks of blight and late in month kill off or cut off potato haulms prior to harvesting.
Grassland: new leys should be sown: existing cocksfoot leys can be shut off to provide some winter grazing; clover grown for seed is harvested; grassland will benefit from irrigation in dry spells.
Livestock: (*a*) Dairy herd: if a period of drought occurs milk yield will fall quickly.
(*b*) Sheep: ewes should be on poor quality food prior to 'flushing' with good food before being put to the ram. Fertility is raised by this method.

SEPTEMBER

Arable: ploughing continues as harvest is cleared.
(*a*) Cereals: harvesting of cereals is completed; land prepared and winter oats sown at end of month.
(*b*) Roots: according to arrangements with the factory, sugar beet lifting may begin at the end of the month.
(*c*) Potatoes: this crop is lifted and put into store.
Grassland: Pastures or leys intended for 'early bite' should be shut off and treated with lime, phosphate or potash as necessary.
Livestock: Dairy herd: cows calving in the autumn should be put on to good grazing. If kale is available, this may be strip-grazed by the dairy herd, but not in frosty conditions.
General: Corn drills and fertiliser drills should be checked over; order fertilisers for future use; hop-picking and the gathering of the apple crop are carried out this month.

Although not specifically mentioned in the calendar milking of the dairy herd, the tending of 'baby-beef' or 'broiler-beef' calves, and of pigs and poultry has to be carried on day by day.

SOME FEATURES OF THE YEARLY WEATHER PATTERN

(N.B. As weather conditions are unpredictable and variable, this chart shows only generalisations)

Month		Weather	Seasons	General Conditions	Weather Conditions	Some notable Weather Events
JANUARY	1–7	Wind and rain	EARLY	The coldest month of the year. Coldest traditionally on St. Hilary's Day. The first part of the month is a stormy one. A renewal of storms takes place at the end of the month.	Rainfall in the early part of the month, followed by a drier period and then at the end of the month by renewed gales and storms.	5 January 1552 Great wind storms over all Western Europe, repeated again. 6 January 1839 The Great Wind: many ships wrecked, houses blown over in Scotland and Northern England. 8-15 January 1552 North Sea storm surges. 11 January 1740 Record cold day in spell which started on 4 January Temp. in London –9°C. 12 January 1818 Severe gale damaged buildings in Edinburgh.
	14–21	Fine cold	WINTER			13 January 1725 Very dry period began, only 15 days with rain at Wells, Somerset, in the next three months.
	28	Wind and rain			Heavy rains and gales.	19 January 1942 Great snowstorm over all Britain. 28 January 1927 Widespread gale damage.
FEBRUARY	1–7	———	LATE	February is a cold month and is often dry although it starts rather stormy.	Fewer gales; but very low temperatures in the middle of the month. This cold is associated with dry conditions.	**1 to 4 February 1814 Last Frost Fair held on the Thames in London.** 2 February 1776 End of severe spell affecting all Europe since 4th January. 3 February 1666 Gales in London. Houses blown down.
	7–14	Fine Cold		High pressure dominates the country and brings cold sometimes foggy or frosty weather.		7 February 1911 Notable drought began. 8 February 1698 Ice 8 inches thick on the North Sea off Suffolk.
	14–	Unsettled				10 February 1579 Thames flooded by melting snow

FEBRUARY	21 28	Fine Cold Wind and rain	Spring Equinox WINTER AND	The end of the month brings a renewal of the depressions which bring stormy weather.		11 February 1895 Lowest temps. in a long cold spell. –27°C at Braemar. Thames blocked by icefloes 9–17. 14 February 1579 Four day snowfall 15 February 1900 All-day snowstorm in Northern England. 16 February 1962 Great Gale. Wind speed of 177 m.p.h. (284 kph) on Uist. 18 February 1684 Rain and thaw after eight weeks freezing. 28 February 1937 Great snowstorm in Wales and Scotland.
MARCH	1 7 ——— 14 ——— 21 28	Fine Wind rain	EARLY SPRING	A boisterous start is followed by high pressure in the middle of the month. This brings real spring-like weather. Another stormy period ends the month.	Many gales with a decrease of rain in the middle of the month.	1 March 1636 Beginning of long dry spell. 5 March 1838 Rain and thaw in London; all snow gone by 8th. 8 March 1674 13 day snowfall and blizzard. 10 March 1929 Day temps. 21°C in Lake District. Ice on lakes because of the cold nights. 16 March 1947 Great gales. 18 March 1886 End of spell of frost and snow. 24 March 1878 Sudden gale. 24 March 1895 Worst gale of the century in Midlands. 29 March 1901 Heavy snow in the North.
APRIL	1 7 14 ——— ———	Wind rain	SPRING	Many showers, fog becomes rare; changeable pressure conditions and much change in the weather.	Abrupt increase in rainfall; fogs rare; late spring snowfall possible.	1 April 1917 Great snowstorm in Northern England. 14 April 1921 Snow in many districts. 18 April 1850 Thunderstorm with tornado in Dublin. 20 April 1893 Early heat wave. 28°C in London.

APRIL	21 28	Changeable conditions	AND EARLY SUMMER	From mid to late April there is considerable influence from high pressure systems and there are fine spells of weather.		24 April 1600 Heavy snowfall. 25 April 1725 Beginning of prolonged rainy spell. 25 April 1950 Deep snow. 27 April 1919 Snow all over Britain. 29 April 1882 Violent S.W. gale.
MAY	1 7 14 21 28	Thundery ——— ——— Fine ———	SPRING and EARLY SUMMER	After a showery start that is associated with depression activity, pressure is changeable between high and low; sometimes cold weather is brought from the north. The end of the month brings the return of the high pressure systems.	The middle of the month is often fine; but there is a liability to late frosts. Thunderstorms become more frequent at the beginning of the month.	1 May 1698 Five inches of snow in Yorkshire. 4 May 1579 Snow 1 ft. deep in London. 5 May 1959 Beginning of long warm spell. 6 May 1911 Beginning of a long warm spell. 12 May 1947 Beginning of a long warm spell. 13 May 1698 Snow in Yorkshire and the South. 16 May 1740 Snow in London. 16 May 1935 Snow at Cambridge and heavy frost. 19 May 1698 Snow in Shropshire. 20 May 1729 Tornado in Kent and Sussex. 21 May 1950 Tornadoes in East England with thunderstorms. 27 May 1821 Snow in London.
JUNE	1 7 14 21 24 28	Wind and rain Fine ——— ——— Hot and thundery	——— MID-SUMMERS DAY	The pressure systems are reforming and there is an increase in cloudy weather; so that temperatures tend to drop at first. Because of these changes there are many thunderstorms.	Fall in temperature at the beginning of the month; frequent thunderstorms; some cold nights.	1 June 1924 Flooding in Central England. 3 June 1962 Record June frosts –6°C at Santon Downham (Norfolk). 4 June 1945 Heavy gales on the West coast. 7 June 1768 Beginning of a record wet summer in England. 9 June 1910 Large hailstones from a very severe storm. 11 June 1667 Beginning of a long dry spell.

JUNE						11 June 1768 Two day downpour. 14 June 1914 Floods and hail damage in London. 17 June 1815 Thunderstorm rains in Belgium delay Napoleon's army at Waterloo. 22 June 1799 Beginning of a long rainy spell. 28 June 1788 Probably the wettest day ever recorded in Somerset.
JULY	1 7 14 21 28	——— ——— Warm period ——— unsettled and thundery	HIGH SUMMER	A series of slow-moving depressions is a common feature of this month especially from the middle of the month onwards. This is the hottest month of the year.	This can be a period of great heat and of heavy thunderstorms.	2 July 1893 Cloudburst on Cheviots. 2 July 1946 Tropical type thunderstorm over South and East England. 4 July 1681 End of four months' spell of east winds in Scotland. 5 July 1666 Extremely hot. 8 July 1893 Thunderstorms and whirlwinds in the North of England. 11 July 1596 A period of severe gales in Scotland lasting into August. 13 July 1808 Very high temperatures in South and East England 20 July 1930 Four days persistent rain in N. Yorks. 22 July 1868 Highest shade temperature ever recorded in England 38.1°C at Tonbridge, Kent. 25 July 1738 Severe hailstorms. Lumps of ice up to 9 inches across fell. 29 July 1956 Violent gale in Channel. 29 July 1588 Spanish Armada entered the Channel after a stormy journey.

AUGUST	1 7 14 21 28	Rain and wind		The first part of the month continues the pattern of July, but by the middle of the month the depression systems are moving south.	Stormy at first, with a tendency to be colder than July. The later part of the month is again stormy.	1 August 1846 Violent thunderstorms. Hail smashed windows. 1–12 August 1938 Very stormy spell. 3 August 1879 Great hailstones smashed roofs. 4 August 1929 Disastrous floods in West Scotland. 8 August 1588 Spanish Armada defeated and carried northwards by strong S.W. winds. 9 August 1911 37.8°C at Greenwich 15 August 1951 Great rains on Exmoor. Lynmouth floods. 17 August 1748 Sleet near coast of Shetland. 20 August 1698 Short fine period in Yorkshire. 31 August 1879 Fine anticyclonic weather ends summer rains.
SEPTEMBER	1 7 14 21	Fine Stormy	HIGH SUMMER AUTUMN	High pressure systems pass across Southern Britain. September is a month of fairly long periods of more settled weather either cold or wet. The latter half is subject to a series of depressions.	Often dry at the beginning but stormy with increasing rainfall at the end.	1 September 1883 Former West Indian hurricane brings heavy rain. 2 September 1741 First general rain after heat and drought since 12 June. 5 September 1725 Beginning of a period of drier weather. 5 September 1958 Tornadoes and giant hail in Sussex. 13 September 1903 High pressure after a notable wet period. 19 September 1666 The first considerable rain quenched the Fire of London. 20 September 1773 Rain and gales in Northern Scotland.

SEPT	28					24 September 1895 Latest known date in any year for a temperature of 30°C. 26 September 1903 Depressions again begin to cross Britain. Rainy period begins.
OCTOBER	1	Fine	AUTUMN	At the beginning the high pressure systems begin to become re-established and after a short stormy spell the weather becomes fine. At the end of the month stormy depressions are more frequent.	The wind and the rain of late September change into a fine period but at the end of the month there is heavy rain and gales.	3 October 1959 29°C. in London 6 October 1921 29°C. in London, latest known date for this. 7 October 1829 Earliest known date for the snow to lie in London. 9 October 1740 N. wind brought very cold wind and frost; coldest October on record. 10 October 1959 First general rain after a long drought. 11 October 1916 8 inches rain near Loch Hourn in W. Highlands. 15 October 1571 Gales and sea floods in the Fens. 20 October 1846 Violent floods in Ireland. 29 October 1954 Renewed flooding of the area flooded by the storms in Ireland. 31 October 1638 Tornadoes in Devon.
	7					
	14	Stormy				
	21	Fine				
	28	Stormy				
NOVEMBER	1		AUTUMN	Sometimes a ridge of high pressure extends across England for short periods at the beginning between the depression storms. This is followed by a period of high pressure when fogs are common.	The first period is wet and is then followed by the main fog period. The end of the month again brings high rainfall.	1 November 1785 Tornado damage in Notts. 2 November 1937 Prolonged rain and flooding. 4 November 1946 Warmest November day on record 20.5°C. at Edinburgh. 6 November 1771 Heavy rain and floods at King's Lynn. 9 November 1931 Violent S. gale in the Channel.
	7	Wind and rain				
	14	Fine Foggy	EARLY WINTER			
	21					
	28	Stormy				

NOVEMBER				At the end of the month strong depressions are again common.		12 November 1740 N. gale with rain, snow and hail. 16 November 1771 Floods in the North-East. 21 November 1696 W. winds and rainy weather returned. 26 November 1948 Smoke fog caused many deaths in London. 26 November–1 December. 30 November 1665 Climax to a month of wind and fog. 30 November 1788 Earliest known case of a long unbroken fog lasting until early January 1789.
DECEMBER	1	———		There is a continuation of the conditions of November with deep depressions passing over the country. This is followed by a period dominated by high pressure but the end of the month sees a recurrence of low pressures.	Heavy rain at first. This is one of the wettest periods of the year. The high pressure brings reduced rainfall.	2 December 1665 Severe frost in London. 4 December 1879 Very severe frost –30.5°C at Blackadder. People frozen to death. 5 Dec. 1695 An interval of snow and frost in the London area after a period of dark misty weather. 8 December 1954 Severe thunderstorms and tornadoes in London. 12 December 1901 N.W. gales in the Channel. 14 December 1890 Coldest known December day in London; temperature never rose above —16°C. 21 December 1607 Onset of long frost. 21 December 1665 Long frost set in; Thames blocked by ice. 25 December 1937 Heavy snowstorm in the South; drifts 20ft. deep. 26 December 1813 Thick smoke fog in London. Lasted to 2nd January. 28 December 1879 W.S.W. gale, Tay bridge disaster.
	7	Wind and rain	EARLY WINTER			
	14	———				
	21	Fine Cold	Winter solstice			
	28	Wind and rain				

7 Living Things: Their Nurture and Uses in Schools

The living plants and animals of our environment offer interesting possibilities for observation and study. It is beyond the scope of this book to deal in detail with all these possibilities but some lines of approach will be indicated for development by the teacher.

WORKING WITH PLANTS

Learning from the garden

Some schools may find it possible to set aside some space for cultivation by the children. Some starting-points for learning are as follows:

(A) THE VALUE OF MULCHING CROPS. Use cabbage plants as the crop and try to obtain comparative results by the use of sawdust, peat, strawy manure, well-rotted leaves, vermiculite, black polythene (with holes cut for the plants to be inserted).

(B) CULTIVATION EXPERIMENTS SUCH AS:

- (i) lettuce plants singled compared with those not singled,
- (ii) radishes weeded compared with those not weeded,
- (iii) potatoes ridged compared with those not ridged,
- (iv) lettuces watered regularly compared with those not watered,
- (v) dwarf beans sown at 5 cm. depth compared with those at 10 cm. depth,
- (iv) crop grown on dug ground compared with crop sown in 8 cm. of sifted compost placed over undug soil.

7:1 A suggested lay-out of small garden plots to examine the effects on a cabbage crop of various types of soil mulches.

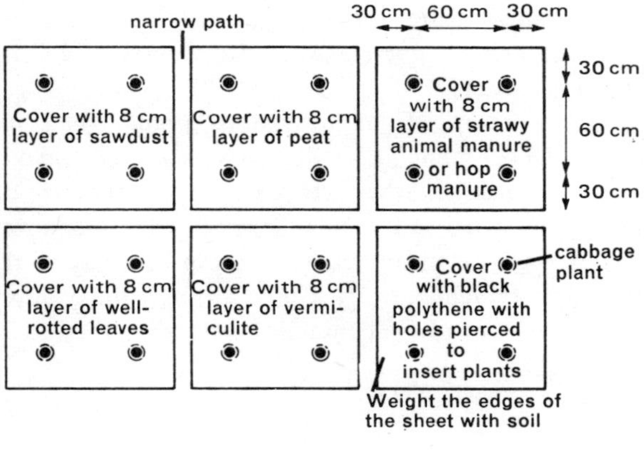

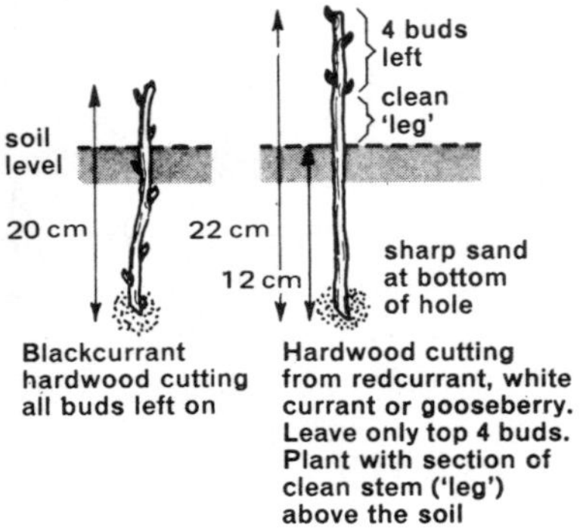

7:2 Methods recommended for the taking of hardwood cuttings of bush fruits.

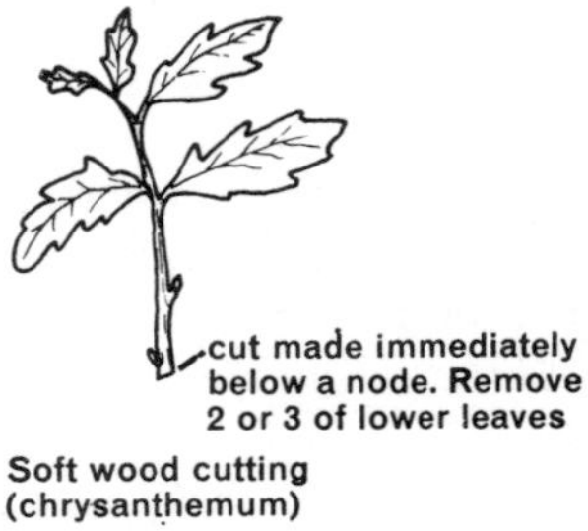

7:3 The preparation of a softwood cutting.

(C) MANURES AND FERTILISERS

(i) Potatoes grown on land manured at 2 bucketsful of farmyard manure per square metre compared with those on land given a complete fertiliser (Growmore) at 60 gm. per square metre.

(ii) Mark out similar narrow strips of soil and lawn and compare the results on (*a*) a radish crop and (*b*) on grass, of using sulphate of ammonia on one strip, superphosphate on another and sulphate of potash on a third, all at a measured rate of 60 gm. per square metre.

(D) WEED STUDIES

(i) Encourage children working in the garden to recognise the weeds that they find. Collections can be taken into school and displayed under 'annuals', 'biennials' and 'perennials'. It is useful with some of the plants to lift them complete and to wash away the adhering soil before displaying them. The books on farm weeds published by Shell and by Blackwell are useful for identification. Also available at various times are free leaflets, containing weed illustrations, issued by various agricultural chemical firms such as I.C.I., May and Baker, Fison's, etc.

(ii) Collections of seeds from the various annual weed plants can be made by the children. This will give some impression of the amount of seed produced and the methods by which they are dispersed. If the seeds are dried and 50 of each species are later sown in pots or seed boxes, germination percentages can be easily worked out and recorded by the children. It will be useful if the children can learn to recognise some of the common weeds when they are in the seedling stage.

(E) PROPAGATION OF PLANTS

(i) Many species of garden plants can be propagated from cuttings of hardwood. In autumn ripened shoots, about 9″ (23 cm.) long, of black currant, redcurrant or gooseberry can be taken and planted firmly to half their depth. With blackcurrants, leave all the buds on the cutting but with the other two, leave only a few buds near the top of the cuttings. Try also deciduous shrubs such as forsythia, *Ribes* (flowering currant), *Lonicera* (honeysuckle), deutzia, philadelphus, and evergreen shrubs such as *Hebe* (veronica), laurel, *Ilex* (holly), *viburnum tinus* are suitable.

(ii) Softwood cuttings. If the school has a garden frame, conservatory or small greenhouse available, then cuttings of young shoots which have not flowered can be taken from such plants as pelargonium (geranium), fuchsia, coleus, pansy, tradescantia, dahlia and chrysanthemum. These cuttings with most leaves removed, should be placed in pots of John Innes compost and arranged around the edge, say, four of five to a pot. Placing the pots in polythene bags tied at the neck will help to hasten root production. Small electrically-heated propagators with a plastic dome cover can now be bought.

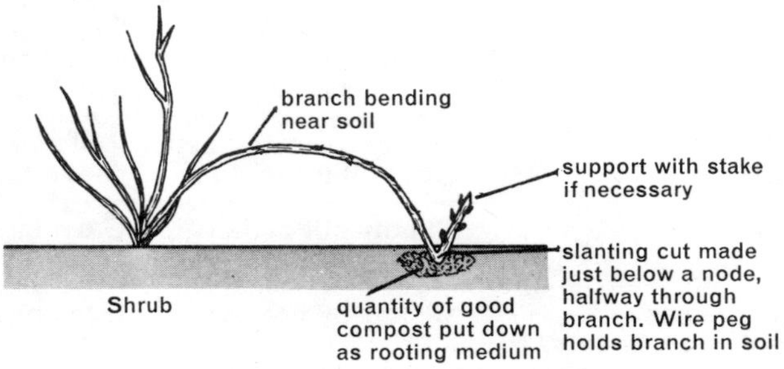

7 : 4 Propagation of a shrub by layering.

(iii) Layering. Some shrubs have branches which droop close to the ground, and with these it is possible to make a slanting cut to half the depth of the stem at a point where a node occurs. Peg down this cut part into the soil so that the thinner end is approximately vertical. When roots have formed the new plant can be finally separated and moved. Forsythia, berberis and escallonia are easily propagated this way.

With blackberries and loganberries the ends of some branches can be pegged into the soil. They will soon form roots. A strawberry plant will readily propagate itself from the runners which it produces.

(iv) Other methods of propagation. The small area of garden should contain examples of plants such as erigeron and michaelmas daisy so that children can try root clump division for propagation. They should also have the opportunity of seeing how gladioli, crocus, tulip, shallots, dahlias, irises and potatoes can propagate themselves vegetatively.

(F) PLANTS OF BOTANICAL INTEREST

It is useful to have plants growing in the garden to illustrate various botanical characteristics. If the school has no facilities for raising half-hardy plants from seed, then some of these plants may be obtainable from nurseries or from Woolworth's stores. Try Thompson & Morgan Ltd., Ipswich, Suffolk for seeds.

Plant (H - hardy HH - half hardy)	*Botanical Features*	*Remarks*
Balsam (camellia-flowered) or *Impatiens* HH	Explosive fruits; rapid transpiration	Easy to grow; keep well-watered
Toadflax *(Linaria cymbalaria)* H	Runners; seed capsule splits across	Easy to grow. Let branches run down over bricks or rocks
Nicotiana affinis HH	Flower opens at dusk; Unusual flower tube	Will stand some shade
Schizanthus hybridus HH	Shoots out pollen	Grow in pot sunk in soil of garden
Canary Creeper *(Tropaeolum canariense)* H	Climbs by petioles	Does best in fertile soil
Ampelopsis H (virginian creeper)	Climbs by suckers	Plant against a wall or woven fence
Anemone St Brigid H	An early flowering plant	Buy the corms
Winter Aconite *(Eranthis hyemalis)* H	A very early flowering plant	Can be planted among shrubs
Morning Glory *(Ipomaea)* HH	Climbs by twining Large size seeds	Buy a plant in August. Give supports
Crocus H	Useful to show life cycle of corm	Avoid yellow ones
Foxglove *(Digitalis)* H	Censer mechanism for seed dispersal	

Pelargonium (Geranium) HH	Some varieties have variegated leaves. Low transpiration rate. Interesting fruit	Plants can be bought. Cuttings can be propagated
Ivy *(Hedera)* H	A root climber	Will grow in shade. Cuttings and layers can be taken
Mesembryanthemum HH	Example of a succulent plant	Do not over-water
Maize (ornamental variety) HH	Shows prop roots. Hybrids show different coloured grains	
Oxalis (wood sorrel) H	Sleep movements of plant; *valdiviensis sp,* shoots out seeds HH	Buy bulbs in autumn. Buy seed
Sweet pea H	Leaf tendrils	
Radish H	Food storage organ Easy germination	
Shallot H	Vegetative reproduction	
Solomon's Seal *(Polygonatum)*	Useful plant for showing rhizome	Buy as plant
Virginian stock H	Useful for showing parts of a plant	Easily grown from seed
Wallflower H	Useful for showing parts of plant	Plants can be bought
Water lily (dwarf form) H	Fruit pulled under water	Buy plant and grow in garden pool

In urban or in other schools where it is impossible to cultivate a small garden, troughs and tubs could be used to provide not only decorative plants but also selected examples from the above list as a basis for practical plant study.

PLANTS IN THE CLASSROOM

(*a*) Pot plants

Classroom conditions can be difficult for plants, but there are some which will be reasonably successful.

Try cacti and succulents in shallow containers. These are useful examples of water storage in plants and, in some cases, of protection from browsing animals. There are opportunities for the cultivation of these from seed, and propagation from cuttings and from broken off leaves can be tried. Pot plants, selected for their hardiness under classroom conditions, can be used for training in the care of plants and also for observation of growth, changes in form, the unfolding of leaves and so on. Some plants which can be recommended are: *Sansevieria laurentii, Tradescantia rosea* and *T. zebrina, Peperomia hederifolia* and *P. magnoliaefolia.*

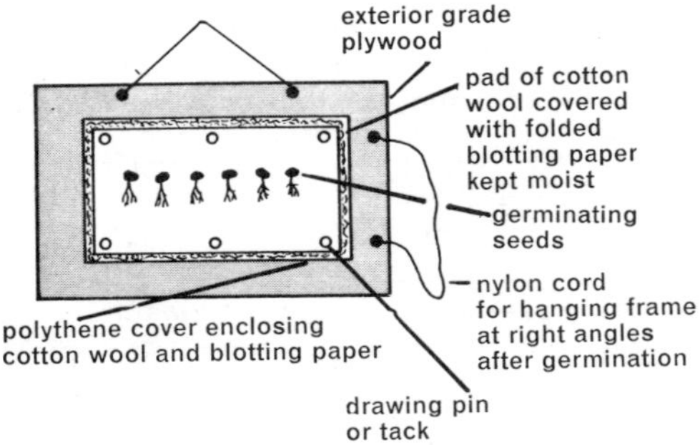

7 : 5 A seed germination 'frame' which can be hung in the classroom.

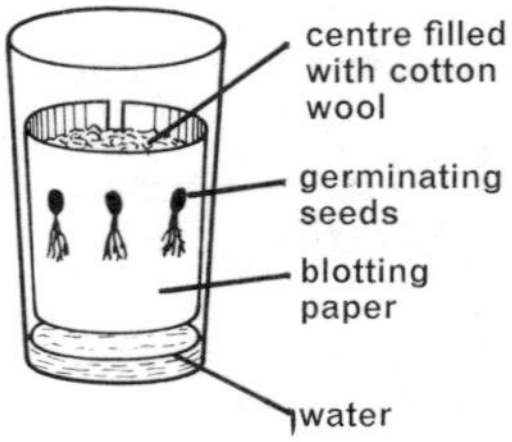

7 : 6 A tumbler used for demonstrating the germination of seeds.

(*b*) Plant studies: seeds

(i) *Seed germination stages* (see also Chapter 5, p. 175)

Children should have the opportunity of setting up simple apparatus for seed germination, and of making frequent observations and recordings of their development.

There are various ways of starting seeds into growth. A hanging frame can be made. Take a piece of exterior quality plywood about 18 × 12 cm., and paint this with Green Solignum (the type which is harmless to plants). Cover an area of this, say 12 × 7·5 cm., with a pad of cotton wool, over which some folded blotting paper should be placed. Make sure that the cotton wool and blotting paper are well moistened. Place groups of seeds such as maize, wheat, mustard, radish, lupin, etc., on the blotting paper, and using drawing pins, fasten these in position by covering with a small sheet of clear polytheme of medium thickness. Water can be added as necessary through spaces between the drawing pins. Similar frames can be made and used to compare seeds with and without water and seeds exposed to light with those in darkness. If the seeds are allowed to germinate and then the frame is moved to hang at right angles to its original position the change of direction of growth of shoot and root can be observed.

Seeds can also be germinated in a glass tumbler. Cut a rectangular-shaped piece of blotting paper to suit the depth of the tumbler. Coil this inside the tumbler and fill the central space with sawdust, peat, vermiculite or foam rubber 'crumbs'. Push seeds such as wheat, barley, peas, beans, nasturtium, calendula down between the glass and the blotting paper. Keep the contents of the tumbler moist always. A third method involves the use of clear, oblong plastic food containers, in which potted meat jars, half filled with sand, can be placed. Using rubber bands, fasten a piece of cotton sheeting over the top of each jar leaving the ends of the sheeting to hang down the sides for the whole length of the jars. Pour water into the plastic container until it reaches half-way up the jars. Place seeds of different kinds

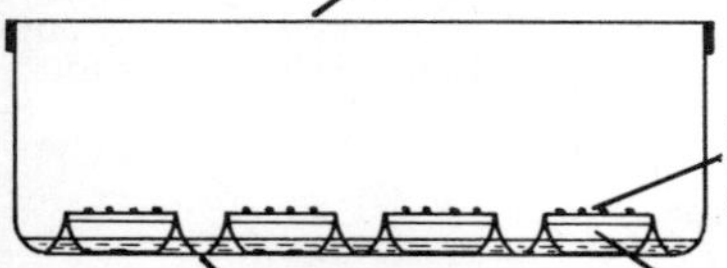

7:7 Using a plastic container for seed germination.

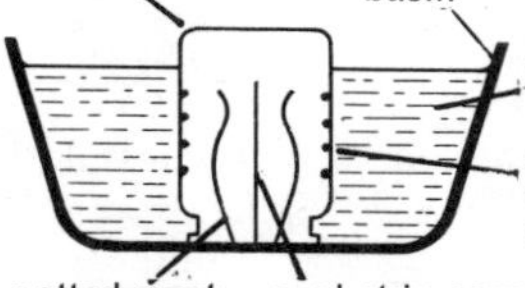

7:8 A demonstration to show that germinating seeds require oxygen.

on the top of each jar and replace the lid of the plastic container. The stages of germination can be observed and recorded.

(ii) *Germination requirements*

Discuss with children the natural conditions under which seeds grow before testing the essential requirements.

Get the children to place similar seeds in jars or test tubes providing each of the following conditions:

1 Seeds on moist cotton wool; jar left open in warmth and light (control).

2 Seeds on dry cotton wool, giving light, warmth, air but no water.

3 Seeds, without cotton wool, well covered with freshly boiled and cooled water. On top of the water pour a covering of boiled olive oil or boiled motor oil. These seeds will have light, warmth, moisture but no air.

4 Seeds on moist cotton wool; jar placed either in a cold place out of doors or in a refrigerator at home or in school. These seeds will have light (not if in refrigerator), moisture, air, but no warmth.

5 Seeds on moist cotton wool; jar covered with an inverted tin. These seeds have warmth, air, moisture but no light. Make sure that those jars requiring moisture are supplied with water regularly. The children should make frequent observations and be able to deduce the requirements of seeds.

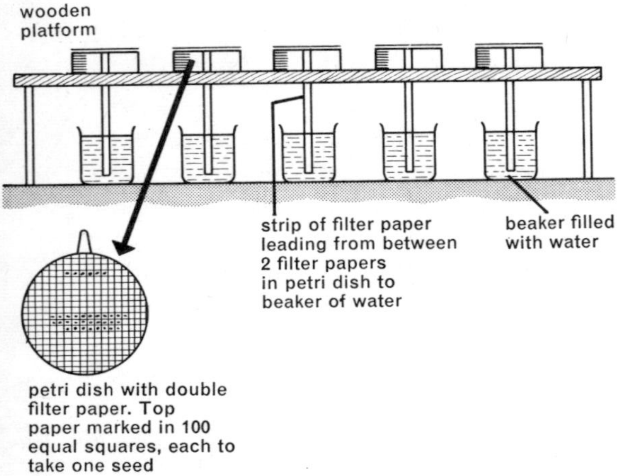

7:9 Simple apparatus used for testing percentage germination of seeds.

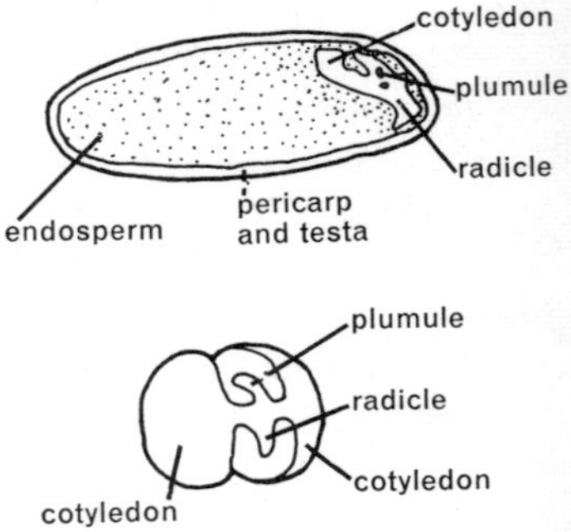

7:10 Sketches to show the structur of the seed of a monocotyledonous plant (wheat) and a dicotyledonous plant (broad bean).

(iii) *Germination percentage*
The viability of seeds varies considerably, and children can test various species to estimate their percentage of germination. Special small plastic germination beakers are available from biological suppliers such as P. K. Dutt and Son Ltd., Bromley Kent, and in these, filter papers marked out in 100 small squares can be used as a base for the seeds.

A second method involves the use of a shelf made from a piece of timber up to 1 m. × 10 cm. × 12 mm. Nail or screw supports to this so that it will stand about six inches (15 cm) above the table. Plastic petri dishes containing two or three filter papers, the top one of which is marked out in 100 squares, can be used for the seeds, placed one in each square. Stand the petri dishes on the shelf and from between the circular filter papers of each dish lead a strip of filter paper into a beaker of water standing at a lower level. Thus water will be supplied steadily to the seeds. Observations, counts and recordings will lead to some useful information about the fertility of seeds. If surplus seeds of previous years have been saved then it may be possible to see how quickly viability is lost. Seed catalogues usually list the minimum germination percentage of common vegetable seeds. Suggest to the children that they might see how much above the legal minimum of percentage germination various seeds appear to be.

(iv) *Seed structure*
Encourage the children to collect seeds of many kinds, and with the larger ones to determine which are monocotyledonous (having one cotyledon or food store) and which are dicotyledonous (having two cotyledons). With the use of hand lens or magnifiers the children can find and sketch the food store area and the part of the seed which will develop into the young plant.

If seeds are to be opened for inspection they should be soaked in water overnight.

An interesting link with geography can be made by making collections of seeds from imported fruits and by also collecting seeds from plants which originated in other countries but which are now grown in Britain, e.g. maize, tobacco, eschscholzia, azalea, etc.

(v) *Seeds and atmospheric gases*

Germinating seeds and oxygen:

Fill a jam jar with water and then empty the water away. Immediately, sprinkle some radish or mustard seeds round the walls of the jar, and place inside it a piece of blotting paper to hold the seeds in position. Take a fairly deep dish of greater diameter than the mouth of the jam jar and stand in the dish a tall type of potted meat jar. In this jar place a strip of cardboard which has been covered with wet iron filings or pierced with about two dozen wet tin tacks. Now two-thirds fill the dish with water and invert the jam jar in the water. The rusting of iron will use up oxygen, the seeds will not develop very much and the water should rise about one-fifth of the way up the jar, representing the proportion of oxygen which has disappeared from the air in the jar. Without a good supply of oxygen, seeds will not develop.

Germinating seeds and carbon dioxide:

Place some dwarf bean seeds on some moist cotton wool in the bottom of a glass jar. Take a cork which will fit the jar, and bore the cork to take two glass tubes, one of which leads from near the base of the jar to a rubber tubing connection to a football pump and the other which leads from the top of the jar into a test tube containing lime water. Let the seeds germinate for about a week and then pump air into the jar. Air from the jar will be forced into the lime water and if this turns milky, carbon dioxide has been produced by the germinating seeds. Set up a control experiment without the seeds.

(vi) *Seeds on the move*

Seeds are produced by a plant to ensure the continuation of the species. To avoid undue competition in the area near the parent plant, some seeds are adapted for travel to a new area through different methods of dispersal. Get children to find and bring annual plants – wild and cultivated – to school. Discuss the amount of seed produced, and the lack of any other method of natural propagation. A groundsel plant can produce two generations in one year. Show this by cultivation in pots in school.

Encourage children to bring seeds and fruits of various kinds and to suggest ways in which the seeds may travel to new habitats. The seeds and fruits can be grouped under headings such as: wind dispersal; dispersal by ejection; dispersal by animals; dispersal by water. A display can be set up or examples can be mounted as charts by the children.

The presence of many weed seeds in soil can be demonstrated by potting some garden soil and making a count of seedlings, removing each as soon as it has been counted.

(*c*) **Plant studies: roots and stems**

(i) *Root hairs*

The importance of root hairs for the intake of dissolved nutrients can be discussed. If mustard seeds are grown on damp plastic foam in a covered glass container it is easy to see the root hairs. They can also be examined by using hand lenses or magnifiers.

When the seedlings are large enough to handle, carefully transfer some to a small pot of seed compost. Take some of the other seedlings and with very fine pointed scissors remove as many root hairs as possible. Then plant the seedlings in a pot of similar compost. Compare the rate of growth.

(ii) *The absorption of plant nutrients*

Obtain three wide-necked bottles. Fill one with water, the second with a mixture of red ink and water and the third with a suspension of congo red. Lift three complete groundsel plants and fix one in each bottle, using Plasticene to support the plants and to seal the bottles. The roots will remove some of the water from each bottle. When this has occurred, lift out the plants and cut lengthwise down the stem. The red ink solution will show, but there will be no sign of uptake of the coloured particles of congo red. Therefore all nutrients must be completely dissolved in soil water before they can be taken into a plant.

(iii) *Osmosis*

The solution within the root hairs is stronger than the soil water containing dissolved plant nutrients. We can show the movement of a weaker solution

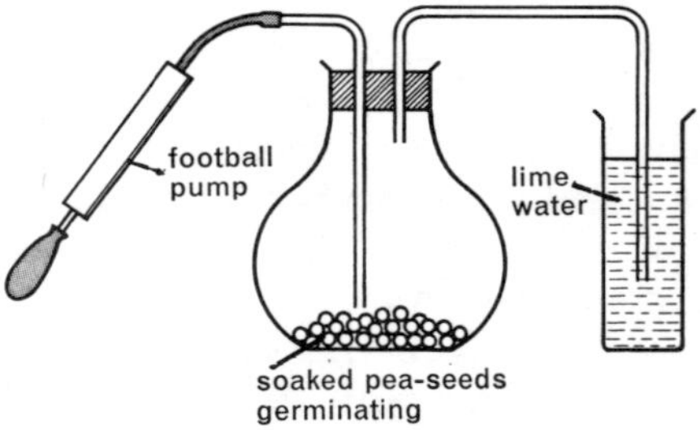

7 : 11 Apparatus which can be used to show that germinating seeds give off carbon dioxide.

into a stronger one in the following way. Take two potatoes, wash and cut off each end. Scoop out a cavity in one of the cut ends of each potato almost to the full depth. With the cavity uppermost remove the peel from about 3 cm. up from the base of each potato. Place each in a separate trough of water. Pour a strong sugar solution into the cavity of one potato, and water into the other. The level of the liquid will rise only where the sugar solution has been used.

(iv) *The upper movement of nutrients through the root*

Obtain a carrot and cut off the tip of the root. Then place the cut end in a solution of red ink and water. Leave it for at least 24 hours and then make a longitudinal or vertical section. It should be possible to trace the upward movement of the coloured liquid.

(v) *The movement of nutrients through the stem*

Cut a short piece off the ends of some celery stems and then freshen the stems by placing them in cold water for a few hours. Then stand the stems in a jar containing red ink, leaving them there for 24 hours. Remove the stems and cut them into short lengths. The upward movement of the coloured liquid can be seen, and some of the tubes can possibly be pulled out from the stems. Encourage the children to try the same thing with young twigs from trees. To illustrate this process more strikingly, the stem of a white carnation flower can be split into three parts using a razor blade. Make the cuts extend about 10 cm. (4″) up the stem and do the cutting under water. Have ready three small beakers each containing a differently coloured ink solution (20% ink). Spread out the split stem so that one of the parts is in each beaker, and observe the flower colour during the next few days. To prevent the stem splitting too far up bind it with Sellotape.

(vi) *Root nodules on leguminous plants*

If a farmer grows a leguminous crop such as clover, lucerne, peas or beans, he may find that the succeeding crop needs very little nitrogenous fertiliser. The roots of any of these plants, or of lupin seedlings cultivated in pots in the classroom can be examined with hand lenses or magnifiers to

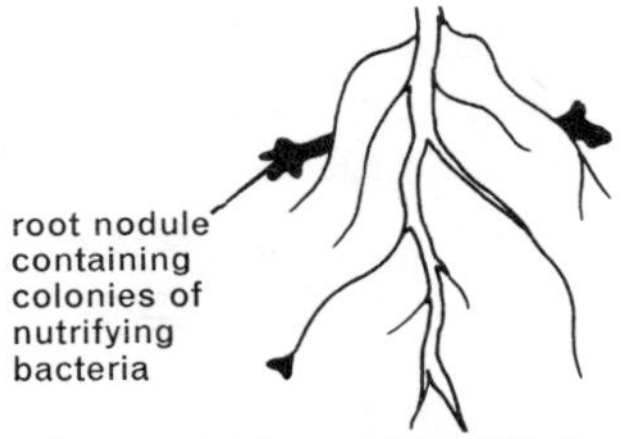

7 : 12 The roots of a leguminous plant, carefully lifted and washed, often reveal nodules containing nitrogen-fixing bacteria.

find the nodules, or small swellings, which contain colonies of nitrogen-fixing bacteria. These bacteria can convert the free nitrogen of soil air into a form which can be used by plants. Children should be encouraged to examine and sketch these nodules.

(vii) *Roots and stems as food storage organs*
Biennial plants normally do not flower and produce seeds until their second year of life. During the first year excess food is manufactured by the plant and stored, often in the *tap roots* which swell considerably. Examples of such plants, which can be easily obtained from the school garden or from the greengrocer, include carrot, parsnip, beetroot, swede, turnip, sugar beet and mangel.

A potato tuber (*stem tuber*), is really an underground stem, swollen with stored food. Having produced many of these tubers, to carry on the species, the original parent plant dies away in the autumn.

Some plants store food in a short, swollen stem which we know as a *corm*. In plants such as the crocus and cuckoo-pint new corms are formed on top of the old; the latter shrivels as the new corm is built up.

In plants which have *rhizomes*, the stem remains below ground, but from it leaves and flowers develop above ground. Couch grass and the iris are examples of such plants.

Some other plants have the top parts of their roots swollen with food stores, and these are known as *root tubers*. The lesser celandine and the dahlia can be quoted as examples.

Encourage children to make collections of these various storage organs, to group and label them. Discuss the ways in which new plants and new storage organs arise from the food of the parent part. If you consult a biology book such as *Progressive Biology Vol.* 2: Perry and Hirons (Blandford), you will find descriptions of how to carry out simple tests for sugar, starch, fats and proteins. Children could thus discover which of the storage organs react to these tests. A useful project could be developed on 'Roots: their uses to man'.

(viii) *The usefulness of stems*
We all appreciate that a stem is useful for transporting food, supporting leaves, flowers and fruits, but children can discover other uses of stems. Examine stems of plants in the environment and again make a grouped and labelled display in the classroom. Here are some suggestions.

(*a*) stems which creep underground: creeping thistle, couch grass.

(*b*) stems which creep on top of the ground: strawberry, silverweed, ground ivy.

(*c*) stems which have tendrils for climbing: virginia creeper, sweet pea, garden pea, vine.

7 : 13 The variegated leaves of *Tradescantia* sp. can be used in photosynthesis demonstrations.

(*d*) stems which twine around supports to reach the light: runner bean, honeysuckle, convolvulus, hop. In which direction do these climb?

(*e*) stems which have protective stinging hairs; stinging nettle.

(*f*) stems which have protective spines or thorns: rose, hawthorn, blackthorn, berberis, pyracantha, thistle.

Discuss with the children the reasons for these various adaptations, linking the plant with the conditions in its natural habitat, wherever possible.

(ix) *Propagation from stems*

In many species, new plants can be encouraged to grow from sections of stem of the parent plant. Try a good number of species, indoors in pots and boxes or outdoors in troughs, deep boxes or the open ground. For outdoors or indoors try hardwood cuttings such as forsythia, berberis, weigela, deutzia, willow, poplar, flowering currant, blackcurrant, red currant, gooseberry. For indoor only, try pelargonium ('geranium') salvia, coleus, viola, dahlia, chrysanthemum. The indoor cuttings should have their pots or boxes enveloped in polythene bags to keep down transpiration. Further hints are given in *Plant Life*. G. A. Perry (Blandford).

(x) *The effect of light on stem growth*

In plant pots grow some seedlings of mustard or radish. When they are about 2·5 cm. (1″) high, cover one pot with an inverted cardboard box with a hole cut near one edge of the top. Observe the direction of growth, then move the box round so that light comes from a different direction. After a few days observe the growth again.

(*d*) **Plant studies: leaves**

(i) *Variety in shapes*

To illustrate the infinite variety of shapes and patterns in nature, make occasional collections of leaves. Children can gradually learn to recognise more of the commoner species by their leaves. If leaves of plants such as lily, iris, grasses and cereals can be included, the children can be shown the parallel vein pattern of these monocotyledons. The majority of leaves will show a branching pattern of veins, typical of dicotyledonous plants.

Freshly-gathered leaves painted or sprayed with clear polyurethane (obtainable from paint and 'do-it-yourself' shops) will usually retain their colour and fresh appearance for some considerable time.

(ii) *Leaf patterns*

While studying plants *in situ* or those brought into or grown in school, it is worthwhile sketching the pattern of leaf arrangement on the stem when viewed from above. The positioning of leaves to obtain the maximum amount of light can usually be seen clearly.

(iii) *Making leaf prints* (see also Chapter 5, p. 166)

Records of leaf shapes can be made by pressing the leaves or by sketching or painting them. Other techniques can also be employed.

Powder colour prints. Make a paste similar to the consistency of cream from powder colour and olive oil. Paint a thin covering of this on to the underside of the leaf. Turn the wet side down on to a sheet of paper or card and cover the leaf with another piece of card. Rub evenly over the top card and then carefully lift the card and the leaf, leaving the shape on the bottom paper or card.

Scribble prints A scribble print can be made by placing a leaf, vein side up, on to a firm flat base. Place a sheet of white kitchen paper over the leaf, and scribble evenly over the leaf with a pencil or cobbler's heel-ball. Cut out the leaf shape, mount and label it.

Spatter prints Press the leaves under a heavy weight for a few hours to make sure that they will lie flat. Place a leaf on a sheet of white paper and fasten leaf and paper down on to a firm base. If required a cardboard frame can be placed around the leaf leaving a clearance of roughly 2·5 cm. all round. Make up some powder colour or water colour paint. Dip an old toothbrush in this and then shake it to remove surplus paint. Hold the bristles upwards and draw the blade of a knife along them, starting at the end nearest the toothbrush handle. When the colour is dry remove the leaf and, if necessary, the cardboard frame.

Smoke prints Find a smooth, round bottle and cover the sides with a thin coating of Vaseline. Fill the bottle with water and replace the cork or screw-top firmly. Hold the bottle over the flame of a candle until there is a good coating of soot. Place a leaf vein side up on a wad of newspaper and then roll the bottle over the leaf. Next place the leaf, vein side up on clean newspaper, and put a sheet of white paper on top. Roll over the white paper and the leaf with a clean round bottle or rolling pin.

Shoe polish prints Using an old toothbrush or a finger put a light covering of shoe polish on to a leaf. Turn the leaf polish side down, on to a sheet of white paper or card. Cover the leaf with another piece of card or paper and rub firmly and smoothly. Lift the top covering and the leaf carefully.

Carbon paper prints On a sheet of white paper place a piece of carbon paper face downwards. Then put a leaf, underside downwards, on to the back of the carbon paper. Cover the leaf with a sheet of paper and rub gently over the surface. Remove the covering paper, the carbon paper and the leaf.

Leaf silhouettes While holding a leaf firmly on a sheet of white paper, rub a piece of latex or plastic foam (synthetic sponge) against a rubber stamp inking pad. Make sure that the leaf does not slip, as you rub outwards all round the leaf edge. Remove the leaf carefully.

Plaster casts Make a block of Plasticine about 1·5 cm. thick and slightly larger than the leaf to be used. Ensure that the top and bottom surfaces are smooth and level. Press the specimen leaf (or twig) into the Plasticine until there is a good deep impression. Remove the specimen and build a 'wall' of Plasticine about half an inch (1·3 cm.) high around the outer edge of the block. Make up into a creamy consistency sufficient Plaster of Paris or Polyfilla, and pour this into the mould. A loop of thin wire, white string or nylon cord can be pushed into the plaster to act as a hanging device for use later. When the plaster material is thoroughly hard, remove the Plasticine. The shape of the specimen can be painted in water colours to match the original.

(iv) *Leaf development from stored food*

Take a carrot, parsnip, turnip, swede or pineapple. Cut off the fleshy part, leaving about 2·5 cm. depth below the point where the leaves emerge. Take off any existing leaves, except in the case of the pineapple. Place these top parts of the vegetable or fruit in a shallow dish of water, placing pebbles on them for support. New leaves will grow and the stored food will diminish.

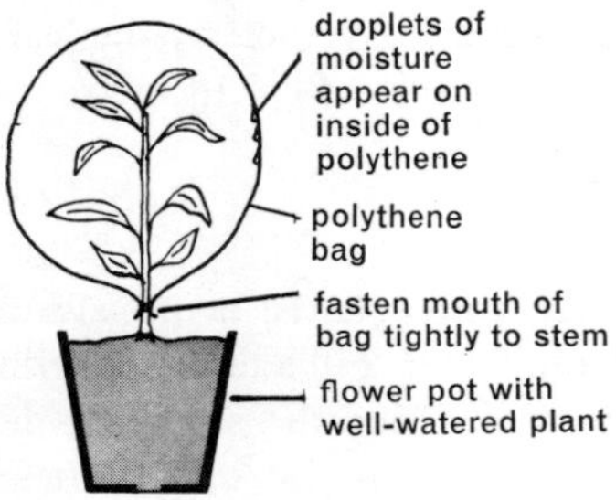

7:14 Transpiration from the leaves of a plant can be demonstrated by this method.

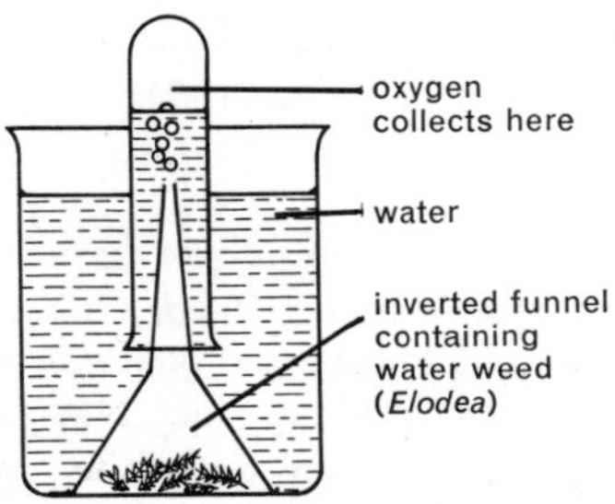

7:15 Using the aquatic plant *Elodea* to show that leaves release oxygen during sunlight.

(v) *Transpiration from leaves*

Transplant into a pot a well-grown plant of shepherd's purse or groundsel or make use of a pot plant. Avoid pelargoniums (geraniums) as these do not transpire freely. Cover the whole plant with a polythene bag, tying the mouth of the bag tightly around the stem just above soil level. Keep the pot watered and put it in a warm place. After a few days, moisture will appear on the inside of the polythene. This could have come only from the leaves and stem.

(vi) *Leaf structure*

If microscopes are available, the undersides of leaves can be examined to locate the stomata. Useful leaves for this are from laurel, rhubarb, lily and an onion bulb. Material should be torn across obliquely. Trim off a tiny piece of the thinnest part and mount it in water on the microscope slide. Discuss the function of stomata with relation to light intensity and loss of stomata with relation to light intensity and loss of water, and the reason why they are found in greater numbers on the underside of leaves. Sketches should be made of what is seen under the microscope. The stomata can be made to close by putting a little strong salt or sugar solution on the tissue.

(vii) *Leaves and photosynthesis*

Keep a large-leaved plant in darkness for 24 hours so that any starch in the leaves will be used up. Place a disc of cork above part of a large leaf and a similar piece below, holding them together by pushing through several pins. Place the plant in sunlight for several hours. Then remove the leaf and the pieces of cork attached, and plunge the leaf into boiling water for about 30 seconds. Next place the leaf in alcohol to extract the chlorophyll. Transfer the leaf into a weak solution of iodine. The parts of the leaf not covered by the cork will turn blue-black indicating the presence of starch formed during exposure to sunshine. No starch is present in the part which has been covered by the cork.

Photosynthesis is confined to daylight hours and takes place most effectively in sunlight. During this process, oxygen is given off by the leaf. Experiment in a similar way with the variegated leaves of coleus or tradescantia.

(viii) *Leaves release oxygen during sunlight*

A water weed such as *Elodea* (obtained cheaply from aquarist or pet store) can be placed under a funnel inverted in a jar of water. Fill a test tube with water and invert the tube over the funnel stem. Place the apparatus in strong sunlight and observe the bubbles of gas which rise into the test tube. After a few hours this gas can be tested with a glowing taper or splint, indicating the presence of oxygen.

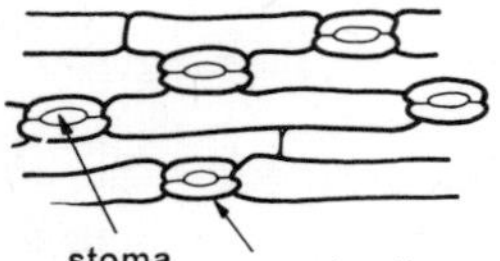

7 : 16 A sketch showing the detail of a stoma of a leaf.

7 : 17 Apparatus which can be used to show the intake of oxygen and the release of carbon dioxide during plant respiration.

(ix) *Leaves and respiration*

Using Plasticine or surgical tape fix a specimen tube or a test tube in the centre of the base of a bowl. In the tube put some water to cover the roots of a small plant such as wallflower or groundsel. Fill the bowl about three-quarters' full with lime water, and invert a jam jar over the tube and plant. Put the apparatus in the dark for about 24 hours. The lime water should turn milky indicating the presence of carbon dioxide, and the level of the water inside the jar should have risen, indicating that oxygen has passed from the jar to the leaves of the plant. These reactions are characteristic of respiration. It is important to discuss the value to the plant of this function, and also the gaseous exchange by plants in relation to man and other living things.

(x) *Leaves for the use of man and other animals*

We have seen that leaves are capable of taking in and using carbon dioxide from the atmosphere and releasing oxygen – a gas that supports animal life – during photosynthesis.

The manufacture of starch by plants provides food for man and other animals, establishing food-chains such as: grasses and clovers → food for cows → milk, cream, butter, cheese, meat for man. Children can be encouraged to think of other similar 'chains'.

Man also eats many forms of leaves, e.g. brussels sprouts, cabbage, chicory, endive, kale, lettuce, spinach. These supply important vitamins in man's diet. For a beverage, the leaves of the tea plant have long been important, while twine and ropes can be made from the leaves of sisal and manila plants.

The link between plants and animals is obvious if we consider how many of our country's list of animals are herbivores or omnivores. There seems excellent scope for children's research and a display on 'Leaves and Life'! Nor must we neglect the collecting, the display and recording in colour of the wealth of autumn tints that leaves assume.

(*e*) Plant studies: flowers

Wild and cultivated plants are usually much easier to recognise when in flower, and fieldwork involving visits to various habitats including gardens will give opportunities of identifying and listing the occurrence of various species. If such visits are impossible, then a range of flowers should be examined in classroom or laboratory, remembering of course that rare flowers should never be collected.

(i) *Flowers and pollination*

The function of flowers should be discussed, including the production and dispersal of pollen, the reception of pollen and the provision of the egg cell. An interesting piece of work can be built up on 'insect attraction'. This will involve collecting and examining wild and cultivated flowers which offer one or more of: nectar; surplus pollen; appealing colour or pattern; appealing scent. Examine also flowers which are wind-pollinated, comparing the amount of pollen produced here with that of some insect-pollinated plants.

(ii) *Flowers which open at night*

Make a collection of some of these such as evening primrose (*Oenothera*), night-scented stock (*Matthiola bicornis*) and tobacco plant (*Nicotiana alba* or *N. affinis*). Discuss the pollination of such plants by night-flying insects, and measure the distance of the nectaries down the corolla tube.

(iii) *Pollen in variety*

Shake the pollen from various species of flowers on to separate pieces of black paper. Examine the pollen with a magnifying glass. Alternatively, shake the pollen on to microscope slides, or squash the anthers and tease out the pollen on to slides. Cover with a cover-glass and examine each slide under low and high power. A wet mount can be made by placing pollen grains in a 50/50 solution of water and glycerine.

(iv) *Germinating pollen grains*

Place a filter paper marked out as four equal segments, in a petri dish and wet the paper with a 15% sucrose solution. Expose only one-quarter at a time, and shake on pollen from a different flower in each quarter. Foxglove, sweet pea, marrow and runner bean could be used. Replace the lid of the petri dish and examine the grains each day for 3 or 4 days. Try this also with 5% and 10% sucrose solutions.

(v) *Insects visiting flowers*

If possible, observation should be kept on various species of flowers. Record the types of insect visitors, the purpose of their visit, the length of stay and if possible the plants that are next visited. Do colours of petals appear to have any effect on which species of insects visit? A simple experiment could be carried out by making paper flowers of different colours and placing honey or sugar syrup on the petals.

(vi) *The value of flowers to man*

A display might be arranged to show pattern in flowers, and those flowers which are highly scented. Children can be invited to bring, select and arrange their favourite flowers.

Other uses of flowers include the production of perfumes, mainly in southern Europe, from the petals of violets (*Viola odorata*), lavender (*Lavendula officinalis*), jasmine (*Jasminum grandiflorum*), orange blossom (*Citrus aurantium*), roses (*Rosa damascena*) and other plants.

(*f*) **Plant studies: fruits**

The confusion over fruits and seeds can probably be ended if we think of a seed as a fertilised ovule containing an embryo, whereas a fruit is a ripened ovary containing one or more seeds.

(i) *Dry fruits and juicy fruits*

If possible, a study of a great variety of fruits should be made in their natural habitat. If land is available a good number can be produced in the school garden. Otherwise a collection can be made and classified in the classroom. Some thought can be given as to why fruits are of different form—for example, pods (peas and beans, gorse, broom, vetch); nuts (acorn, hazel nut, brazil nut, filbert nut, coconut); berries (currant, bilberry, tomato, gooseberry). A connection will usually be seen between structure of the fruits and the need for dispersal of the seeds.

In towns, observation of fruits displayed in greengrocers' shops and on market stalls will yield a good deal of information as a basis for further studies.

(ii) *Fruits as food for animals*

Animals, including man, make great use of fruits as food. Usually man is in competition for these fruits. From observations and collected materials it is possible to build up a 'fruit menu' list for various sections of the animal kingdom. Something on these lines might be attempted:

Apple – man; birds; larvae of codlin moth; larvae of apple sawfly; wasps.
Blackberry – man; birds; mice; wasps; bluebottles.
Hips – man; birds; mice.
Hazel nuts – man; squirrels; mice.

(iii) *Fruits from home and overseas fruit farms*

By questions asked at the fruiterer's shop, by collecting specimens and by labels from various canned fruits the theme can be developed on a geographical basis to locate the countries of origin and to discover the ways in which these fruits are farmed. The main fruit-growing areas of Britain, too, can be located.

(iv) *Fruits from the home garden*

A list of these will allow us to classify them, for example, as tree fruits, bush fruits, cane fruits and 'runner' fruits. In the school garden, too, there is a need to know how these various plants should be cultivated and cared for.

(v) *Fruits for beverages, essences and flavourings*

Work on this theme will lead us to (1) soft drinks made from orange, lemon, lime and grapefruit (2) alcoholic drinks such as beer, made from the fruits of the hop plant and fermented wines made from grapes, cider apples, pears and many other fruits either commercially or in the home (3) fruit juices, served at the beginning of meals. Alcoholic drinks lead on to a study of fermentation (yeast plants), possible discussions on alcoholism, 'drinking and driving', and maybe a visit to a brewery. Oils and juices from some fruits are used in flavourings. Vanilla essence is taken from the fruit of a climbing plant found in India and Sri Lanka, and almond flavouring is extracted from bitter almonds grown in Morocco.

'Your Good Health' could well be the title of a piece of work embracing the various aspects of beverages made from fruit.

(vi) *Protecting fruit from damage*

Common pests and diseases of fruits can be studied in a practical way. Useful pamphlets are usually available from such firms as Murphy; May and Baker; I.C.I. (Plant Protection Ltd.), Fison's, etc. Your seedsman's shop often has examples for free distribution.

From fruit damage and the life histories of common pests, the work could move on to the study of chemicals which are used as protective sprays.

PLANTS IN THEIR ENVIRONMENTS

(see also Chapter 3).

Wherever possible, it is of paramount importance that plants should be studied *in situ* and in relationship with soils, climatic conditions and animals. Because many urban schools have only limited facilities for this a good deal of emphasis has been placed on studies in the classroom and on the school site.

Space available does not permit detailed studies of the many habitats in existence, although work of this kind will be suggested in several of the children's books available in the Environmental Studies series. The reader is also referred to *Progressive Biology 1* and *2*: Perry and Hirons (Blandford Press) and to *Nature Study for Primary Schools:* E. Proctor (Evans).

Whether in town or in country, you may be able to find several of the following habitats natural or man-made, near enough to be used for observation and recording.

A cultivated garden	Hedgerow
A neglected or derelict garden	Deciduous woodland
Pond	Coniferous woodland
Stream or river	Copse
Lake	Roadside verge
Park	Rubbish tip
Wall with plants	Disused railway track
Farm	Greengrocer's shop
Museum (with natural history section)	Sea shore
Rain water tank	Salt marsh
Heathland	Meadow land
Chalkland	School playing field
Bog	Sand dunes
Mountain sides	School garden pond
Waste spaces	Quarry (disused)
Decaying tree stump	Rotten tree trunk

Devise appropriate but simple problems for children to answer (N.B. the following are obviously not appropriate to all habitats).

From where have these plants come?

Why are they successful here?

What species of plants and animals are present?

Are they adapted in any way to the conditions, e.g. aquatic plants or plants of heath and chalk land?

Can we construct an outline sketch-map of the habitat?

What direction does the habitat face?

Does slope or elevation have any effect on the flora and fauna present?

Is there any evidence of animal tracks, trails and signs?

Is a quadrat or transect of any value in our studies?

Do shade and exposure to sunshine have any effect on plant life?

Which species of plants and animals have you seen evidence of in other habitats as well as in this one? Why do you think they occur in both?

What can you find out about the depth, the type, the fertility, the acidity of the soil in the habitat?

What evidence can you find of food-chains in the habitat?

What effect have human beings had upon the plant and animal life?

Do any of the animals make use of plants other than for food?

Which birds make their homes in this habitat and why do they choose it?

Has the name of this area any historical connections?

Can you find examples of any non-flowering plants? If so, can you suggest why they succeed in this habitat?

Does the area produce anything of value to man?

Is the area of any value for leisure activities?

Is the vegetation static or is it gradually changing its species?

What happens to the plants and animals when they die in this habitat?

LIVING ANIMALS IN SCHOOLS

Children of all ages delight in having living things to observe and handle. Some authorities are now setting up mobile zoos in pantechnicons so that children may be made aware of the wide range of animal life. Other authorities are setting up animal loan schemes so that animals may be borrowed for short periods. These new ideas overcome the problems of keeping animals in schools but are no substitute for the school's own animals. These schemes are meant to augment, to widen the experience, not to replace.

There are many problems arising from keeping animals in schools but they can often be easily overcome. Before we decide to keep an animal in the school we must ask ourselves some questions.

1 *Can we feed it?*

Do we know upon what it feeds? If the answer to this after reading and research is no, then the animals must be released. We know that rabbits and guinea pigs can be readily fed but what about that caterpillar brought in, in a matchbox? If its food plant is unknown the child must return it to the place where it was found. Can we ensure that we can feed it throughout the year and every day if the animal requires this? The problem of the long holiday is paramount here. There are caretakers *and* caretakers: some will feed the animals, some will not! Try to get your caretaker on your side early on, and introduce him to the animals you are rearing. Ask his advice if necessary. Involve him in what you are doing. Sometimes this works the oracle and he will volunteer his help. Do not forget the children. I have often farmed out animals to 'foster homes' during a vacation and both the animals and the children have been better for it. A word of warning: ask the children early – well before the start of the vacation – and do get a note from dad to say that he is willing. Better still, if possible, get dad to call. All this is made very much easier if your animals are somewhat unusual – a parent may refuse a rabbit but relish a raccoon! Children living near the school may be willing to come to school to feed and clean the animals. In this case a roster may be drawn up, and duplicated so that the child knows his day. Have 'reserves' and inform the caretaker so that he's in the picture. Many schools have 'Animal Defenders' among their numbers and these children will usually be very keen to help.

2 *Can we house it properly?*
Do we know the best type of container for the animals? How much space does it require? Will it thrive under school conditions? The answers to these problems will be given as far as is possible in the section dealing with the animal.

3 *Is the animal worth having?*
Do not be tempted to buy an animal whose sole quality is that it is rare or bizarre. I was persuaded some time ago to buy a 'Jack Dempsey' cichlid – a large tropical fish, some 6″ (15 cm.) from head to tail. He does nothing of interest and my search for a female has to date been unsuccessful. He dominates a huge tank in solitary splendour as nothing can live with him. Every day I feed him vast quantities of worms. My tank of guppies is infinitely more interesting, for children can see the eyes of the young within the female, watch mating behaviour and condition them to tapping. The law of diminishing return applies here. It is not worth the vast labour in care and nurture of an animal if the intrinsic interest of the specimen is negligible.

4 *Smell*
Many animals have an objectionable smell. Unfortunately, the people in a room tend to get accustomed and immune to this and accept it. To an outsider entering such a room the assault on his nose can be overwhelming.

5 *Cleaning*
Children must take their part in the cleaning of the animal cages. It can be quite a chore. I am always amazed by the lack of squeamishness on the part of children. They will clean out cages with abandon. They tend to adopt the manner of the class teacher and if he shows distaste then the class will adopt the attitude. These chores teach the children responsibility, for ownership involves responsibility.

7 : 18 Hydra.

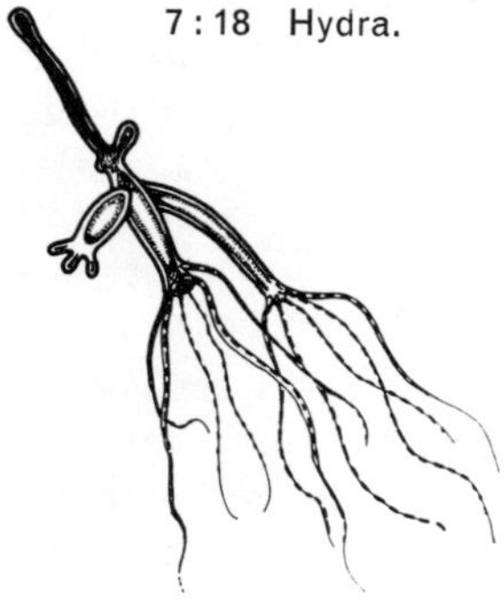

7 : 19 Flatworm.

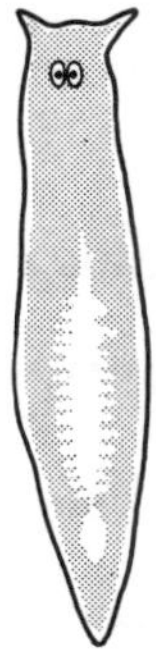

NOTES ON SPECIES OF ANIMALS FOR SCHOOL USE

There is a tendency for teachers to look to the furry animals (mammals) for their class animals. I should like to advocate some easier, simple and perhaps more interesting variations.

THE LOWER ANIMALS

Protozoa and hydra

Protozoa will undoubtedly enter the classroom in jars of pond water but their small size makes their study unrewarding.

Small sticks, leaves, etc. from ponds will often have *Hydra* attached to them. Look for *Hydra* with a hand lens. If found transfer the stick, or portion with *Hydra* to a jam jar half full of the original pond water. Replace jam jar top with a few holes punched in it. They require living food – water fleas, which are readily obtained from ponds – once a week. They are most interesting to observe, particularly their behaviour when you have just introduced food.

Flatworms

These are common in ponds and lakes.

They are unusual creatures to keep but are suggested because of their powers of regeneration. Keep in jam jars of pond water with black paper sleeve – they like darkness. Feed weekly on chopped worm, chopped liver or boiled egg yolk. It is a good idea to transfer them to another 'feeding dish' containing the food, leave them for twenty minutes and then return them to their 'tank'. In this way fouling of the aquarium water is prevented.

Cut planarians in half; separate the halves and observe, regularly, what is happening. All one needs is a hand lens and a sharp knife or razor blade. A pinch of Epsom salts added to a saucer of pond water will keep them still by narcotisation for microscopic examination.

How do they react to light?

How do they react to tapping the container or touching with a pin? Planaria are the subject of some advanced work in learning theory. By feeding Planaria on Planaria that have developed conditioned reflexes, the fed Planaria appear to be conditioned more readily!

Earthworms

These may be kept to show their role in tilling the soil, fertilising it by dragging down leaves, or as food for fishes, frogs and some reptiles. They may be collected at night, after a good rain, or they can be brought to the surface in the day by adding an eggcupful of formalin (from chemists) to a gallon of water and watering this over a square metre of ground. As they

7:20 Garden snail.

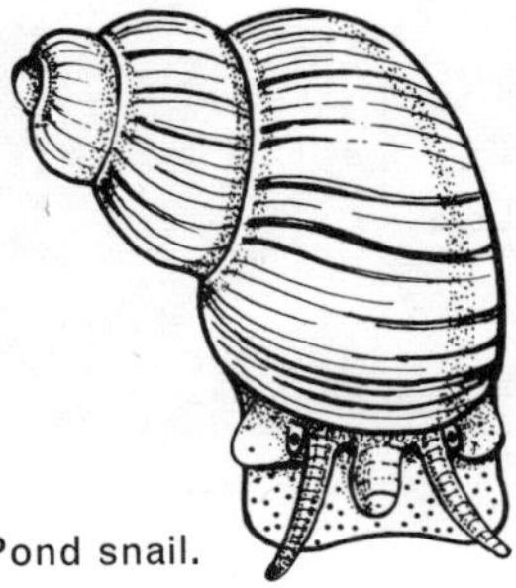

7:21 Pond snail.

emerge, wash them in a bucket of water and place on the surface of 10 cm. depth of soil in a plastic washing-up bowl. Add a second dose of the above solution to the square metre of soil after fifteen minutes to bring out those from greater depths. Leave them overnight in soil in the covered plastic bowl. The next day the worms can be transferred to the wormery.

'Watering' patches of soil in different places can be a rewarding exercise for children. Do the number of worms per square metre vary in different places – wood, field, etc.? How many worms per hectare if 'x' number are present in a square metre?

Worms can be kept in a wormery whose width need not exceed 2 cm. For breeding healthy worms, in 60 × 60 × 30 cm. wooden boxes, put in a 2 cm. layer of crocks or pebbles and 15 cm. of peat and good garden soil. Wet the soil periodically to keep it moist but do not wet through. This will hold two dozen worms. Add lettuce leaves, or bread and milk, to the surface periodically as food. Add different types of leaves; is there any preference? At what rate do they bury leaves?

Snails

Best found in evening on moist herbage, fallen logs and in dead leaves. Land snails can be kept in old aquaria or sweet jar. Add 5 or 6 cm. of good garden soil with a third of peat and also a few pieces of ground chalk or limestone kept moist. Have glass lid (Sellotape the cut edge) on tank. Feed snails on lettuce, cabbage, flour paste, mashed potato. Do they have food preferences? Remove the food before it decays. Avoid getting your tank too warm.

If conditions are correct they will breed. They are hermaphodites so no need to worry about males and females. If too dry they will aestivate – a type of hibernation. Note how they look in this condition. To awaken from aestivation soak in tepid water. Watch how they move over the glass of the tank. Some interesting work has been done in getting them to pull weights up slopes.

7 : 22 Woodlouse.

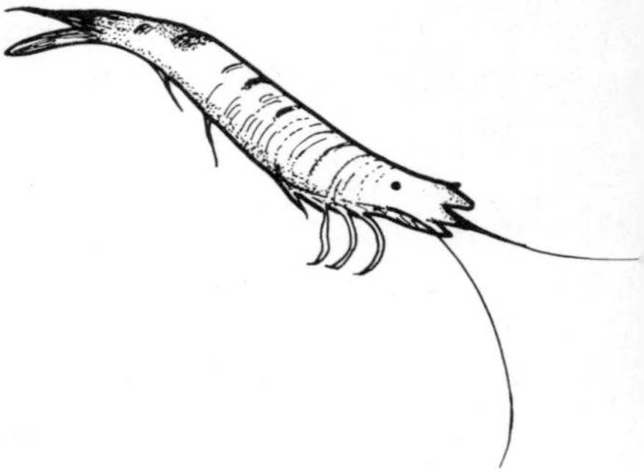

7 : 23 Brine shrimp.

Slugs

Can be kept as above. Rewarding for study. If black paper is placed inside container they will produce their slime trail and their journeys can be recorded.

Pond snails

Every aquarium should have its colony of pond snails. They help to keep down the green growth (algae) on the tank sides. If too much light falls on the tank not even the snails will be able to cope. They will undoubtedly lay eggs on the tank sides and the development of the eggs can be watched with a hand lens.

Woodlice

Can usually be found in damp situations, under rotting logs and piles of stones. They can be kept in an old aquarium tank set up as for snails. Feed with bits of ripe fruit, apples, raw potato. They will also take meat scraps.

They may not appeal to many as pets but are interesting creatures in that they are very primitive land animals. They require a large quantity of moisture in the air. Make a long tube out of celluloid and block one end with wet and the other with dry cotton wool. A woodlouse is introduced in the centre. Will it move to the wet cotton wool end or the dry? How do they react to light?

Brine shrimps

These are obtained from aquarium shops as eggs. They are now being supplied as part of a kit with a microscope (*sic*).

They are useful as a readily obtained, easily reared water animal with some interesting behavioural characteristics. They also provide excellent food for young fish.

Make up some artificial sea water for these shrimps live in salt water

7 : 24 Cockroach.

7 : 25 Stick insect.

lakes. 30–40 gms. of salt (cooking) in 1 litre of aquarium water or rain water. A sweet jar makes a good container – half full of water. Keep container in moderate light and do not disturb. When the eggs hatch, young are fed on scrapings from aquarium tank sides, i.e. green algae. When they become adults they swim so that they lie on their backs. If you put black paper over the top half of the sweet jar and illuminate from below the brine shrimps will turn over. They are sensitive to light and keep the light so that their ventral surface is facing it. They may breed for you in the sweet jars. If so remove the eggs and dry them. They will keep for several years in airtight bottles.

INSECTS

There seem to be as many methods for insects as there are insects, so only a selection will be outlined. Methods for collection of insects have been given in an earlier section (page 171).

Cockroaches

Not many schools will be interested in keeping cockroaches in the classroom. Some children, however, are fascinated by them and even delight in handling them. You may have such a child in your class. Give him his head and start him with a colony. Only recently a 15-year-old girl was able to disprove all the old ideas on the life cycle of the cockroach by her first-hand observation. Cockroaches are often called black-beetles but as they are neither black nor beetles, the term, perhaps, should be avoided.

They are readily housed in small aquarium tanks with 5 cm. of sawdust, with a sheet of newspaper on the surface – they do not like light – and a potted meat jar containing water-soaked cotton wool. They will take bread, sugar, apple and the like. Small scraps of food, removed before they rot, are sufficient.

If you keep cockroaches make sure the lid fits tightly – female cleaners are particularly averse to them. Remember if you show your dislike the majority of the class will respond in a similar way. In defence of the cockroach, they are very clean animals, useful scavengers, and do not harbour bacteria harmful to man.

Stick insects

These are most readily reared in classrooms and really need no introduction. Most teachers seem to like them, perhaps because they move slowly and deliberately. Could it be that quick, darting movements of things frighten us more than appearance?

A simple cage for stick and other insects is shown.

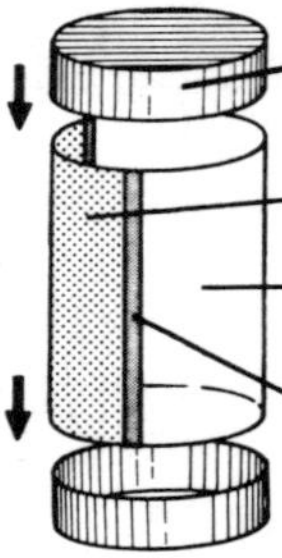

7 : 26 A simple cage for insects.

Things to do with Stick Insects

Record lengths daily or weekly; make graphs to show growth. Is this unusual – do other animals grow in this way? Compare growth of insect with say growth in length of mouse – any differences?

How many eggs laid by one female? Can males be found? How many of eggs laid hatch? Compare life of stick insect with say, that of cockroach or butterfly. Do the young which hatch resemble adults in each case? Leads on to the types of insect life cycles, complete and incomplete metamorphosis. How much do they eat, of a privet leaf, in say 1 hour. Is this a constant rate throughout the day or does it vary? For this technique see 'Butterflies and Moths' section which follows.

Butterflies and moths

If necessary, various types may be obtained from Worldwide Butterflies Ltd., Seafields House, Charmouth, Bridport, Dorset.

Breeding and rearing

Eggs may be brought into the school with the leaves upon which they are found. Remember to note the plant because the eggs are laid on the food plant for the larvae (caterpillars). The leaves with eggs can be kept in plastic sandwich boxes. When the caterpillars develop they require fresh leaves daily and the box should be cleaned daily. The leaves should be dry and a double thickness of blotting paper on the bottom of box achieves this. You may need to distribute your larvae over several boxes if your rearing is successful.

Eggs should be observed with a hand lens and the interesting surface sculpturing noted. Growth of the caterpillars may be recorded; if this is recorded in the form of a graph interesting discussion may start. Does the caterpillar just keep growing or does it grow in jerks? Do not handle caterpillars when they are moulting.

How much do caterpillars consume? One probably has not the delicate balances necessary to weigh the actual amount consumed by a caterpillar in say a morning but one can get an idea by the following technique. Place a food leaf on graph paper and draw the outline. Place the leaf in with the caterpillar which is under experiment and let it feed for a given time then remove the leaf. (Where does the caterpillar start to eat the leaf?)

Place the eaten leaf on graph paper and calculate the area eaten; see Fig. 7:29. What proportion of the leaf has the caterpillar eaten? One may in this way, compare eating rates at different ages in its caterpillar life or under different temperatures. If one wishes to talk about weight of leaf eaten this is rather difficult as the leaf will be losing weight due to water loss all the time. However, one can cut out thick cardboard, the shape of the actual leaf fed, and weigh it. Allow the caterpillar to feed for a given period, then remove leaf. Place over the thick card. Draw around the part that has been eaten. Cut out the 'eaten' part from the cardboard. Weigh the 'eaten' cardboard. How much has been eaten, i.e. what proportion of the actual leaf has been eaten? If the same type of cardboard is always used for this experiment then the cardboard equivalent of leaves is a good quantitative measure of feeding.

Pupae (chrysalides)

These should be left in the cages until they are hard enough to handle – say, a week. They should be stored in clean tins in a cold, dry place.

Imagines (adults)

These will require large containers which can be simply made. There are many types and you may find it easier to modify the equipment to suit what you find easily available. See Fig. 7:28.

The base of the box should be filled with peat or coconut fibre and the top covered with a fine moss, the feathery type that comes up with lawn raking is excellent. Sink your wide-bottomed narrow-necked (glue pot?) water jar for the food plant into the peat. For butterflies and moths the

7:27 A species of butterfly.

7 : 31 Valerian flowers.

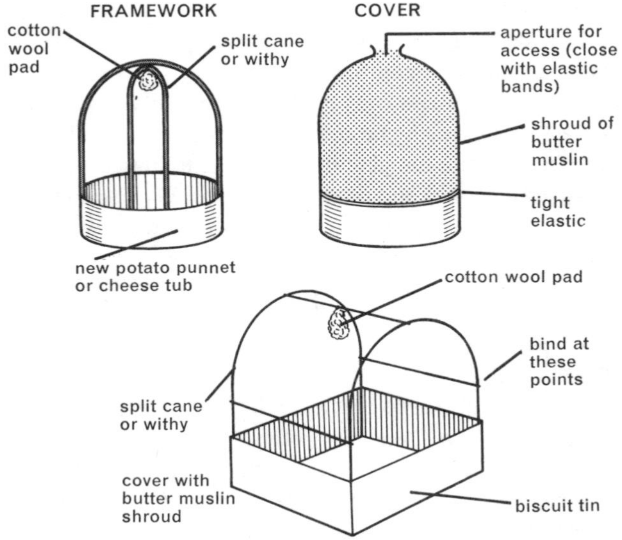

7 : 28 Rearing cages for butterflies and moths.

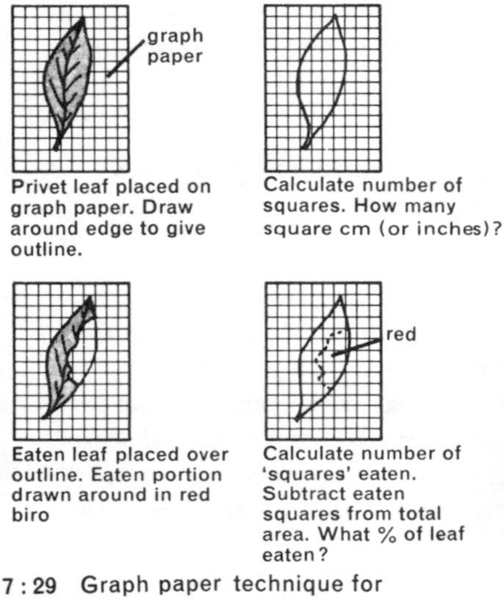

7 : 29 Graph paper technique for recording leaf consumption.

7 : 30 Buddleia flowers.

food plants can be such flowers as Buddleia or Valerian. Do not let the flowers touch the covers.

The insects will sip the nectar from these plants by means of their long proboscis. It is easier to feed the adults on a cotton-wool pad soaked in a mixture of honey or sugar and water. This may be placed in the top of the cage. With practice you can get them to feed by holding them between finger and thumb and placing their feet on the cotton-wool pad. As they 'taste' through their feet they may start to push out their 'watch-spring coiled' proboscis into the sugary liquid. If they require persuasion, carefully insert a pin into the centre of the 'spring' of the proboscis, unroll it and dip it into the pad.

You will have discovered the correct type of food plant for your particular caterpillars and this should be placed in the cage. If the food plant is readily available, e.g. White Dead Nettle, it may be grown in a pot and the pot sunk into the peat. (Remember to water!) You should have no difficulty now in getting your imagines to mate and lay their eggs on the food plants.

Things to do

Note the feeding habits of the adult. If breeding, do they prefer dilute sugar or strong sugar solution? If sugar solution is placed on different coloured paper, do they show any colour preference?

Record dates of egg laying, date and percentage hatching of eggs. Various moults (ecdysis) of caterpillars, percentages at each stage of development. Length of pupation.

Feeding methods of caterpillars? Consumption of leaves.

Ants

These are relatively difficult to maintain in the classroom but are worth the attempt as they are fascinating creatures. They can be kept in plaster of Paris containers (formicaria) which should be kept moist. A mould is made out of greased wood or Plasticine to produce a block some 10 cm. × 4 cm. × 12 mm. high. Place on a sheet of glass. Into the bottom of the mould place a glass microscope slide, on top of the slide a sliver of balsa wood, say 2 × 6·5 cm. × 3 mm. In front of this slide place a piece of wood, 2·5 cm. × 12 mm. × 6 mm. (See Fig. 7:32.)

Carefully pour in plaster of Paris mixture so that the slide, wood, etc. are not disturbed. When plaster is dry remove mould. Remove slide and wood sliver. Remove piece of wood. The end product should appear as shown.

With a needle or wire make a hole through from outside to nesting chamber. Keep slide on housing, make a sugar paper sleeve to fit the container and insert into sleeve. Keep the well in the container topped up with water. Several such containers may be made. They may be kept on a wooden base supported by four 6″–9″ (15–23 cm.) nails. The ends of the

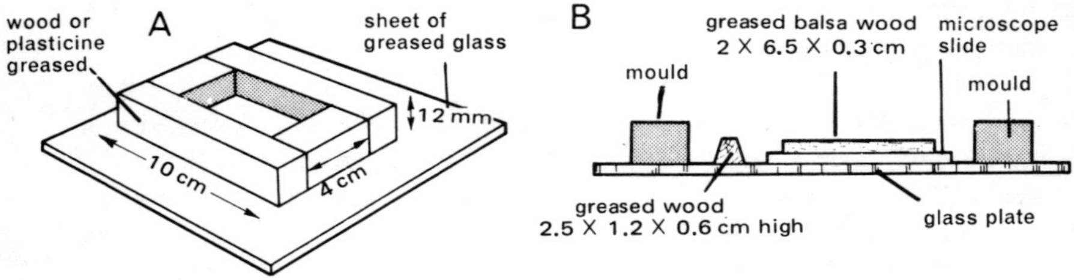

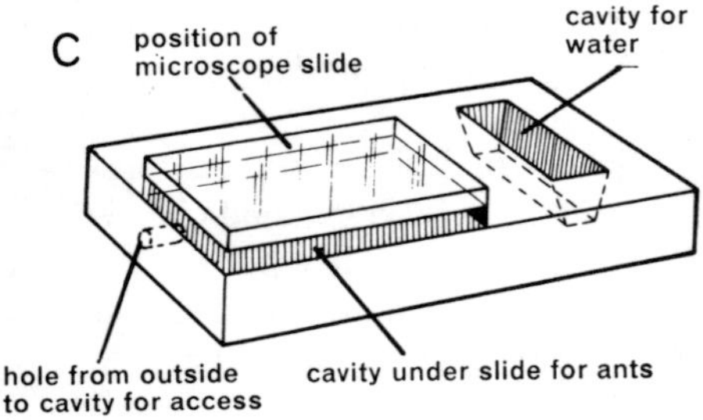

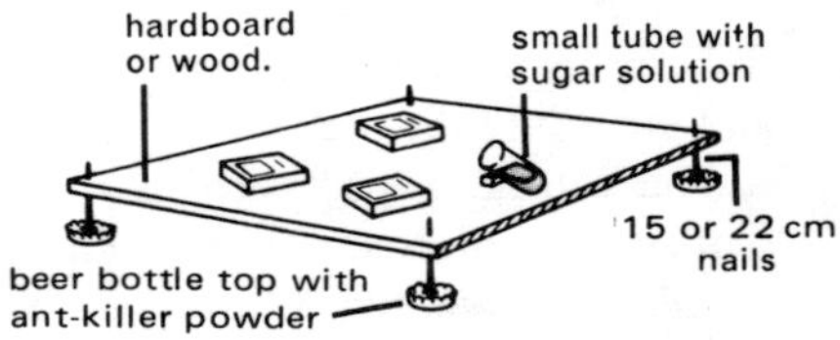

7 : 33 Ant table with several formicaria.

7 : 32 Construction of a formicarium. *(a)* the mould *(b)* section through mould showing 'formers' *(c)* completed formicarium.

nails rest in small 'cups' of ant powder; the nails can be placed on a zinc bath and this filled with water or oil.

If the ants are brought in with soil they can be removed from the soil by placing a table lamp over it. If the nesting boxes are damp the ants will be seen to remove their larvae and pupae to the damp boxes. If the hole from the outside to nesting chamber is oversmall ants will have problems getting grubs in. Note the 'co-operation' in moving 'grubs' about. Feed the ants on dilute sugar solution.

Silk worms

These are often kept by schools but I find them difficult. Eggs can be obtained from Silk Worm Farm, Ayot House, Ayot St. Lawrence, Herts. When the eggs arrive it is as well to retain them in the refrigerator until mulberry leaves are available. A white mulberry bush is reasonable in price and can be planted in a tub or in the school garden. (Children sing about the mulberry bush – how many have seen one?) Cut mulberry into strips, say 12 mm. wide for the young caterpillars. They may be kept in shoe boxes or shoe-box lids as they do not stray from food. Keep the caterpillars out of draughts. After several months, when they show signs of pupation by moving into a corner and weaving their head around, they can be placed individually into paper cones with top tucked in. After placing in cone wait 10–12 days, then shake the paper cone. If it rattles there is a sound pupa inside. The silk must be removed at this stage by soaking in warm water, then if pulled at the sides you will find a single strand in a continuous thread.

Lettuce may be used if mulberry is unobtainable but the results are not so good. If you start on mulberry the caterpillars will not switch to the lettuce. The converse however, is possible.

Some methods for insects

A 'type-collection' of insects may be required. Children are great collectors and a good well-labelled collection is a real aid to identification.

Killing

Cyanide killing bottles are best kept out of children's hands. Insects can be killed by cutting up laurel leaves, bruising them and packing them 5 cm. deep in an airtight jar. Cover the laurel leaf surface with cotton wool. When the insects are dead they will have become stiff and they *must* be relaxed before they can be mounted.

Killing – other techniques

1. For hard bodied insects such as beetles drop into boiling water as the other method takes several hours (this is humane).
2. Strong household ammonia for butterflies and moths.
3. Ethyl acetate, to be used only by teacher – beware of harmful vapour (obtainable from Boots).

Relaxing

An Oxo-tin or plastic sandwich box containing a thin pad of foam plastic soaked in boiled water is required. The insect is placed upon pad and the lid replaced – a high humidity is required to relax the insects. If very serious work is intended a commercial relaxing fluid from a Biological Supply House is required to replace the boiled water as this prevents fungal growth. Leave insect in relaxing tin for two or three days when the wings will have become limp and easily moved. It is now ready for setting.

Setting

The purpose of setting is to display the insect in a suitable way and then allow it to dry in this position. Pin through the thorax with a stainless steel

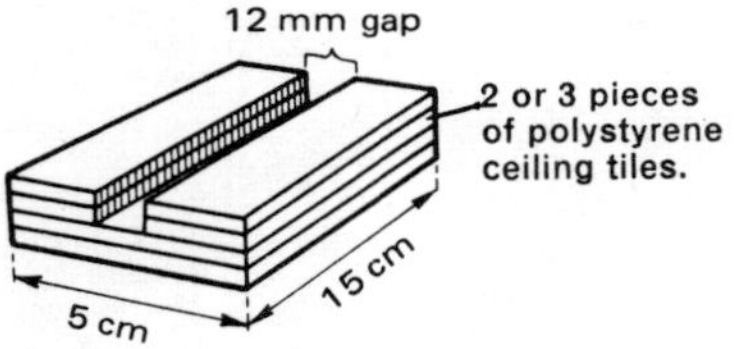

7 : 34a Polystyrene tile setting board.

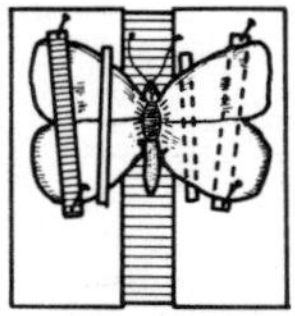

7 : 34b Butterfly on setting board.

pin (not dressmaker pins which may rust). A setting board should be bought or made (Fig. 7:34a).

Put the insect's body into the groove and strap down the wings with two strips of transparent paper on each side.

Allow large insects to dry out for at least three weeks and large-bodied moths require a month. After this time the insects are transferred to their mountings. Fix the data label on pin underneath the insect and store in an insect cabinet containing a bag of moth balls or Mothax. Wooden cigar boxes make good cabinets.

AQUARIA

Setting up

Buy, if you can afford it, several smaller tanks rather than one large. Make sure that the tank has a large surface to volume ratio. One goldfish bowl if filled to the top is just about the poorest type of container (see Fig. 7:35).

Angle-iron tanks are excellent, better than all-glass ones. It is cheaper to replace a pane than buy a new tank. The new stainless steel-framed tanks are very good but expensive. Battery jars, quarter full of water can be used, and many schools are finding that tanks made of modern forms of plastic are very satisfactory and are cheaper than the glass types.

Obtain several pounds of aquarium compost (gravel) from a pet shop – (about 3–6 mm. grade is best). You can find and wash your own but this is laborious! The gravel should be placed in the tanks so that it covers the front angle iron and slopes to about 4–5 cm. at the back. Fill your tank with tap water and leave for 24 hours. This gives the chlorine time to escape to

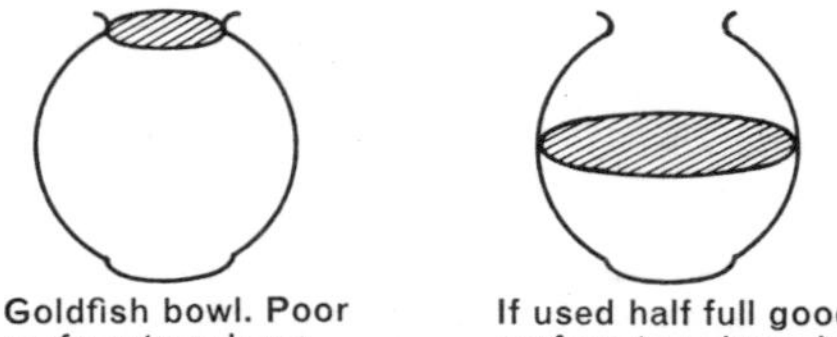

Goldfish bowl. Poor surface to volume ratio

If used half full good surface to volume but little volume.

7 : 35 Correct water level in a goldfish bowl.

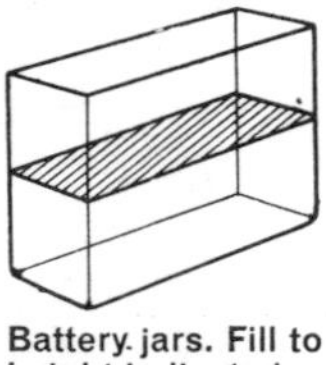

7 : 36a Correct water level in a battery jar.

Battery jars. Fill to height indicated otherwise poor surface to volume ratio.

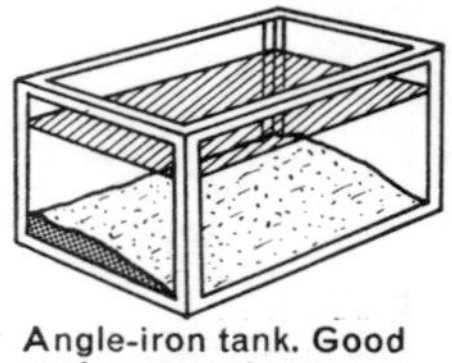

7 : 36b Angle-iron tank with good surface/volume ratio.

Angle-iron tank. Good surface to volume ratio. Note how gravel slopes upwards to back of tank.

7 : 37 Sticklebacks afford interesting observations.

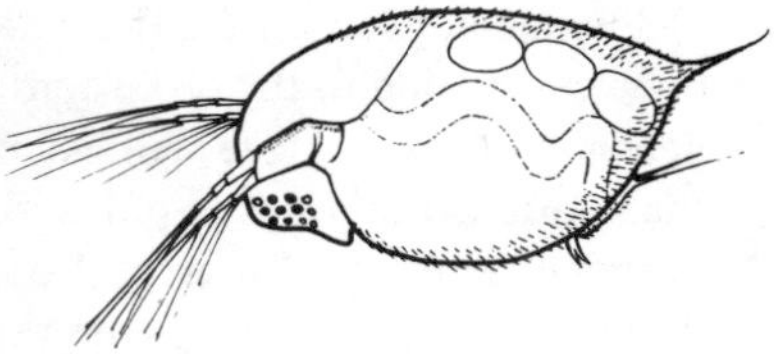

7 : 38 Water fleas provide excellent live food.

the air. If you are keeping pond fish then pond water is the best as no waiting is required. As you fill pour the water on to a saucer at the bottom of the tank so that your gravel does not get too disturbed. Arrange your plants along the back of the tank in clumps, if you feel they are necessary: they make it look good but they are certainly not essential. The old idea that they put oxygen into the water is correct but they cannot actually add more than the water will hold. The surface of the water will absorb as much oxygen as is necessary provided it is large enough – but do not overstock with fish. If surface to volume ratio is good then the temperature of the water will determine how much oxygen it can hold; the higher the temperature the less held. It has been said that in ponds overstocked with fish and having masses of floating duckweed (reducing effective surface area) and plenty of submerged plants; the pond may be short of oxygen after a very warm night and the fish may suffocate. At night both plants and animals compete for the oxygen in the pond and the plants are not releasing any because, obviously, photosynthesis is at a standstill in darkness.

Classrooms are relatively warm compared with ponds and the fish may tolerate the rise in temperature but if the tank is overstocked they will suffocate because the water is holding less oxygen. A rough guide for small fish is 75 sq. cm. of surface area for each 2·5cm. of fish. Larger fish, over 8 cm. require about 150 sq. cm. of water surface per 2·5 cm. of fish. One wonders how goldfish survive in bowls!

7 : 39(a) & (b) Two types of wet vivaria used for housing amphibia.

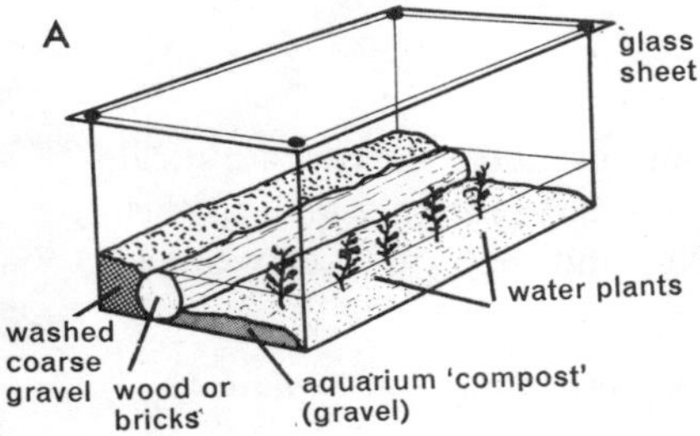

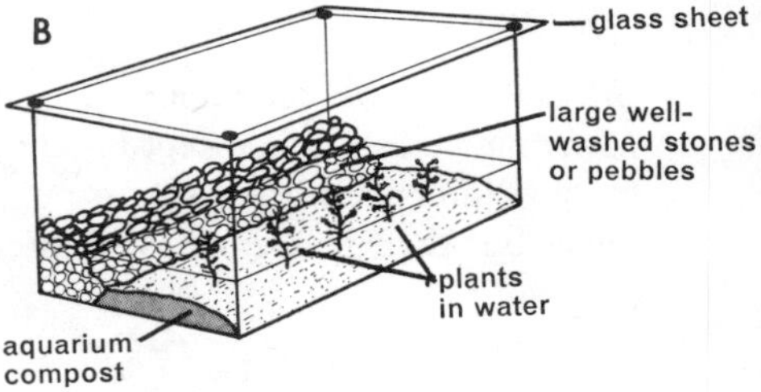

The usual position for the tank is a window-sill but this is probably the poorest position in the classroom. Too much light enters the tank and large deposits of green algae will accumulate on the sides. This is good for the snails but as the purpose of keeping fish is to observe how they behave and as the algae produce a green 'soup' then the point of keeping them is lost. Paste blue sugar paper on the three sides of the tank to exclude light. Do not be tempted to paint pretty pictures on the 'backcloth' for they seldom look effective. There are no hard and fast criteria about light; one just has to adjust the amount of light-shielding until your plants are healthy, and there is minimal algal growth.

A glass cover for the tank is essential – it keeps out chalk and other dust, prevents excessive water loss and prevents the fish from jumping out! The glass edges should be bound with Sellotape or sticking plaster to prevent nasty cuts. If the glass is placed directly on to an angle-iron tank top it will speed up rusting. Cut a cork into four pieces, say 6 mm. thick, and stick these down on each corner of the tank. This lifts the glass, prevents rusting and allows air to reach the water surface facilitating gaseous exchange at the surface.

Aeration

The value of an aerator or pump is limited. It apparently adds little to the total oxygen content of the tank but may help in setting up water movements to bring more water into contact with air and thus help the natural process of diffusion. Tanks can be kept without such an expensive item.

Feeding

In general, the tendency is to overfeed fish and this results in the uneaten remains falling to the bottom of the tank where they are acted upon by bacteria, so that in really bad conditions the fish are living in a bacterial 'soup'. The results of underfeeding are less obvious as the fish can stand short periods of starvation without external signs. Hence feeding has its problems.

Living foods are the best as they live on for a short time in the water without dying and decaying. Hence it is more difficult to overfeed. Some live foods are often obtainable in season from pet shops and from ponds (see below).

Sticklebacks in the aquarium

Many native fish can be kept in schools but just about the best are sticklebacks. Unfortunately these are pugnacious and require a tank to themselves but their behaviour is so interesting and they are so easy to keep,

7 : 40 Mealworms: a useful food especially in winter.

that they really do deserve a place in a school. Males and females will live together happily except at the breeding season when each male will choose his own territory. Unless you have a large tank it is as well to keep just one male with several females.

When the males start to develop their red throats and blue eyes it is time to return your surplus males to the pond or lake. Keep a lively one! The mating behaviour has been thoroughly investigated by Tinbergen in *Social Behaviour in Animals* and will not be detailed here. The account is fascinating and well worth reading. Sticklebacks require plants and pond weeds during breeding as the male requires them to construct his nest. Children will be delighted with the mating behaviour and it can be observed readily in a classroom tank. They may even wish to try out some simple experiments on the fish. Try pushing a red Biro top on a wire towards a male in breeding condition. They have been seen to make threatening approaches to Royal Mail vans parked 27 metres away in the road! Is shape important? Which shape attracts the male?

If you have a large tank, say over 60 cm. long, try having two males. They will each set up a territory. As a male moves from his base he becomes progressively more timid so that somewhere the two territories meet. The closer one male gets to the other's base the more fierce the owner gets in his threats and the more timid the intruder becomes.

It is difficult to keep other native fish as they soon outgrow the tank but young carp, rudd and gudgeon can be kept. However, I suggest sticklebacks! Goldfish are too well known to need introduction and are not native.

Live foods

(1) *Daphnia* – '*water fleas*' (Fig. 7:38)

May be cultured in the school. A large sweet jar is filled with pond water and a jam jar full of rotten leaves from the bottom of a pond is added. Put in pieces of lettuce leaf, adding more as they rot and decay. The resulting water-fleas will be useful for feeding to fish or for observation in their own right. Observe heart-beat with microscope. Look for eggs in female (female has curved end to intestine, male has straight tube).

(2) *Tubifex worms* – place in bowl after purchase and run cold water from the tap over them. Should form a tight red ball. Keep in dish with gentle stream of water.

(3) *Mosquito and Midge larvae and pupae* – collect from pond surfaces.

(4) *White worms* – these have to be cultured in school but provide a very valuable food available throughout the year. Can be purchased with full instructions from biological suppliers.

(5) *Earthworms* are a very valuable food for most fishes. Unfortunately they have to be cut up rather small and this is messy and should not be performed in front of young children.

(6) *Maggots* (*Blowfly larvae*). These are interesting in their own right and provide a readily available source of living material for urban schools. Purchase from a fishing tackle shop. Observe them under a hand lens. Place two or three in a glass tube and partially cover with dark paper. What do they do? Try different-coloured cellophane. Record their activity at different temperature. Feed on meat and vary amount for different groups. (Adult flies will have to be killed.)

(7) *Mealworms* (*Tenebrio beetle larvae*). The larvae or mealworms can be purchased from most pet shops and from any Biological Supply House. They provide an easily maintained source of living material. The mealworms are a valuable food for large fish, amphibia and reptiles. Culture the worms in battery jars, large jam jars or sweet bottles filled to within 8–10 cm. of the top with bran or oatmeal. Add pieces of raw carrot or potato periodically. A close fitting lid of perforated zinc, gauze or plastic mesh is required. The larvae must be kept warm at about 26° C (80° F), so place the container on a radiator. Life cycle takes about four to six months so colony will take some time to get established (Fig. 7:40).

Prepared foods. There are many types and it is profitable to change your type periodically so that the fish stand a better chance of getting a balanced diet. Kitchen scraps of liver, boiled egg, fish and meat are useful additions to a diet of prepared foods. When feeding prepared foods experiment initially with the amounts. The fish should be able to consume what you give them in 5 to 10 minutes.

Pond life

The best water for pond life is the actual water from the pond, topped up when necessary with more pond water. If pond water is unavailable then use rain water or cold tap water which has stood for 24 hours. Identification of pond creatures can be aided by many books and leaflets (see bibliography). Some creatures are aggressively carnivorous and have to be avoided in a community tank, e.g. dragonfly nymphs, Diving beetles and their nymphs.

TROPICAL FRESHWATER TANKS

These are more expensive to set up but broaden the scope of fish-keeping beyond sticklebacks and goldfish. The tanks are set up as mentioned previously but as the water temperature is best kept between 23°–26° C (75°–80° F) some form of heating and heating control by means of a thermostat is necessary. In order to check that your heating system is working correctly a thermometer is required. The floating buoy-type is probably best as the 'stick-on' type invariably falls off and one has to grub about on the tank bottom to retrieve it.

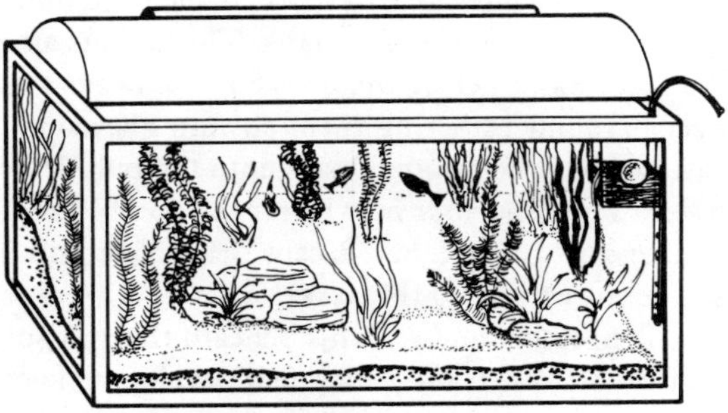

7:41 A fully equipped tropical tank.

If there is no electric power source in the classroom then abandon the idea of tropical fish. The other methods (gas etc.) are cumbersome and too unreliable.

Tropical plants can be obtained from any good aquarist and are not expensive. They should be planted as indicated earlier.

FISH

Guppies. These make very good subjects for the class tank. They are live-bearers and the black eyes of the young can be seen inside the gravid (pregnant) females. The male has a long modified fin for introducing sperms. Females produce about 20 young fish every four to five weeks.

Swordtails. So named because the male has a long sword-like extension to his tail fin. If fed correctly the male will be quite large when his 'sword' is fully developed. There is a dominance developed in male swordtails, one being as it were, king over the others, taking first place for food, females, etc. Several colours are available. Try breeding using different 'crosses'.

Mollies. Normally grey but the all-black form is commonly on sale. More difficult to get to breed. When breeding these fish in a community tank, keep plenty of plants on or near the surface for the young fry to hide in.

Siamese Fighting Fish. These are dealt with here because of their wonderful reproductive behaviour.

As is often the case, the mature male fighting fish is a splendid creature whereas the female is dowdy in comparison. Males have wonderfully veiled fins when mature and are about 5 cm. long, while females mature at about 4 cm. long. The male may be kept alone in a tank prior to breeding. Feed him well on live foods. The female is introduced either directly into the tank or floated in a jam jar in the tank for a few hours. If all is well when the pair get together a really dramatic courtship commences. The male constructs a nest of bubbles in the corner of the tank and when this job is completed tries to persuade the female to follow him under the nest. As the female sheds her eggs a white cloud of sperm is shed and the eggs and sperm fall together towards the bottom of the tank. The parents are motionless for a fraction of a second but before the now-fertilised eggs reach the bottom the male sweeps around gathering them all into his mouth. After he has caught the last he spits them individually into the bubble nest on the surface of the water. The behaviour may be repeated until the female is spent. It is now kindness to remove her because the male will attack without warning if she ventures near to the nest.

He is an excellent father and remains beneath the nest spitting back any eggs that fall from it. When the young fish develop he keeps them all together until he leaves the young to fend for themselves.

This behaviour is readily seen in a classroom and provokes real interest, wonderful descriptive writing and delightful drawings, which are well worth the effort and cost in setting up. Also you can recoup your costs by selling some of the progeny back to the pet shop! You cannot keep more than one male as they really fight. Place a mirror next to the tank near a mature fighting fish and watch his reactions!

Some interesting aquatic animals

Dytiscus larvae (Golden-edged water beetle – *Dytiscus marginalis*). Most interesting animals! I know a person who has kept a pair as pets very happily for several years. They travel around the country in the car when necessary. The larvae are commonly brought up when pond dipping. They are well worth keeping in a small tank on their own. Aggressive, fierce creatures, they will attack and devour tadpoles, but may be fed on mealworms, maggots and white worm. Observe the feeding behaviour.

If you wish to follow the whole life cycle a fairly complicated arrangement is required. The larvae pupate by the pond edge so when the larvae go off their food they should be housed as in the diagram (Fig. 7:43).

After pupation the adults will emerge and may enter the water. They should be removed and placed in a larger tank; if possible a pair should be kept together. The female's wing covers are grooved whereas the male's are

7 : 42 Dytiscus larva – fierce but interesting.

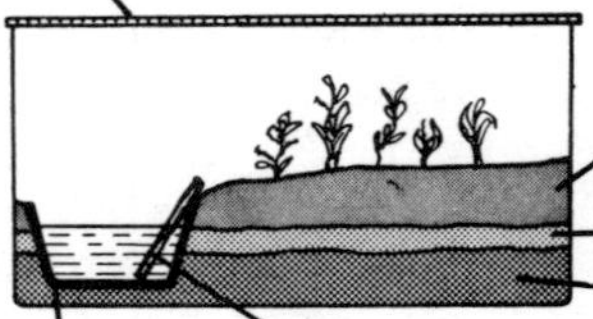

7 : 43 Housing for Dytiscus larvae.

smooth. He also has a 'disc' on the first pair of legs. The adults fly and hence a cover is needed over their tank. They breed in spring and summer the female laying eggs in slits in reeds by the water bank. Modify the tank shown, replacing turf by reed clump and keep very moist. With luck eggs will develop and larvae will move into the water. Feed adults weekly by placing piece of meat on string in tank for half an hour. They will suck out 'juice'.

WATER SPIDERS. Need a separate tank but this need be only a large pickle or sweet jar. The lid of the jar needs a few small holes punched in it. Feed on dead flies, water-louse (*Acellus*), or blood worms. A nest will be made in amongst the water weeds. This is in the form of a web, not used as a trap but as a home. Water spiders are difficult to find but are available from L. Haig, Beam Brook, Newdigate, Surrey.

Caddis fly larvae. These are detritus feeders, consuming small pieces of organic matter.

RIVER LIFE

Trout. Useful in winter when little life is stirring outside. I have had some very good years with trout, rearing a very high proportion of eggs through to 5 cm. fish. In other years the mortality rate has been very high. They are readily kept in schools. All that is needed is a sink and a tap which can be left running. They may be purchased from The Midland Fishery, Nailsworth, Glos., from January to March. The eggs will arrive surrounded by damp sphagnum moss at the 'eyed-stage'.

Transfer the eggs to a pie dish or shallow plastic box and fill with tap water. Examine the eggs carefully; some may be unhealthy and diseased, and should be discarded. Diseased eggs will look rather like boiled egg white while healthy eggs will be clear and transparent. Set up the aquarium as shown in the diagram, observing regularly and discarding diseased specimens.

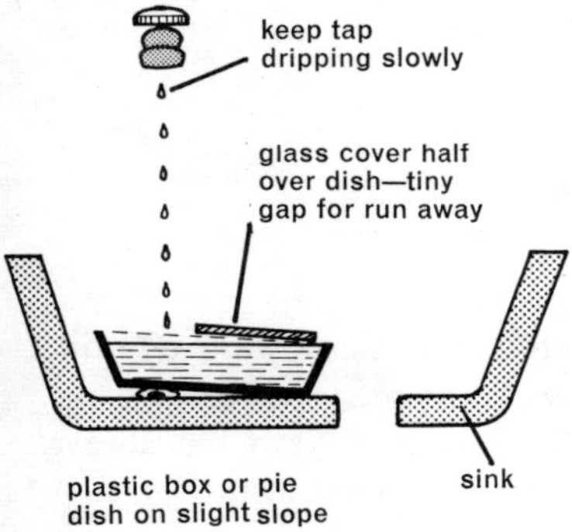

7 : 44 Trout-rearing aquarium.

7 : 45 Young trout – alevin.

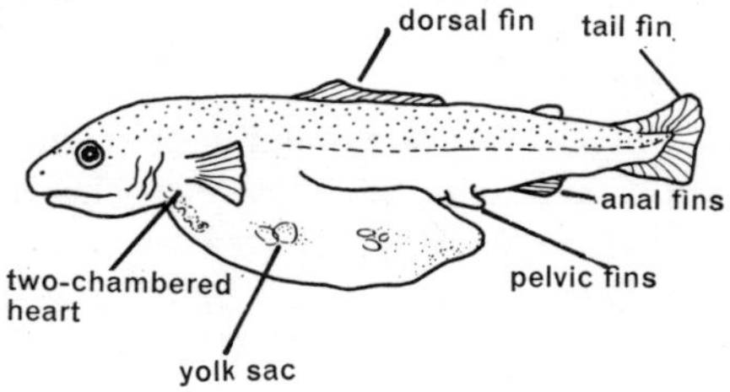

In some areas the tap water may be unsuitable for the trout or a tap may not be available. In these circumstances have a large container open to the air and holding tap water. This will be at room temperature and will rapidly lose its chlorine to the atmosphere. Twice a day replace the water in the 'trout-tank' with the 'stand-by' water; at the same time top up the 'stand-by' water from the tap. The containers for the developing trout may be quite shallow.

After four or five days, depending on temperature, since development is delayed by very low temperatures, the young alevin emerge from the egg case. The yolk sac is attached externally to the alevin and this provides its nourishment for about six weeks.

After this time it is absorbed and the trout are termed fry; they now feed and should be transferred to a deeper tank. If possible small crustacea (water fleas) from ponds or culture tank should be provided. The fry should be fed very small amounts. Egg yolk is a good substitute and 'liqui-fry' is excellent while very small liver scrapings are useful. Many schools successfully rear trout to 10–15 cm. and then release them into suitable streams.

Observations should be made at all stages and drawings and other records made. Do all the eggs develop at the same time? When fish are at the fry stage do any patterns of dominance emerge? Is there a 'king' fish? If a dominant fish emerges how is the dominance shown? Investigate food preferences of the young fish by dropping various flies on to the water film. Will they take worms of any kind?

SEA WATER AQUARIA

Not recommended for schools away from sea and without access to supplies of sea water. They can be kept but there are many difficulties. The main problem is to keep the tank cool and therefore the summer months are best avoided.

As this will be a technique for relatively few schools a specialised book in this field should be consulted (see bibliography).

AMPHIBIA

Newts

Three species are found in the United Kingdom.

1 Common or Smooth Newt – has a smooth body without warts on skin.
2 Great Warty or Crested Newt – has a very warty skin.
3 Palmate Newt – May be confused with the Common Newt but always has a white throat. The Common Newt has spots on the throat.

Eggs. The eggs are shed singly after internal fertilisation. The female fastens each one to the underside of a water plant leaf so search for them among the pond weed. The eggs are laid normally in early April but laying may continue through to July.

Tadpoles. Tadpoles develop three pairs of pink feathery gills on each side of the head. These are retained until the lungs develop. The front legs develop before the hind, the reverse of frog tadpoles. From being shed to leaving the water takes about 14–16 weeks for Palmate and Common Newts and about 20 weeks for the Great Warty Newt. The July-laid eggs remain as tadpoles in the ponds through the winter. The April-laid eggs will develop and the young newt emerge from the pond in early autumn to hibernate on the land.

Care of newt tadpoles. If you find eggs or tadpoles do not be tempted to collect too many. A dozen or so eggs and half a dozen tadpoles are enough. Set up a tank as for fish for the receipt of your tadpoles. Lower the collecting jar into the tank so that the tadpoles swim out. Do not pour the tadpoles and water in as they are delicate creatures. You will wish to feed your tadpoles carefully so that you have as many young newts as you had tadpoles. Newts are carnivorous throughout their life. Any of the live foods

7 : 46 Newts are of great interest to children.

mentioned earlier (p. 232) are suitable. After they have spent some weeks as tadpoles they will leave the water. By floating wood or cork in the tank they can emerge on to it and can be removed to the adult vivarium.

Young newts. These feed on minute insects and are very difficult to rear. It is a kindness to release them after a few days' observation.

Adult newts. These can be kept and bred in schools. They require a wet vivarium. An aquarium tank at least 60 × 30 × 25 cm. is required. Fill the bottom up to say, 5 cm. with a mixture of peaty loam on a 2·5 cm. bed of gravel. Cover the surface with well-rotted leaf mould. You may plant in this mosses, small ferns or Tradescantia to make it more attractive and to provide shade. Bark, stones or plant pots should be arranged in the vivarium to provide hiding places. Sink a shallow dish into the compost so that its rim is level with the compost surface. Keep the dish filled with fresh clean water. Cover the tank with a perforated zinc lid bent like a shoe-box lid or with a glass sheet resting on 6 mm. corks on tank corners. Feed on slugs, insects and small pieces of meat and liver. They feed normally at night but may become tame enough to take food dangled in front of them.

Breeding tank for newts. A pair of newts should be placed in the breeding tank in late March. If they spawn they should be removed back to the wet vivarium as they are not only carnivorous but also cannibalistic.

Frogs and toads

The Common Frog only is described as the Edible and Marsh Frog have very local distribution and the Common Toad only is dealt with as the Natterjack is also very localised.

The Common Frog has been recorded as living for twelve years in captivity. They can be distinguished readily from toads by the black triangular patch that runs from just in front of the eye over the circular external ear-

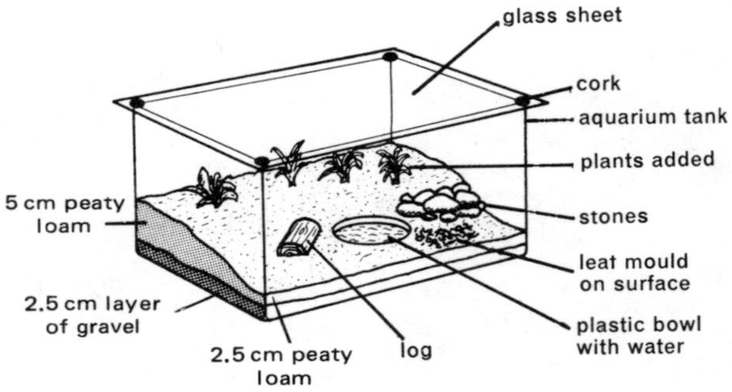

7 : 47 A breeding tank for newts.

drum (normally darker). They possess teeth in the upper jaw but these are absent in toads. The tongue of the frog is 'hinged' at the front of the mouth unlike the toad's which is fastened at the back. The hind feet are fully webbed in the frog but partially webbed in the toad. The Common Toad usually has a very warty skin through which venom is secreted. The large glands on the head produce a cream-like venom which can be squirted some distance. If handling toads do so very gently to avoid a 'squirt' which is very painful in the eye.

The males can readily be distinguished from females in the breeding season as the former have the nuptial pad on the hand.

FROGS

Tadpoles. Set up an aquarium as for fish. The young tadpoles are herbivorous initially and will require green plants, so make sure some are planted. Do not keep more than a dozen tadpoles as they really require careful feeding. Eggs need no introduction but are shed much earlier in the year than is commonly realised – beginning February to mid-March. They are laid in masses in shallow water. Development from the egg to the young frog takes about three months. It is wellnigh impossible to get frogs to breed in schools so that you will have to collect the spawn. Young frogs are difficult to feed and should be released after a few days' observation. Tadpoles scrape the algae off aquatic plants with their horny jaws. If there is a shortage of aquatic plants a few pieces of bruised lettuce leaves on the water surface suffice. When the external gills are absorbed the frogs become carnivores and require meat. They may be fed on a strip of meat dangled in the tank on a string; an earthworm will do but children may react adversely to this. Take care that the strip of meat is not allowed to decay; remove after say, half an hour. Feed daily. If tadpoles die do not remove them for their 'cannibal brothers' will dispose of them. When tadpoles have four legs and the tail is being absorbed float wood on the water for them to crawl upon.

It is difficult to keep adult frogs in school as they usually refuse food and become very nervous. They may be brought in for a short time for observation and then it is kind to release them.

TOADS

Treat toad spawn and tadpoles as for frogs.

Adults. These may be kept either singly or paired in the 'wet' vivarium previously described. If a white saucer is placed in the tank and used as a feeding base it will encourage the toads to become tame. If you want them really tame handle them gently, daily. Feed toads on worms, mealworms and assorted insects.

Salamanders (Spotted or European Salamander – black with yellow blotches)

Salamanders require a wet vivarium. They will thrive in schools but as they hide for most of the day, feeding at night, their use is limited. They will however, breed readily (viviparous) in captivity entering the water to deposit the young, so have a large water bowl in tank. The young salamander tadpoles live in water for about four months and may be fed on live foods, e.g. Daphnia. Treat as for young newts.

The adult colours are developed after about six months. Feed adults on earthworms and slugs and mealworms.

Experimental work with amphibia

1 Effect of temperature on tadpole development. If frog or toad spawn is separated into two batches and kept at two contrasting temperatures, say separated by —12° C (10° F), what effect does it have on growth rates?

2 Effect of varying water depths.

3 Effect of crowding.

4 Effect of feeding on live food, e.g. fresh chopped earthworm as opposed to proprietary foods, e.g. Brosiam fish food.

5 Feeding in frogs and toads. The animals will snap at moving food. If a mealworm is placed close the animal will take it. By feeding a mealworm at varying distances from the animal its eyesight can be gauged. Some most interesting work has been done with tame toads by placing them on revolving turntables and putting mealworms on a stationary base near by. They take the 'worm' very accurately. Similarly one could revolve a worm around a stationary toad! This to my knowledge has not been attempted in schools!

6 If you have a breeding pair of newts does the female show any preference in the type of plant chosen for laying its eggs? Try various plants in the aquarium.

REPTILES

Lizards

May be housed simply in a 'dry vivarium'. Strip light, incandescent *not* fluorescent, in roof aids visibility and keeps lizard warm. They still require sunlight and should be placed in a sunny spot.

A dry vivarium is an aquarium tank with a 2–3 cm. layer of sand and some old plant pots as hiding places. The roof should be of perforated zinc and well-fitting.

Three types of lizards occur in the United Kingdom:

1 Common, or Viviparous lizard (*Lacerta vivipa*)

Five to six inches (15–17 cm.) long when mature and variously marked. Bears young alive rather than laying eggs. Feeds on insects and grubs; enjoys mealworms.

2 Sand lizard (*Lacerta agilis*)
Larger than Common lizard. Male is olive or dark brown on the back and bright emerald green on sides. Female is greenish brown. This species has a very localised distribution on sandy heaths in Lancashire, Dorset, Hampshire and Surrey.
3 Slow-worm or blindworm (*Anguis fragilis*)
This is really a limbless lizard. A good sized specimen would be between 30–45 cm., half of this being its tail.
Makes a good pet in school. Thrives in the dry vivarium but prefers damper conditions than the other two. Feed on Garden slugs but will also take insects and small earthworms as well as mealworms.
Never attempt to hold lizards by the tail. These will be shed and the new tail that develops is not as attractive as the original!

Work with reptiles
1 Effect of temperature upon their activity.
2 Lizards can be conditioned to come to feed at the sound of a bell or whistle. This might be worth trying.
3 Growth rate may be recorded.
4 Food preferences.

BIRDS

We feel that birds should not be kept in schools. Although they are not difficult to manage they tend to be noisy, as anyone who has attempted to teach in a room with a canary will testify! They are common as pets in homes and children are generally familiar with them. Moreover they can be readily borrowed when required. However there may be people who wish to try their hand at breeding and behaviour studies so a brief outline follows.
Cage. The all-wire cage is not really ideal as the birds are susceptible to draughts. The cage design is relatively unimportant provided it is not kept in a draught. The main characteristic of the cage should be to give good movement space. A wooden cage, say 60 × 45 × 45 cm. with a wire front (purchased cheaply from pet shop) is ideal. Arrange perches at either end of cage – one high, one low – so that the bird can open its wings in movement. Floor has removable tray with bird sand (expensive) or newspaper (cheap). Clean regularly, scrubbing perches weekly.

Feeding

Canaries
Require seed, water and grit. The mixed seed sold by pet shops is suitable, the bird selecting the seed it likes best. A spray of green food, e.g. chickweed, dandelion, groundsel, lettuce or a piece of apple should be given daily.

Budgerigars
Proprietary foods are very suitable and the additions mentioned for canaries. Millet sprays should be provided occasionally as a titbit.

Zebra Finch
A very attractive bird, quieter than canary or budgerigar and more likely to be a novelty to children. Feed on seed mixture of small yellow millet, small canary and white millet, or a proprietary brand of British Finch mixture with additions as for budgerigar and canaries.

Bird Table – observations can be made of species and food preferences. Full details on construction of bird tables and nesting boxes are obtainable free from the Royal Society for the Protection of Birds (pp. 119–22).

MAMMALS

The rat

Handling
It is most important if albino (white) or other rats are to be kept that they be handled regularly. They will become very tame and friendly if they are treated carefully. They are however temperamental and there is always the risk of a bite.

The photograph demonstrates the correct way to hold a rat. Note the index finger is placed under the neck, the remainder of the fingers support the belly while the thumb is placed over the neck. All movements should be slow and gentle. For demonstration the 'root' of the tail is held in one hand and the body of the animal supported by the other.

Housing
A professionally-made all-wire cage is quite expensive and so might place it out of the range of the schools. A very simple cage incorporating many desirable features can be made very cheaply. Two types are shown in Fig. 7:48, 49.

In the bottom of the bowl is dry peat or sawdust. Advantage of this type of cage is that it never gets urine soaked and it can be sterilised readily with really hot water and 'Dettol'.

Feeding
A simple food hopper is required in the cage. A plastic dropping bottle for water is also required. Diet – rats are rather demanding and the best plan is to obtain a ready mixed complete diet as supplied by Dixon & Sons, Ware, Herts. or Harris Biological Supplies Ltd., Weston-super-Mare, Somerset.

Even though the diet is complete, children will enjoy feeding green food and roots periodically.

Cleaning
Thorough cleansing of the cage is required every week and so a spare

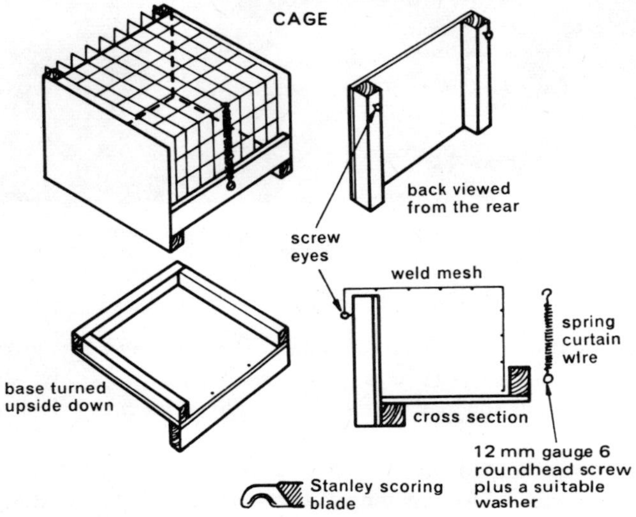

7 : 48 An easily-made case for small mammals.

housing cage is required during this period. Feeding bottle and hopper will also require cleaning. If the cages are cleaned regularly there is no reason why the animals should smell.

Average classroom temperatures of 14°–21° C (60°–70° F) are suitable for rats; in fact, they will tolerate colder conditions if they are provided with more bedding material – shredded paper, wood-wool, etc. Rapid changes of temperature are to be avoided as they lead to respiratory and other infections.

Breeding

A breeding pair should be between 3 and 12 months old. The sexes can be distinguished by the fact that the distance between the anus and the genital papilla is greater in the male than in a female of similar age.

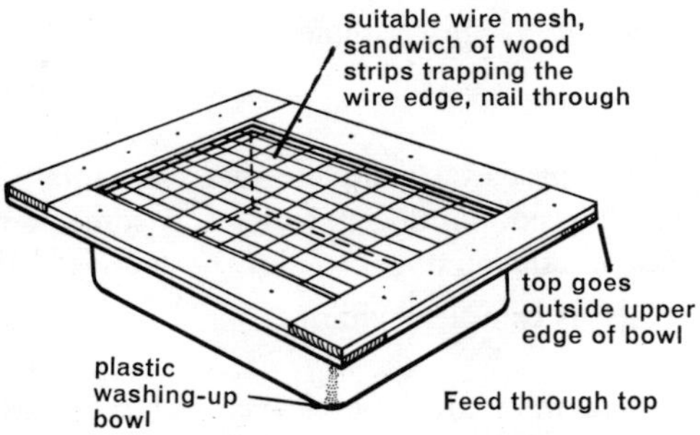

7 : 49 'Washing-up bowl' cage.

7 : 50 The correct method of holding a tame rat.

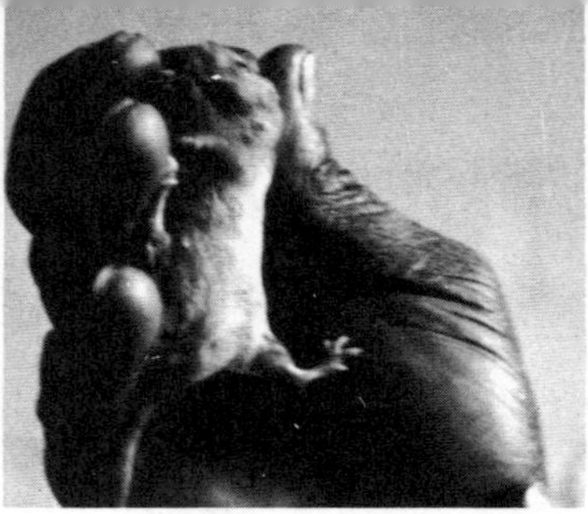

7 : 51 The correct method of holding a tame mouse.

Leave male with female for up to 20 days; then he may be removed. As the gestation period is 21–22 days, young should arrive quickly. Do not disturb the mother as she may eat the young. The number in a litter varies from 3 to 12.

Young are helpless at birth. Eyes open on or about the 15th day and the young start to take solid food. Young can be weaned at three weeks and the sexes should be separated at eight weeks to prevent early breeding. In captivity rats will live for about three years.

The mouse

Mice nearly always smell! If you wish to keep mice the plastic cage described for the rat is very suitable and will house a breeding pair. The design of the cage is such that the occupants are unable to climb the slippery polythene walls. Do not, therefore, place food hoppers in positions where the young baby mice can climb up and squeeze through the weldmesh. Various types of mice including genetically pure strains can be obtained. Try the main biological suppliers, e.g. Philip Harris Ltd., 63 Ludgate Hill, Birmingham 3.

Handling

Lift the mouse by the tail near to its 'root' and then turn the hand so that the mouse rests upon it. If this is done quietly, carefully and regularly mice rarely bite.

Feeding

Mice can be fed on a prepared complete diet (see 'rats'). Mixed grain, wheat, oats, millet, linseed, sunflower fruits and some fresh vegetables, e.g. cabbage, lettuce, dandelion may be fed if the complete diet is not purchased. Feed at the same time each day.

Cleaning

Because of their smell mice must be cleaned out more frequently than most mammals – twice weekly, so have a spare cage. Clean as for rats.

Breeding
A breeding pair should be about 3 months old. The period of gestation is from 19–21 days and the number in a litter varies from about 6 to 12. If the male is left with the female then he will mate immediately after the birth of the young. If this takes place a new litter will be produced in a few weeks. If the male is removed prior to parturition then the female will not mate again while suckling the litter, i.e. for about three weeks. The female should not be disturbed after parturition otherwise she may eat her young. Separate the mother from the litter at about a month if necessary. Males may be housed together but they tend to fight as they become mature and if this happens you will wish to keep them separate. The males can be distinguished from the females at maturity by the appearance of the testes – swellings at the base of the tail.

Cavies or guinea pigs

Our domesticated form is one of the many types of cavies found in South America on the plains of Uruguay and Brazil. When Europeans arrived on this continent the inhabitants had domesticated the guinea pig some hundreds of years before.

May be kept in pairs, small units or in colonies. They may be kept out of doors in a sheltered spot but ensure that the hutch is above the ground. Better kept outside as their grunts and squeaks are disturbing in the classroom. A family unit would require a hutch say 60 × 90 × 60 cm. high, a boar and three sows one 120 × 60 × 60 cm. high.

Handling
The guinea pig is normally easily handled but may become intractable if with litter. They should be held with both hands.

Feeding
Guinea pigs are herbivores and should always have hay available. They should be fed on mixed grains (see mice) or rolled oats, about 60 gm. daily. Roots and green vegetables, e.g. dandelion, coltsfoot, clover, apple peel, apple cores can also be given. They do not require water if a good supply of green vegetables is available, but it is safest to give them a bowl.

Breeding
Guinea pigs should be about 6 months' old for breeding. They can be sexed by separating the inguinal skin when the boar's penis will appear round and the sow's vulva as a slit. Both are anterior to the anus. The gestation period is about ten weeks and normally three or four young are born in a very advanced state with eyes open and the milk teeth shed. A few hours after birth they will run with their mother and will nibble grain on the second day. They are suckled for 14 days and may be separated from

parents at two to three weeks. The female will mate on the day young are born as in mice – post-parturition mating – otherwise she will not mate while suckling.

Hamsters

The Golden hamster has been described as the cleanest, least troublesome and most convenient small mammal for classroom observation. Although this mantle may now have fallen on the 'Mongolian Gerbil' (see later) it is nevertheless an excellent animal for schools.

Unknown, except to a few specialists, twenty years ago, the hamster has achieved tremendous popularity. The Golden hamsters in the United Kingdom today have probably all descended from an adult female and twelve young which were brought to Jerusalem in 1930 and bred in captivity.

The cage recommended for mice and rats is quite suitable, or an aquarium tank 45 × 30 × 30 cm. with 12 mm. mesh wire netting or 'weld-mesh' as a lid. The cage should be kept warm in winter, otherwise hibernation occurs. Normal classroom temperature is suitable.

Handling

Most hamsters can be handled easily. They are held as for rats. Care is necessary with older females who may bite. These animals, like the others mentioned, should be handled and fondled regularly to give them confidence. Handling during the day also disturbs their normal nocturnal habit.

Feeding

Feed once a day, in the afternoon preferably. They may be fed on assorted cereals, peas, beans, nuts, dried brown bread, bread and milk. A few pieces of carrot or green vegetables are needed every day. Beware of overfeeding as the animal carries off surplus food in its cheek pouches and hides this in dark corners of the cage. This stored food is rarely eaten and it indicates overfeeding if a surplus is accumulating daily. This stored food may rot and cause disease in the cage so it should be removed.

Cleaning

Cages should be thoroughly cleaned weekly. Hamsters habitually choose an area in the cage in which to urinate. If a shallow tray is placed in this position and covered with the sawdust or peat it may be removed daily thus keeping the cage from smelling.

Breeding

For breeding, hamsters should be about 10–15 weeks old even though they are sexually mature at 5–6 weeks. They breed all the year round but mainly in May to October. The reproductive life of the female is about twelve months and she may rear three litters during this time. Breeding requires some care. The female is more pugnacious than the male and should always be transferred to his cage. Choose a female about the same size as the male. Females are in season every 4–5 days and indicate this by an air of restlessness and by small cries. At this time if the back is gently stroked the tail will be raised. On introduction of the doe to the buck's cage watch to see if he is attacked. If so, remove doe and repeat again the next day trying if necessary for three or four days. They may mate several times for up to fifteen minutes at a time. The female goes into a mating trance and should be removed as soon as she starts to move about. Gestation lasts 15–17 days and the doe may profitably be given more milk and food during this time. Nest material such as hay should obviously be provided. Do not disturb the nest during cleaning. When the litter is produced do not disturb until the second day. Usually 5 to 12 young are produced in a litter. Young hamsters are helpless at birth. Their eyes do not open for about 14 days but at a week old they may be sampling the mother's food store. They develop rapidly once their eyes are open, leaving the nest and moving about in the cage. They should be removed from the doe when they are 1 month old. They may be housed together for some time but once they start to fight they must be separated and treated as adults.

Mongolian Gerbils (*Merione unginculatus*)

These may well become more popular than the hamster. They were only introduced into the United Kingdom in November 1964. They were rather expensive at first, but are now available at a reasonable price.

Their natural habitat is desert or semi-desert regions where they live in large communities in subterranean burrows.

Housing

The polythene cage recommended is suitable as is an aquarium modified as for hamsters. A breeding pair require 929 sq. cm. and group cages should have about 129 sq. cm. per animal. Peat or sawdust is required on the floor

7:52 The Golden hamster.

7:53 Mother gerbil and family

plus cotton wool or wood-wool for bedding. Feeding hoppers must be fastened to the side of the cage or bedded on the floor of the cage. They should not be put on the surface of bedding as the animals have been known to suffocate under the hopper. A water bottle is required.

They will thrive and even breed at temperatures of 0° C (32° F) if they have good bedding but thrive best at 'school temperature', i.e. 14°–21° C (60°–70° F.)

Handling

It is perfectly safe to handle Mongolian Gerbils at all stages as they very rarely bite. Even pregnant females and breeding pairs with suckling young may be handled. Recently weaned juveniles are very lively and although safe may get loose! Gerbils show intense inquisitiveness and will explore any new object or hand placed in their cage.

Feeding

Can be fed on complete diet as for rats – diet 41B being very suitable. Grain mixtures as for mice are also suitable; they particularly like maize and oats (whole). If water is provided they do not need vegetables but they enjoy cabbage, carrots and lettuce.

Cleaning

Cages are practically odourless as the animal only produces one or two drops of highly concentrated urine per day and the faeces are completely dry. Hence the cage need only be cleaned weekly and sterilised monthly. This is obviously a boon to schools. It is possible to leave the cleaning for fortnightly or even monthly periods.

Breeding

Select a pair of pubertal animals if possible and keep these as a breeding pair for their lives. In this case there is no possibility of friction. If a breeding pair is set up from adults they must be carefully observed, as for hamsters, and separated if fighting occurs.

Females, when in season, every 4–7 days, show an intense behaviour pattern, drumming with the hind feet and indicating general alertness. The period of gestation is 24–26 days and the litter may contain 1 to 12 young with a mean litter size of around 4–5. The young are naked and their eyes are closed. Hair starts to develop at 5 days and the eyes open at 16–20 days. Young start to nibble solids at about 10 days. They should be weaned from the parents at 21 days. The female will produce one litter every 30 to 40 days.

Although the Mongolian Gerbil was recently a newcomer to this country its appearance, behaviour and ease of handling ensure that it is now a most popular pet and classroom animal.

Rabbits

Require little comment. Best kept outside, for unless they are very regularly cleaned, smells tend to develop. Indoor hutches should be cleaned every day to prevent smells. Also they appear to be healthier if kept out of doors. In the authors' opinion rabbits require such large living quarters (e.g. for a small variety a cage 60 × 60 × 45 cm. high) that they are unsuitable for urban schools particularly when there are smaller alternative animals available.

Housing

Sawdust required on bottom of hutch. Hay required as bedding material and food.

Handling

The left hand is passed over the body and under the belly just behind the front legs while the right hand supports the rump of the animal. Do not hold them by their ears!

Feeding

Twice daily. Early in the morning and in the late afternoon. In the mornings they may be fed on old bread (one slice) or ½ teacupful of crushed oats, a few greens in the morning – mixed from kitchen garden vegetables, potato peelings (dry) grasses, clover, etc.

In the evening the oats or bread plus a large amount of the greens. In winter any peelings that are available may be used, e.g. cabbage, carrot, apple, pear, turnip, swede. Do not feed rhubarb leaves as these are poisonous. Many people are unaware that they eat their soft night pellets (faeces) to obtain digested cellulose from them.

Water should be available but is rarely taken when plenty of greens are supplied.

Cleaning

Weekly outdoors, daily indoors. Really good scour out with disinfectant periodically.

Breeding

Six to nine months old before paired, depending on size. Small breeds are mature earlier than large breeds. Take the doe to the buck's hutch. Mating usually occurs within a few minutes. If the doe is aggressive to the buck or avoids him by jumping about the hutch she should be removed and a new attempt made two days later. Gestation lasts for 28–30 days. The young are naked, eyes are closed. Hair starts to develop after 5 days; after 10–11 days eyes are open and at three weeks' old they move around in the cage. Young should be removed from the doe when they are about 6–8 weeks old. Males and females may be segregated into separate hutches at three months. When first removed from mother young rabbits should be fed three or four times a day. They should be handled regularly on emergence from the nest otherwise they become wild and intractable as adults.

Recommended Books

Bolger, F. J., *Smaller Livestock at Home and School*, Blandford.

Hvass H., *Reptiles of the World*, Methuen.

Kettlewell, H. B. D., *Your Book of Butterflies & Moths*, Faber & Faber, 1963.

Leutscher, A., *A Study of Reptiles and Amphibians*, Blandford.

Lodewijks, J. M., *Tropical Fish in the Aquarium*, Blandford.

Savory, T., *Spiders & Other Arachnids*, E.U.P., 1964.

Southern, H. N., *Handbook of British Mammals*, Blackwell.

Vevers, G., *Reptiles and Amphibians in Colour*. Blandford, 1972.

Walker, Braz, *Tropical Fish in Colour*, Blandford, 1971.

8 Discovering Past Environments

(This chapter has been contributed by D. J. Steel and L. Taylor, Senior Lecturers in History, Berkshire College of Education.)

Local history projects should develop naturally from the geographical and biological exploration of the environment, but only too often they end up just on the wrong side of that fine line that divides history from antiquarianism. In studying Domesday, examining potsherds or visiting an ancient church, the children must not be allowed to forget the people who toiled in the fields, cooked with the pots or worshipped in the church.

It is not necessarily obvious to a child that his environment owes as much to man as to nature. He is apt to think that 'God made the country, and man made the town', failing to appreciate either the full extent of man's transformation of the countryside, or the way in which the siting and development of the town has been largely conditioned by natural factors.

The methods used by the teacher to give children some understanding of the interaction between past societies and their environment must vary according to circumstances. For example, the urban child may be able to grasp quite readily the historical changes in his own neighbourhood, but the teacher may have to resort to different techniques to give him an understanding of the more subtle processes at work in the countryside.

To understand these social forces, the child needs to examine many different kinds of evidence and to ask continually what a particular object, building or document can tell him about the community which produced it. By constantly questioning, he will learn something of the techniques of the historian.

I – THE NEIGHBOURHOOD

Because his own knowledge and experience are limited, a child's attention should initially be focused on an area much smaller than a region, county, town or even a parish, and on a period of time relatively close to the present. The aspects of his environment most familiar to the child are on his own doorstep. Similarly, the only period of time he fully understands is one closely related to his own life span, and that of his parents. Thus, it is unwise to attempt a historical project until the child has a thorough understanding of his environment as it is today. From this, he can proceed backwards in time by easy stages, first by questioning his parents, and later by interviewing elderly relatives and neighbours. If a historical project has been started in this way, not only is its relevance felt by the children, but they are unlikely in its later stages to forget that history is about real people.

1. Questions to Parents

Parents' memories will provide many leads to be followed up, but much depends upon the questions the child asks. A teacher may assume too readily that the pupil has enough knowledge of the recent past to ask the right ones. It may not have occurred to a child living on a relatively new housing estate that there were fields there not so long ago. Similarly, one living in a remote village may not realise that it is only since car-ownership has become so widespread that there has been ease of communication with the outside world. In both cases an understanding of the immediate past can give meaning to more remote historical changes such as the growth of towns or the advent of the railways in the nineteenth century.

Most of the questions to parents should be highly specific. For example:

(i) How long have you lived in the area?
(ii) Has it grown since you first came? (or 'in your lifetime' if the parent was born there).
(iii) What new building or demolition has occurred during this period? Please describe in each case what was there previously.
(iv) Was your school any different from mine?
(v) Did your family have a car when you were a child? If not, how did you travel?
(vi) Did you watch the television when you were a child? If not, what did you do in your spare time?
(vii) Where did you play when you were a child?
(viii) Where did you work when you first left school, and how did you travel to work?

Once specific information has been obtained, there is no reason why one or two more general questions should not be included in order to give scope for expression of opinion, e.g.

(ix) Do you think things have changed very much since you were young? If so, in what way?
(x) Do you think young people are as happy now as they were a generation ago?

Although some of these questions may seem unrelated to an environmental study, a great deal of indirect evidence will, in fact, emerge about the pattern of life a generation or more ago, how it has changed, and the ways in which the environment has been modified to accommodate these changes, e.g. the widening of roads as a result of increased car-ownership, or the part played by television in the transforming of cinemas into bingo halls.

2. Information from elderly relatives and neighbours

(*a*) When the child has understood how changes in the environment are directly related to changes in the patterns of human behaviour, it is possible to go further back in time by talking to elderly relatives and neighbours. Care should be taken to ensure that such old people are either already known to the child, or have been previously contacted by the teacher. From them the child is likely to obtain vivid accounts of what it was like to go to school, work or church when they were young. Whether or not they spent their youth in the immediate district (and on new housing estates most will not have done), they will still be able to give the children a vivid impression of the way in which environmental changes occur. They will probably remember walking across fields where houses, factories or roads now stand, and fishing or swimming in rivers and streams now polluted.

(*b*) At this stage, it is probably better for the questions not to be too specific, as some elderly people dislike questionnaires, and prefer to talk about those things which they remember best. The older the person interviewed, the greater will be the information which is new to the child, and it is important that this stage of the project should not be hurried. Any changes revealed should be discussed in class, and complemented by fieldwork.

(*c*) Usually old people can not only describe the society and the environment of their youth, but will remember their parents' memories, and sometimes those of their grandparents and great-grandparents. As with the information obtained from parents, memories of life in a different area may illustrate general points which the teacher may apply to the place being studied.

(*d*) Wherever possible, children should tape-record these memories. The tapes can then be used for extensive classroom discussion and further work.

3. Family documents

Teachers are prone to forget that the children themselves can often provide interesting old photographs which they have obtained from elderly relatives. If the family has long been resident in the area, there may be other relevant documents in the home, such as local papers, letters, diaries, programmes of local entertainments and parish magazines. The variety of documents obtainable is described in D. J. Steel and L. Taylor's *Family History in Schools* (Phillimore, 1970).

4. School log books

Not only the home, but the school itself (or neighbouring schools) can provide important source material for local history. Ever since the 1870 Education Act, schools have kept log books recording attendance, accidents, punishments, illnesses and inspectors' reports on the work, health and discipline of the school and the competence of the teachers. Using only material which is over fifty years old, so as to avoid embarrassment to living people, children can transcribe passages, analyse attendance figures, record reasons for absence from school (such as harvest-time or the lack of boots), and learn about pupil-teachers, discipline and payment by results. Besides the log book, the school may possess other items such as old photographs, early plans of the school, attendance registers, old textbooks and exercise books, all of which can be used to stimulate discussion and projects.

5. Maps and fieldwork

Initially, maps should be made of the area as it was in the parents' and grandparents' youth. Here the *Historian's Guide to Ordnance Survey Maps* (National Council of Social Service 1964) will prove indispensable. Fieldwork and map-work should always run concurrently. Whereas in a new town or a modern suburb, a survey of buildings may reveal little of immediate significance, enormous changes may be revealed by comparing a 1910 six-inch to the mile O.S. map with the latest edition. Conversely, in a rural area, changes such as factory farming or the bulldozing of hedges may not be shown on a map, but will be more readily apparent on the ground. Even in singularly unpromising areas, fieldwork may not prove entirely unfruitful. Few suburbs or new towns are without the occasional old church, houses or inns, and, in some cases, street names may recall old lanes, farms or former prominent families.

6. Buildings

A brief description of the more important buildings in an area will be found in the relevant county volume of N. Pevsner's *The Buildings of England* (Penguin). However, not only these but most other buildings will repay careful examination. As well as churches, houses and inns, there may be old farms or factories, markets, shops, chapels (many now put to other uses), bridges and viaducts, almshouses, almost certainly a railway station and perhaps a hospital or a former workhouse. Note should be taken of building materials and methods of construction, and where possible of room sizes and amenities. Children should be made aware that sometimes a relatively modern façade conceals an older building.

A recognition of architectural styles will come only by increasing familiarity with the details which provide evidence as to the age or period. The children should be encouraged to observe carefully, and to sketch or photograph features such as windows, porches, chimneys, plaques or coats of arms. Even a relatively homogeneous area like a Victorian working-class suburb can provide plenty of scope and variety if a careful study is made of housing densities, house size and decoration. While some houses have plain frontages, others may have bow-windows and may be decorated with polychromatic bricks, dog-tooth mouldings, stone and stucco, which are used to convey subtle social differences. Much help may be obtained on these points from John Penoyre and Michael Ryan's *The Observer's Book of Architecture* (Warne). Some useful books devoted to particular types of buildings, such as farm houses or inns, are given in the booklist, as are several works on industrial archaeology, which will prove invaluable if old mills, factories or mines are found in the area.

II – THE PARISH

Interviews with elderly people, work on family and school documents, map work and fieldwork, if effectively co-ordinated should have given the children some idea of the character of a relatively small area at various periods, and an understanding of how and why changes occur. The time may now have come to widen the study to include a whole parish (or in urban areas, perhaps a whole borough). The natural starting point for such a study is the parish church.

1. Church and churchyard

The architectural and decorative aspects of churches are covered by children's books such as *The I Spy Book of Churches* or P. Thornhill's *The Parish Church* (Methuen's *Finding Out* series) and adult works such as G. H. Cook's *The English Mediaeval Parish Church* (Phoenix House 1955) or J. Betjeman's *Collins' Guide to English Parish Churches* (Collins 1958). Also there is often a church guide containing architectural information. However, this is unlikely to tell us much about the parishioners, and it is they who are our main concern. The children might start by studying the tombs, hatchments, or plaques commemorating prominent local families. Other monuments might tell of railway and mine accidents, epidemics and the death of soldiers and sailors in battle or, more significantly, of disease. Whether it is a country church redolent of the aristocracy and gentry or a town church which recalls local dignitaries and merchants, it can provide names and dates which can be followed up in *Burke's Peerage* and *Landed Gentry*, in the *Dictionary of National Biography*, and, if the local library is well equipped, in books of local worthies, in the *Gentleman's Magazine* or in old copies of the local newspaper. Similarly, a survey of gravestones in the adjacent churchyard may provoke interesting questions about families still living in the neighbourhood, or about infant mortality. The inscriptions may also demonstrate changes in artistic styles and religious attitudes (e.g. the replacement of stylised eighteenth-century cherubs by the nineteenth-century crosses brought back by the Oxford Movement). Unfortunately, tombstones are disappearing at an alarming rate, not only through erosion and subsidence but also through the deliberate clearance of churchyards. Only too often, no record of the inscriptions has been made. Children can be of immense service in preserving the information for future generations by copying the tombstones in their locality. The Institute of Heraldic and Genealogical Studies, Northgate, Canterbury, Kent, offers annual prizes to children who produce the best record of inscriptions in a local churchyard, and welcomes enquiries about the scheme. Two comprehensive works on inscriptions are K. Esdaile's *English Church Monuments 1510–1840* (O.U.P. 1946) and F. Burgess' *English Churchyard Memorials* (Lutterworth Press 1963).

2. Parish documents

These may still be found in the Parish Chest but have usually been deposited in the County Record Office, the addresses and opening hours of which are listed in the H.M.S.O. booklet, *Record Repositories in Great Britain* (3rd edition 1968). Although many county record offices, such as that of Essex, welcome school-children, most cannot accommodate large numbers, and the teacher may find it easier for the children to work from photocopies. There are many documents which children can effectively use, as the Department of Education and Science demonstrate in their pamphlet No. 54 *Archives and Education* (1968). The Parish documents which most appeal to children are those concerned with the operation of the Poor Law. By an act of 1662 it was necessary to have a legal 'settlement' in the parish, and persons likely to become paupers could be compulsorily removed to their parish of origin after examination by a magistrate. There are usually accounts of the Overseers of the Poor, bundles of settlement and removal certificates and copies of examinations, which are often, in effect mini-biographies. When photocopies of these documents are used in the classroom, children are often shocked to find the extent to which people's freedom was restricted by 'authority', and especially by the removal of pregnant women so that their children would not be born in the parish and become a burden on the ratepayers. For the background to Poor Law records, the best short account is J. J. and A. J. Bagley's *The English Poor Law* (Macmillan 1966).

The Parish Registers of baptisms, marriages and burials may extend back to the seventeenth century, or in exceptional cases, as far back as 1538. In these, children can trace families found on tombstones or still resident in the area, which may possibly include those of members of the class. Furthermore the registers give scope for obtaining information of the intensely personal kind (age at marriage, size of family, infant mortality etc.) described in Peter Laslett's *The World We Have Lost* (Methuen 1965). The techniques are outlined in *An Introduction to English Historical Demography*, edited by E. A. Wrigley (Weidenfeld & Nicolson 1966), though they need considerable simplification for work with children.

Other parish documents which might repay study are records of charities, churchwardens', constables' and surveyors' accounts and vestry minutes. An indispensable guide to all parish records is the late W. E. Tate's *The Parish Chest* (C.U.P. 3rd edition 1969).

3. Tithe and enclosure maps

In reconstructing the past character of an area, enclosure and tithe maps are especially useful. These may usually be consulted in local record offices. Many of these maps are so huge that photocopying is normally impossible and the parts required must be traced. Excellent reproductions can be obtained by putting the tracing on a Xerox machine with a piece of white paper on top. The resulting photocopies can be shaded to indicate different landowners, information which is vital for reconstructing the social history of the area.

4. Newspapers

Although copies of local newspapers may be brought in occasionally by the children, it will probably prove necessary to consult the files at a local library or newspaper office. Because they contain so much information, it may be best to photocopy parts of a few editions at key periods and to make an intensive study of these. The reports, illustrations, obituaries and above all the advertisements will provide many exciting clues to the history of the area, sometimes as far back as the eighteenth century.

5. Commercial directories, gazetteers and guide books

Although there are commercial directories extant for London from the late eighteenth century, only the larger towns possess them before the 1830s. A list and brief description of those available will be found in the *Guide to the National and Provincial Directories of England and Wales, excluding London, published before* 1856 (Royal Historical Society, 1950). Beginning with a general description of the area, they usually proceed to list the principal inhabitants, professional men, shops, markets and the times of coaches, carriers' carts, canal and, later, railway services. From the information they provide, children can make graphs showing the vicissitudes of trade and transport in the locality. Many libraries may also have

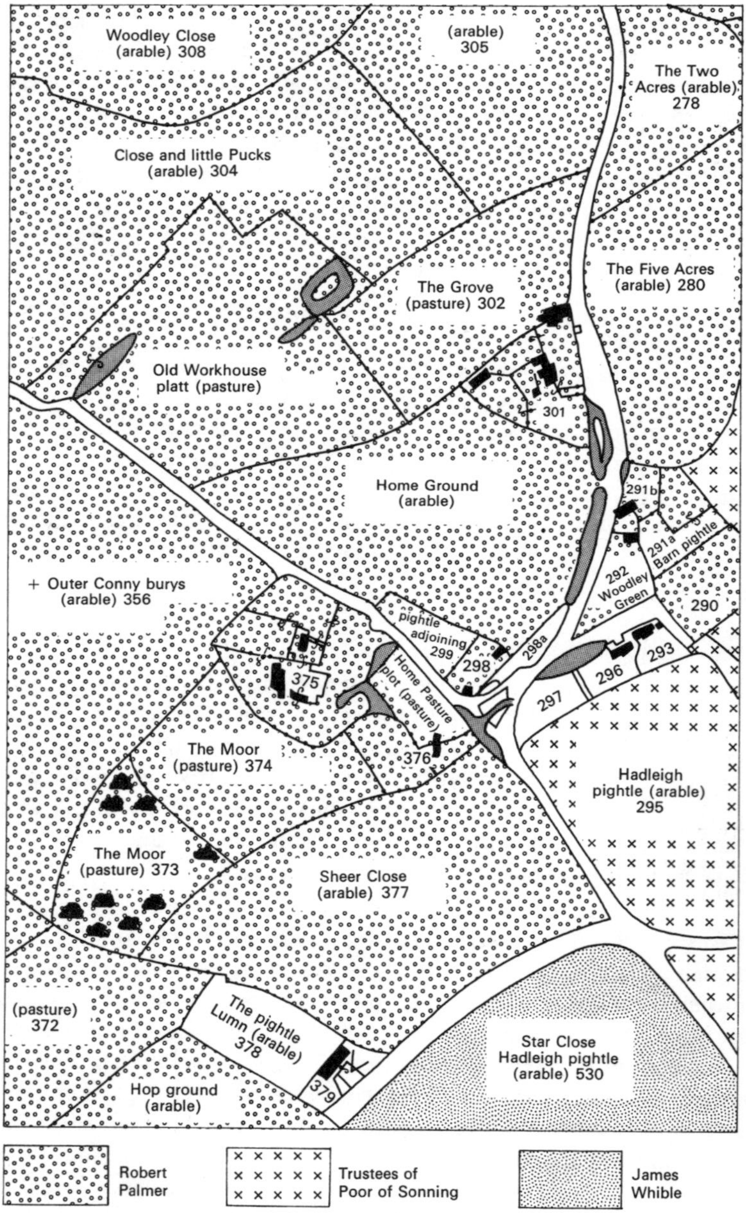

Section of an 1844 tithe map shaded to indicate land ownership copies of Lewis's *Topographical Dictionary of England* (various editions 1831 to 1849).

As more people travelled from the eighteenth century onwards, so a demand for guide books grew. There are many eighteenth- and early nineteenth-century road-books and, for the latter part of the nineteenth century, Murray's *Handbooks for Travellers* and the Ward Lock *Red Guides*.

6. Census returns

Decennial censuses have been held in Britain since 1801 and the published reports give substantial statistical breakdowns which can be utilised to study occupations, although unfortunately the statistics are based on the county and not the parish. For the 1841, 1851 and 1861 censuses, the enumerators' returns containing details for each household can be consulted at the Public Record Office, Chancery Lane, London, W.C.2. Many local libraries have already obtained microfilm copies for their own areas, and others might respond favourably if asked to do so. Children in the upper age groups may be interested in tracing streets in the area, discovering the size of households and the occupations of the people. If their families are local, they may wish to study the returns for their own ancestors.

7. Wills and inventories

Wills were until 1858 proved by the ecclesiastical courts and may still be in diocesan registries, though usually, they too have been deposited in county record offices. The present location of wills may be ascertained from A. J. Camp's *Wills and Their Whereabouts* (Phillimore 1963). As important as the wills are the inventories which usually accompanied them, and the exciting work that can be done on these is outlined in John West's *Village Records* (Macmillan 1962) pp. 92–131. A useful printed collection of inventories with an excellent introduction is F. W. Steer's *Farm and Cottage Inventories of Mid Essex 1634–1749* (reprinted Phillimore 1969).

8. Other records

Space precludes mention here of further records such as those of the manor, Quarter Sessions and local firms, and above all the letters and papers of prominent local families. For information on these as well as the records already mentioned, the best guides are F. G. Emmison's *Archives and Local History* (Methuen 1966) and J. West's *Village Records* (Macmillan 1962). The Historical Association (see p. 263) has included in the journal *History* an excellent series entitled *Short Guides to Records*, and copies of individual articles are available very cheaply. In using records, even younger children can be trained to read old handwriting which to the inexpert eye appears quite illegible. An invaluable and inexpensive aid is F. G. Emmison's *How to Read Local Archives 1550–1750* (Historical Association 1967). A fuller work providing plenty of photocopies for practice reading is Hilda E. P. Grieve's *Examples of English Handwriting 1150–1750* (Essex Record Office 1959). For some areas, made-up sets of local documents are already provided by the Record Office, the Museum Schools' Service or a local University or College of Education. Some of these are listed in J. Fines' 'Archives in Schools' in *History*, vol. LIII, No. 179 (October 1968), pp. 348–356. In any case, the experienced teacher will be able to build up his own collection of photocopies for classroom use.

9. **Pictures**

Most museums and art galleries have collections of local paintings, engravings and drawings. Their artistic merits vary considerably, but sketches made by the rector's daughter may be as valuable historically as the masterpieces of Constable or Doré. Many museums, libraries and record offices also have old photographs (sometimes in albums) and picture postcards of streets and buildings or of distant views of the area. Old local histories may contain illustrations not available elsewhere. By placing them alongside contemporary photographs, changes which are not apparent on maps can be more easily discerned.

10. **Printed histories**

The children should be introduced to printed sources only after they have found out a fair amount of information about the locality from interviews, fieldwork, maps and documents. Otherwise children are apt to feel 'It's all in the book. Why should I bother to do it the hard way?'. In fact, if an environmental history project is developed from the child's own experience, when he comes to use printed sources he will appreciate their limitations. The earlier Victoria County Histories tend to emphasise architecture and the history of landed families at the expense of social history, though this has been remedied in more recently completed volumes. The same criticism can be made of most town and parish histories, although there are some excellent exceptions. Published memoirs and biographies of local worthies may prove more useful, although often the best secondary sources for reconstructing the past life of the neighbourhood are not the specifically 'local' books at all, but general works on social history such as M. and C. H. B. Quennell's *A History of Everyday Things in England* (Batsford, brought right up to date by S. E. Ellacott, 1968), Longman's *Then and There* and *Evidence in Pictures* series and Methuen's *Get to Know* series,

Children of all ages can be introduced to extracts from contemporary surveys such as Mayhew's *London Labour and the London Poor* (Selections, O.U.P. 1965), and older children can cope with adult works such as G. E. and K. R. Fussell's *The English Countryman: His Life and Work 1500–1900* (1955), W. J. Reader's *Life in Victorian England* (1964), and Nicolas Bentley's *The Victorian Scene* (Weidenfeld & Nicolson, 1969). Biographies and memoirs such as Elizabeth Ashby's *Joseph Ashby of Tysoe, 1859–1919* (C.U.P. 1961), the life of a former Warwickshire farm labourer, give a vivid account of a past way of life. So, too, do accounts of occupations, such as G. Sturt's *The Wheelwright's Shop* (C.U.P. 1960) and James Arnold's *The Shell Book of Country Crafts* (John Baker 1968). To relate previous societies more specifically to their local environment the teacher will need to be familiar with works such as W. G. Hoskins' *The Making of the English Landscape* (Hodder and Stoughton 1955). H. C. Darby's *Historical Geography of England before 1800* (C.U.P. 1936, New edition 1948), J. Finberg's *Exploring Villages* (Routledge and Kegan Paul 1958), and A. E. Smailes' *The Geography of Towns* (Hutchinson, second edition 1957) and perhaps with some more specialised works on the type of environment being studied such as H. J. Dyos's *Victorian Suburb: A Study of the Growth of Camberwell* (1966). Three absolutely indispensable works for the effective co-ordination of information derived from archives, secondary sources and fieldwork are W. G. Hoskins's *Local History in England* (Longmans 1959), the same author's *Fieldwork in Local History* (Faber and Faber, 1967) and R. Douch's *Local History and the Teacher* (Routledge 1967).

11. **Literature**

Teachers tend to neglect the wealth of historical material in literary works of all kinds. Yet novels such as those of Charles Dickens, Elizabeth Gaskell or H. G. Wells give a rich insight into rural or urban life in the past. Often vivid descriptions are given of actual places, and it is very likely that there has been a local novelist of some standing, such as Hardy (Wessex), the Brontë sisters (Yorkshire Moors), Flora Thompson (Oxfordshire), Mary Russell Mitford (Berkshire), Arnold Bennett (Staffordshire) or D. H. Lawrence (Nottinghamshire). Although some of the appropriate books by these writers may be too difficult for the children to read themselves, descriptive passages may be read to them or duplicated for use in the classroom.

III – THE WIDER ENVIRONMENT

Many teachers may wish to confine themselves to the study of one parish at a single period in the past, and indeed they will be wise to do so if the time for the project is limited. However, when a whole year is available for an environmental studies project, and when classes have concentrated in the first term upon the immediate neighbourhood of the school and in the second upon the parish, teachers may wish to broaden the project in the third term to include a larger area, and to select a more remote period for study (e.g. The Middle Ages). To visit surviving sites and monuments of this period will normally require a day-long coach trip. However, it is important that, wherever possible, this stage of the project should utilize the accumulated experience of the previous two terms, and that the techniques and sources outlined earlier are still used. Otherwise a day visit becomes, not an enriching educational experience, but little more than an outing.

1. Information on historic sites and buildings

(a) Ministry of Works

Information about sites in the care of the Department of the Environment will be found in the following H.M.S.O. Publications:

(i) *General*

Sectional list No. 27 Ancient Monuments and Historic Buildings in the care of the Department of the Environment, open to the public.

(ii) *Regional*

Vol. I Northern England
Vol. II Southern England
Vol. III East Anglia and the Midlands
Vol. IV South Wales and Monmouthshire
Vol. V North Wales
Vol. VI Scotland

(iii) *Specialised*

Castles
Abbeys
Scottish Castles
Scottish Abbeys
Castles of Northern Ireland
Abbeys of Northern Ireland
A Look at the Monasteries of North-East Yorkshire.

There are also individual guides to the monuments which set the sites in historical perspective and are well illustrated. A list of these is obtainable free from H.M.S.O., P.O. Box 569, London, S.E.1.

(b) Historical Monuments Commission

The Royal Commission on Ancient and Historical Monuments and Construction produce the following County inventories. (Those marked with an asterisk are out of print but may be consulted at a local library.)

Buckinghamshire
- *Vol. I South
- *Vol. II North

Dorset West
Cambridge (City)
Essex
- *Vol. I North-West
- *Vol. II Central and South-West
- *Vol. III North-East
- *Vol. IV South-East

Herefordshire
- *Vol. I South-West
- *Vol. II East
- *Vol. III North-West

**Hertfordshire*
Huntingdonshire
London
- *Vol. I Westminster Abbey
- *Vol. II West London
- *Vol. III Roman London
- *Vol. IV The City
- *Vol. V East London

**Middlesex*
Oxford
**Westmorland*
York (City)

Wales
Anglesey
Caernarvonshire
- Vol. I East
- Vol. II Central

Scotland
City of Edinburgh
Roxburghshire
Selkirk
Stirlingshire

(c) *Ordnance Survey Historical Maps*

The Ordnance Survey publish a series of maps showing archaeological and historical sites (see p. 128).

(d) *The National Trust*

The National Trust publish guides to their properties. A list may be obtained from The National Trust, 42 Queen's Gate, London, S.W.1.

(e) *Other Useful Publications*

Thomas, N. *Guide to Prehistoric England*. County lists of sites.
The Shell & B.P. Guide to Britain. George Rainbird and Ebury Press. 1964.
Shilling Guides (for each county). Shell Mex and B.P. Ltd.
The Shell County Guides, ed. John Betjeman and John Piper. Faber and Faber.
The Little Guides. Methuen. Provide information on buildings and their contents.
Historic Houses, Castles and Gardens in Great Britain and Ireland. Index Publications – published annually.
The Buildings of England Series, ed. N. Pevsner. Penguin. Available for most counties.
Murray's *Architectural Guides*, ed. J. Betjeman and J. Piper.

(f) *Other sources of information*

The Historical Association, 59a, Kennington Park Road, London, S.E.11, publishes a number of handbooks of primary interest to local historians in the series of 'Helps for students of History'. It has some hundred branches at home and abroad. Many of these have local history study groups or co-operate with local extra-mural departments etc. Details of the Association and its publications can be obtained from the above address.

The Standing Conference for Local History, 26, Bedford Square, London, W.C.1, can supply a list of its member County Local History Committees.

2. Aims of visits

If the children are out for a whole day, it is not desirable to cram in as many visits as possible. Such a girdling of the area often blurs impressions. Rather, the teacher should strive to convey to the children something of the atmosphere of the site when it was in active use. The rigours of life in an Iron Age fort set high on the Downs can perhaps be appreciated only on a cold, blustery day. The problems in attacking the same fort can be understood most easily by mounting a mock assault; only then will the children realise the difficulty of approaching unobserved from any direction, or the exertion needed to clamber up slopes (now grass covered, but once much steeper and of soft white chalk) with the defenders hurling down stones and spears. It may even be necessary to make several visits to a single site, as the children become confused or bored if they are asked to look for too many things in too short a time. Furthermore, it is important that the slower children are given adequate time to complete worksheets.

3. Types of visit

Four kinds of day visits are envisaged:

(*a*) *Focus*

Here a visit is made to a single site in the locality, and the children's whole attention is focused on it in order to give them a depth impression. For children of 9–13 years, this is probably the most useful kind of visit.

(*b*) *Thematic*

Here one journey takes in several relatively minor visits, all of which are connected chronologically and culturally. If the nineteenth century is being studied, one day trip might include a disused brickworks, oasthouses, a windmill, a watermill and a rural craftsman at work. For the medieval period the visits might be to a section of medieval town wall, a crusader's tomb, a market cross and the medieval collection in a local museum.

(*c*) *Linear*

A different sort of 'visit' would involve walking an ancient ridge-way, visiting the hill forts, burial mounds and ditches en route. Some teachers may wish to organise the walking of a lengthy stretch at weekends or during the school holidays. Similar walks can be made along the tow-paths of rivers or canals and along disused railway tracks.

(d) Sample

The teacher may wish to visit a building or site some distance away (e.g. a castle in a good state of preservation, or a Roman site) because it is an example of a type of building which was once represented in the locality and has since disappeared, or else is in a poor state of preservation. In some cases, old pictures and descriptions of the latter may have survived. Useful though visits to general places of interest are for other aspects of history teaching, in the context of an environmental study it is important that such buildings should not present such unusual features as to make them unique (e.g. a visit to Verulamium would help children to recreate Silchester, but a visit to the Tower of London would not help them to recreate Farnham Castle, Surrey).

(e) Museums

Information on museums can be found on pages 40–46. A museum visit requires extensive preparation. Many museums now produce worksheets appropriate for different age-groups, and these can be obtained from the museum when arrangements are being made for the visit. Many museums have established school services. A list of these is given on pages 41–3. A few of these, such as Reading, not only lend artefacts and models, but have a substantial collection of documentary units, films and filmstrips for loan. A copy of the catalogue should be obtained.

4. **Preparing for a visit**

(a) The site

Before taking the class on an educational visit, a teacher should first send away for a guide-book, and ask for a list of any other available materials such as worksheets, postcards and transparencies. This should be followed up by a personal visit in order to devise a scheme of work. The teacher may also feel the need to acquire more detailed background information, such as that provided by a good general history. For example, Sheppard Frere's *Britannia* is indispensable for setting a Roman site in the context of the Roman occupation.

(b) The route

The teacher should be familiar not only with the site but also with the route to it. Coach drivers are rarely expert map-readers, and school parties have been known to fail to arrive at their official destination. Also drivers are sometimes reluctant to take 41-seater, 2½-metre-wide coaches down narrow winding country lanes. A carefully planned route need not be the shortest, but should include several items of historical interest, and perhaps draw attention to an important factor relating to the siting of the monument (e.g. a river may be obscured from the castle by modern buildings and the shortest approach may not touch it). Children should be issued with a duplicated sketch map taken from the 1″ or $2\frac{1}{2}$″ O.S. map showing the siting of the monument and the principal points of interest along the route.

(*c*) *Preliminary work in the classroom*

A visit is worthwhile only if the children have enough background information to imagine the monument or site as it once was. Background information should be given where possible by reference to an important episode in the history of the monument (e.g. an attack upon the castle during the Civil War), and certainly by the use of visual material, such as pictures, films and filmstrips.

(*d*) *Films and filmstrips*

A wide variety of films and filmstrips is available. A comprehensive list can be found in *Visual Aids: Films, Filmstrips and Transparencies, Part II. History, Civics and Economics*, produced by The Educational Foundation for Visual Aids, 33, Queen Anne Street, London, W.1. The commonest medieval sites visited are castles, cathedrals and abbeys. For these the following films and filmstrips are useful.

(i) *Castles*

Medieval Castle. Sound film. 18 mins. Gaumont British Instructional. 1950. Distributed by Rank.
Lets Visit Britain's Castles. E.F.V.A. 1947.
Medieval Building: Part I. The Castle. Gaumont British Instructional. 1947. Distributed by Rank.
Medieval Life: The Castle. Common Ground. 1949.
The Story of the Castle. British Transport. 1956.

(ii) *Cathedrals*

Cathedral City. Sound film. 21 mins. Rank. 1949. (Based on Canterbury.)
I Live in a Cathedral City. E.P. 1950. (Also based on Canterbury.)
Cathedrals and Abbeys. British Instructional Films. 1950.
Medieval Building, Part II: The Cathedral. Gaumont British Instructional. 1947–50. Distributed by Rank.

(iii) *Monasteries*

Medieval Monastery. Sound film. Gaumont British Instructional. Distributed by Rank. 17 mins.
The Monastery. Common Ground. 1953.
Medieval Building, Part V: The Monastery. Gaumont British Instructional. Distributed by Rank.
The Monks of Kirkstall Abbey. E.F.V.A. 1952.

(*e*) *Books*

A list of books suitable for teachers and children will be found on pages 269–271.

5. Worksheets

Whether the type of site visited is a Roman villa, a medieval cathedral, castle or abbey, or a nineteenth-century railway cutting, certain fundamental questions need to be considered:

(*a*) When was it built?

(*b*) Why was it built?

(*c*) Is there any surviving evidence as to its original function?

(*d*) Who built it?

(*e*) Why was this particular site chosen?

(*f*) How large a labour force was needed to build it? Where did it come from? Was it voluntary or forced labour?

(*g*) What sort of building materials were used? Where did they come from? How were they transported?

(*h*) If the monument or site was built today, what tools and machines would be used? How many of these were available to the builders at the time? How long did it take to build?

(*i*) Are there signs of successive rebuilding?

(*j*) Is it still in use? If not when was it vacated and why?

(*k*) If it is still in use, does it still serve its original purpose?

(*l*) If the building is in a poor state of preservation:

(i) How did it fall into a state of decay?

(ii) What happened to the missing building materials?

Such questions as these, adapted to the particular site, can be used as a basis for worksheets for preparation, for the actual visit, and for follow-up work in the classroom. Wherever possible the emphasis should be placed on surviving features which may give the children clues to some of these important questions. In addition every monument will provide a host of more specific questions. Here are some examples for different types of sites:

(*a*) *Roman villa*

(i) Why are the Roman remains so far below the surface? Where has the earth on top come from?

(ii) If you had not been told that the site was a Roman one, how many things do you observe which would have indicated this?

(*b*) *Medieval castle*

(i) In how many different ways could the castle be defended?

(ii) What are the square holes in the walls of the keep for?

(*c*) *Medieval monastery*

(i) Mark on your plan (*a*) where the monks ate, (*b*) where they slept.

(ii) By pacing the distance estimate (*a*) how long, (*b*) how wide, the abbey church was. Is this larger or smaller than your own parish church?

(*d*) *A railway cutting*

(i) Why was a cutting dug instead of making a tunnel?

(ii) What happened to the excavated earth?

6. **Administration**

There will be numerous minor but important administrative points to attend to. The teacher must ensure that the children wear suitable clothing and have plastic macs with them even on days which promise to be fine. They should also have with them the appropriate equipment for measuring and recording information, including cameras if possible. If several sites are visited, each child should also be given a duplicated list of times and meeting places. The prudent teacher will have a couple of spare children's plastic macs, and perhaps a spare packed lunch. Most emergencies can be covered by a first-aid box, needle and thread and safety pins, toilet paper, soap and paper towels. Helpful extras are a pair of binoculars, a 20 metre measuring tape, and paper and heelball for making rubbings. On a previous visit the teacher should also have discovered for each site the nearest toilets and public telephone.

7. **Follow-up work in the classroom**

(*a*) *Workbooks*

A visit should always be followed by full discussion. In their notebooks, the children will have sketches, diagrams and snippets of information which will need to be sorted, redrawn and amplified into a full-scale report.

(*b*) *Imaginative writing and drama*

As the Plowden Report emphasises, visits can provide the stimulus for vivid creative writing and for dramatic reconstructions.

(*c*) *Models*

Groups of children can be engaged on making large models, e.g. a Roman amphitheatre or forum or a Romano-British village, a medieval castle, monastery or manor house, a tithe barn, an open field system, a Georgian terrace, a tin mine, a windmill, a mid-Victorian textile mill or slate quarry.

EXHIBITIONS

Many teachers will wish to incorporate the results of the children's researches in an exhibition, and here, the National Council of Social Service's booklet, *Local History Exhibitions – How to Present and Plan them* is helpful. Exhibitions are eminently desirable so long as their structure does not inhibit the children's freedom in exploring the aspects or sources which interest them most.

Whether the children are listening to old people, studying or drawing maps, visiting the area, working with archives, reading works of literature or preparing for an exhibition, the aim must always be to give them some insight into the behaviour of people – the way they have been affected by their environment and the way in which they in turn have shaped it.

BOOK LIST

Bibliography

Kuhlicke, F. W. and Emmison, F. G. *English Local History Handlist.* Historical Association 'Helps for Students of History', No. 69, 4th edn., 1969.

General

Anderson, M. D. *History by the Highway.* Faber. 1967.
Douch, R. *Local History and the Teacher.* Routledge. 1967.
Finberg, J. *Exploring Villages.* Routledge. 1958.
Grigson, G. *The Shell Country Alphabet.* Michael Joseph. 1966.
Hoskins, W. G. *Local History in England.* Longman. 1959.
Hoskins, W. G. *Fieldwork in Local History.* Faber & Faber. 1967.
Hoskins, W. G. *The Making of the English Landscape.* Hodder & Stoughton. 1955.

For Children

Corcoran, J. X. W. P. *The Young Field Archaeologist's Guide.* Bell. 1966.
Grigson, G. *Looking and Finding.* Phoenix House.
Mills, D. R. *The English Village.* 'Local Search' series. Routledge. An excellent introduction for both teacher and pupil.
Perry, G. A. *Farms and Farm Life.* Blandford.
Reeves, M. *The Medieval Village.* 'Then & There.' Longmans.
Reeves, M. *The Medieval Town.* 'Then & There.' Longmans.
Vince, J. N. T. *History All Around You.* Wheaton.

Oral Information

Steel, D. J. and Taylor, L. *Family History in Schools.* Phillimore. 1970.
Steel, D. J. and Taylor, L. *Talking to Grand-dad.* Phillimore. 1970.

Maps and Directories

Harley, J. B. *The Historian's Guide to Ordnance Survey Maps.* National Council of Social Service. 1964.

Archives

Emmison, F. G. *Archives and Local History.* Methuen. 1966.
Emmison, F. G. *How to Read Local Archives* 1550–1750. Historical Association. 1967.
Emmison, F. G. and Gray, I. *County Records.* Historical Association. 1961.

Fines, J. 'Archives in School', *History LIII*, No. 179. October, 1968.
H.M.S.O. *Archives and Education.* 1968.
H.M.S.O. *Census Reports of Great Britain*, 1801–1931.
H.M.S.O. *List of Record Repositories in Great Britain*. 1968.
Steel, D. J. (ed.) *National Index of Parish Registers.* Phillimore for the Society of Genealogists, 1966–1970. Vol. 1, General; Vol. II, Nonconformists; Vol. V, South Midlands and Welsh Border; Vol. XII, Scottish Sources.
Tate, W. E. *The Parish Chest.* O.U.P. new edn. 1969. An indispensable guide.

Churches, Cathedrals and Abbeys
Betjeman, J. (ed.) *Collins Guide to English Parish Churches.* Collins revised edn. 1959.
Blatch, M. *Parish Churches of England in Colour.* Blandford. 1974.
Burgess, F. *English Churchyard Memorials.* Lutterworth Press. 1963.

For Children
Gittings, C. *Brasses & Brass Rubbings.* Blandford. 1970.
Purton, Rowland *Churches and Religions.* Blandford. 1972.
Thornhill, P. *The Parish Church.* ('Get to Know' series.) Methuen. 1951.

Castles
Toy, S. *The Castles of Great Britain*. Heinemann. 1953.

For Children
Reeves, M. *The Medieval Castle.* ('Then and There.') Longmans. 1963.
Sellmann, R. R. *Castles and Fortresses.* ('Outline' series.) Methuen. 1962.

Houses and Homes
Barley, M. W. *The English Farmhouse and Cottage.* London. 1961.
Council for British Archaeology. *The Investigation of Smaller Domestic Buildings.* Pamphlet.
Yarwood, D. *The English Home.* Batsford. 1956.

For Children
Hammersley, A. *Towns and Town Life.* Blandford. 1969.
Penoyre, J. and Ryan, M. *The Observer's Book of Architecture.* Warne. 1958.
Perry, G. A. *Villages and Village Life*. Blandford. 1970.

Slidefolios
Houses and Their History Slide Centre.
Towns (3). Slide Centre.

Archaeology
Hudson, K. *Industrial Archaeology, an Introduction*. John Baker. 1967.
Ordnance Survey. *Field Archaeology. Some Notes for Beginners.* H.M.S.O. 1963.
Pannell, J. P. M. *Techniques of Industrial Archaeology*. David & Charles. 1966.
Rix, M. *Industrial Archaeology*. Historical Association. 1967.
See also The Regional Archaeologies. Heinemann Educational.

Transport
Coleman, T. *The Railway Navvies*. Hutchinson. 1965.
Duckham, B. F. 'Inland Waterways. Some Sources for their History.' *Amateur Historian*. Vol. 6, No. 1.
Joyce, J. *Pocket Encyclopaedia of Trams in Colour.* Blandford. 1970.
Kaye, D. *Pocket Encyclopaedia of Buses and Trolleybuses* (3 vols.), Blandford.
Nock, O. S. *Pocket Encyclopaedia of British Steam Locomotives.* Blandford. 1964.
Nock, O. S. *Steam Railways of Britain in Colour.* Blandford. 1967.

Rolt, L. T. C. *The Inland Waterways of England*. Allen & Unwin. 1962.
Simmons, J. *Transport.* Studio Vista. 1962.
Williams, H. *Farm Tractors*. Blandford 1974.

For Children

Fry, L. *Railways*. ('How Things Developed.') Ward Lock. 1960.
Greenwood, M. O. *Roads and Canals in the 18th Century*. ('Then and There'.) Longman. 1957.
Halson, G. R. *Discovering Railways.* Univ. of London Press. 1961.
Hammersley, A. *Roads and Road Transport.* Blandford. 1970.
Metcalfe, L. *Bridges and Bridgebuilding.* Blandford. 1970.
Thornhill, P. *Inland Waterways.* ('Get to Know.') Methuen. 1959.
Vince, J. *River and Canal Transport.* Blandford. 1970.
Hammersley, A. and Perry, G. A. *Railways and Rail Transport*. Blandford. 1971.

Periodicals

Almost every edition of the Historical Association's periodical, *Teaching History*, devotes some space to work on local history currently being done in schools. Many other relevant articles will also be found in *The Local Historian* (formerly the *Amateur Historian*), published by the National Council of Social Service, and perhaps in some of the more specialist periodicals, such as *Industrial Archaeology* or *Journal of Transport History.* Most counties have a local historical or archaeological journal, and the indexes to past volumes should be consulted.

Appendix 1

TEACHERS' GUIDES AND CLASS BOOKS, ASSOCIATED PROGRAMMES

in *Approaches to Environmental Studies* scheme

CLASS BOOKS

1. Towns and Town Life
2. World of Water
3. Weather and Life
4. Air We Need
5. Farms and Farm Life
6. Roads and Road Transport

Teachers' Guide 1
covering titles 1–6

7. River and Canal Transport
8. Buildings and Building Sites
9. Villages and Village Life
10. Railways and Rail Transport
11. Minerals, Mines and Mining
12. Bridges and Bridge-Building

Teachers' Guide 2
covering titles 7–12

13. Churches and Religions
14. Communications: Signs to Satellites
15. The Post Office and Its Services
16. Fire and the Fire Service
17. Ports and Sea Transport
18. Police and the Police Service

Teachers' Guide 3
covering titles 13–18

19. Pollution and Life
20. Parks and Open Spaces
21. Shops, Stores and Markets
22. Power Supplies

Teachers' Guide 4
covering titles 19–24

PROGRAMMES

1. Traffic
2. The Highway Code for Pedestrians
3. Farmers and Their Animals
4. Farmers and the Crops They Grow
5. Railways Today
6. The Growth of Railways
7. Weather Recording
8. Houses and Their History
9. Building a House
10. The Growth of Roads

A Programmed Approach to
Environmental Studies:
Guide to programmes 1–10

Appendix 2

SOUND AND TELEVISION BROADCASTS

The teacher should not overlook the valuable help available from sound and television broadcasts, and from the appropriate pamphlets for pupils and teachers' notes which are published. The B.B.C. Annual Programme, covering radio and television broadcasts for schools is available in two parts (5–13 and 9–18 age-groups) from the School Broadcasting Council at the appropriate address: (*a*) The Langham, Portland Place, London, W1A 1AA, (*b*) 5, Queen Street, Edinburgh, 2, (*c*) Broadcasting House, Llandaff, Cardiff, CF5 2YQ. Registered schools will automatically receive the booklet in advance, so that a selection can be planned. Some programmes are listed under 'Environmental Studies', but, in addition, there are programmes under history, geography, biology, nature and science which can be of real value in approaches through the environment.

The Independent Television Authority (I.T.A.) also put out valuable television broadcasts for schools, and in schools where a television receiver is available teachers can select programmes about local and wider environments. Details of these programmes and of children's pamphlets and teachers' notes may be obtained from the Education Office (Schools Information) at the appropriate address.

Teachers may wish to tape-record B.B.C. radio programmes for use at some future date before the end of the school academic year. Some B.B.C. and I.T.V. television programmes for schools are available on hire, as 16 mm. films, from the E.F.V.A. library, and audio-visual equipment is available (although expensive!) to re-show some T.V. programmes which have been recorded in cassette form.

Apart from the B.B.C., the following Independent Television companies are the main producers of educational programmes:

ATV Network Ltd.,
ATV House,
17 Great Cumberland Place
London, W.1

Thames Television Ltd.,
Television House,
306, Euston Road,
London, N.W.1

Granada Television Ltd.,
Television Centre,
Manchester, 3

Yorkshire Television,
Television Centre,
Leeds, 3

Other companies which initiate local educational programmes are:

Grampian TV Ltd.,
Queens Cross,
Aberdeen,
AB9 2XJ

Scottish TV Ltd.,
Theatre Royal,
Hope Street,
Glasgow, C.2

HTV Ltd.,
Bristol Studios,
Bath Road,
Bristol, 4

Ulster TV Ltd.,
Havelock House,
Ormeau Road,
Belfast BT7 1AB

Appendix 3

VISUAL AIDS PRODUCED IN ASSOCIATION WITH 'APPROACHES TO ENVIRONMENTAL STUDIES'

The text of this book and the associated pupils' books and programmes are fully supported by single slides, slidefolios and film loops, specially prepared by THE SLIDE CENTRE for these publications. A note to this effect is made in the appropriate place throughout the books. They are as follows:

1. SLIDEFOLIOS
   (*a*) based on the Class Books.
   Each FOLIO contains twelve 35-mm. double-frame colour slides mounted in white heatsealed card mounts suitable for standard slide projectors or viewers. The slides are packed in plastic packs and are supported by descriptive texts.
   (*b*) based on the Programmed Texts.
   These contain fifteen 35-mm. double-frame colour slides mounted in white heatsealed card mounts. These slides are packed in a specially designed quarto-sized plastic sheet, which can be stored (along with the Programmed Texts) in a ring binder. This will facilitate easy handling on the part of the children.

Although designed primarily for use with the class books and programmes, each Slidefolio contains a set of fully descriptive notes which enables it to be used independently.

SLIDEFOLIOS

Based on Class Books

Farms and Farm Life (16 slides)

1. Farm Animals and Machinery
2. Farm Buildings and Crops

The Air We Need (12 slides)

1. Air and Air Pressure
2. Winds and Their Origin and How Animals Breathe
3. Aerodynamics and Animals that Fly

The World of Water (12 slides)

1. Water and Living Things
2. Water and Its Properties Part 1
3. Water and Its Properties Part 2

Towns and Town Life (12 slides)

1. Building Types and Materials Part 1 to Victorian Times
2. Building Types and Materials Part 2 Victorian Times to the Present Day
3. Types of Towns

Building and Building Sites (12 slides)
1. Buying and Preparing the Site
2. Foundations and Materials
3. Main Structure
4. Installation of Services

Roads and Road Transport (12 slides)
1. Before the Motor Car
2. The Advent of the Motor Car
3. Roads and Road Making

Villages and Village Life (12 slides)
1. Village Sites
2. Typical Buildings in a Village
3. Things Seen in a Village

River and Canal Transport (12 slides)
1. Rivers and Waterways
2. History and Development of Canals
3. Things seen on our Canals and Waterways

Weather and Life (12 slides)
1. Clouds and Weather Signs
2. Weather Recording
3. Weather in the Past

Bridges and Bridge-building (12 slides)
1. History of Bridges and Bridge-building
2. Types of bridge construction
3. Looking at bridges

Churches and Religions (12 slides)
1. The Parish Church
2. Places of Worship
3. Church People, Services and Festivals
4. The Social Work of the Christian Church

Minerals, Mines and Mining (12 slides)
1. Coal-mining in Britain, Past and Present
2. Metals and Minerals in Britain
3. Minerals, Metals and Precious Stones

Ports and Sea Transport (12 slides)
1. Ports and Harbours
2. Cargo and Cargo Ships
3. Docks Equipment and Shipping Control

Based on Programmes
Railways at Work (15 slides)
Farms and Farming (15 slides)
Houses and Their History (15 slides),
Weather Recording (15 slides)

2. FILM LOOPS

These loops have been prepared for use either independently or in conjunction with the appropriate Programmed Texts. Each loop has an approximate running time of $3\frac{1}{2}$ to 4 minutes and is housed in a plastic cassette which protects it from dust, dirt and finger-marks. The subjects are filmed on Standard 8-mm film in full colour and the loops can be shown on any standard 8-mm loop projector.

Colour Film Loops available:
How a canal lock works
Traffic

In addition there are also available a considerable number of supporting slides, details of which it is not possible to give here, but for which lists are available from: The Slide Centre, Portman House, 17 Brodrick Road, London, S.W.17.

Index